Walt Disney's

Donald Duck

by Carl Barks

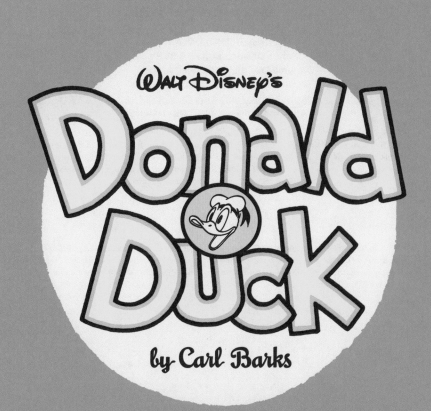

Publisher and Executive Editor: GARY GROTH
Senior Editor: J. MICHAEL CATRON
Color Editor: MIKE BAEHR
Colorist: RICH TOMMASO
Series Design: JACOB COVEY
Volume Design: KEELI McCARTHY
Production: PAUL BARESH
Editorial Consultant: DAVID GERSTEIN
Associate Publisher: ERIC REYNOLDS

Fantagraphics Books, Inc.
7563 Lake City Way NE
Seattle WA 98115

To receive a free catalog of more books like this, as well as an amazing variety of
cutting-edge graphic novels, classic comic book and newspaper strip collections, eclectic prose novels, uniquely
insightful cultural criticism, and other fine works of artistry, call (800) 657-1100 or visit Fantagraphics.com.
Follow us on Twitter at @fantagraphics and on Facebook at facebook.com/fantagraphics.

Special thanks to: Thomas Jensen and Kim Weston

First printing, June 2015
ISBN 978-1-60699-834-2
Printed in Singapore
Library of Congress Control Number: 2014957446

Boxed sets of some titles are available at select locations.

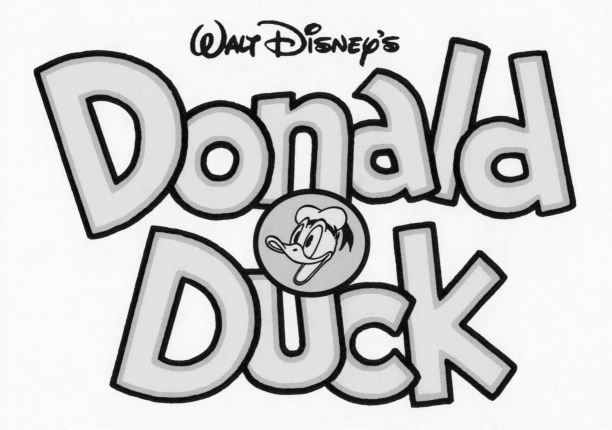

Walt Disney's

Donald Duck

"The Pixilated Parrot"

by Carl Barks

FANTAGRAPHICS BOOKS

Contents

All comics stories written and drawn by Carl Barks except as noted.

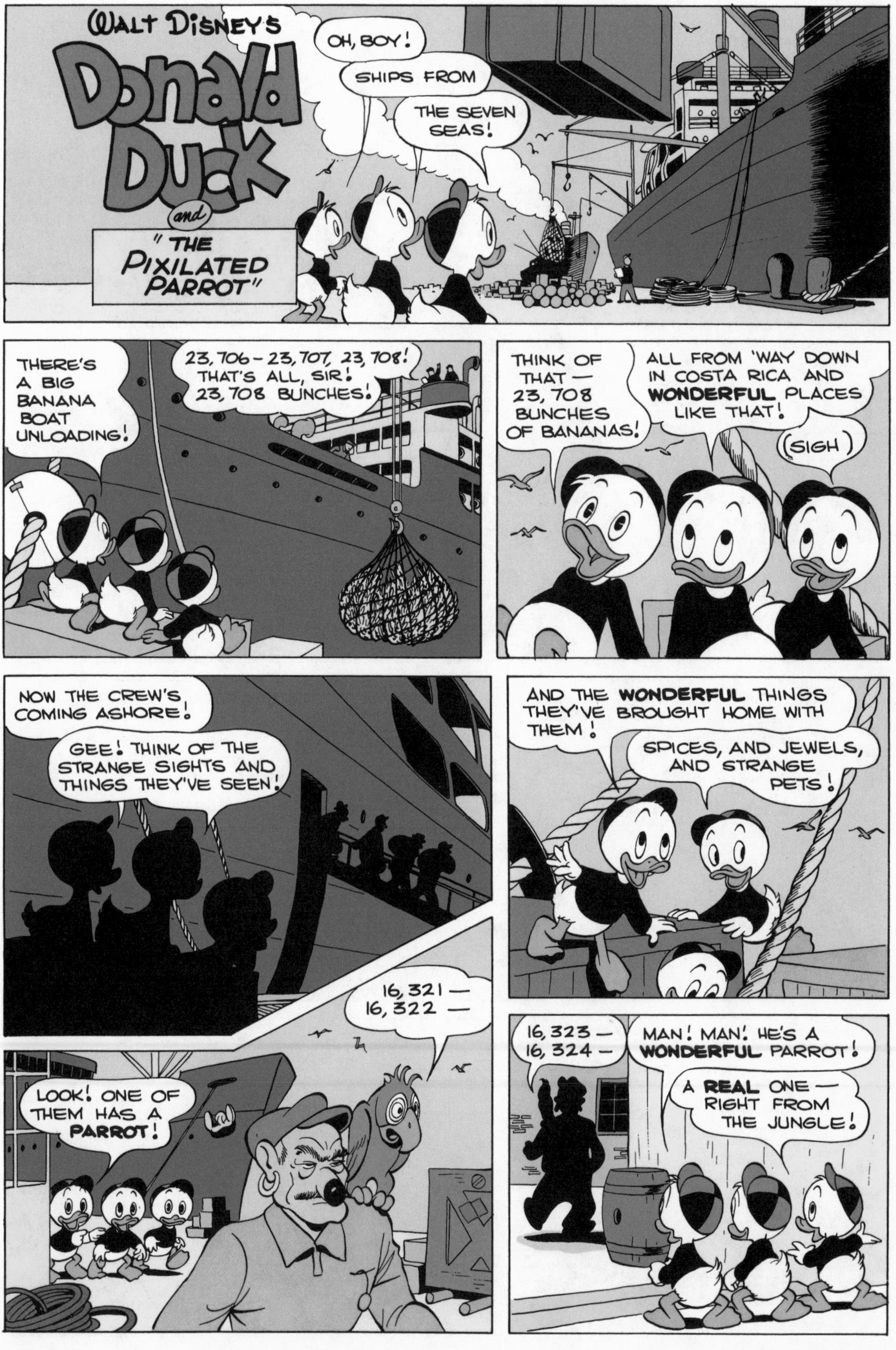

WALT DISNEY'S
Donald Duck
and
"THE PIXILATED PARROT"
OH, BOY!
SHIPS FROM
THE SEVEN SEAS!
THERE'S A BIG BANANA BOAT UNLOADING!
23,706 – 23,707, 23,708! THAT'S ALL, SIR! 23,708 BUNCHES!
THINK OF THAT — 23,708 BUNCHES OF BANANAS!
ALL FROM 'WAY DOWN IN COSTA RICA AND WONDERFUL PLACES LIKE THAT!
(SIGH)
NOW THE CREW'S COMING ASHORE!
GEE! THINK OF THE STRANGE SIGHTS AND THINGS THEY'VE SEEN!
AND THE WONDERFUL THINGS THEY'VE BROUGHT HOME WITH THEM!
SPICES, AND JEWELS, AND STRANGE PETS!
LOOK! ONE OF THEM HAS A PARROT!
16,321 — 16,322 —
16,323 — 16,324 —
MAN! MAN! HE'S A WONDERFUL PARROT!
A REAL ONE — RIGHT FROM THE JUNGLE!

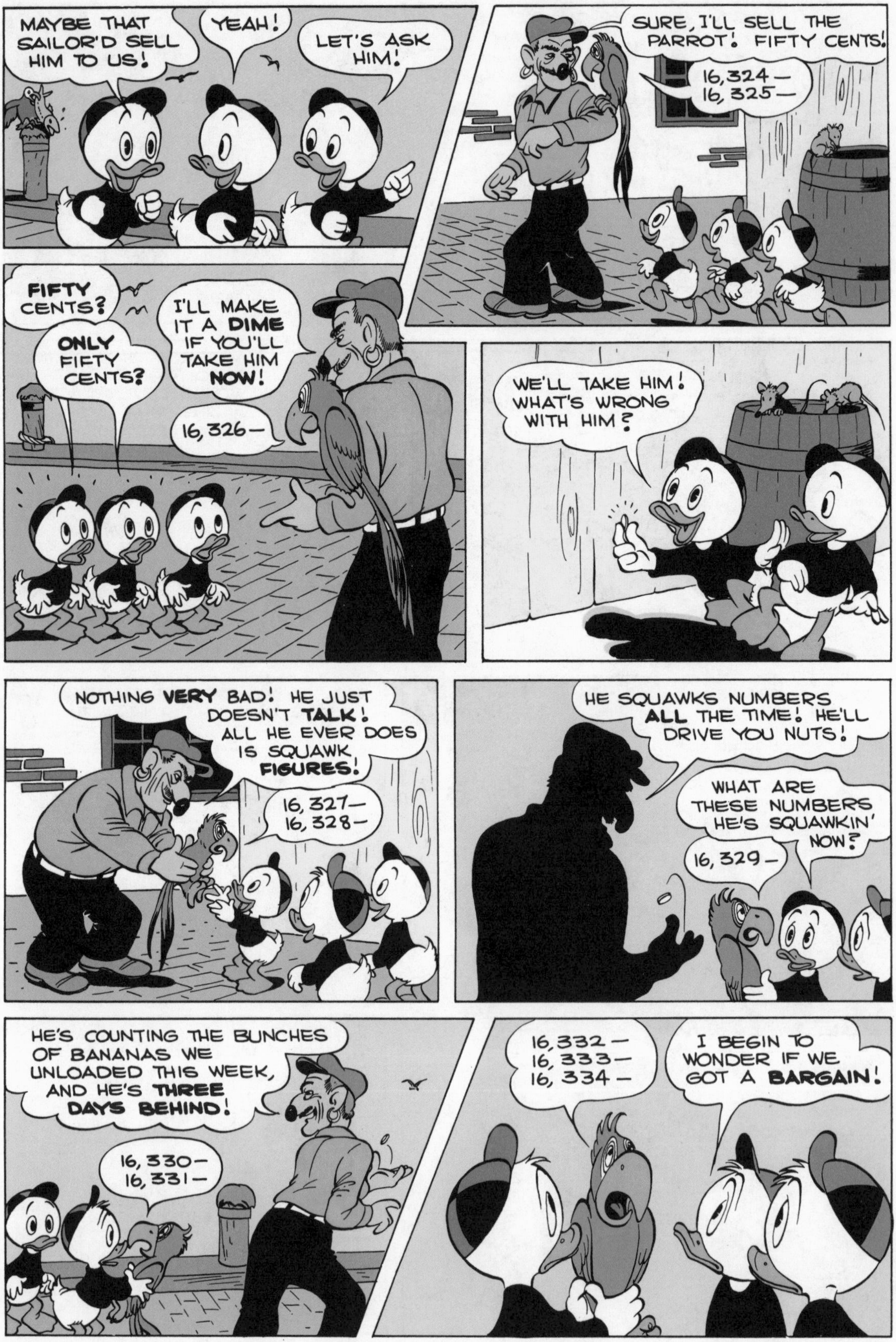
MAYBE THAT SAILOR'D SELL HIM TO US!
YEAH!
LET'S ASK HIM!
SURE, I'LL SELL THE PARROT! FIFTY CENTS!
16,324— 16,325—
FIFTY CENTS?
ONLY FIFTY CENTS?
I'LL MAKE IT A DIME IF YOU'LL TAKE HIM NOW!
16,326—
WE'LL TAKE HIM! WHAT'S WRONG WITH HIM?
NOTHING VERY BAD! HE JUST DOESN'T TALK! ALL HE EVER DOES IS SQUAWK FIGURES!
16,327— 16,328—
HE SQUAWKS NUMBERS ALL THE TIME! HE'LL DRIVE YOU NUTS!
WHAT ARE THESE NUMBERS HE'S SQUAWKIN' NOW?
16,329—
HE'S COUNTING THE BUNCHES OF BANANAS WE UNLOADED THIS WEEK, AND HE'S THREE DAYS BEHIND!
16,330— 16,331—
16,332— 16,333— 16,334—
I BEGIN TO WONDER IF WE GOT A BARGAIN!

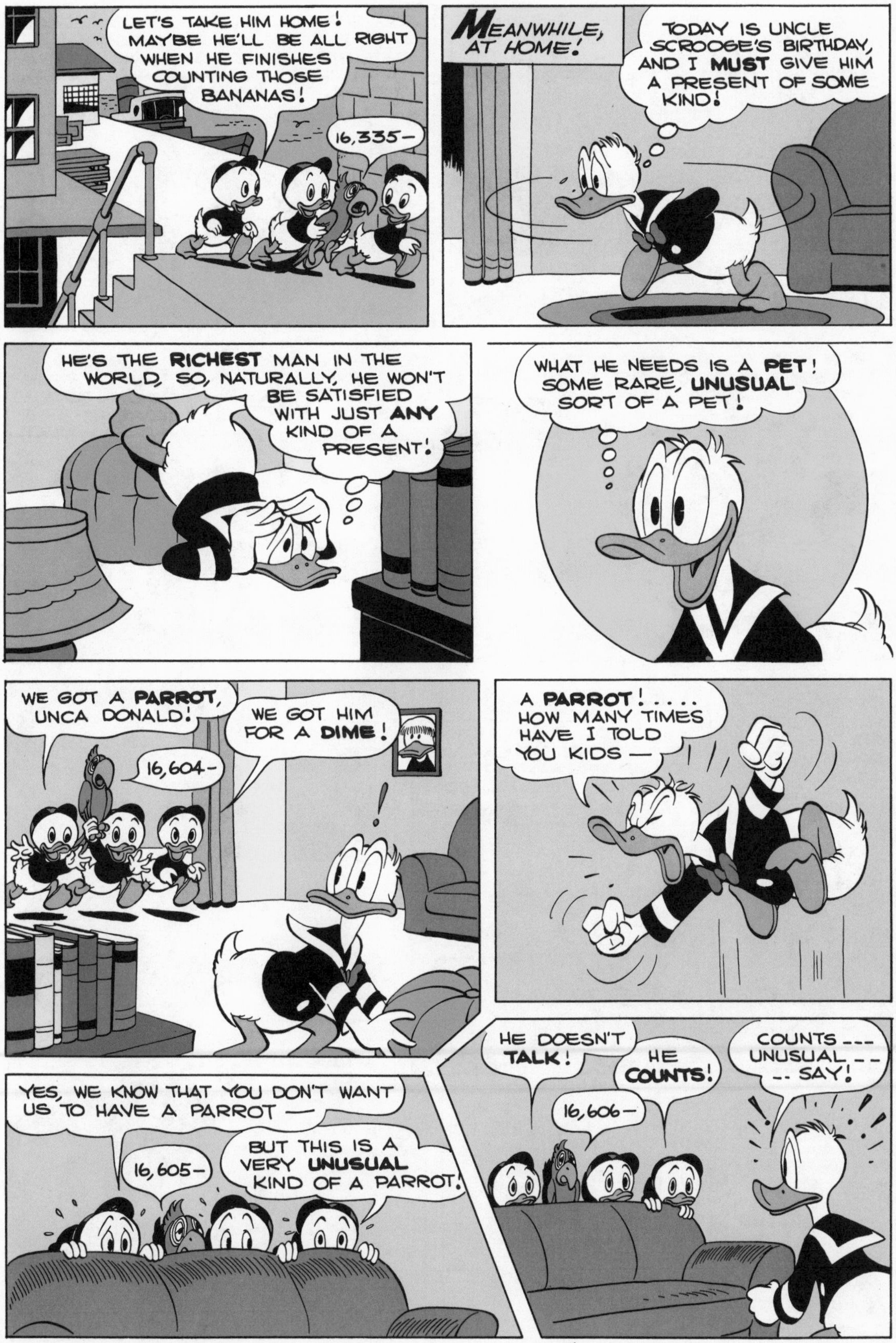
LET'S TAKE HIM HOME! MAYBE HE'LL BE ALL RIGHT WHEN HE FINISHES COUNTING THOSE BANANAS!
16,335—
MEANWHILE, AT HOME!
TODAY IS UNCLE SCROOGE'S BIRTHDAY, AND I MUST GIVE HIM A PRESENT OF SOME KIND!
HE'S THE RICHEST MAN IN THE WORLD, SO, NATURALLY, HE WON'T BE SATISFIED WITH JUST ANY KIND OF A PRESENT!
WHAT HE NEEDS IS A PET! SOME RARE, UNUSUAL SORT OF A PET!
WE GOT A PARROT, UNCA DONALD!
WE GOT HIM FOR A DIME!
16,604—
A PARROT!..... HOW MANY TIMES HAVE I TOLD YOU KIDS —
YES, WE KNOW THAT YOU DON'T WANT US TO HAVE A PARROT —
16,605—
BUT THIS IS A VERY UNUSUAL KIND OF A PARROT!
HE DOESN'T TALK!
HE COUNTS!
16,606—
COUNTS --- UNUSUAL --- SAY!

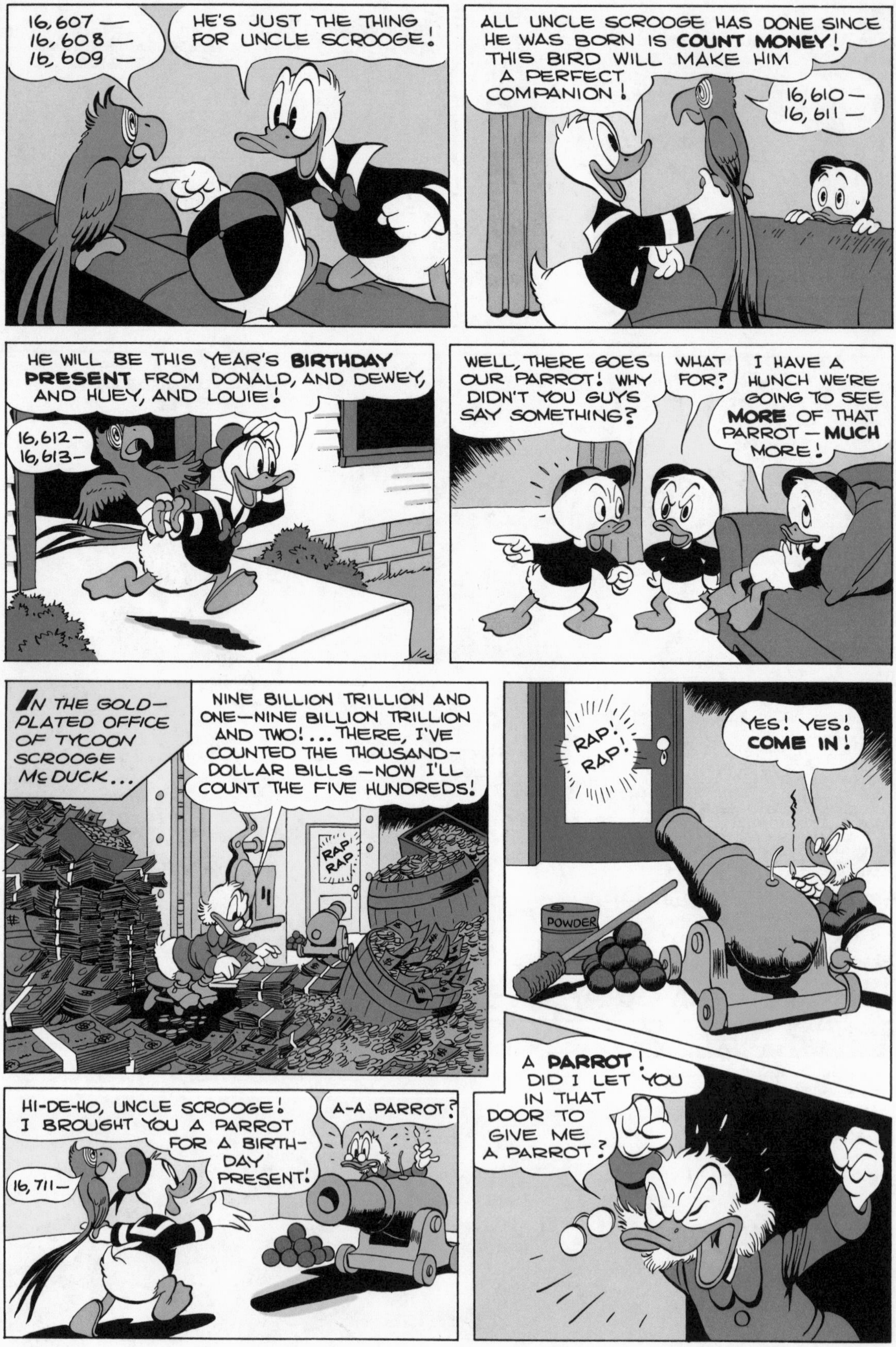
16,607 —
16,608 —
16,609 —
HE'S JUST THE THING FOR UNCLE SCROOGE!
ALL UNCLE SCROOGE HAS DONE SINCE HE WAS BORN IS COUNT MONEY! THIS BIRD WILL MAKE HIM A PERFECT COMPANION!
16,610 —
16,611 —
HE WILL BE THIS YEAR'S BIRTHDAY PRESENT FROM DONALD, AND DEWEY, AND HUEY, AND LOUIE!
16,612 —
16,613 —
WELL, THERE GOES OUR PARROT! WHY DIDN'T YOU GUYS SAY SOMETHING?
WHAT FOR?
I HAVE A HUNCH WE'RE GOING TO SEE MORE OF THAT PARROT — MUCH MORE!
IN THE GOLD-PLATED OFFICE OF TYCOON SCROOGE McDUCK...
NINE BILLION TRILLION AND ONE—NINE BILLION TRILLION AND TWO!... THERE, I'VE COUNTED THE THOUSAND-DOLLAR BILLS — NOW I'LL COUNT THE FIVE HUNDREDS!
RAP! RAP!
RAP! RAP!
YES! YES! COME IN!
POWDER
HI-DE-HO, UNCLE SCROOGE! I BROUGHT YOU A PARROT FOR A BIRTHDAY PRESENT!
16,711 —
A-A PARROT?
A PARROT! DID I LET YOU IN THAT DOOR TO GIVE ME A PARROT?

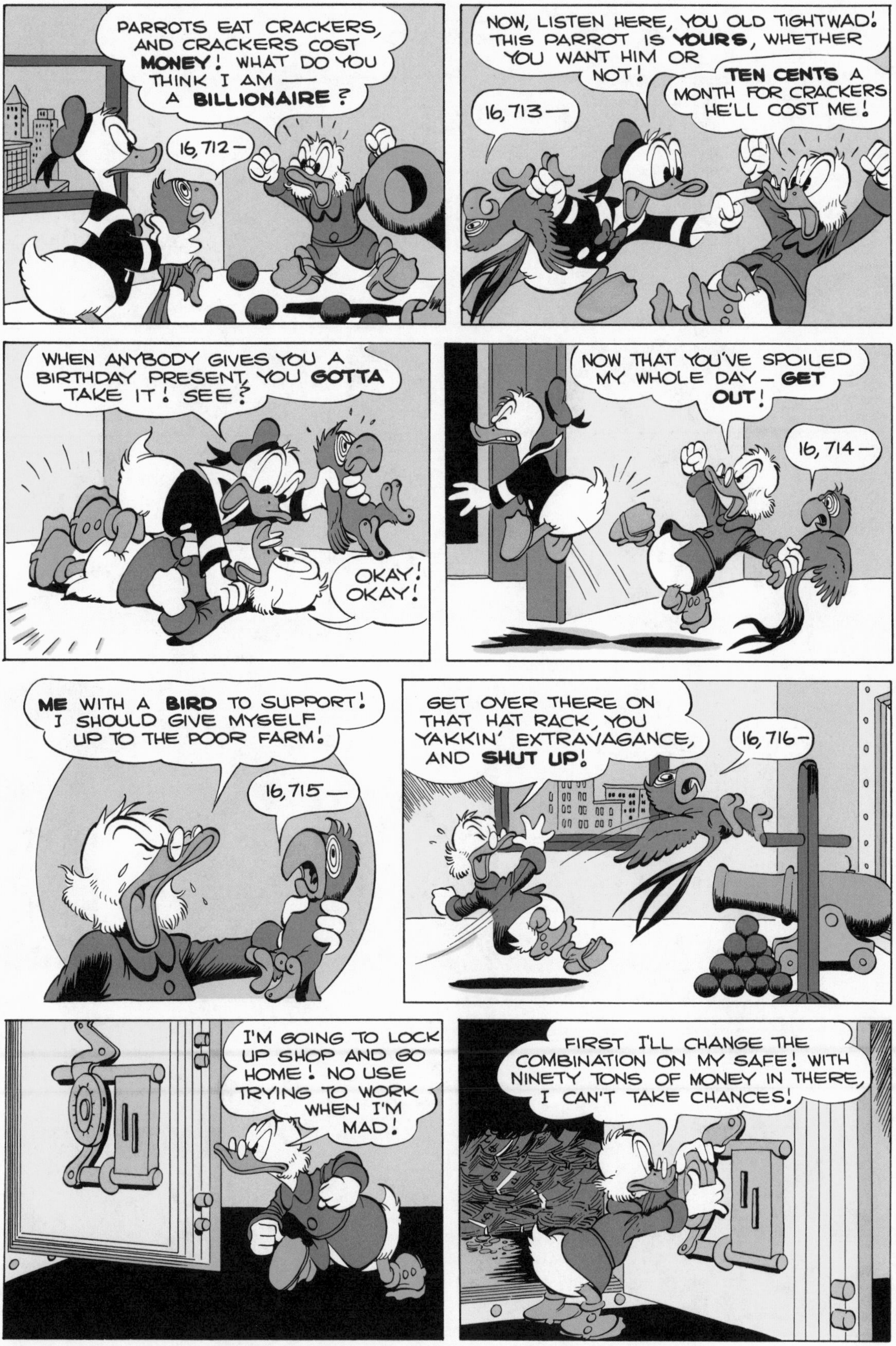
PARROTS EAT CRACKERS, AND CRACKERS COST MONEY! WHAT DO YOU THINK I AM — A BILLIONAIRE?
16,712—
NOW, LISTEN HERE, YOU OLD TIGHTWAD! THIS PARROT IS YOURS, WHETHER YOU WANT HIM OR NOT!
TEN CENTS A MONTH FOR CRACKERS HE'LL COST ME!
16,713—
WHEN ANYBODY GIVES YOU A BIRTHDAY PRESENT, YOU GOTTA TAKE IT! SEE?
OKAY! OKAY!
NOW THAT YOU'VE SPOILED MY WHOLE DAY — GET OUT!
16,714—
ME WITH A BIRD TO SUPPORT! I SHOULD GIVE MYSELF UP TO THE POOR FARM!
16,715—
GET OVER THERE ON THAT HAT RACK, YOU YAKKIN' EXTRAVAGANCE, AND SHUT UP!
16,716—
I'M GOING TO LOCK UP SHOP AND GO HOME! NO USE TRYING TO WORK WHEN I'M MAD!
FIRST I'LL CHANGE THE COMBINATION ON MY SAFE! WITH NINETY TONS OF MONEY IN THERE, I CAN'T TAKE CHANCES!

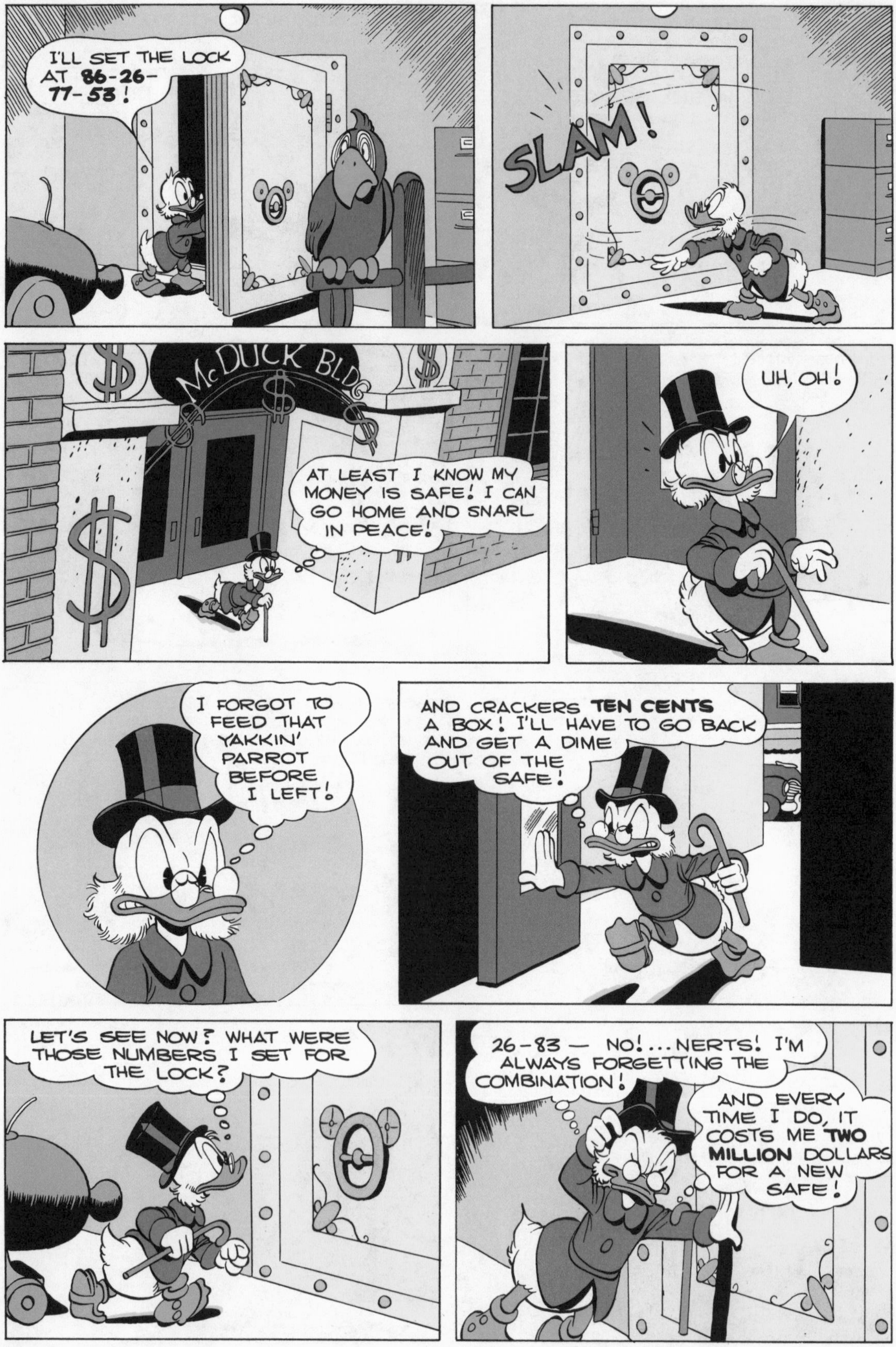
I'LL SET THE LOCK AT 86-26-77-53!
SLAM!
McDUCK BLDG
AT LEAST I KNOW MY MONEY IS SAFE! I CAN GO HOME AND SNARL IN PEACE!
UH, OH!
I FORGOT TO FEED THAT YAKKIN' PARROT BEFORE I LEFT!
AND CRACKERS **TEN CENTS** A BOX! I'LL HAVE TO GO BACK AND GET A DIME OUT OF THE SAFE!
LET'S SEE NOW? WHAT WERE THOSE NUMBERS I SET FOR THE LOCK?
26-83 — NO!...NERTS! I'M ALWAYS FORGETTING THE COMBINATION!
AND EVERY TIME I DO, IT COSTS ME **TWO MILLION** DOLLARS FOR A NEW SAFE!

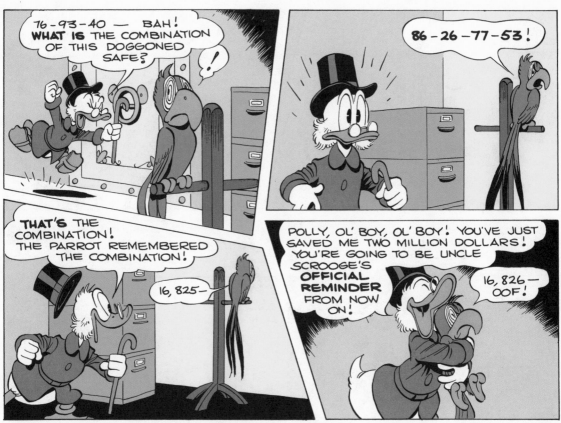

76 - 93 - 40 — BAH! **WHAT IS** THE COMBINATION OF THIS DOGGONED SAFE?

86 - 26 - 77 - 53!

THAT'S THE COMBINATION! THE PARROT REMEMBERED THE COMBINATION!

16,825 —

POLLY, OL' BOY, OL' BOY! YOU'VE JUST SAVED ME TWO MILLION DOLLARS! YOU'RE GOING TO BE UNCLE SCROOGE'S **OFFICIAL REMINDER** FROM NOW ON!

16,826 — OOF!

HERE! YOU CAN HAVE THIS TOP DRAWER FOR YOUR HOME — AND **CRACKERS** — YOU CAN HAVE A **DIME'S** WORTH EVERY **WEEK!**

THAT NIGHT!

AT LAST I CAN GIVE MY TIRED OLD MEMORY A REST! IF I FORGET THE COMBINATION OF MY SAFE — BINGO! — THE PARROT TELLS ME!

*A*T THE OFFICE, POLLY, FULL OF CRACKERS, AND COZY IN HIS WARM QUARTERS, SETTLES DOWN FOR A NIGHT OF COUNTING BANANAS!

17,440 — 17,441 — 17,442 —

*M*IDNIGHT! THERE IT IS, BUTCH! TH' **RICHEST SAFE** IN TH' WOILD!

SCROOGE McDUCK'S SAFE! LET'S CRACK IT!

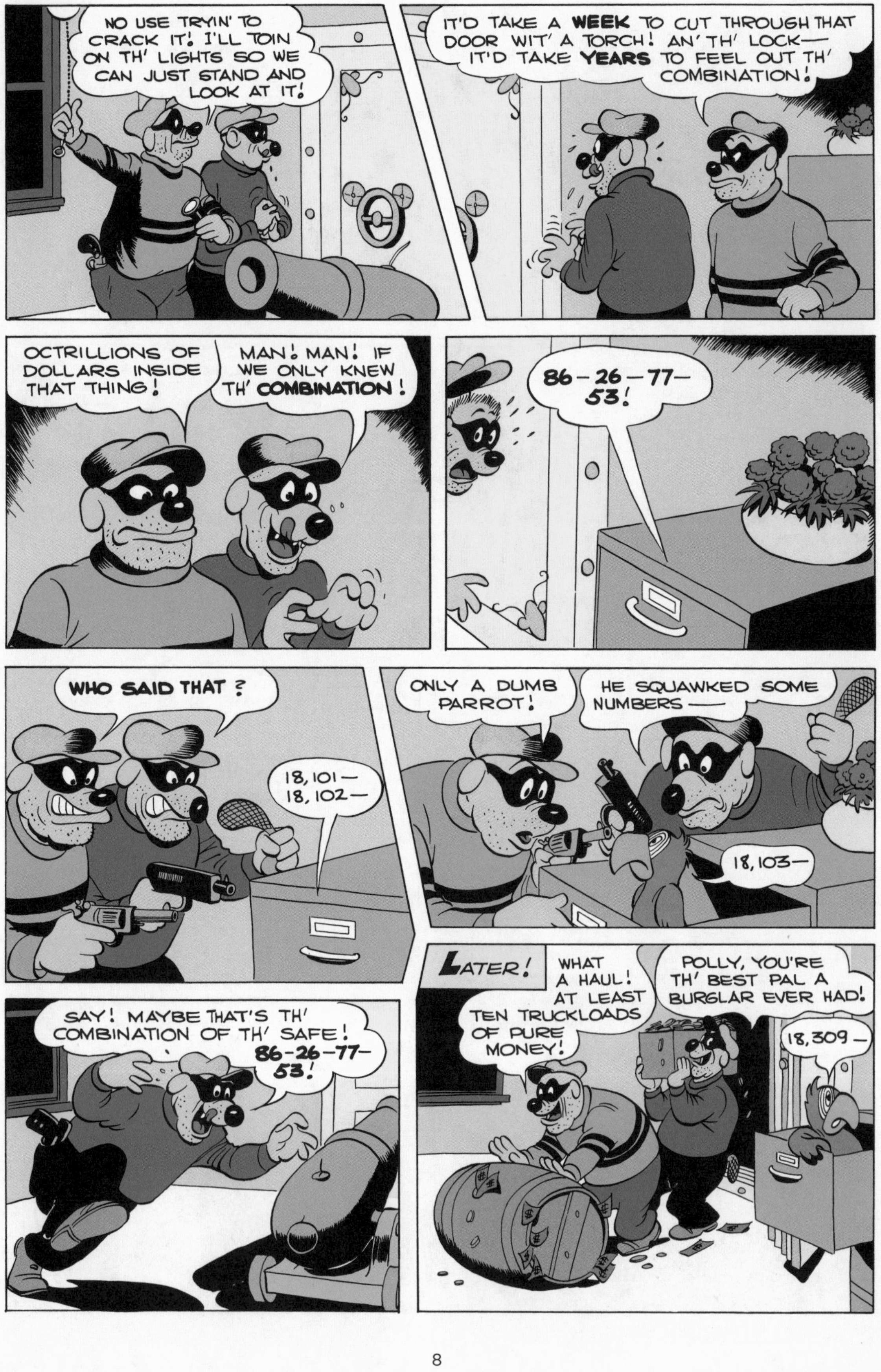
NO USE TRYIN' TO CRACK IT! I'LL TOIN ON TH' LIGHTS SO WE CAN JUST STAND AND LOOK AT IT!
IT'D TAKE A WEEK TO CUT THROUGH THAT DOOR WIT' A TORCH! AN' TH' LOCK— IT'D TAKE YEARS TO FEEL OUT TH' COMBINATION!
OCTRILLIONS OF DOLLARS INSIDE THAT THING!
MAN! MAN! IF WE ONLY KNEW TH' COMBINATION!
86—26—77—53!
WHO SAID THAT ?
18,101— 18,102—
ONLY A DUMB PARROT!
HE SQUAWKED SOME NUMBERS —
18,103—
SAY! MAYBE THAT'S TH' COMBINATION OF TH' SAFE! 86-26-77-53!
LATER!
WHAT A HAUL! AT LEAST TEN TRUCKLOADS OF PURE MONEY!
POLLY, YOU'RE TH' BEST PAL A BURGLAR EVER HAD!
18,309 —

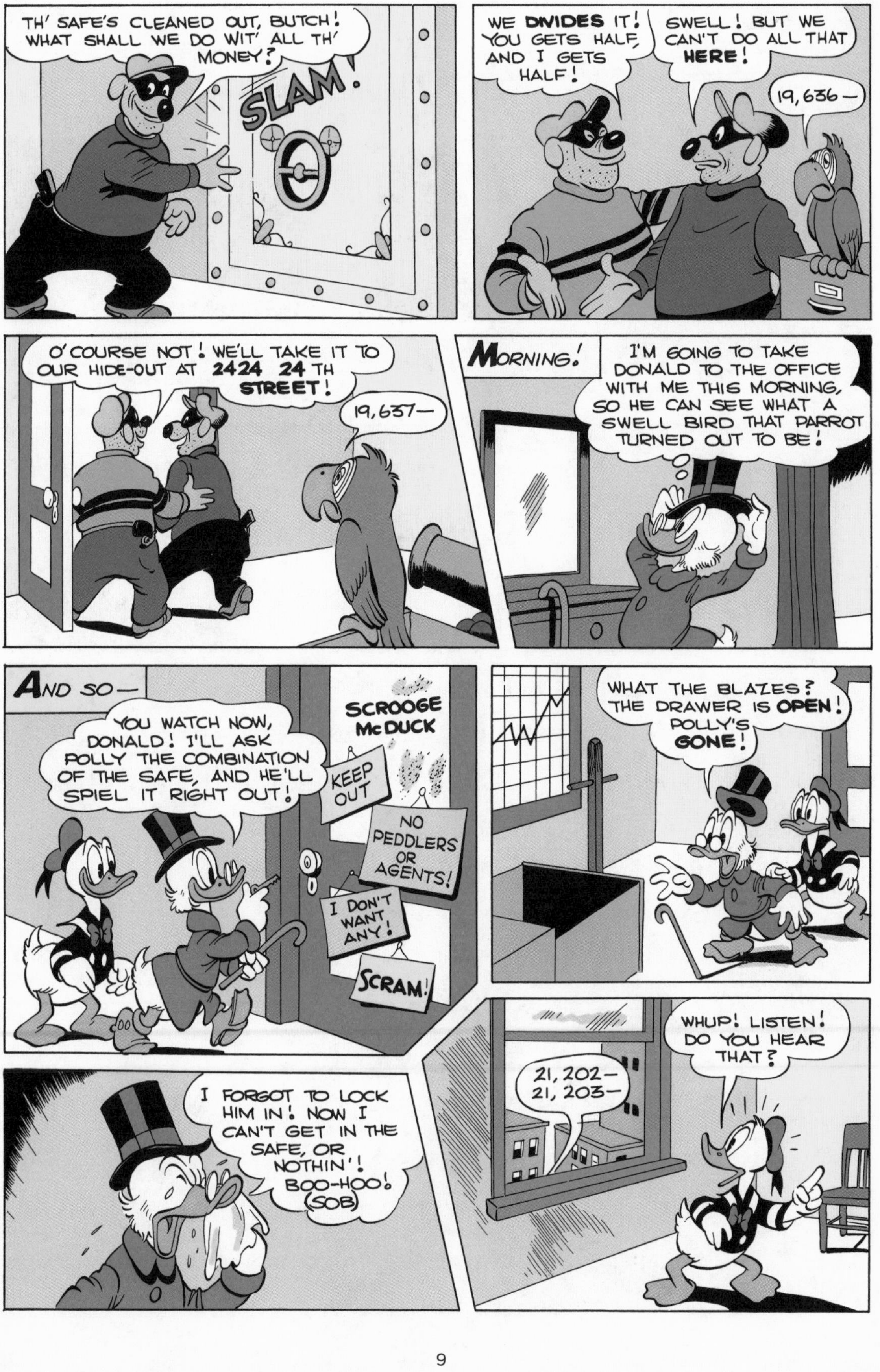
TH' SAFE'S CLEANED OUT, BUTCH! WHAT SHALL WE DO WIT' ALL TH' MONEY?
SLAM!
WE DIVIDES IT! YOU GETS HALF, AND I GETS HALF!
SWELL! BUT WE CAN'T DO ALL THAT HERE!
19,636—
O'COURSE NOT! WE'LL TAKE IT TO OUR HIDE-OUT AT 2424 24 TH STREET!
19,637—
MORNING!
I'M GOING TO TAKE DONALD TO THE OFFICE WITH ME THIS MORNING, SO HE CAN SEE WHAT A SWELL BIRD THAT PARROT TURNED OUT TO BE!
AND SO—
YOU WATCH NOW, DONALD! I'LL ASK POLLY THE COMBINATION OF THE SAFE, AND HE'LL SPIEL IT RIGHT OUT!
SCROOGE McDUCK
KEEP OUT
NO PEDDLERS OR AGENTS!
I DON'T WANT ANY!
SCRAM!
WHAT THE BLAZES? THE DRAWER IS OPEN! POLLY'S GONE!
I FORGOT TO LOCK HIM IN! NOW I CAN'T GET IN THE SAFE, OR NOTHIN'! BOO-HOO! (SOB)
WHUP! LISTEN! DO YOU HEAR THAT?
21,202— 21,203—

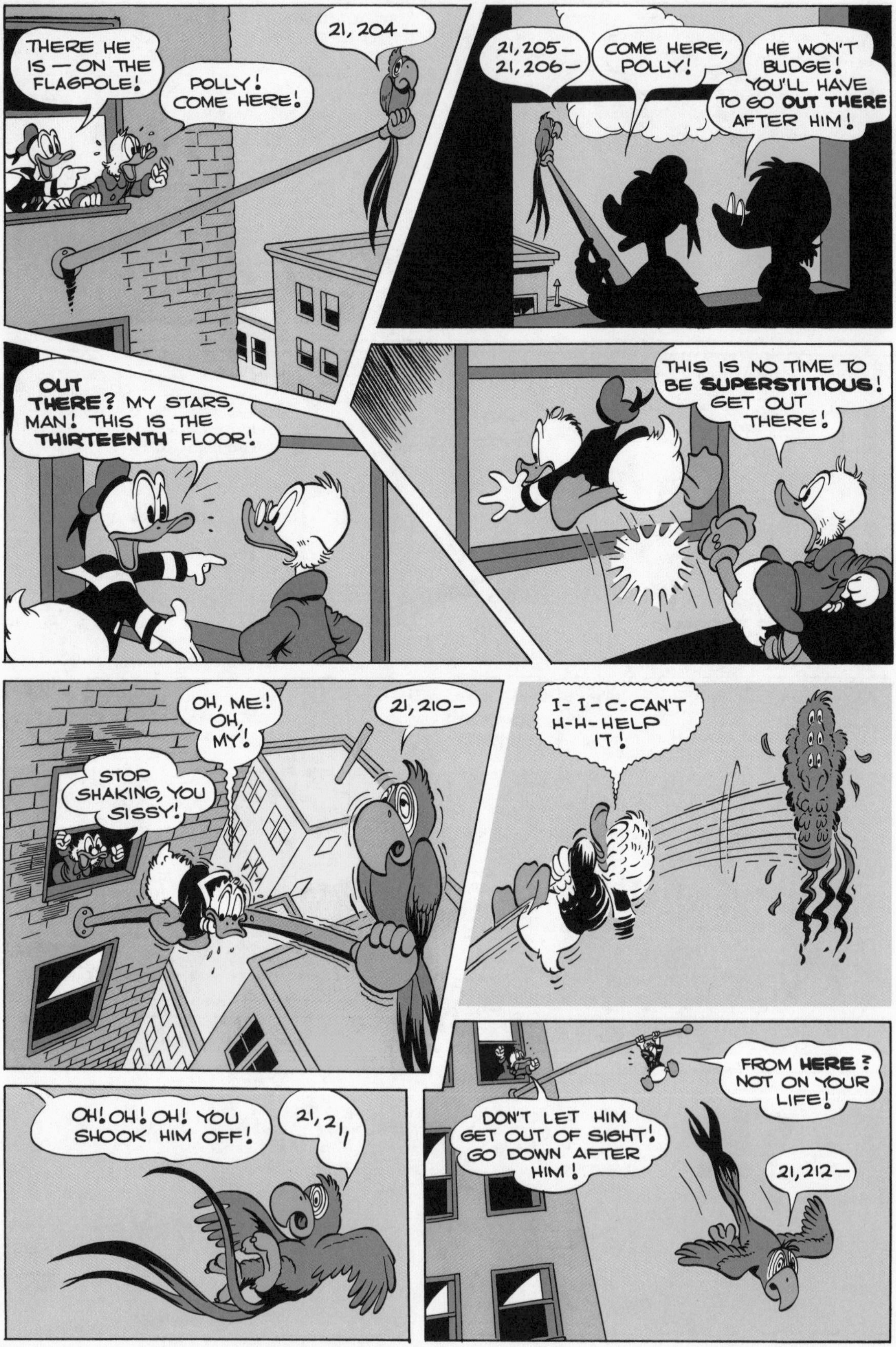
THERE HE IS — ON THE FLAGPOLE!
POLLY! COME HERE!
21,204 —
21,205 — 21,206 —
COME HERE, POLLY!
HE WON'T BUDGE! YOU'LL HAVE TO GO OUT THERE AFTER HIM!
OUT THERE? MY STARS, MAN! THIS IS THE THIRTEENTH FLOOR!
THIS IS NO TIME TO BE SUPERSTITIOUS! GET OUT THERE!
OH, ME! OH, MY!
21,210 —
STOP SHAKING, YOU SISSY!
I-I-C-CAN'T H-H-HELP IT!
OH! OH! OH! YOU SHOOK HIM OFF!
21,211
DON'T LET HIM GET OUT OF SIGHT! GO DOWN AFTER HIM!
FROM HERE? NOT ON YOUR LIFE!
21,212 —

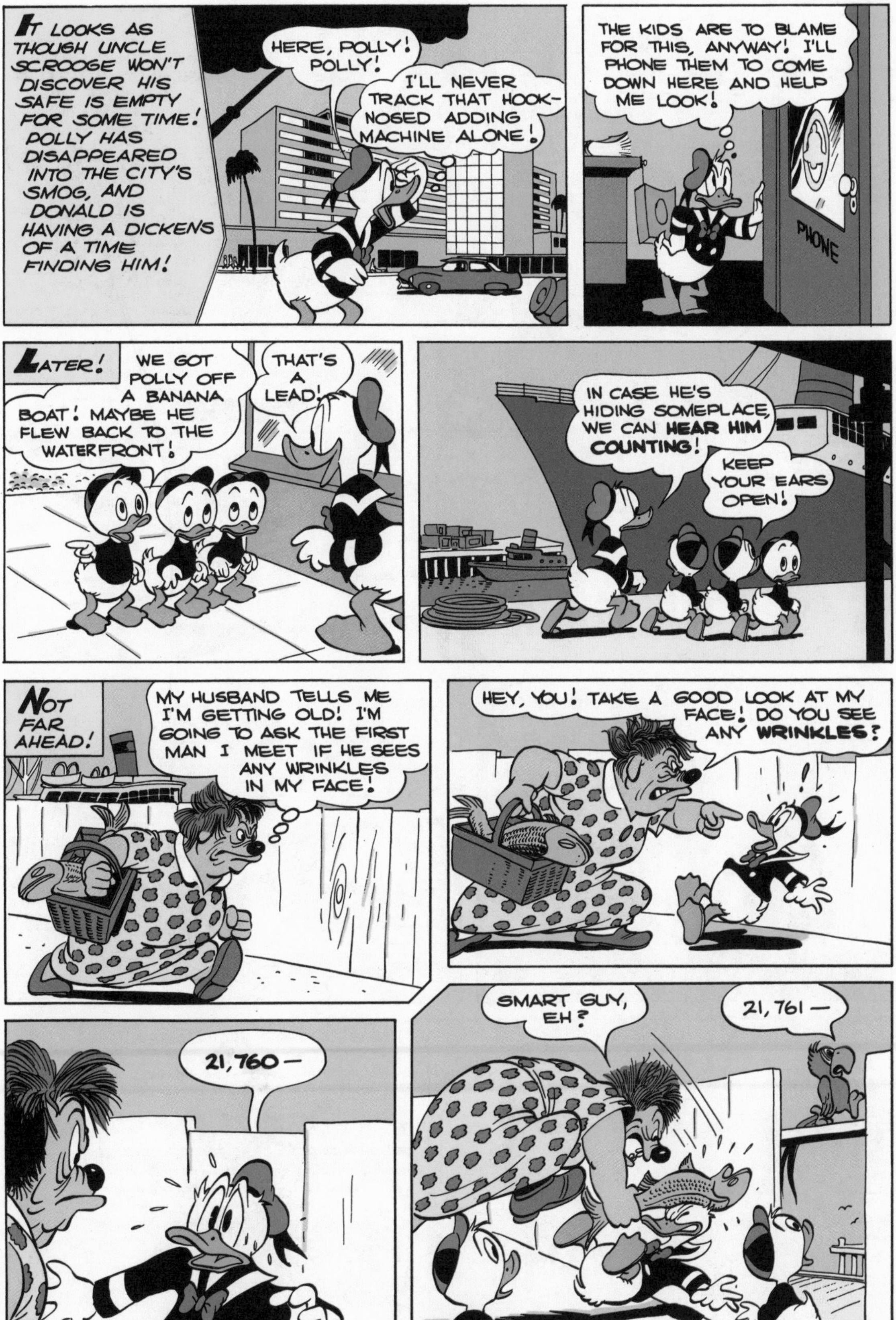
IT LOOKS AS THOUGH UNCLE SCROOGE WON'T DISCOVER HIS SAFE IS EMPTY FOR SOME TIME! POLLY HAS DISAPPEARED INTO THE CITY'S SMOG, AND DONALD IS HAVING A DICKENS OF A TIME FINDING HIM!
HERE, POLLY! POLLY!
I'LL NEVER TRACK THAT HOOK-NOSED ADDING MACHINE ALONE!
THE KIDS ARE TO BLAME FOR THIS, ANYWAY! I'LL PHONE THEM TO COME DOWN HERE AND HELP ME LOOK!
PHONE
LATER!
WE GOT POLLY OFF A BANANA BOAT! MAYBE HE FLEW BACK TO THE WATERFRONT!
THAT'S A LEAD!
IN CASE HE'S HIDING SOMEPLACE, WE CAN HEAR HIM COUNTING!
KEEP YOUR EARS OPEN!
NOT FAR AHEAD!
MY HUSBAND TELLS ME I'M GETTING OLD! I'M GOING TO ASK THE FIRST MAN I MEET IF HE SEES ANY WRINKLES IN MY FACE!
HEY, YOU! TAKE A GOOD LOOK AT MY FACE! DO YOU SEE ANY WRINKLES?
21,760 —
SMART GUY, EH?
21,761 —

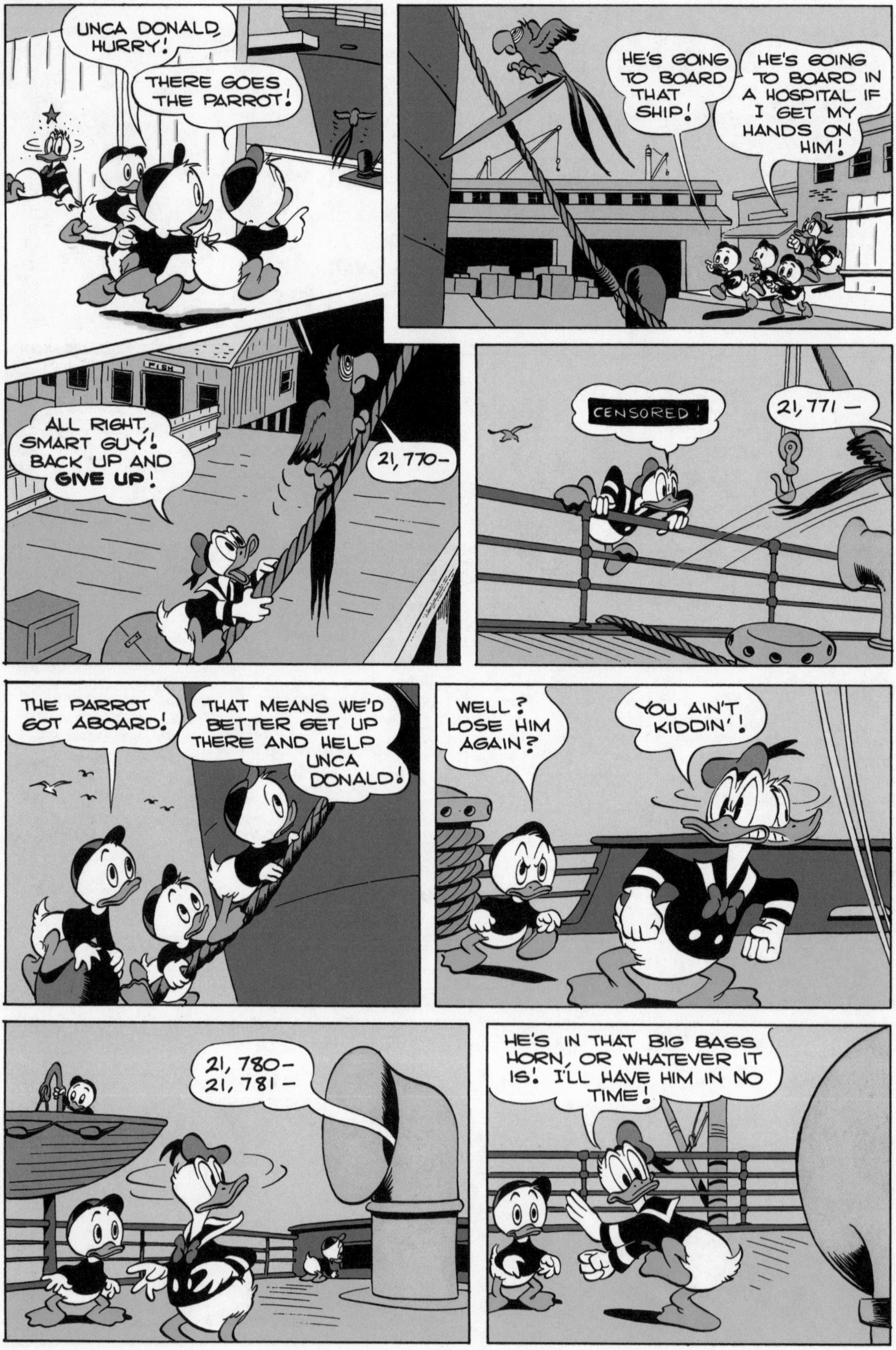
UNCA DONALD, HURRY!
THERE GOES THE PARROT!
HE'S GOING TO BOARD THAT SHIP!
HE'S GOING TO BOARD IN A HOSPITAL IF I GET MY HANDS ON HIM!
FISH
ALL RIGHT, SMART GUY! BACK UP AND GIVE UP!
21,770–
CENSORED!
21,771 –
THE PARROT GOT ABOARD!
THAT MEANS WE'D BETTER GET UP THERE AND HELP UNCA DONALD!
WELL? LOSE HIM AGAIN?
YOU AIN'T KIDDIN'!
21,780–
21,781 –
HE'S IN THAT BIG BASS HORN, OR WHATEVER IT IS! I'LL HAVE HIM IN NO TIME!

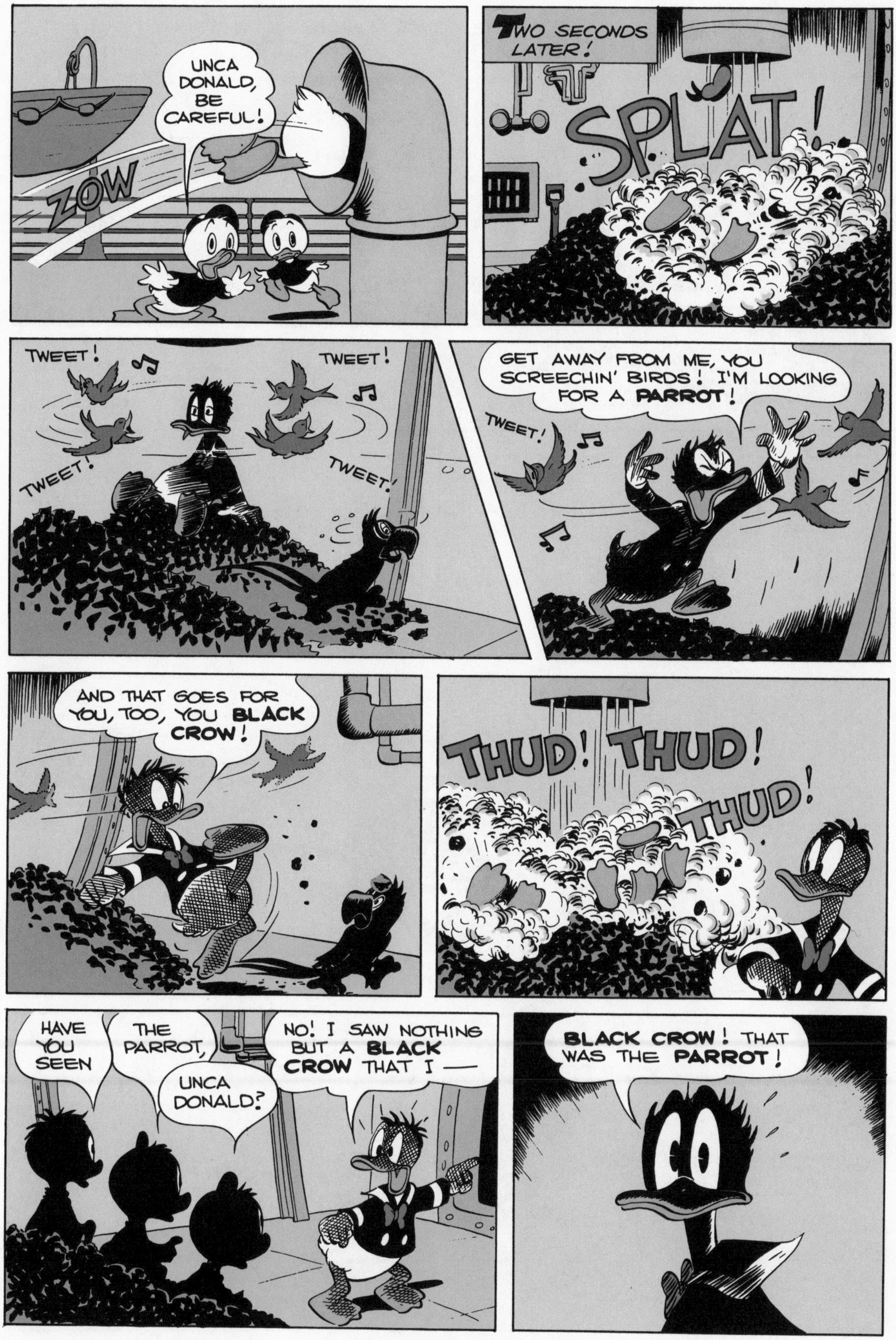
UNCA DONALD, BE CAREFUL!
ZOW
TWO SECONDS LATER!
SPLAT!
TWEET!
TWEET!
TWEET!
TWEET!
GET AWAY FROM ME, YOU SCREECHIN' BIRDS! I'M LOOKING FOR A **PARROT**!
TWEET!
AND THAT GOES FOR YOU, TOO, YOU **BLACK CROW**!
THUD! THUD!
THUD!
HAVE YOU SEEN
THE PARROT,
UNCA DONALD?
NO! I SAW NOTHING BUT A **BLACK CROW** THAT I —
BLACK CROW! THAT WAS THE **PARROT**!

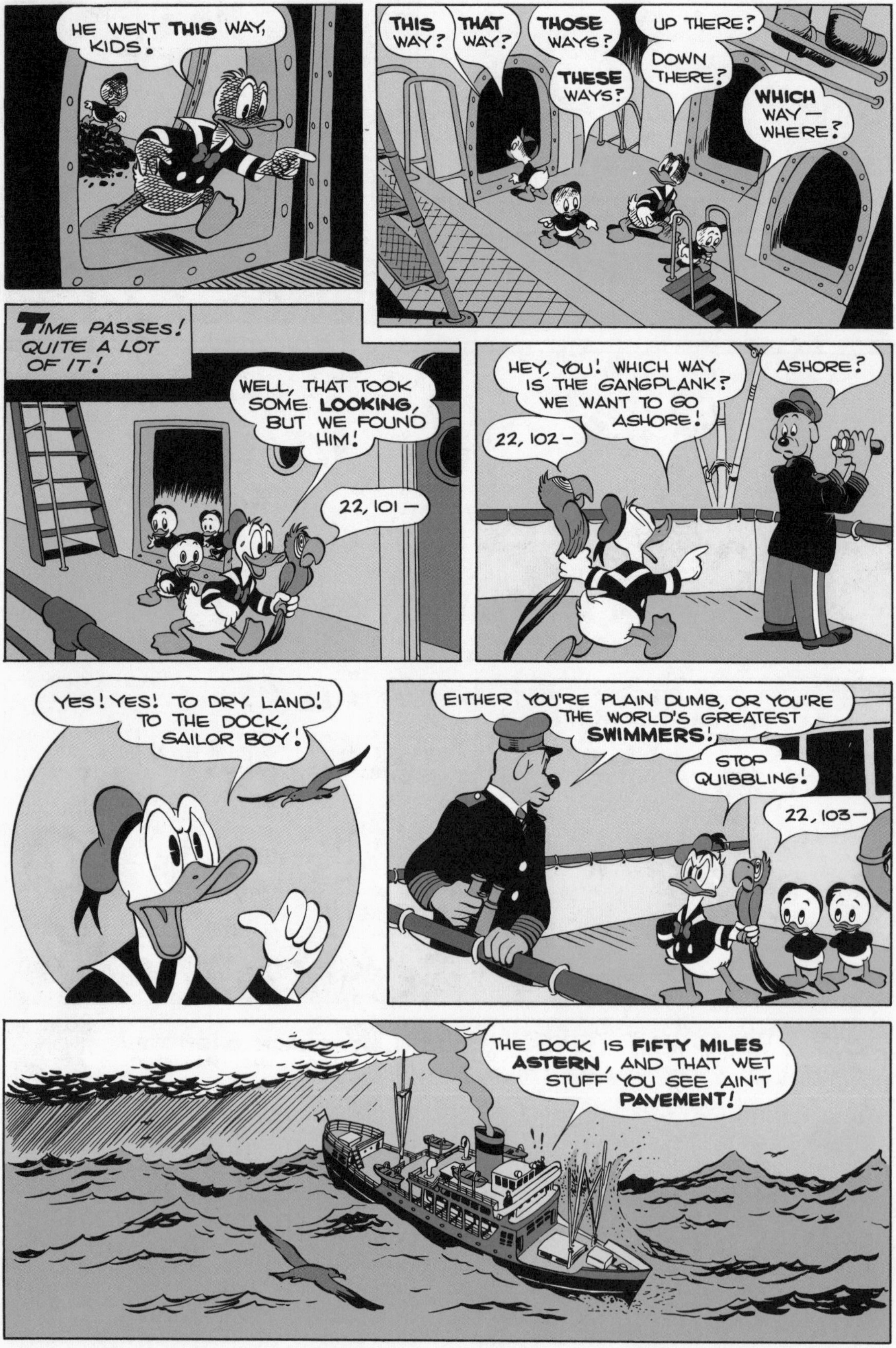

HE WENT THIS WAY, KIDS!
THIS WAY?
THAT WAY?
THOSE WAYS?
THESE WAYS?
UP THERE?
DOWN THERE?
WHICH WAY— WHERE?
TIME PASSES! QUITE A LOT OF IT!
WELL, THAT TOOK SOME LOOKING, BUT WE FOUND HIM!
22, 101—
HEY, YOU! WHICH WAY IS THE GANGPLANK? WE WANT TO GO ASHORE!
22, 102—
ASHORE?
YES! YES! TO DRY LAND! TO THE DOCK, SAILOR BOY!
EITHER YOU'RE PLAIN DUMB, OR YOU'RE THE WORLD'S GREATEST SWIMMERS!
STOP QUIBBLING!
22, 103—
THE DOCK IS FIFTY MILES ASTERN, AND THAT WET STUFF YOU SEE AIN'T PAVEMENT!
!!

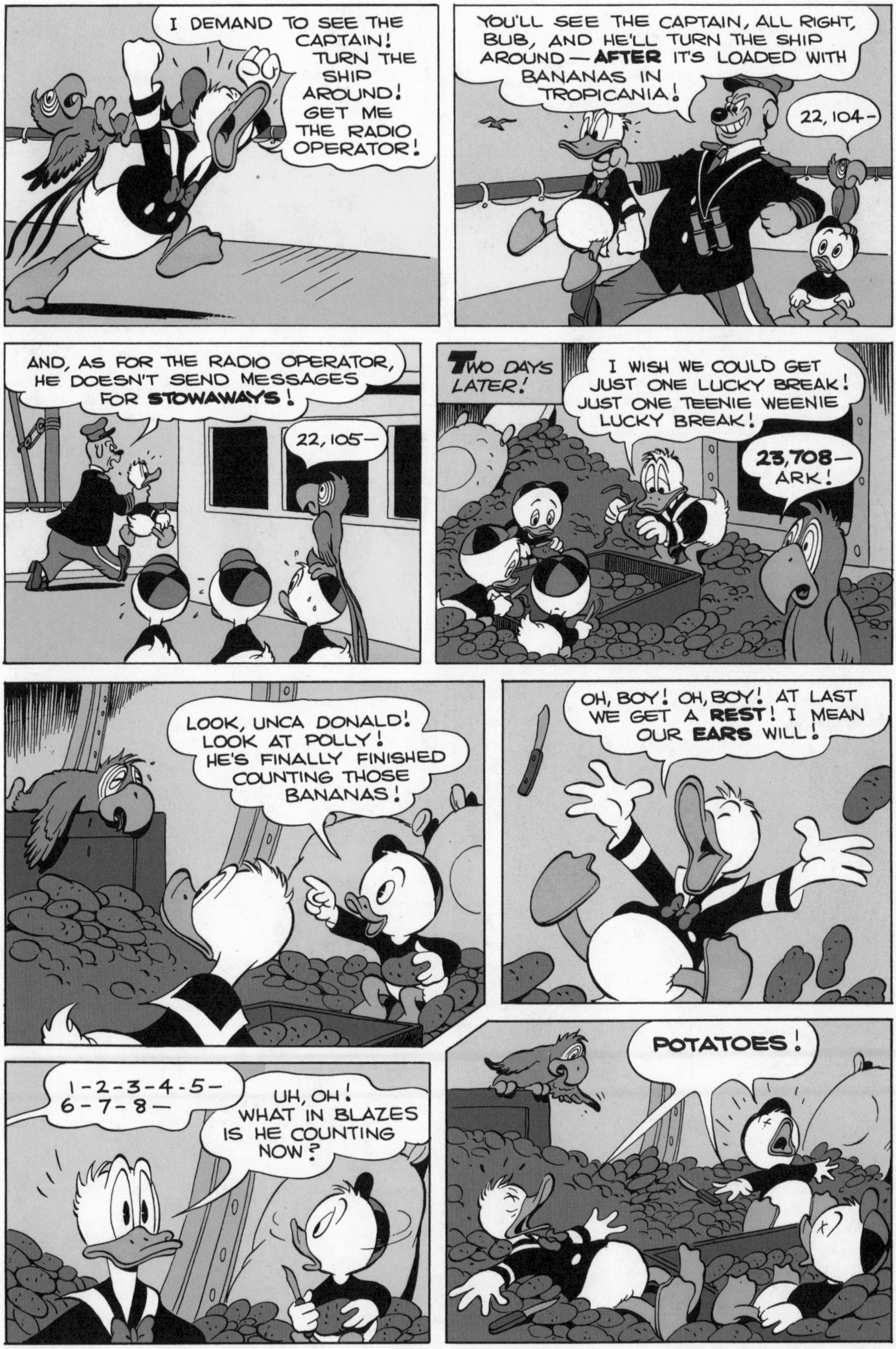
I DEMAND TO SEE THE CAPTAIN! TURN THE SHIP AROUND! GET ME THE RADIO OPERATOR!
YOU'LL SEE THE CAPTAIN, ALL RIGHT, BUB, AND HE'LL TURN THE SHIP AROUND—AFTER IT'S LOADED WITH BANANAS IN TROPICANIA!
22,104-
AND, AS FOR THE RADIO OPERATOR, HE DOESN'T SEND MESSAGES FOR STOWAWAYS!
22,105—
TWO DAYS LATER!
I WISH WE COULD GET JUST ONE LUCKY BREAK! JUST ONE TEENIE WEENIE LUCKY BREAK!
23,708— ARK!
LOOK, UNCA DONALD! LOOK AT POLLY! HE'S FINALLY FINISHED COUNTING THOSE BANANAS!
OH, BOY! OH, BOY! AT LAST WE GET A REST! I MEAN OUR EARS WILL!
1-2-3-4-5— 6-7-8—
UH, OH! WHAT IN BLAZES IS HE COUNTING NOW?
POTATOES!

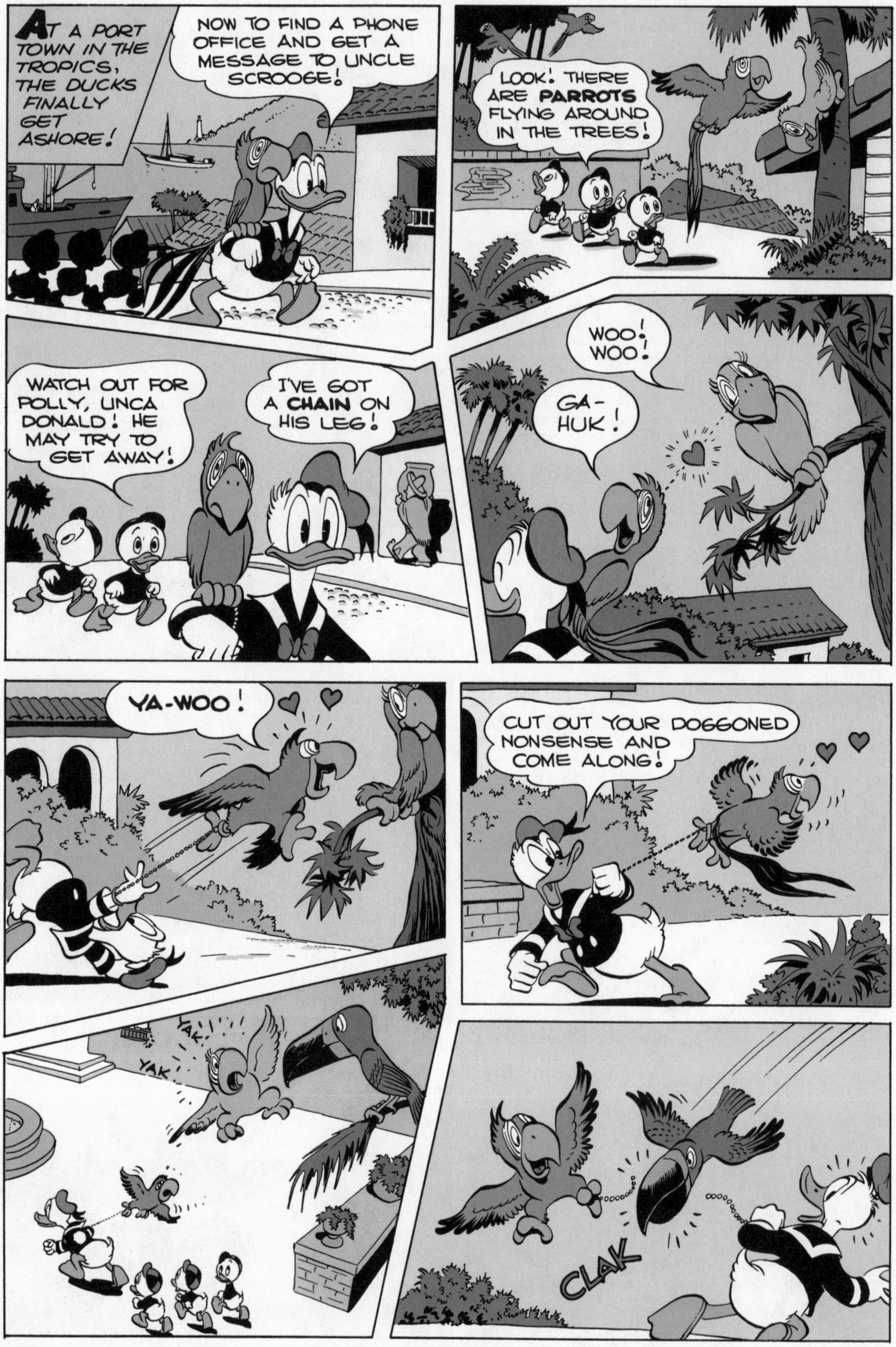
AT A PORT TOWN IN THE TROPICS, THE DUCKS FINALLY GET ASHORE!
NOW TO FIND A PHONE OFFICE AND GET A MESSAGE TO UNCLE SCROOGE!
LOOK! THERE ARE PARROTS FLYING AROUND IN THE TREES!
WATCH OUT FOR POLLY, UNCA DONALD! HE MAY TRY TO GET AWAY!
I'VE GOT A CHAIN ON HIS LEG!
WOO! WOO!
GA-HUK!
YA-WOO!
CUT OUT YOUR DOGGONED NONSENSE AND COME ALONG!
YAK
YAK
CLAK

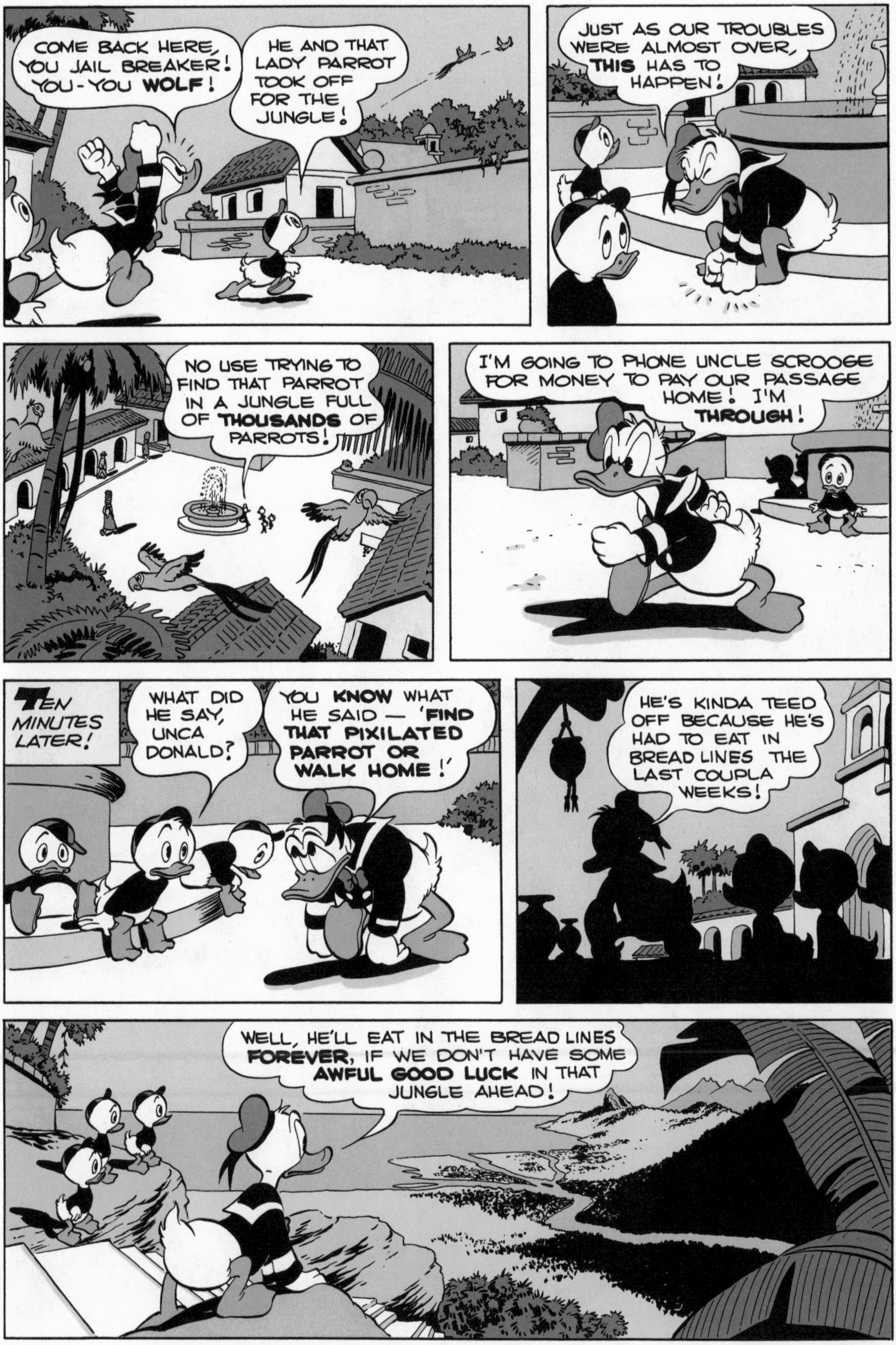
COME BACK HERE, YOU JAIL BREAKER! YOU-YOU **WOLF**!
HE AND THAT LADY PARROT TOOK OFF FOR THE JUNGLE!
JUST AS OUR TROUBLES WERE ALMOST OVER, **THIS** HAS TO HAPPEN!
NO USE TRYING TO FIND THAT PARROT IN A JUNGLE FULL OF **THOUSANDS** OF PARROTS!
I'M GOING TO PHONE UNCLE SCROOGE FOR MONEY TO PAY OUR PASSAGE HOME! I'M **THROUGH**!
TEN MINUTES LATER!
WHAT DID HE SAY, UNCA DONALD?
YOU **KNOW** WHAT HE SAID — **'FIND THAT PIXILATED PARROT OR WALK HOME!'**
HE'S KINDA TEED OFF BECAUSE HE'S HAD TO EAT IN BREAD LINES THE LAST COUPLA WEEKS!
WELL, HE'LL EAT IN THE BREAD LINES **FOREVER**, IF WE DON'T HAVE SOME **AWFUL GOOD LUCK** IN THAT JUNGLE AHEAD!

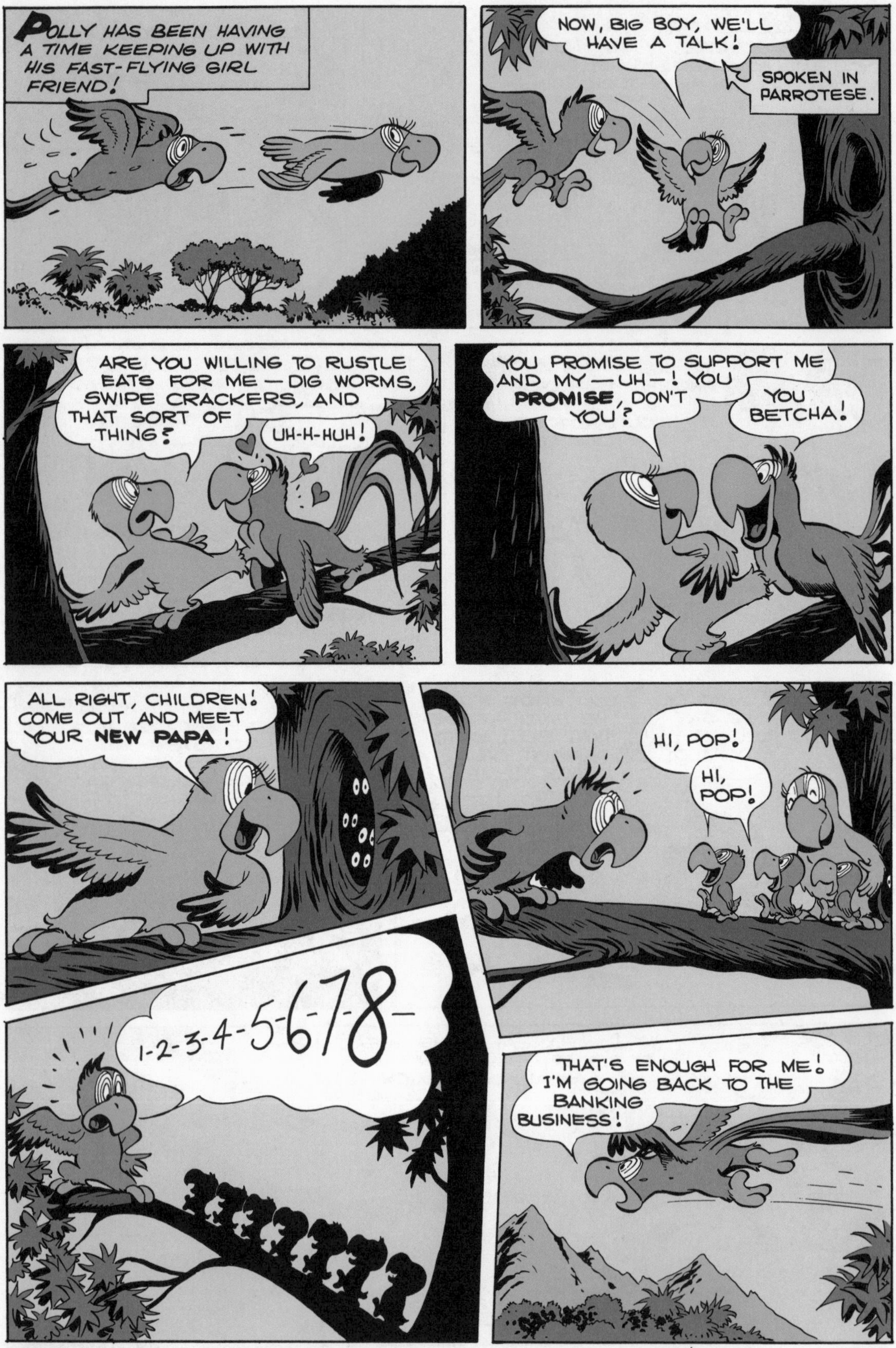
POLLY HAS BEEN HAVING A TIME KEEPING UP WITH HIS FAST-FLYING GIRL FRIEND!
NOW, BIG BOY, WE'LL HAVE A TALK!
SPOKEN IN PARROTESE.
ARE YOU WILLING TO RUSTLE EATS FOR ME — DIG WORMS, SWIPE CRACKERS, AND THAT SORT OF THING?
UH-H-HUH!
YOU PROMISE TO SUPPORT ME AND MY — UH —! YOU PROMISE, DON'T YOU?
YOU BETCHA!
ALL RIGHT, CHILDREN! COME OUT AND MEET YOUR NEW PAPA!
HI, POP!
HI, POP!
1-2-3-4-5-6-7-8—
THAT'S ENOUGH FOR ME! I'M GOING BACK TO THE BANKING BUSINESS!

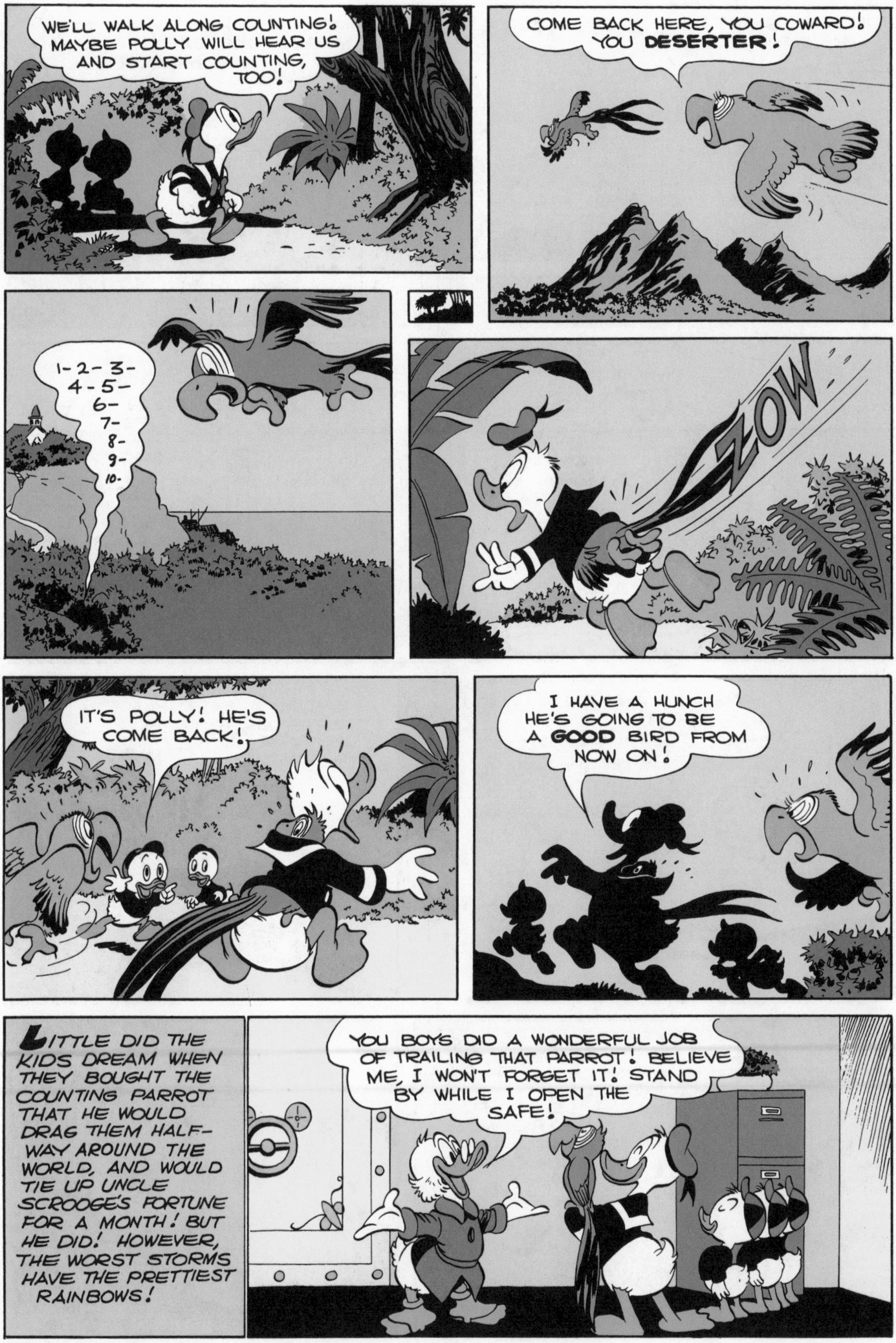
WE'LL WALK ALONG COUNTING! MAYBE POLLY WILL HEAR US AND START COUNTING, TOO!
COME BACK HERE, YOU COWARD! YOU **DESERTER**!
1-2-3-4-5-6-7-8-9-10-
ZOW
IT'S POLLY! HE'S COME BACK!
I HAVE A HUNCH HE'S GOING TO BE A **GOOD** BIRD FROM NOW ON!
LITTLE DID THE KIDS DREAM WHEN THEY BOUGHT THE COUNTING PARROT THAT HE WOULD DRAG THEM HALF-WAY AROUND THE WORLD, AND WOULD TIE UP UNCLE SCROOGE'S FORTUNE FOR A MONTH! BUT HE DID! HOWEVER, THE WORST STORMS HAVE THE PRETTIEST RAINBOWS!
YOU BOYS DID A WONDERFUL JOB OF TRAILING THAT PARROT! BELIEVE ME, I WON'T FORGET IT! STAND BY WHILE I OPEN THE SAFE!

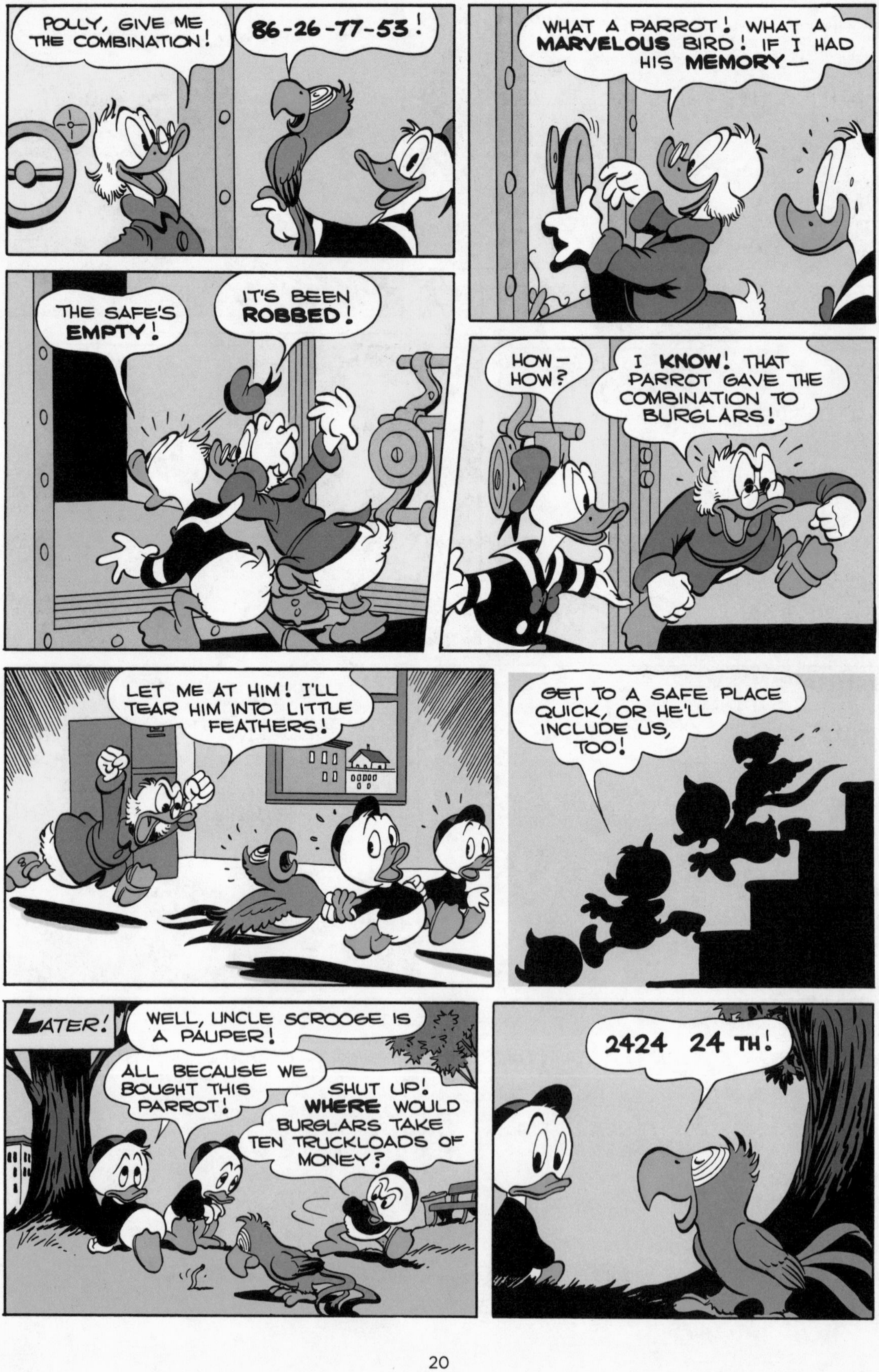
POLLY, GIVE ME THE COMBINATION!
86-26-77-53!
WHAT A PARROT! WHAT A MARVELOUS BIRD! IF I HAD HIS MEMORY—
THE SAFE'S EMPTY!
IT'S BEEN ROBBED!
HOW— HOW?
I KNOW! THAT PARROT GAVE THE COMBINATION TO BURGLARS!
LET ME AT HIM! I'LL TEAR HIM INTO LITTLE FEATHERS!
GET TO A SAFE PLACE QUICK, OR HE'LL INCLUDE US, TOO!
LATER!
WELL, UNCLE SCROOGE IS A PAUPER!
ALL BECAUSE WE BOUGHT THIS PARROT!
SHUT UP! WHERE WOULD BURGLARS TAKE TEN TRUCKLOADS OF MONEY?
2424 24 TH!

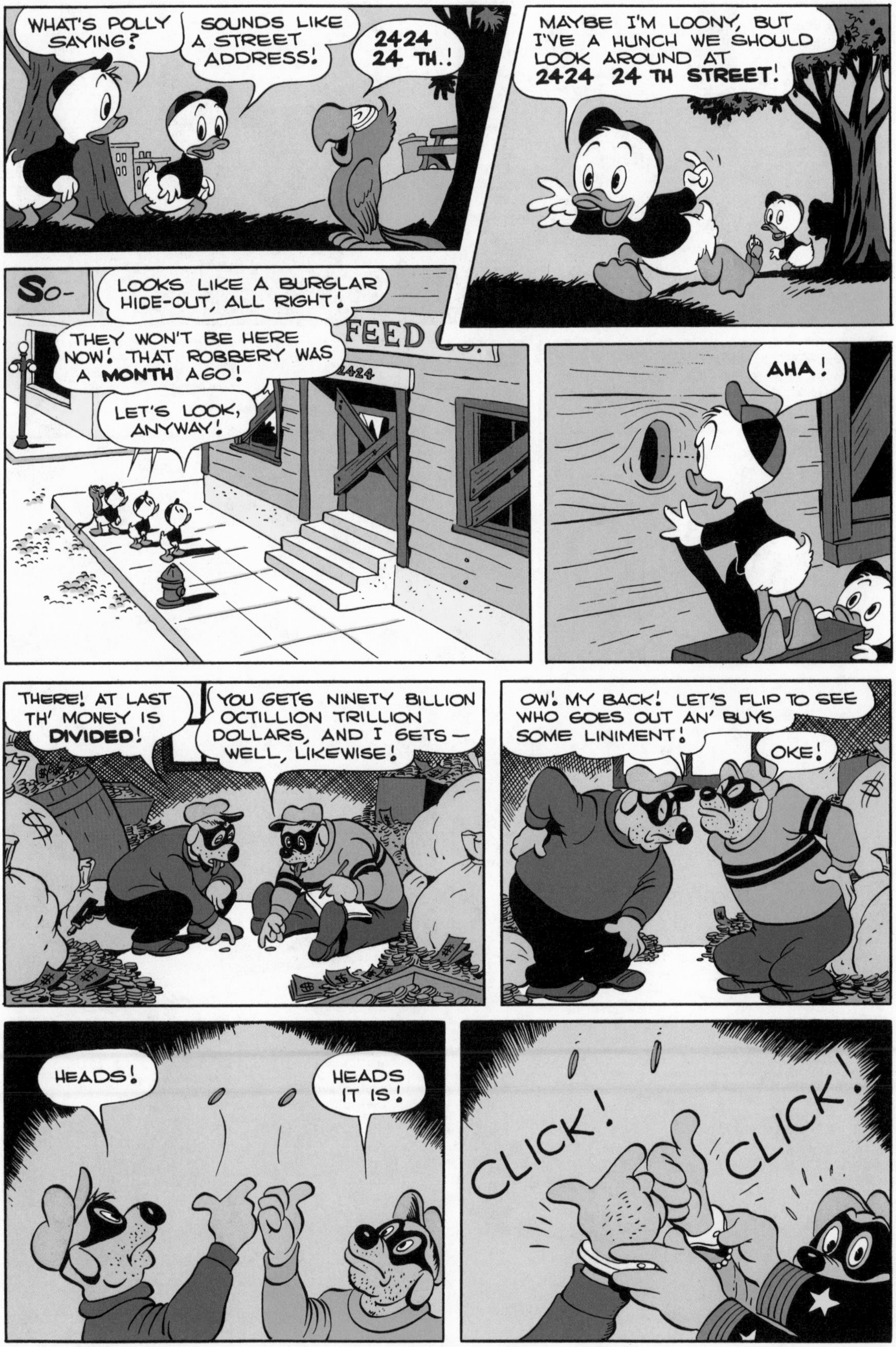
WHAT'S POLLY SAYING?
SOUNDS LIKE A STREET ADDRESS!
2424 24 TH.!
MAYBE I'M LOONY, BUT I'VE A HUNCH WE SHOULD LOOK AROUND AT 2424 24 TH STREET!
SO-
LOOKS LIKE A BURGLAR HIDE-OUT, ALL RIGHT!
THEY WON'T BE HERE NOW! THAT ROBBERY WAS A MONTH AGO!
LET'S LOOK, ANYWAY!
FEED CO.
2424
AHA!
THERE! AT LAST TH' MONEY IS DIVIDED!
YOU GETS NINETY BILLION OCTILLION TRILLION DOLLARS, AND I GETS— WELL, LIKEWISE!
OW! MY BACK! LET'S FLIP TO SEE WHO GOES OUT AN' BUYS SOME LINIMENT!
OKE!
HEADS!
HEADS IT IS!
CLICK!
CLICK!

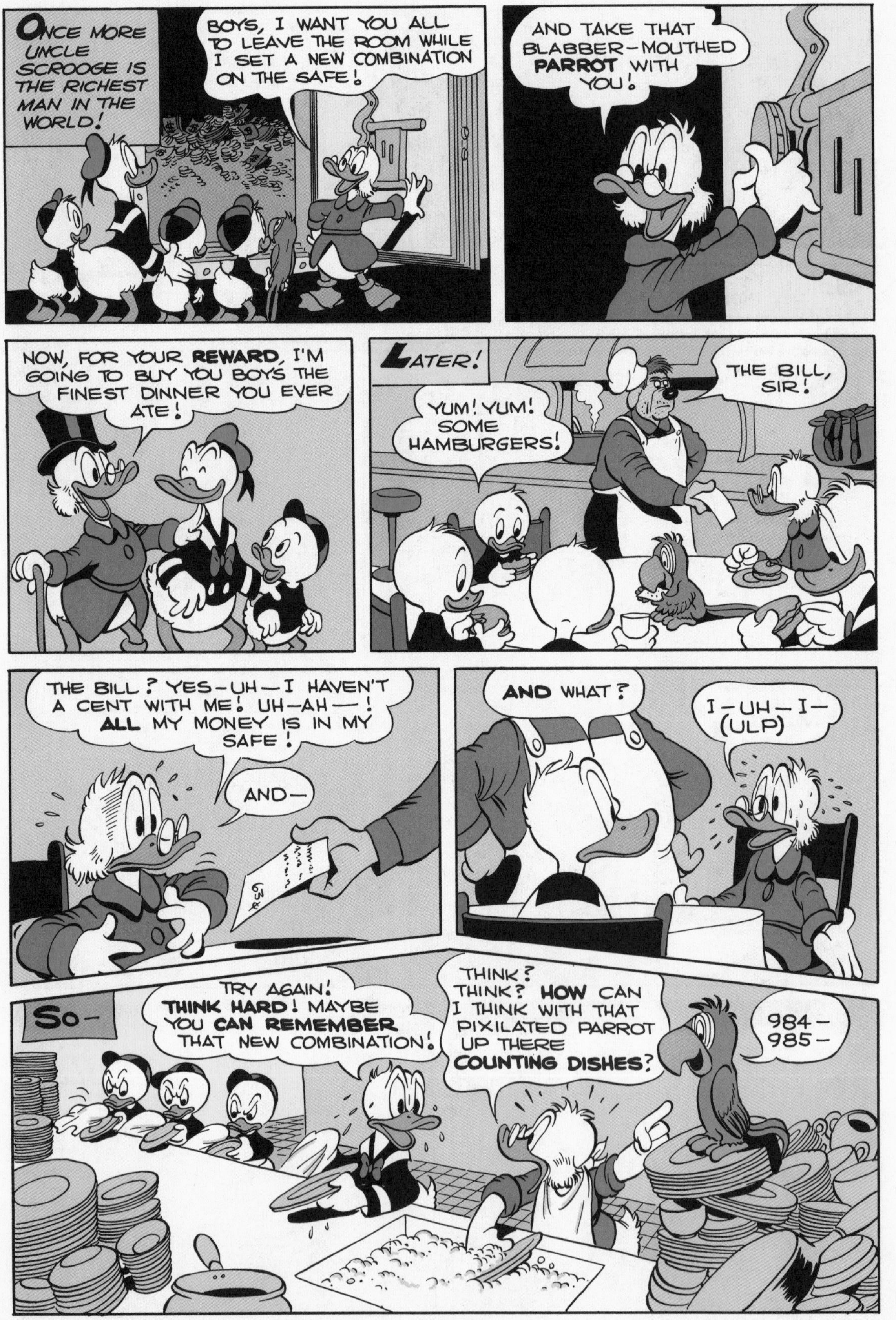
ONCE MORE UNCLE SCROOGE IS THE RICHEST MAN IN THE WORLD!
BOYS, I WANT YOU ALL TO LEAVE THE ROOM WHILE I SET A NEW COMBINATION ON THE SAFE!
AND TAKE THAT BLABBER-MOUTHED PARROT WITH YOU!
NOW, FOR YOUR REWARD, I'M GOING TO BUY YOU BOYS THE FINEST DINNER YOU EVER ATE!
LATER!
YUM! YUM! SOME HAMBURGERS!
THE BILL, SIR!
THE BILL? YES-UH—I HAVEN'T A CENT WITH ME! UH-AH—! ALL MY MONEY IS IN MY SAFE!
AND-
AND WHAT?
I-UH-I- (ULP)
SO-
TRY AGAIN! THINK HARD! MAYBE YOU CAN REMEMBER THAT NEW COMBINATION!
THINK? THINK? HOW CAN I THINK WITH THAT PIXILATED PARROT UP THERE COUNTING DISHES?
984- 985-

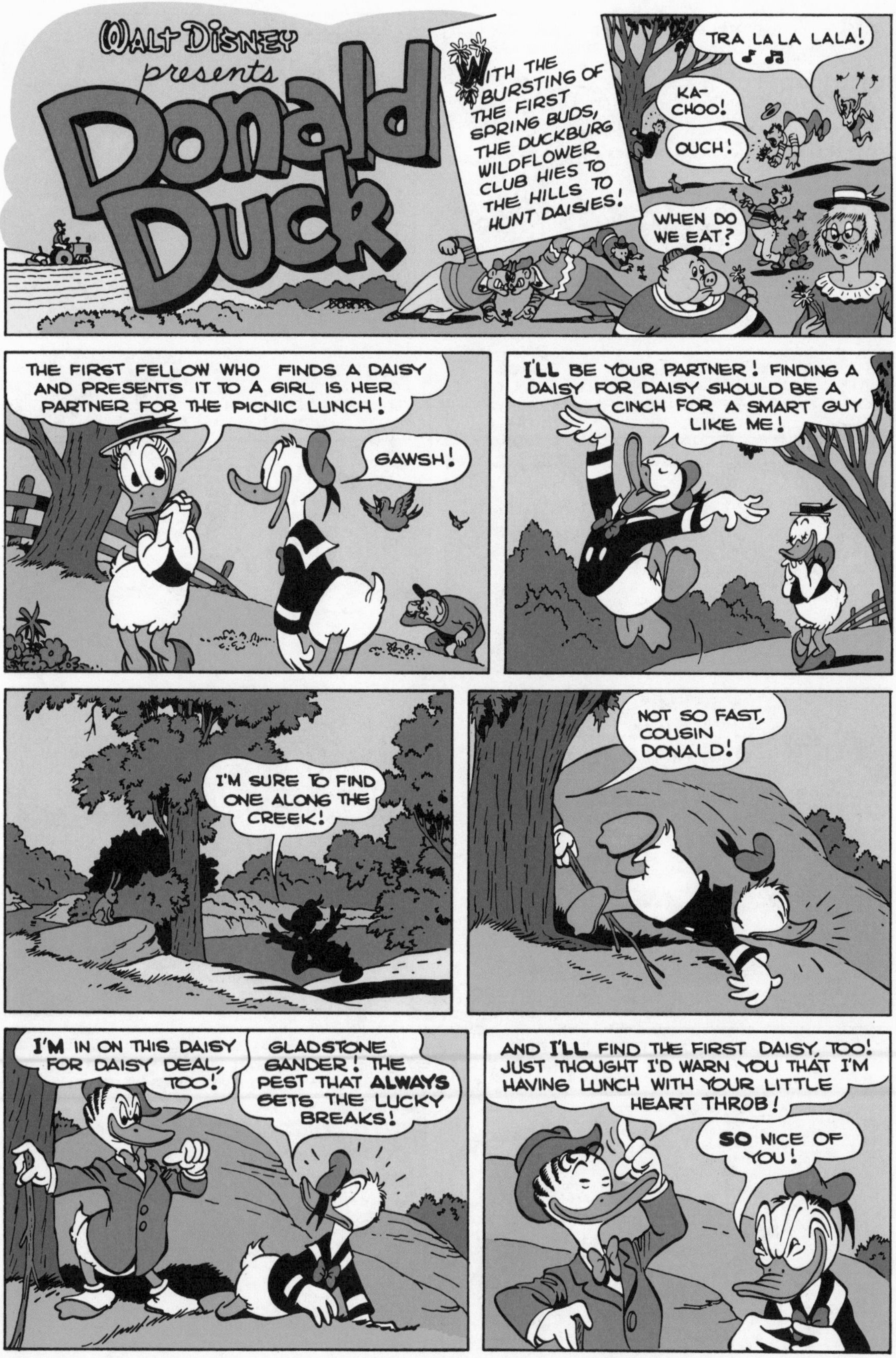
WALT DISNEY
presents
Donald Duck
WITH THE BURSTING OF THE FIRST SPRING BUDS, THE DUCKBURG WILDFLOWER CLUB HIES TO THE HILLS TO HUNT DAISIES!
TRA LA LA LALA!
KA-CHOO!
OUCH!
WHEN DO WE EAT?
THE FIRST FELLOW WHO FINDS A DAISY AND PRESENTS IT TO A GIRL IS HER PARTNER FOR THE PICNIC LUNCH!
GAWSH!
I'LL BE YOUR PARTNER! FINDING A DAISY FOR DAISY SHOULD BE A CINCH FOR A SMART GUY LIKE ME!
I'M SURE TO FIND ONE ALONG THE CREEK!
NOT SO FAST, COUSIN DONALD!
I'M IN ON THIS DAISY FOR DAISY DEAL, TOO!
GLADSTONE GANDER! THE PEST THAT ALWAYS GETS THE LUCKY BREAKS!
AND I'LL FIND THE FIRST DAISY, TOO! JUST THOUGHT I'D WARN YOU THAT I'M HAVING LUNCH WITH YOUR LITTLE HEART THROB!
SO NICE OF YOU!

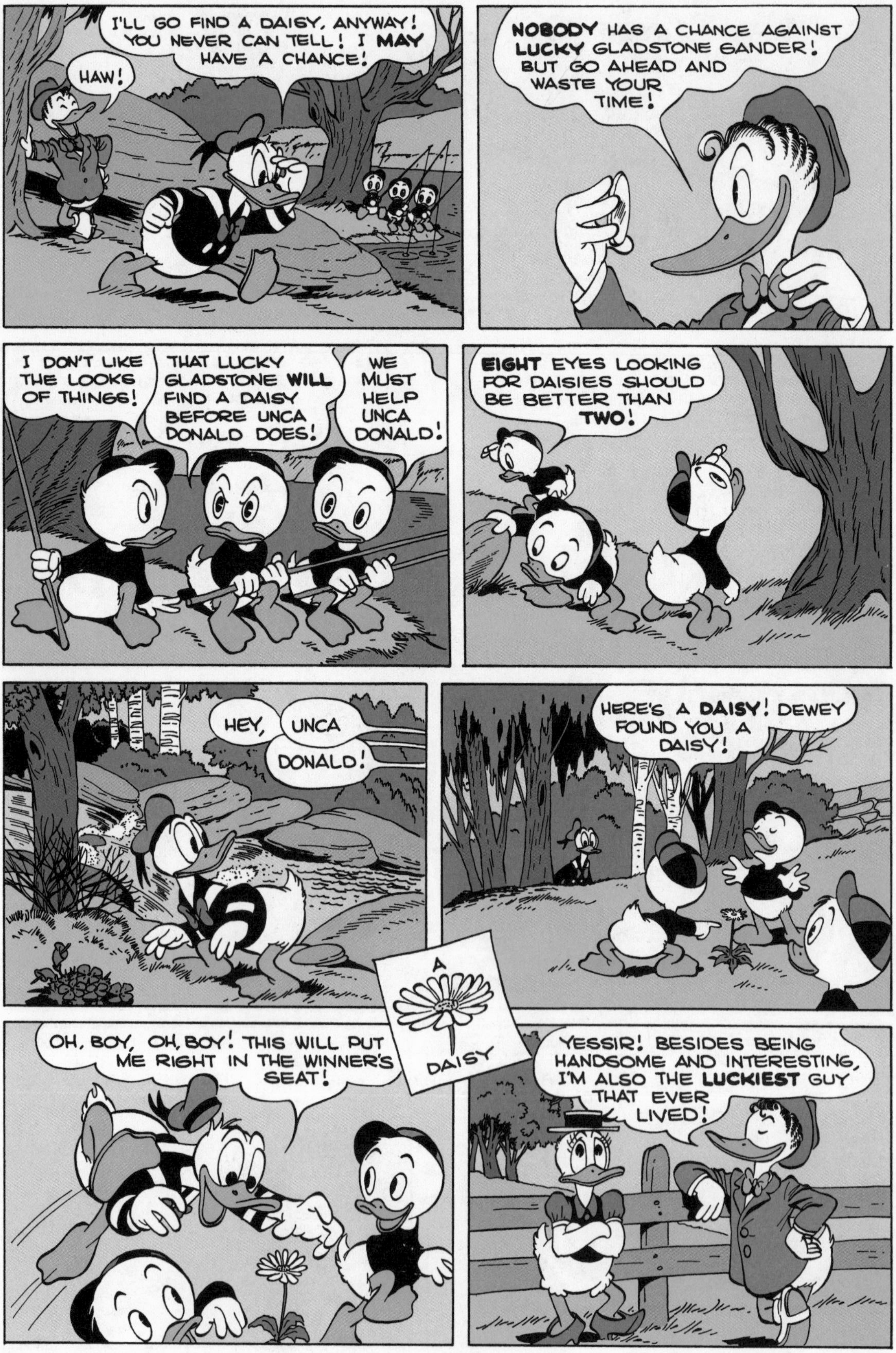
I'LL GO FIND A DAISY, ANYWAY! YOU NEVER CAN TELL! I MAY HAVE A CHANCE!
HAW!
NOBODY HAS A CHANCE AGAINST LUCKY GLADSTONE GANDER! BUT GO AHEAD AND WASTE YOUR TIME!
I DON'T LIKE THE LOOKS OF THINGS!
THAT LUCKY GLADSTONE WILL FIND A DAISY BEFORE UNCA DONALD DOES!
WE MUST HELP UNCA DONALD!
EIGHT EYES LOOKING FOR DAISIES SHOULD BE BETTER THAN TWO!
HEY, UNCA
DONALD!
HERE'S A DAISY! DEWEY FOUND YOU A DAISY!
A DAISY
OH, BOY, OH, BOY! THIS WILL PUT ME RIGHT IN THE WINNER'S SEAT!
YESSIR! BESIDES BEING HANDSOME AND INTERESTING, I'M ALSO THE LUCKIEST GUY THAT EVER LIVED!

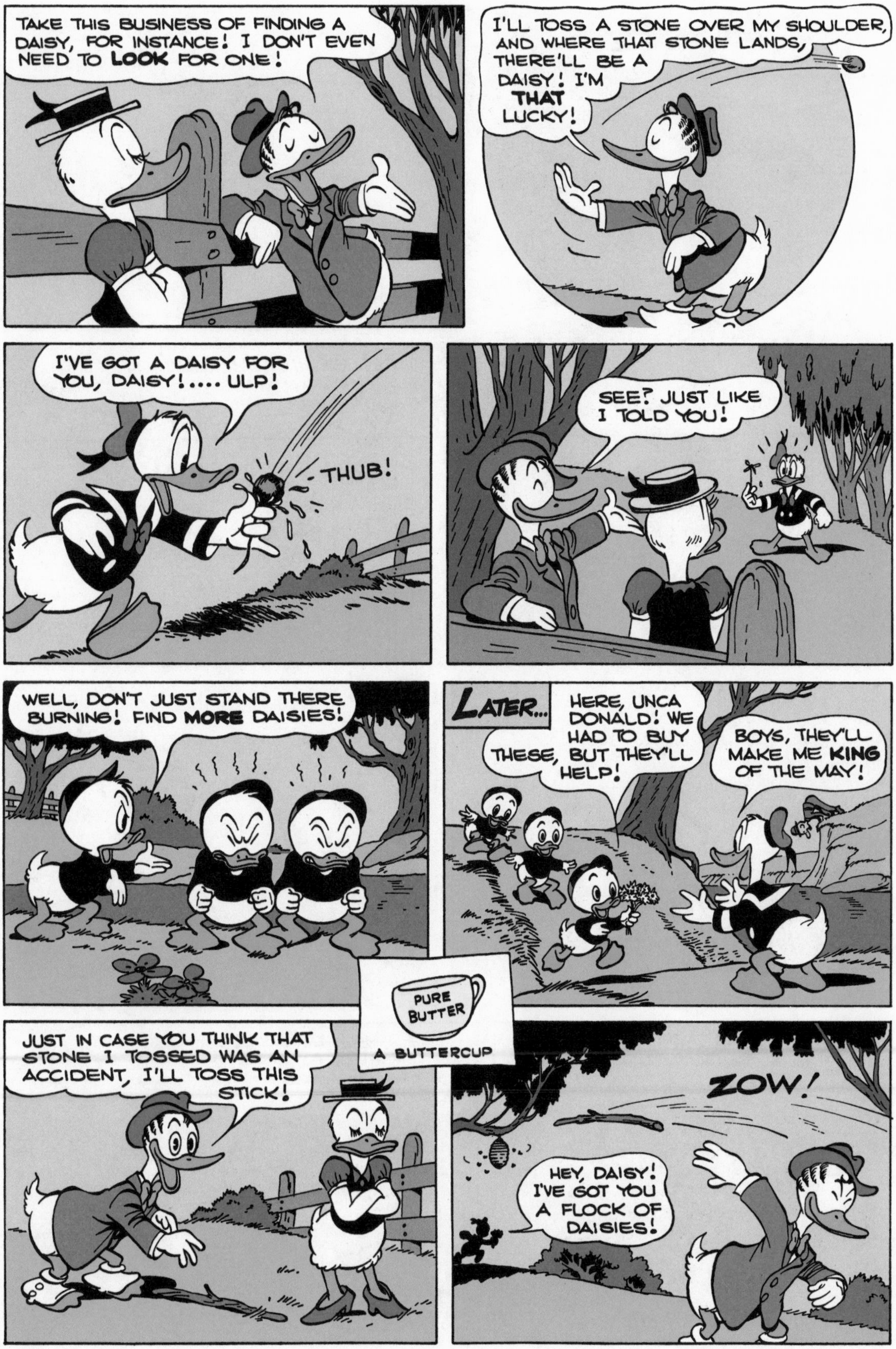
TAKE THIS BUSINESS OF FINDING A DAISY, FOR INSTANCE! I DON'T EVEN NEED TO **LOOK** FOR ONE!
I'LL TOSS A STONE OVER MY SHOULDER, AND WHERE THAT STONE LANDS, THERE'LL BE A DAISY! I'M **THAT** LUCKY!
I'VE GOT A DAISY FOR YOU, DAISY!.... ULP!
THUB!
SEE? JUST LIKE I TOLD YOU!
WELL, DON'T JUST STAND THERE BURNING! FIND **MORE** DAISIES!
LATER...
HERE, UNCA DONALD! WE HAD TO BUY THESE, BUT THEY'LL HELP!
BOYS, THEY'LL MAKE ME **KING** OF THE MAY!
PURE BUTTER
A BUTTERCUP
JUST IN CASE YOU THINK THAT STONE I TOSSED WAS AN ACCIDENT, I'LL TOSS THIS STICK!
ZOW!
HEY, DAISY! I'VE GOT YOU A FLOCK OF DAISIES!

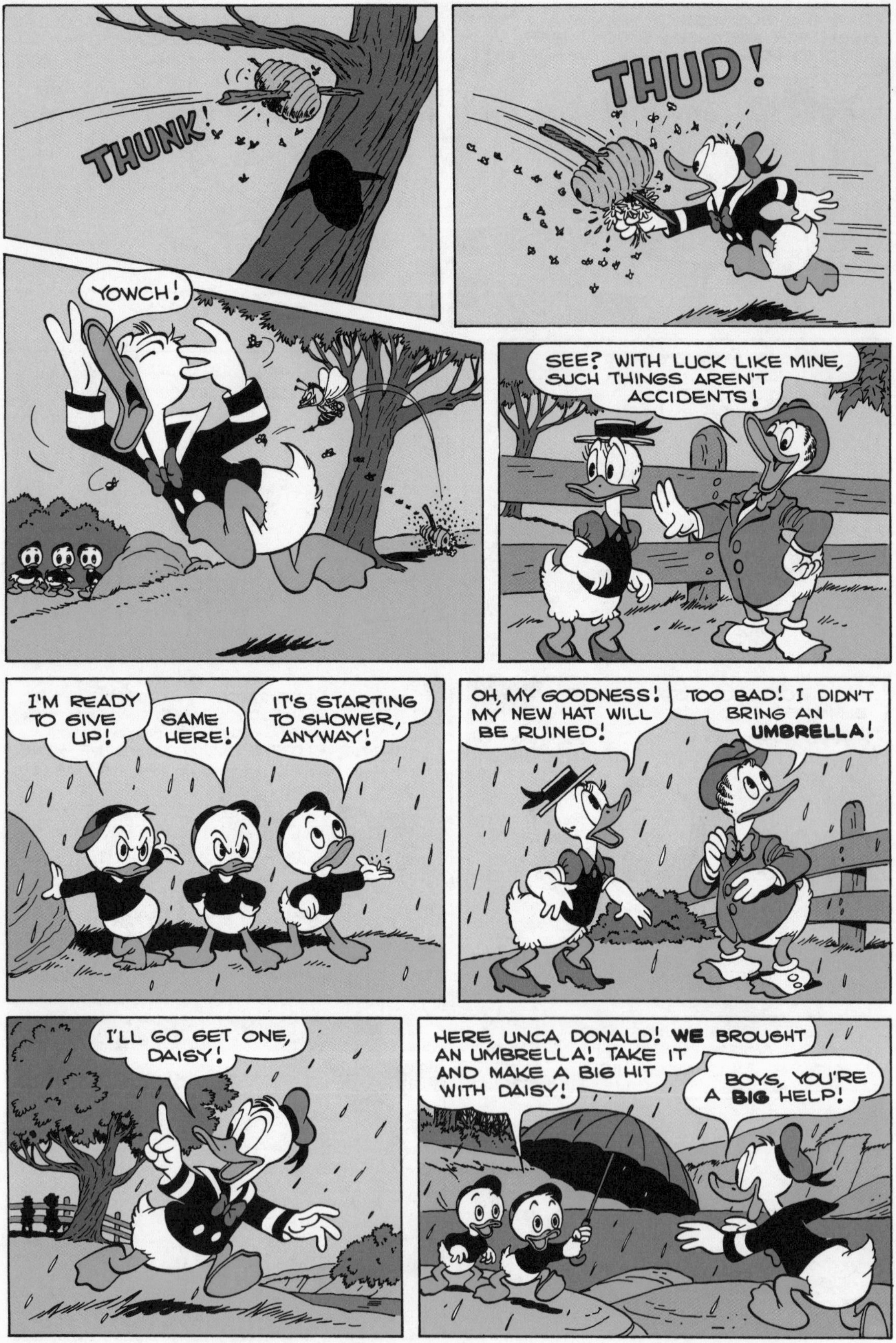
THUNK!
THUD!
YOWCH!
SEE? WITH LUCK LIKE MINE, SUCH THINGS AREN'T ACCIDENTS!
I'M READY TO GIVE UP!
SAME HERE!
IT'S STARTING TO SHOWER, ANYWAY!
OH, MY GOODNESS! MY NEW HAT WILL BE RUINED!
TOO BAD! I DIDN'T BRING AN UMBRELLA!
I'LL GO GET ONE, DAISY!
HERE, UNCA DONALD! WE BROUGHT AN UMBRELLA! TAKE IT AND MAKE A BIG HIT WITH DAISY!
BOYS, YOU'RE A BIG HELP!

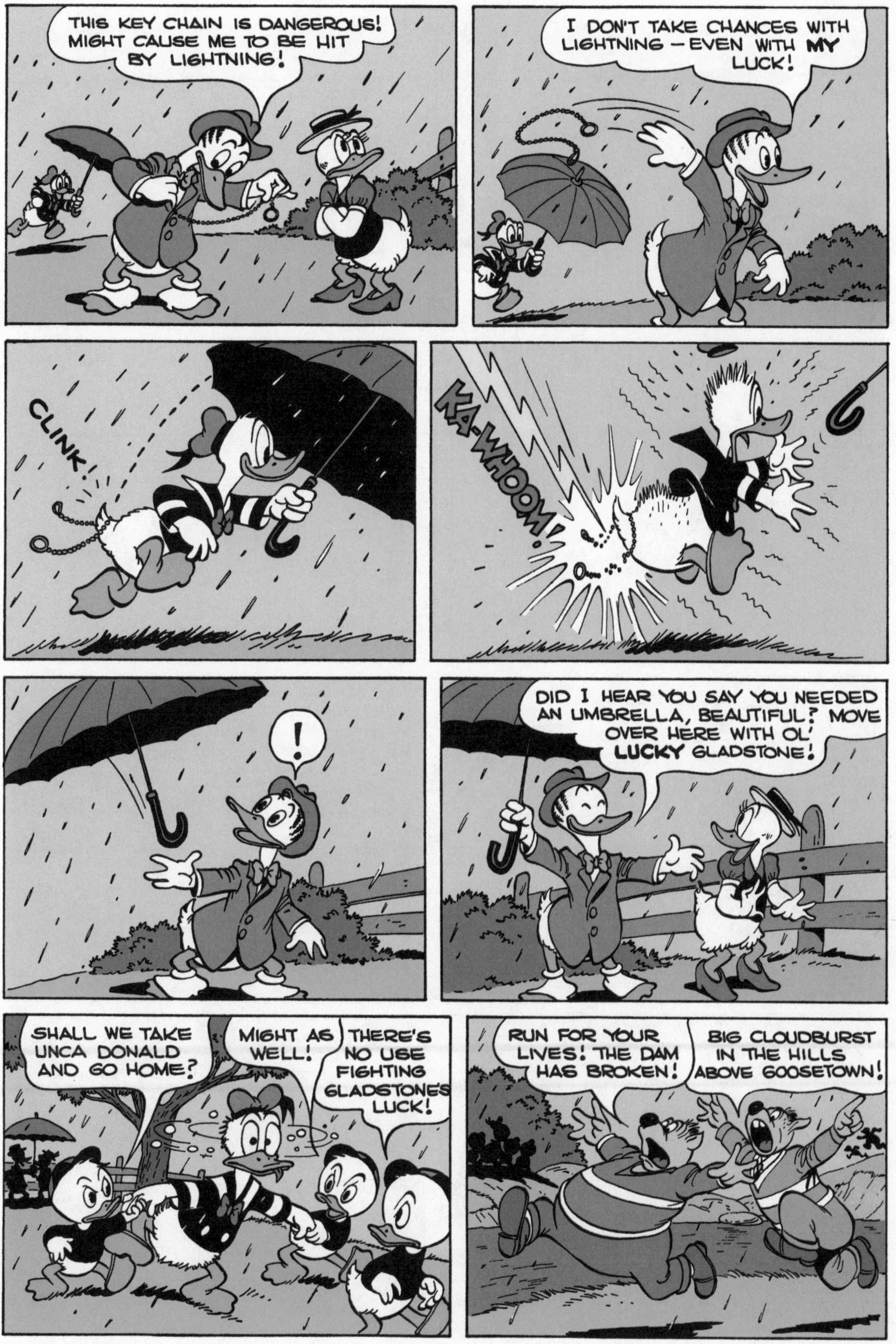
THIS KEY CHAIN IS DANGEROUS! MIGHT CAUSE ME TO BE HIT BY LIGHTNING!
I DON'T TAKE CHANCES WITH LIGHTNING — EVEN WITH MY LUCK!
CLINK!
KA-WHOOM!
!
DID I HEAR YOU SAY YOU NEEDED AN UMBRELLA, BEAUTIFUL? MOVE OVER HERE WITH OL' LUCKY GLADSTONE!
SHALL WE TAKE UNCA DONALD AND GO HOME?
MIGHT AS WELL!
THERE'S NO USE FIGHTING GLADSTONE'S LUCK!
RUN FOR YOUR LIVES! THE DAM HAS BROKEN!
BIG CLOUDBURST IN THE HILLS ABOVE GOOSETOWN!

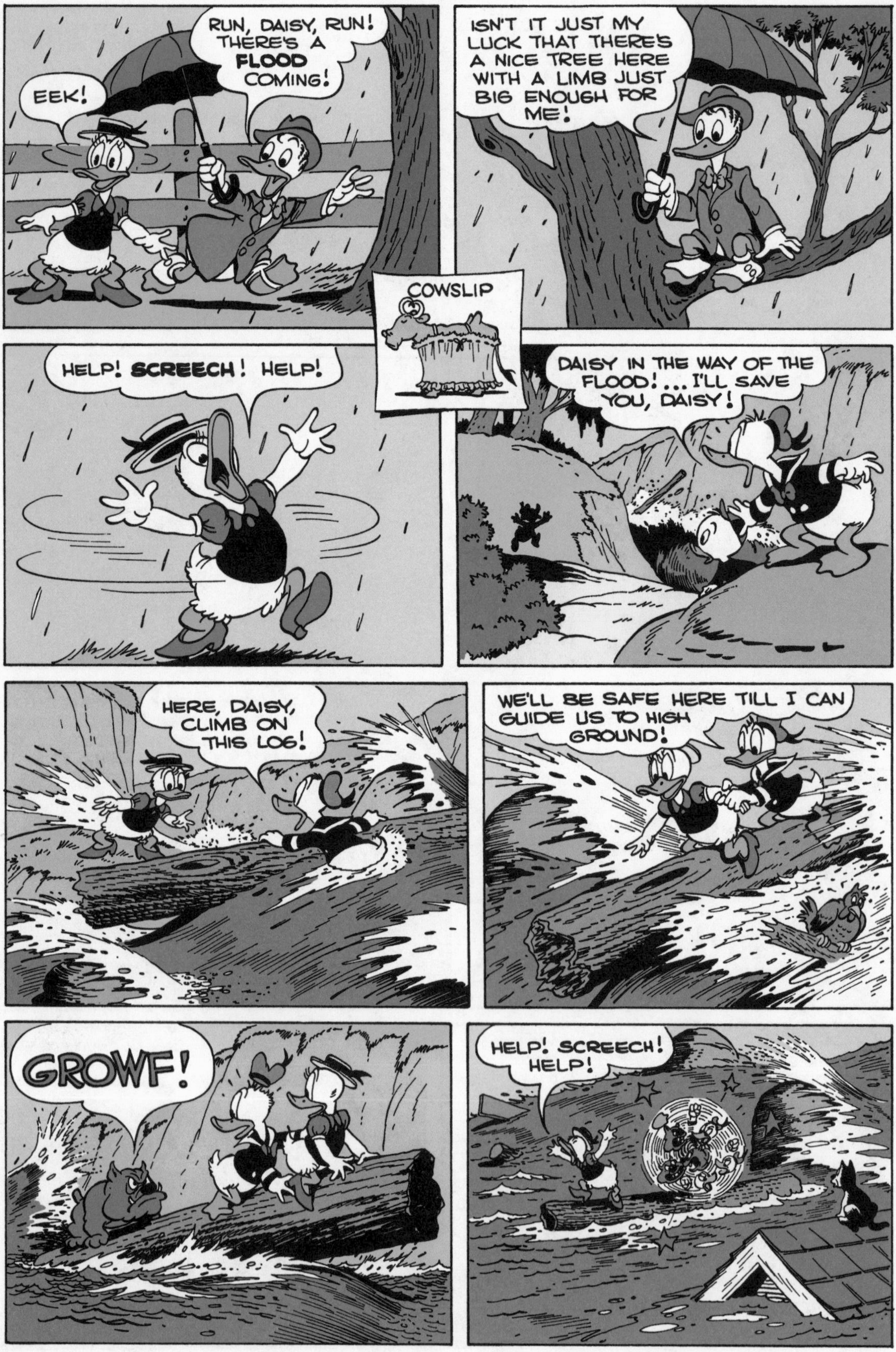
EEK!
RUN, DAISY, RUN! THERE'S A FLOOD COMING!
ISN'T IT JUST MY LUCK THAT THERE'S A NICE TREE HERE WITH A LIMB JUST BIG ENOUGH FOR ME!
COWSLIP
HELP! SCREECH! HELP!
DAISY IN THE WAY OF THE FLOOD! ... I'LL SAVE YOU, DAISY!
HERE, DAISY, CLIMB ON THIS LOG!
WE'LL BE SAFE HERE TILL I CAN GUIDE US TO HIGH GROUND!
GROWF!
HELP! SCREECH! HELP!

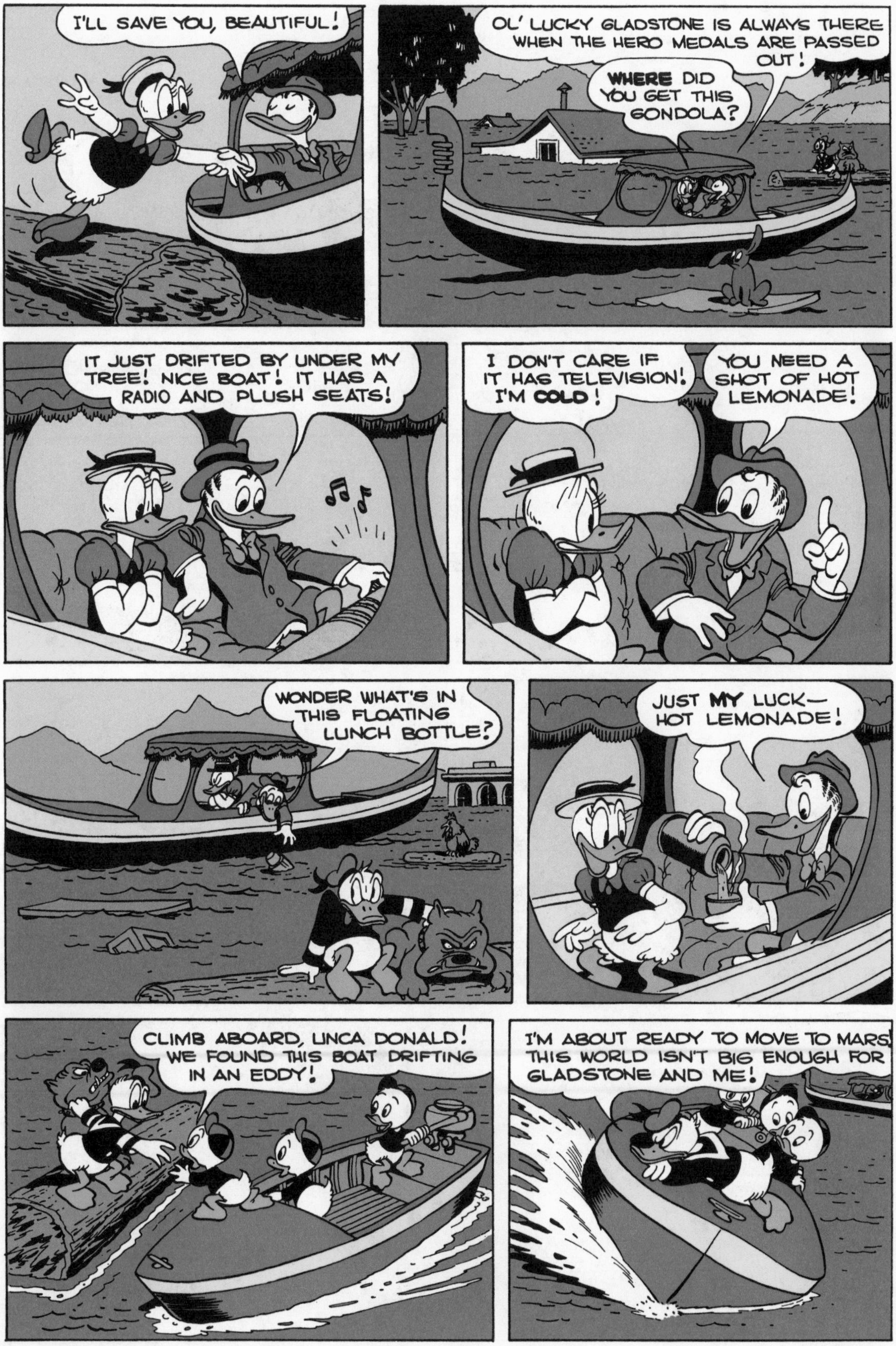
I'LL SAVE YOU, BEAUTIFUL!
OL' LUCKY GLADSTONE IS ALWAYS THERE WHEN THE HERO MEDALS ARE PASSED OUT!
WHERE DID YOU GET THIS GONDOLA?
IT JUST DRIFTED BY UNDER MY TREE! NICE BOAT! IT HAS A RADIO AND PLUSH SEATS!
I DON'T CARE IF IT HAS TELEVISION! I'M COLD!
YOU NEED A SHOT OF HOT LEMONADE!
WONDER WHAT'S IN THIS FLOATING LUNCH BOTTLE?
JUST MY LUCK— HOT LEMONADE!
CLIMB ABOARD, UNCA DONALD! WE FOUND THIS BOAT DRIFTING IN AN EDDY!
I'M ABOUT READY TO MOVE TO MARS! THIS WORLD ISN'T BIG ENOUGH FOR GLADSTONE AND ME!

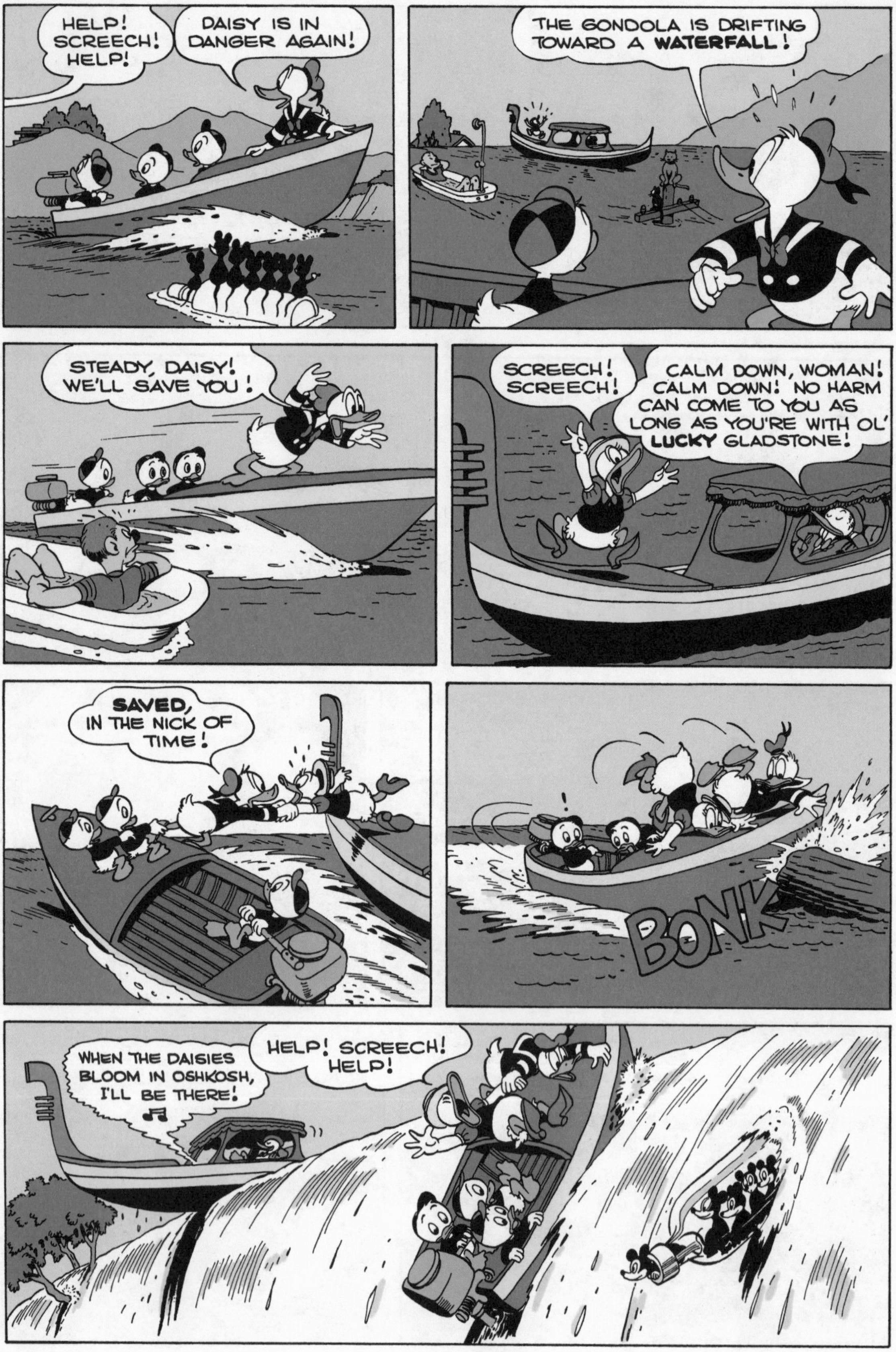
HELP! SCREECH! HELP!
DAISY IS IN DANGER AGAIN!
THE GONDOLA IS DRIFTING TOWARD A **WATERFALL**!
STEADY, DAISY! WE'LL SAVE YOU!
SCREECH! SCREECH!
CALM DOWN, WOMAN! CALM DOWN! NO HARM CAN COME TO YOU AS LONG AS YOU'RE WITH OL' **LUCKY** GLADSTONE!
SAVED, IN THE NICK OF TIME!
BONK
WHEN THE DAISIES BLOOM IN OSHKOSH, I'LL BE THERE!
HELP! SCREECH! HELP!

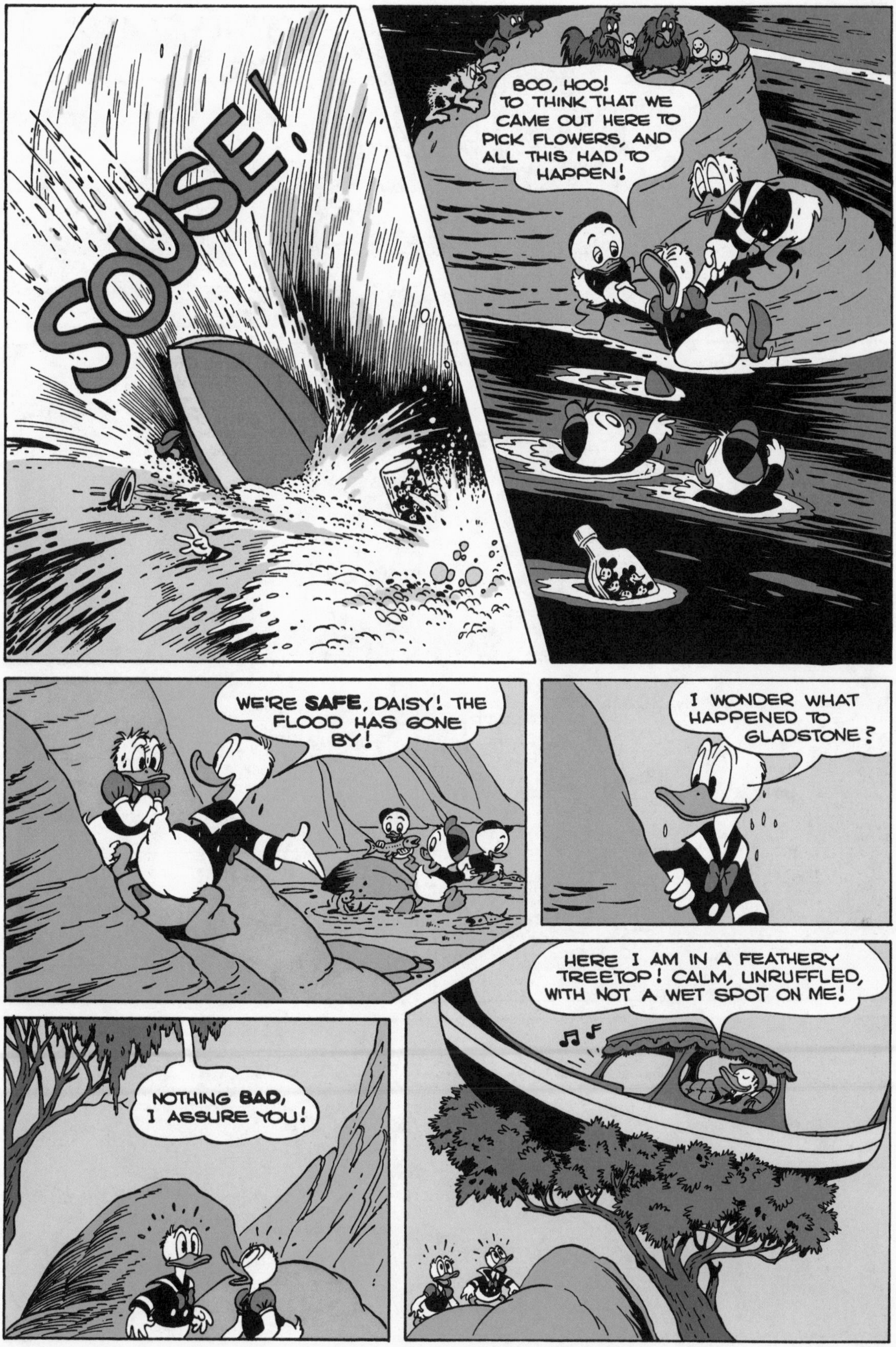
SOUSE!
BOO, HOO! TO THINK THAT WE CAME OUT HERE TO PICK FLOWERS, AND ALL THIS HAD TO HAPPEN!
WE'RE SAFE, DAISY! THE FLOOD HAS GONE BY!
I WONDER WHAT HAPPENED TO GLADSTONE?
NOTHING BAD, I ASSURE YOU!
HERE I AM IN A FEATHERY TREETOP! CALM, UNRUFFLED, WITH NOT A WET SPOT ON ME!

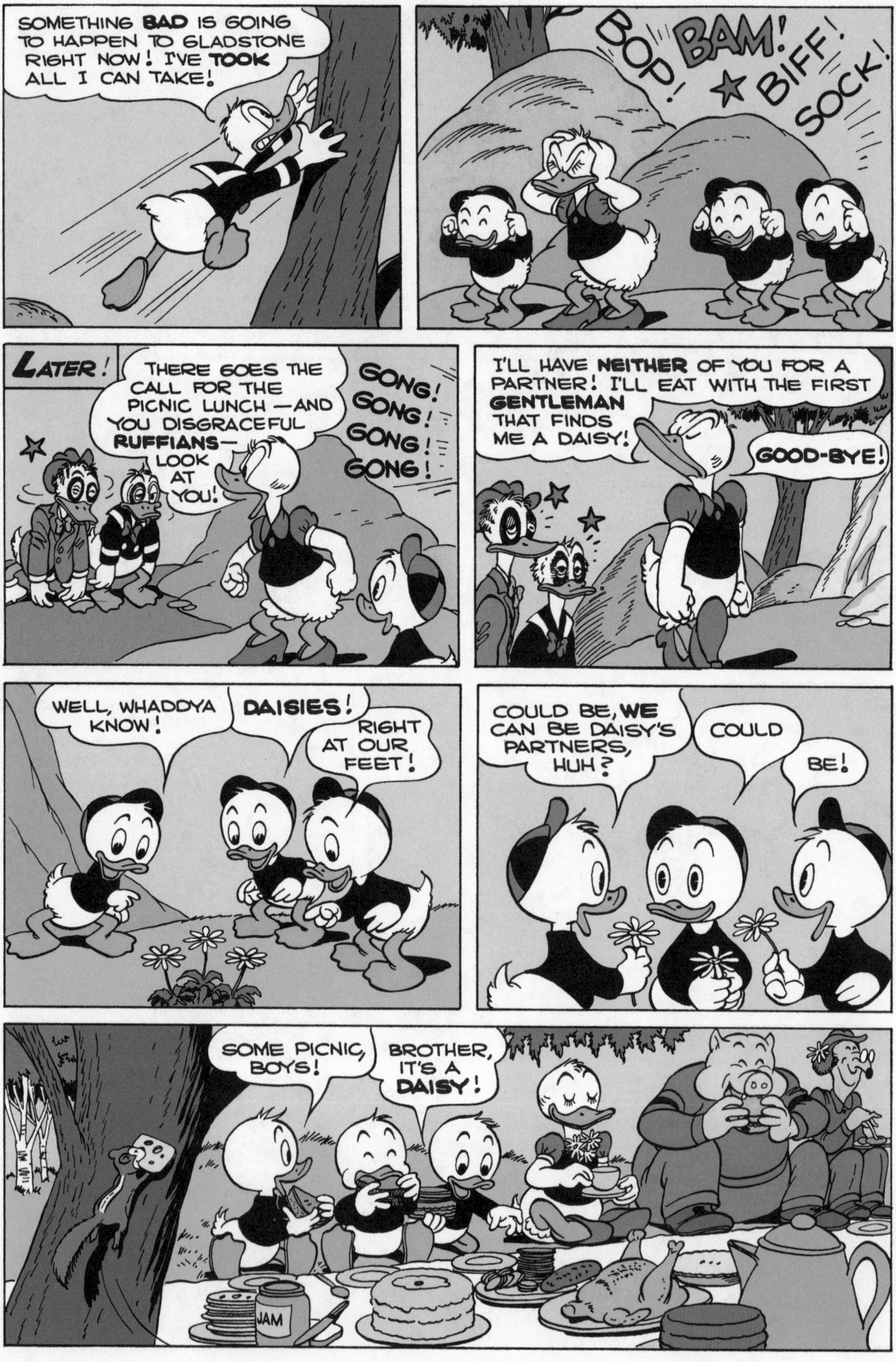
SOMETHING BAD IS GOING TO HAPPEN TO GLADSTONE RIGHT NOW! I'VE TOOK ALL I CAN TAKE!
BOP! BAM! BIFF! SOCK!
LATER!
THERE GOES THE CALL FOR THE PICNIC LUNCH—AND YOU DISGRACEFUL RUFFIANS—LOOK AT YOU!
GONG! GONG! GONG! GONG!
I'LL HAVE NEITHER OF YOU FOR A PARTNER! I'LL EAT WITH THE FIRST GENTLEMAN THAT FINDS ME A DAISY!
GOOD-BYE!
WELL, WHADDYA KNOW!
DAISIES!
RIGHT AT OUR FEET!
COULD BE, WE CAN BE DAISY'S PARTNERS, HUH?
COULD
BE!
SOME PICNIC, BOYS!
BROTHER, IT'S A DAISY!
JAM

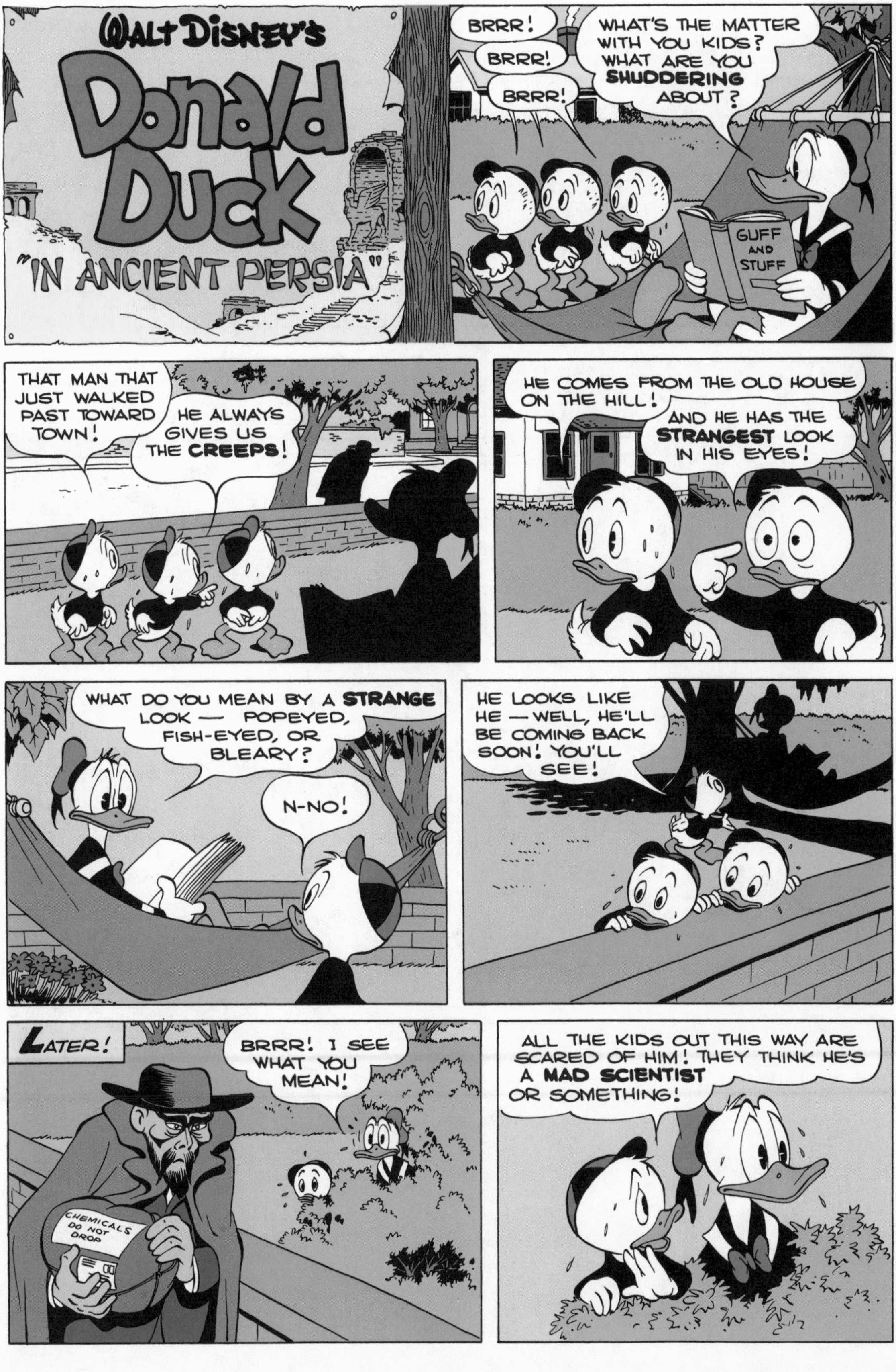
WALT DISNEY'S
Donald Duck
"IN ANCIENT PERSIA"
BRRR!
BRRR!
BRRR!
WHAT'S THE MATTER WITH YOU KIDS? WHAT ARE YOU SHUDDERING ABOUT?
GUFF AND STUFF
THAT MAN THAT JUST WALKED PAST TOWARD TOWN!
HE ALWAYS GIVES US THE CREEPS!
HE COMES FROM THE OLD HOUSE ON THE HILL!
AND HE HAS THE STRANGEST LOOK IN HIS EYES!
WHAT DO YOU MEAN BY A STRANGE LOOK — POPEYED, FISH-EYED, OR BLEARY?
N-NO!
HE LOOKS LIKE HE — WELL, HE'LL BE COMING BACK SOON! YOU'LL SEE!
LATER!
BRRR! I SEE WHAT YOU MEAN!
CHEMICALS DO NOT DROP
ALL THE KIDS OUT THIS WAY ARE SCARED OF HIM! THEY THINK HE'S A MAD SCIENTIST OR SOMETHING!

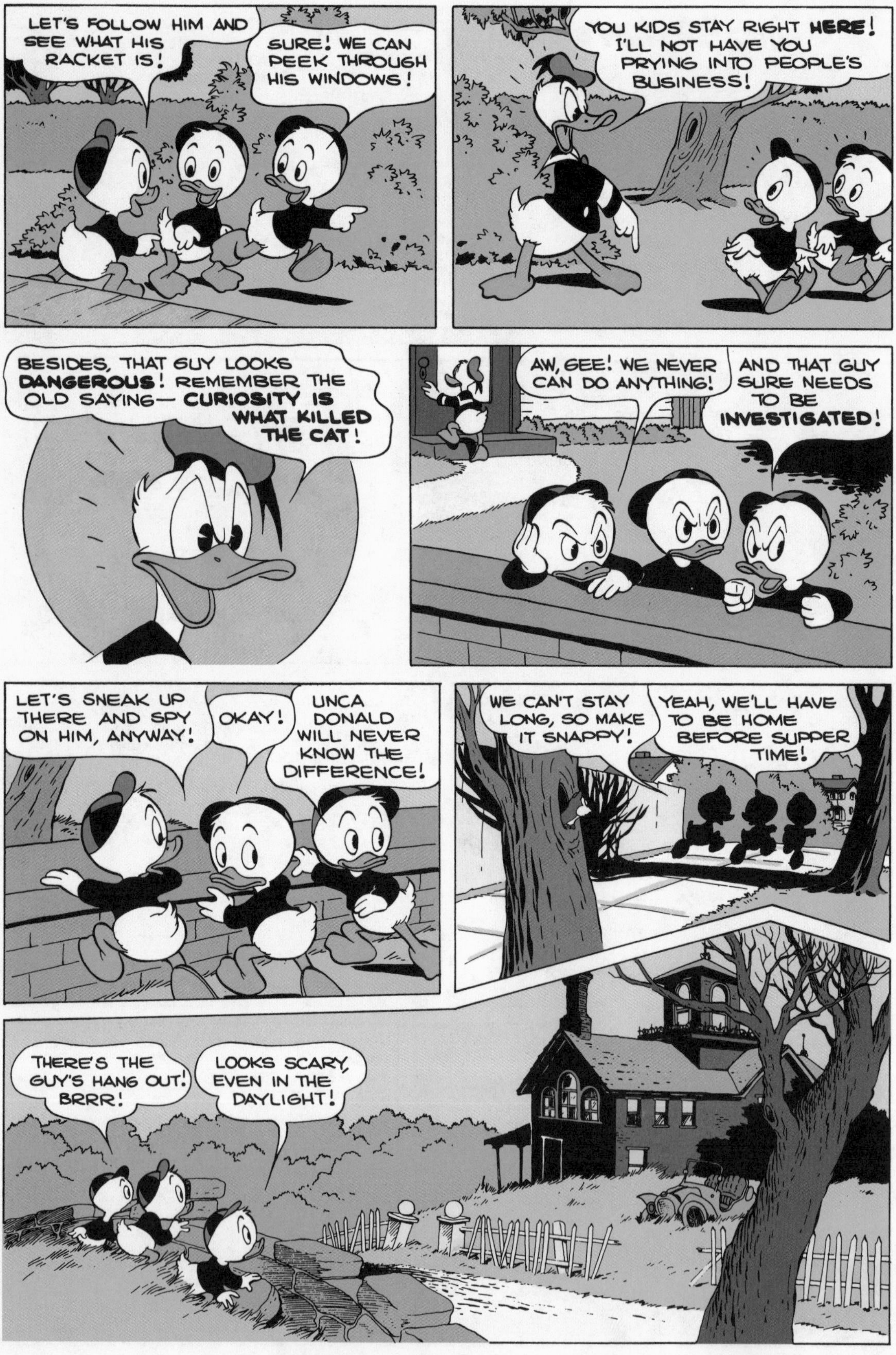
LET'S FOLLOW HIM AND SEE WHAT HIS RACKET IS!
SURE! WE CAN PEEK THROUGH HIS WINDOWS!
YOU KIDS STAY RIGHT HERE! I'LL NOT HAVE YOU PRYING INTO PEOPLE'S BUSINESS!
BESIDES, THAT GUY LOOKS DANGEROUS! REMEMBER THE OLD SAYING— CURIOSITY IS WHAT KILLED THE CAT!
AW, GEE! WE NEVER CAN DO ANYTHING!
AND THAT GUY SURE NEEDS TO BE INVESTIGATED!
LET'S SNEAK UP THERE AND SPY ON HIM, ANYWAY!
OKAY!
UNCA DONALD WILL NEVER KNOW THE DIFFERENCE!
WE CAN'T STAY LONG, SO MAKE IT SNAPPY!
YEAH, WE'LL HAVE TO BE HOME BEFORE SUPPER TIME!
THERE'S THE GUY'S HANG OUT! BRRR!
LOOKS SCARY, EVEN IN THE DAYLIGHT!

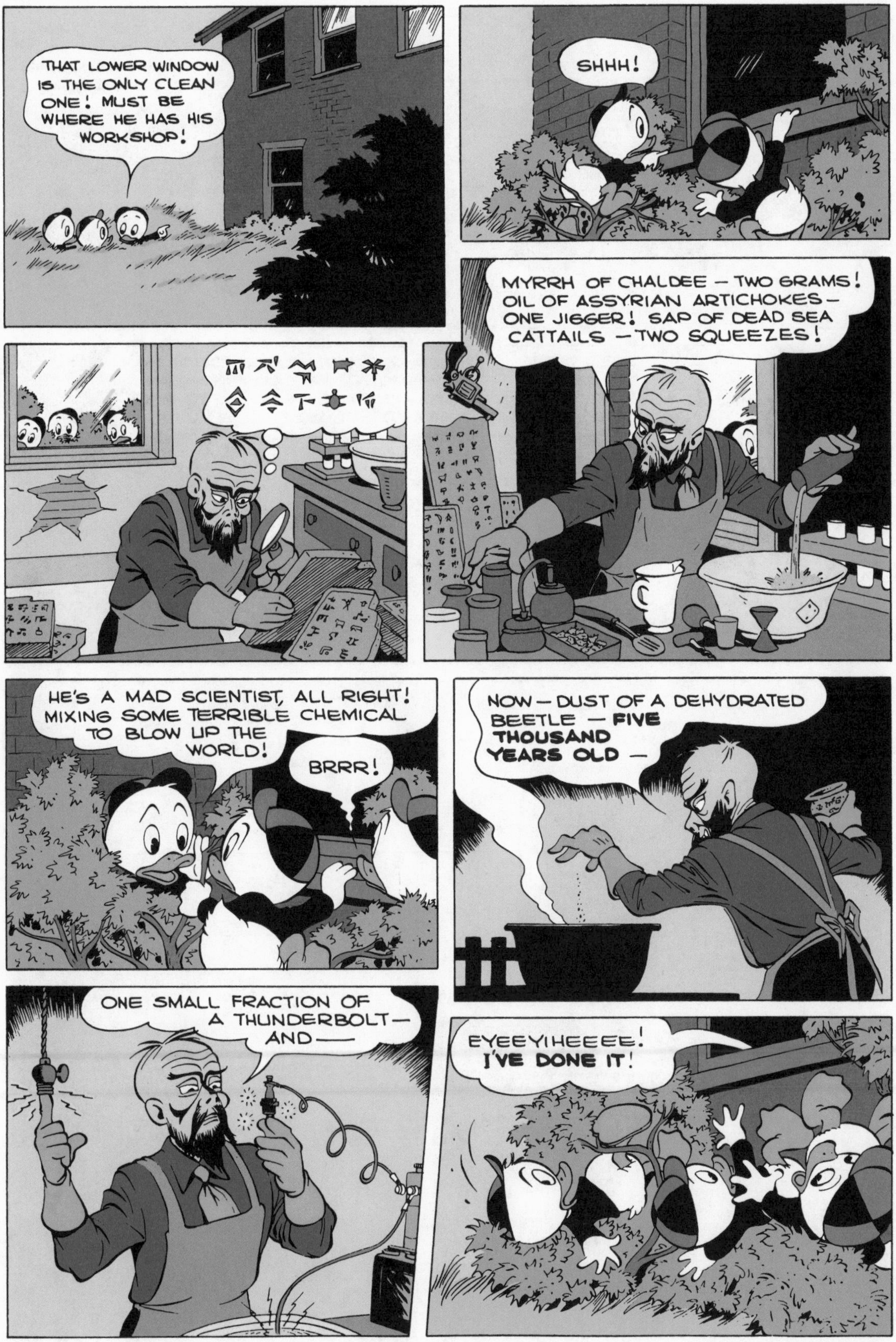
THAT LOWER WINDOW IS THE ONLY CLEAN ONE! MUST BE WHERE HE HAS HIS WORKSHOP!
SHHH!
MYRRH OF CHALDEE — TWO GRAMS! OIL OF ASSYRIAN ARTICHOKES — ONE JIGGER! SAP OF DEAD SEA CATTAILS — TWO SQUEEZES!
HE'S A MAD SCIENTIST, ALL RIGHT! MIXING SOME TERRIBLE CHEMICAL TO BLOW UP THE WORLD!
BRRR!
NOW — DUST OF A DEHYDRATED BEETLE — FIVE THOUSAND YEARS OLD —
ONE SMALL FRACTION OF A THUNDERBOLT — AND —
EYEEYIHEEEE! I'VE DONE IT!

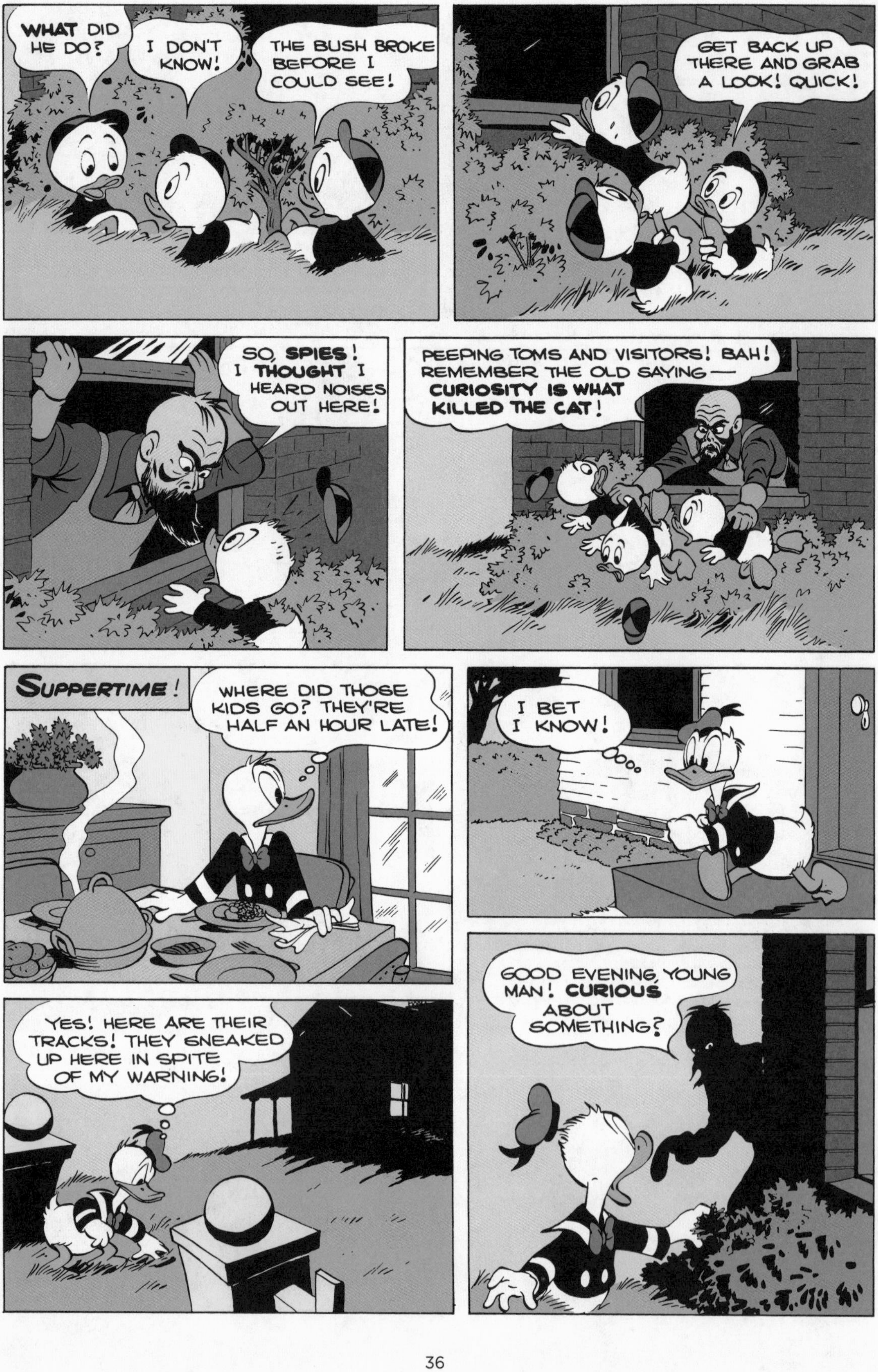
WHAT DID HE DO?
I DON'T KNOW!
THE BUSH BROKE BEFORE I COULD SEE!
GET BACK UP THERE AND GRAB A LOOK! QUICK!
SO, SPIES! I THOUGHT I HEARD NOISES OUT HERE!
PEEPING TOMS AND VISITORS! BAH! REMEMBER THE OLD SAYING— CURIOSITY IS WHAT KILLED THE CAT!
SUPPERTIME!
WHERE DID THOSE KIDS GO? THEY'RE HALF AN HOUR LATE!
I BET I KNOW!
YES! HERE ARE THEIR TRACKS! THEY SNEAKED UP HERE IN SPITE OF MY WARNING!
GOOD EVENING, YOUNG MAN! CURIOUS ABOUT SOMETHING?

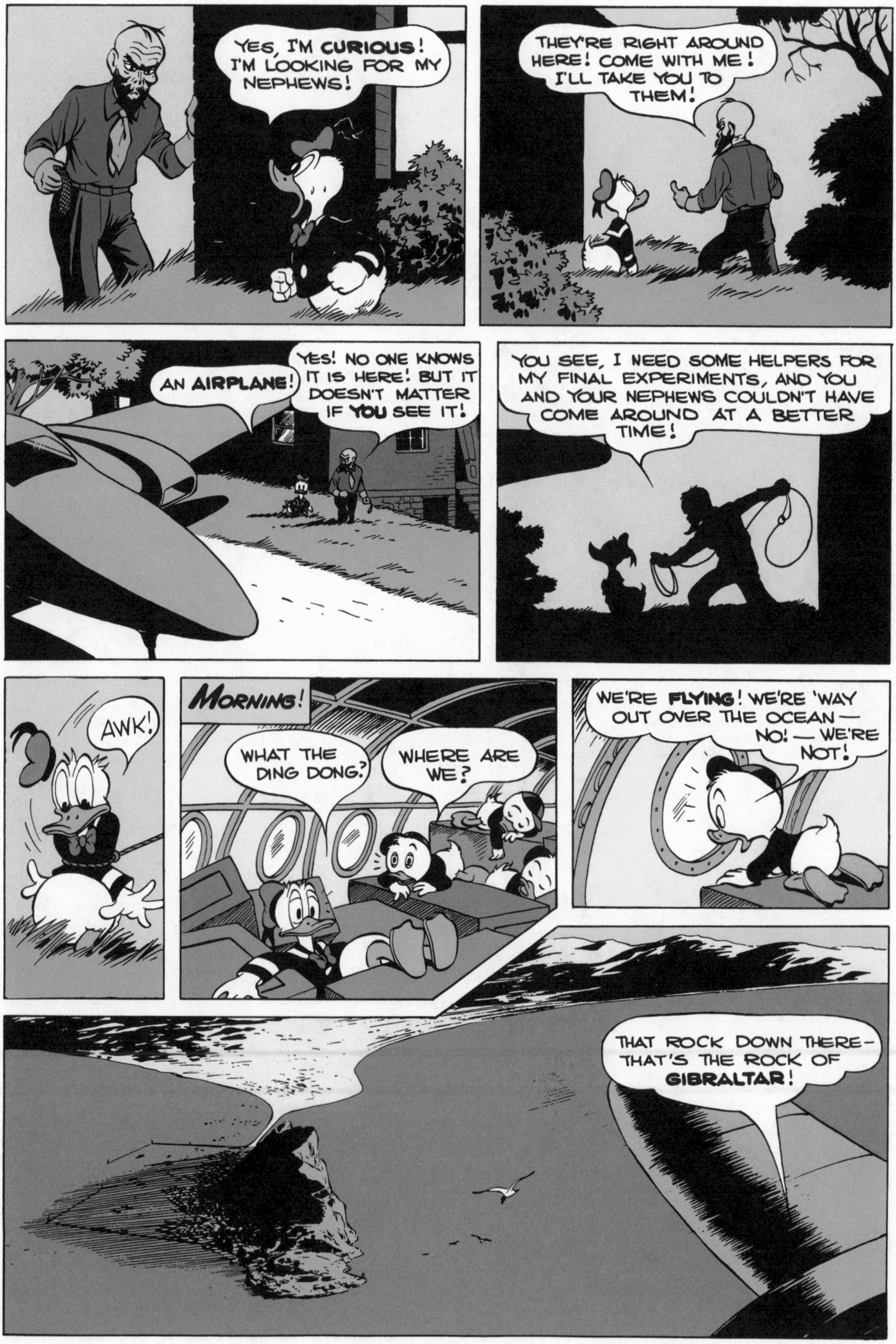
YES, I'M CURIOUS! I'M LOOKING FOR MY NEPHEWS!
THEY'RE RIGHT AROUND HERE! COME WITH ME! I'LL TAKE YOU TO THEM!
AN AIRPLANE!
YES! NO ONE KNOWS IT IS HERE! BUT IT DOESN'T MATTER IF YOU SEE IT!
YOU SEE, I NEED SOME HELPERS FOR MY FINAL EXPERIMENTS, AND YOU AND YOUR NEPHEWS COULDN'T HAVE COME AROUND AT A BETTER TIME!
AWK!
MORNING!
WHAT THE DING DONG?
WHERE ARE WE?
WE'RE FLYING! WE'RE 'WAY OUT OVER THE OCEAN — NO! — WE'RE NOT!
THAT ROCK DOWN THERE— THAT'S THE ROCK OF GIBRALTAR!

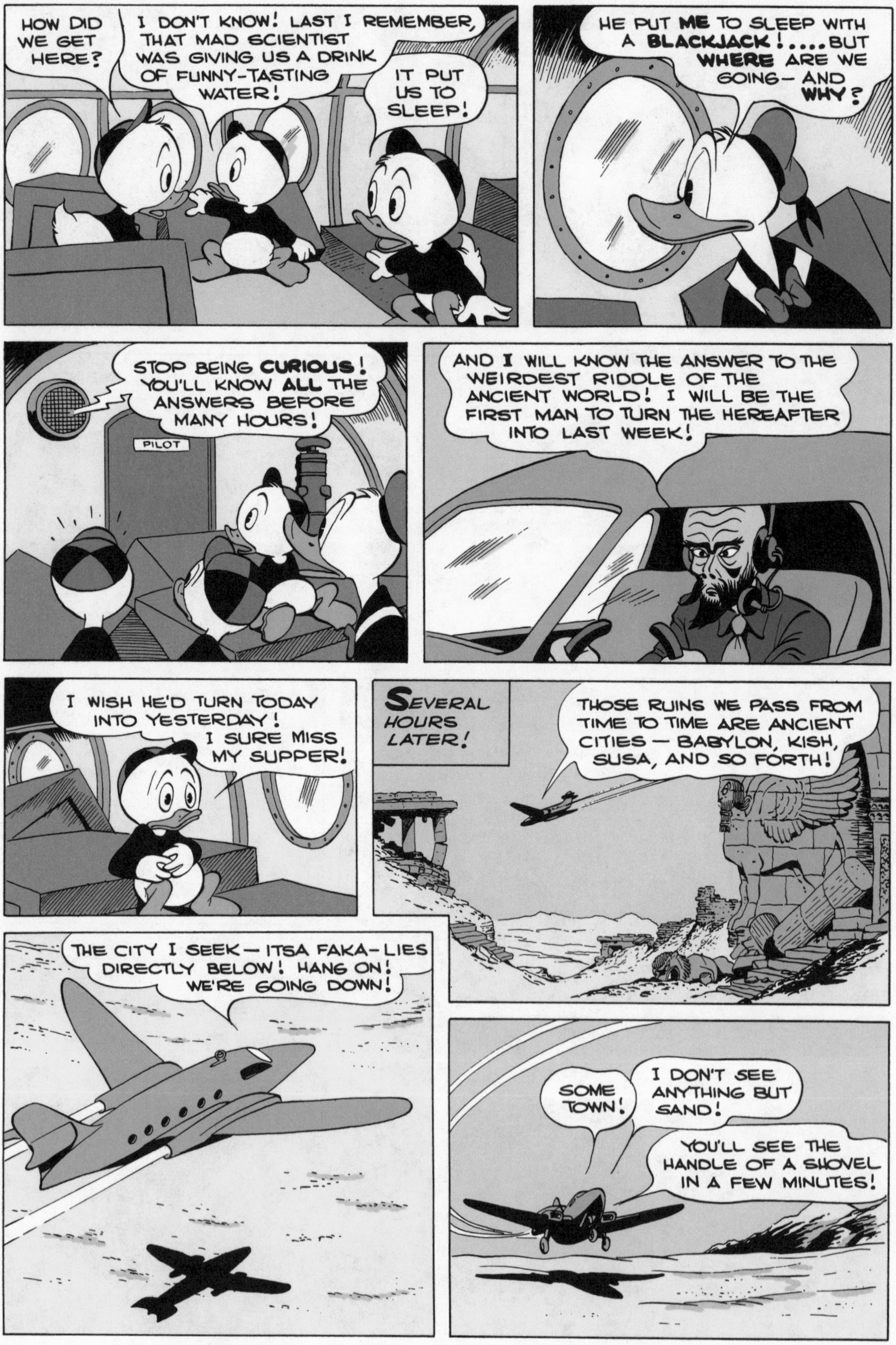
HOW DID WE GET HERE?
I DON'T KNOW! LAST I REMEMBER, THAT MAD SCIENTIST WAS GIVING US A DRINK OF FUNNY-TASTING WATER!
IT PUT US TO SLEEP!
HE PUT ME TO SLEEP WITH A BLACKJACK!....BUT WHERE ARE WE GOING— AND WHY?
STOP BEING CURIOUS! YOU'LL KNOW ALL THE ANSWERS BEFORE MANY HOURS!
PILOT
AND I WILL KNOW THE ANSWER TO THE WEIRDEST RIDDLE OF THE ANCIENT WORLD! I WILL BE THE FIRST MAN TO TURN THE HEREAFTER INTO LAST WEEK!
I WISH HE'D TURN TODAY INTO YESTERDAY! I SURE MISS MY SUPPER!
SEVERAL HOURS LATER!
THOSE RUINS WE PASS FROM TIME TO TIME ARE ANCIENT CITIES — BABYLON, KISH, SUSA, AND SO FORTH!
THE CITY I SEEK — ITSA FAKA — LIES DIRECTLY BELOW! HANG ON! WE'RE GOING DOWN!
SOME TOWN!
I DON'T SEE ANYTHING BUT SAND!
YOU'LL SEE THE HANDLE OF A SHOVEL IN A FEW MINUTES!

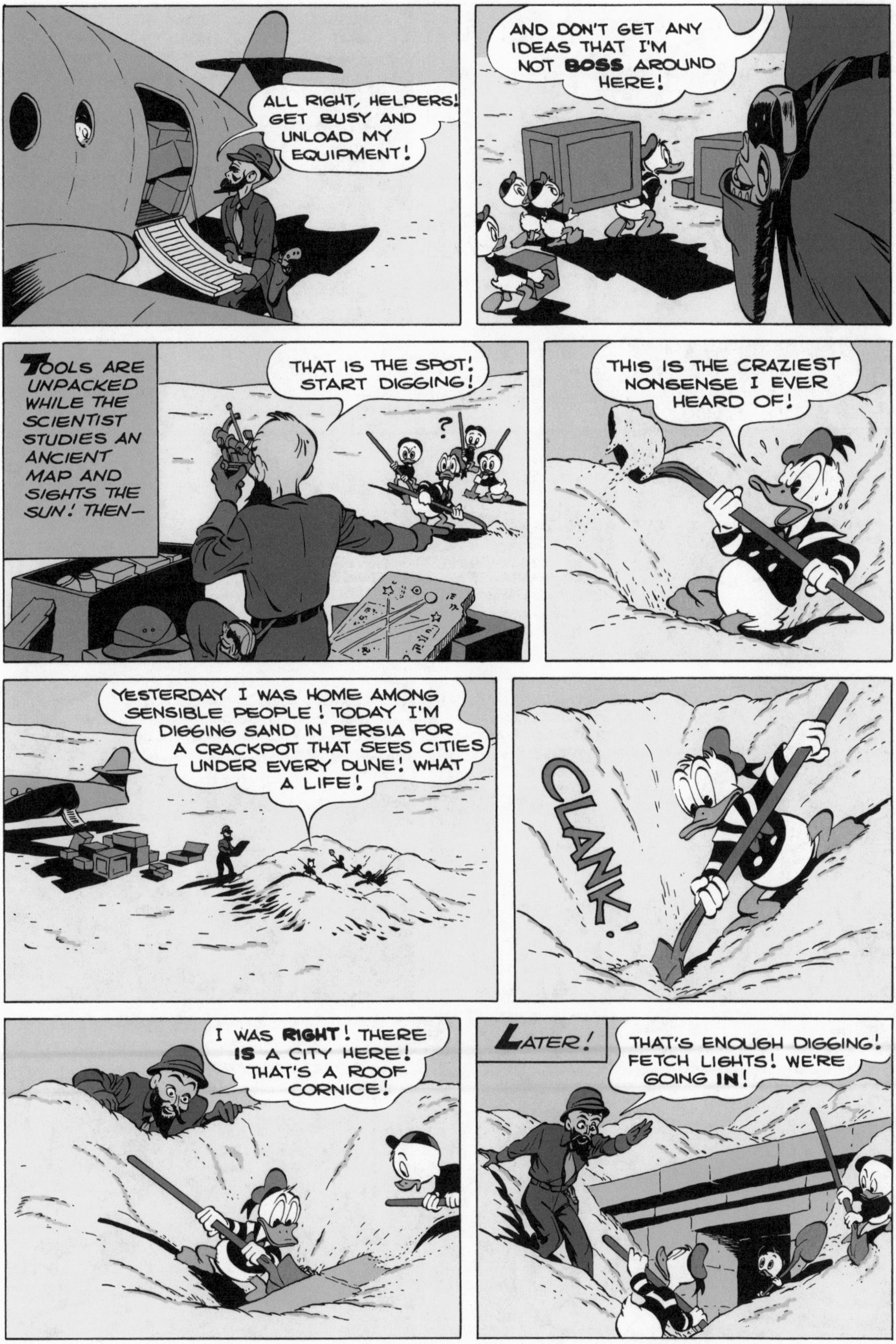
ALL RIGHT, HELPERS! GET BUSY AND UNLOAD MY EQUIPMENT!
AND DON'T GET ANY IDEAS THAT I'M NOT BOSS AROUND HERE!
TOOLS ARE UNPACKED WHILE THE SCIENTIST STUDIES AN ANCIENT MAP AND SIGHTS THE SUN! THEN—
THAT IS THE SPOT! START DIGGING!
?
THIS IS THE CRAZIEST NONSENSE I EVER HEARD OF!
YESTERDAY I WAS HOME AMONG SENSIBLE PEOPLE! TODAY I'M DIGGING SAND IN PERSIA FOR A CRACKPOT THAT SEES CITIES UNDER EVERY DUNE! WHAT A LIFE!
CLANK!
I WAS RIGHT! THERE IS A CITY HERE! THAT'S A ROOF CORNICE!
LATER!
THAT'S ENOUGH DIGGING! FETCH LIGHTS! WE'RE GOING IN!

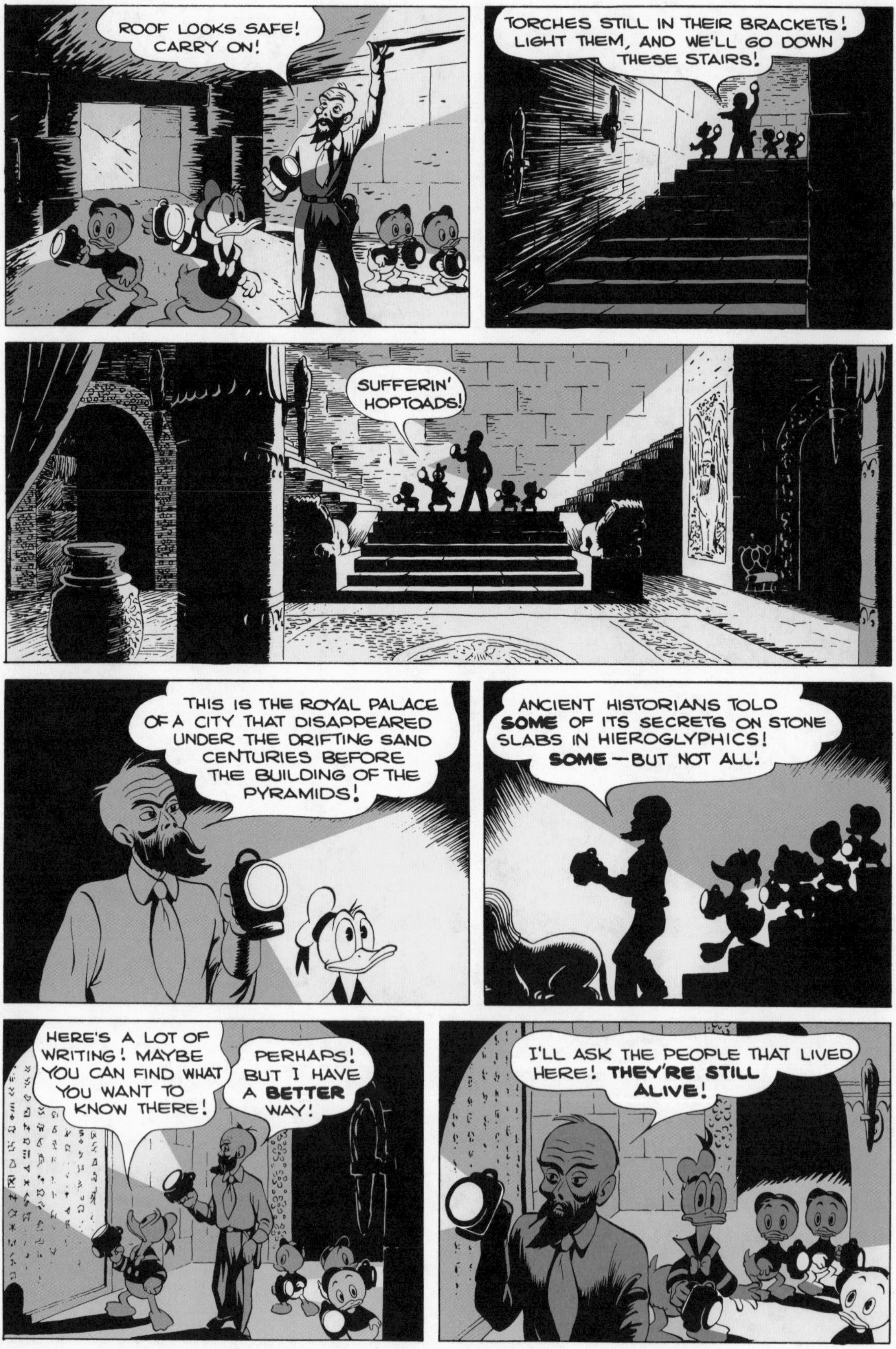
ROOF LOOKS SAFE! CARRY ON!
TORCHES STILL IN THEIR BRACKETS! LIGHT THEM, AND WE'LL GO DOWN THESE STAIRS!
SUFFERIN' HOPTOADS!
THIS IS THE ROYAL PALACE OF A CITY THAT DISAPPEARED UNDER THE DRIFTING SAND CENTURIES BEFORE THE BUILDING OF THE PYRAMIDS!
ANCIENT HISTORIANS TOLD SOME OF ITS SECRETS ON STONE SLABS IN HIEROGLYPHICS! SOME—BUT NOT ALL!
HERE'S A LOT OF WRITING! MAYBE YOU CAN FIND WHAT YOU WANT TO KNOW THERE!
PERHAPS! BUT I HAVE A BETTER WAY!
I'LL ASK THE PEOPLE THAT LIVED HERE! THEY'RE STILL ALIVE!

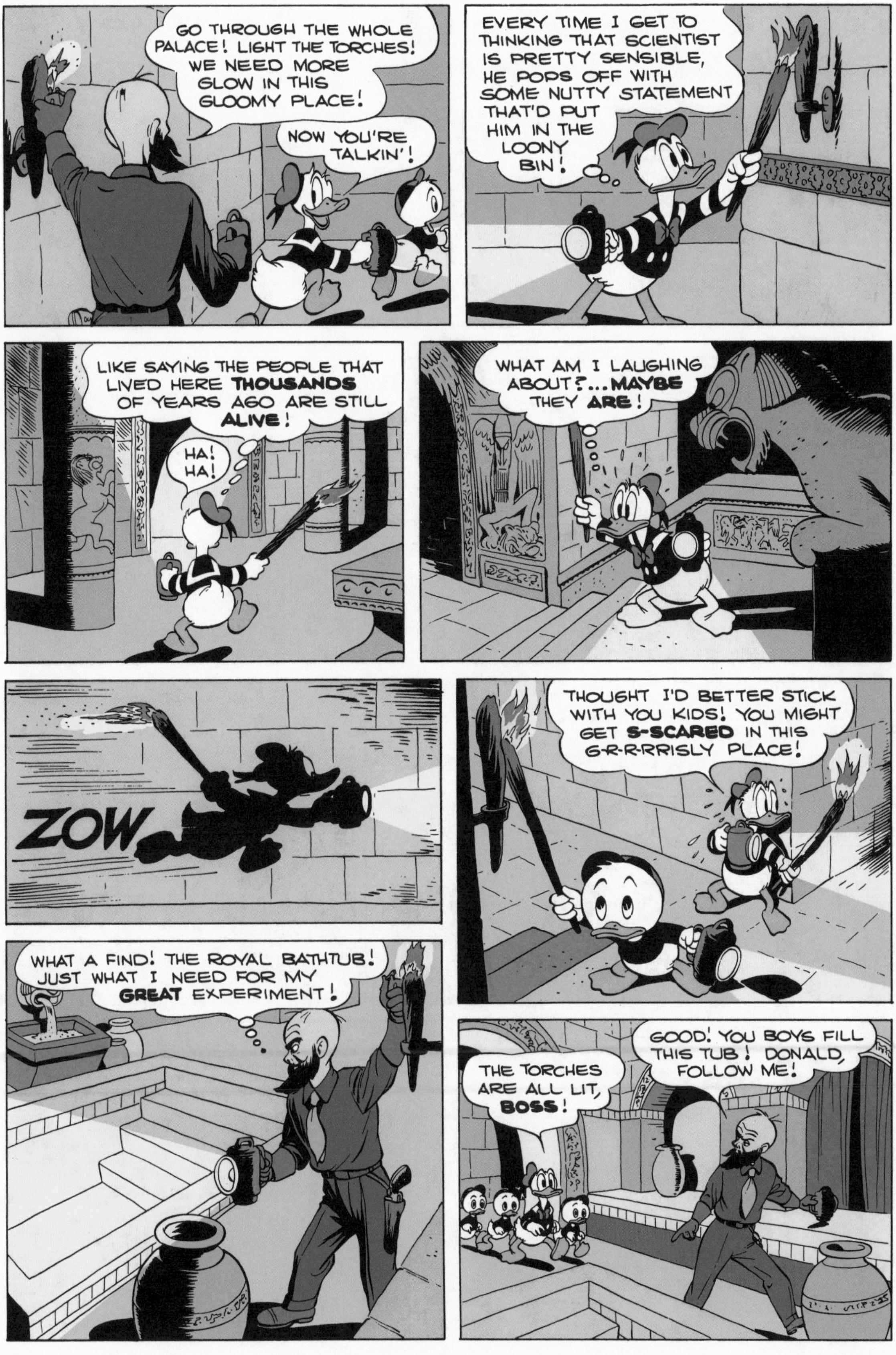
GO THROUGH THE WHOLE PALACE! LIGHT THE TORCHES! WE NEED MORE GLOW IN THIS GLOOMY PLACE!
NOW YOU'RE TALKIN'!
EVERY TIME I GET TO THINKING THAT SCIENTIST IS PRETTY SENSIBLE, HE POPS OFF WITH SOME NUTTY STATEMENT THAT'D PUT HIM IN THE LOONY BIN!
LIKE SAYING THE PEOPLE THAT LIVED HERE THOUSANDS OF YEARS AGO ARE STILL ALIVE!
HA! HA!
WHAT AM I LAUGHING ABOUT?...MAYBE THEY ARE!
ZOW
THOUGHT I'D BETTER STICK WITH YOU KIDS! YOU MIGHT GET S-SCARED IN THIS G-R-R-RRISLY PLACE!
WHAT A FIND! THE ROYAL BATHTUB! JUST WHAT I NEED FOR MY GREAT EXPERIMENT!
THE TORCHES ARE ALL LIT, BOSS!
GOOD! YOU BOYS FILL THIS TUB! DONALD, FOLLOW ME!

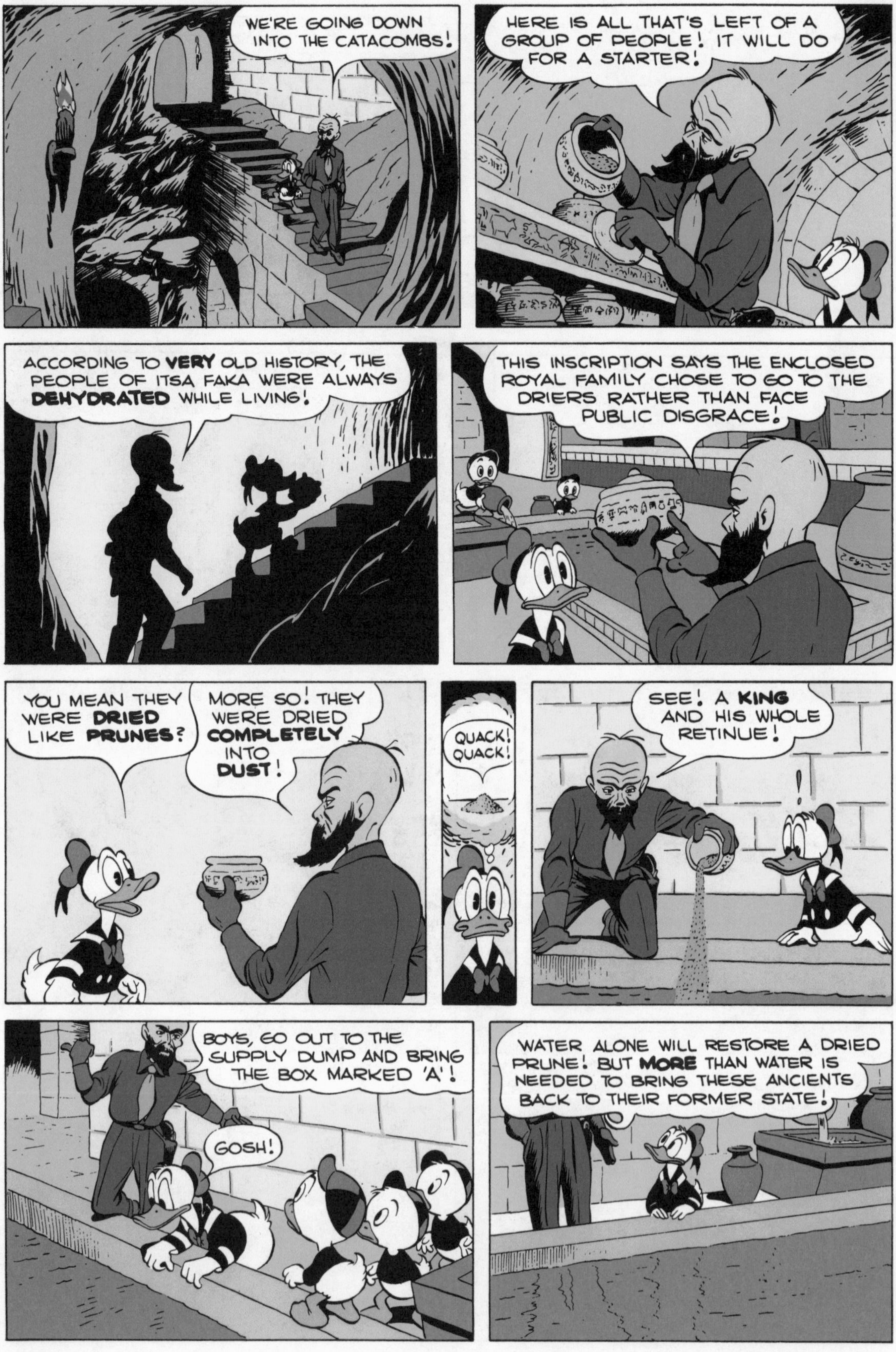
WE'RE GOING DOWN INTO THE CATACOMBS!
HERE IS ALL THAT'S LEFT OF A GROUP OF PEOPLE! IT WILL DO FOR A STARTER!
ACCORDING TO VERY OLD HISTORY, THE PEOPLE OF ITSA FAKA WERE ALWAYS DEHYDRATED WHILE LIVING!
THIS INSCRIPTION SAYS THE ENCLOSED ROYAL FAMILY CHOSE TO GO TO THE DRIERS RATHER THAN FACE PUBLIC DISGRACE!
YOU MEAN THEY WERE DRIED LIKE PRUNES?
MORE SO! THEY WERE DRIED COMPLETELY INTO DUST!
QUACK! QUACK!
SEE! A KING AND HIS WHOLE RETINUE!
!
BOYS, GO OUT TO THE SUPPLY DUMP AND BRING THE BOX MARKED 'A'!
GOSH!
WATER ALONE WILL RESTORE A DRIED PRUNE! BUT MORE THAN WATER IS NEEDED TO BRING THESE ANCIENTS BACK TO THEIR FORMER STATE!

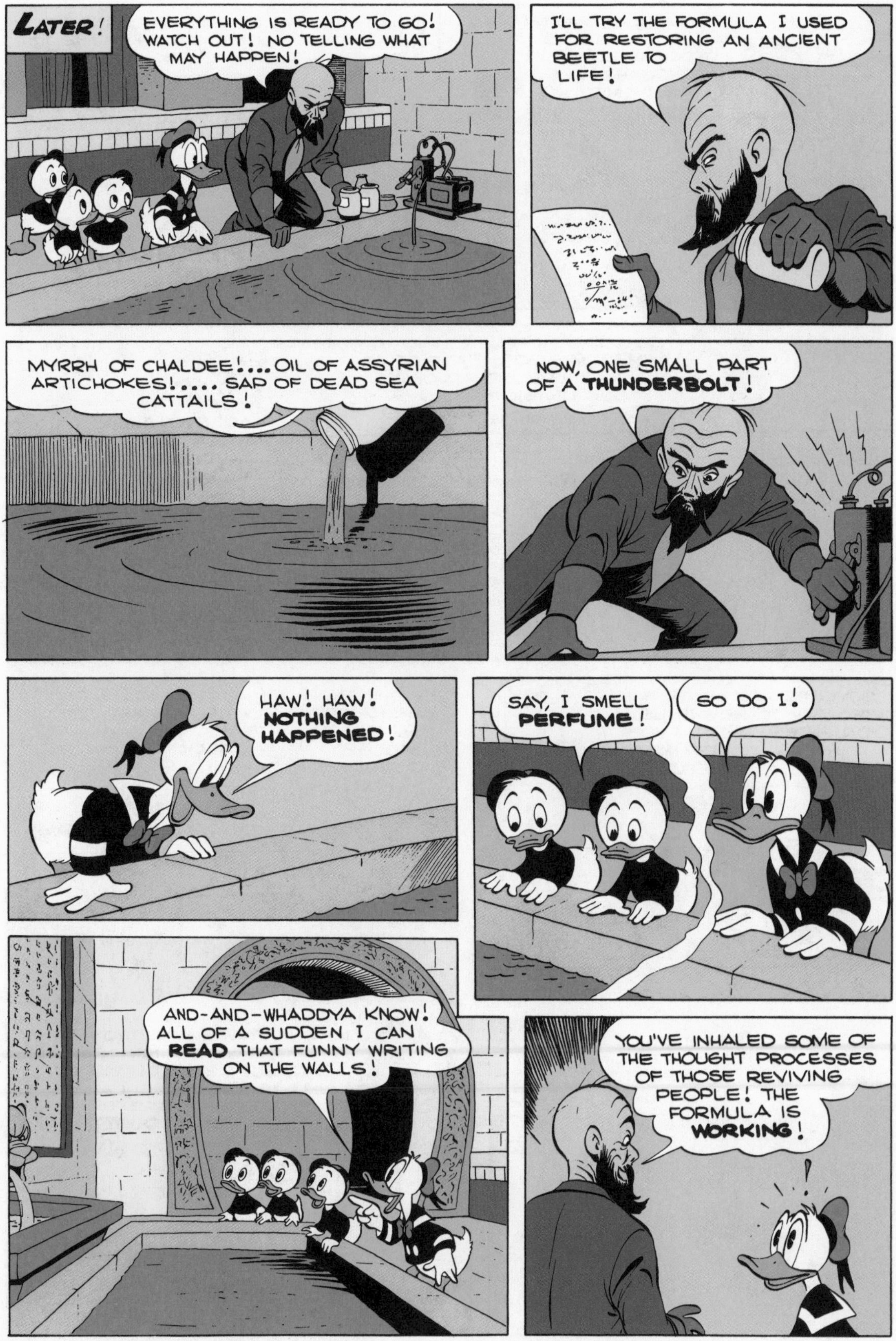
LATER!
EVERYTHING IS READY TO GO! WATCH OUT! NO TELLING WHAT MAY HAPPEN!
I'LL TRY THE FORMULA I USED FOR RESTORING AN ANCIENT BEETLE TO LIFE!
MYRRH OF CHALDEE!... OIL OF ASSYRIAN ARTICHOKES!.... SAP OF DEAD SEA CATTAILS!
NOW, ONE SMALL PART OF A THUNDERBOLT!
HAW! HAW! NOTHING HAPPENED!
SAY, I SMELL PERFUME!
SO DO I!
AND-AND-WHADDYA KNOW! ALL OF A SUDDEN I CAN READ THAT FUNNY WRITING ON THE WALLS!
YOU'VE INHALED SOME OF THE THOUGHT PROCESSES OF THOSE REVIVING PEOPLE! THE FORMULA IS WORKING!
!

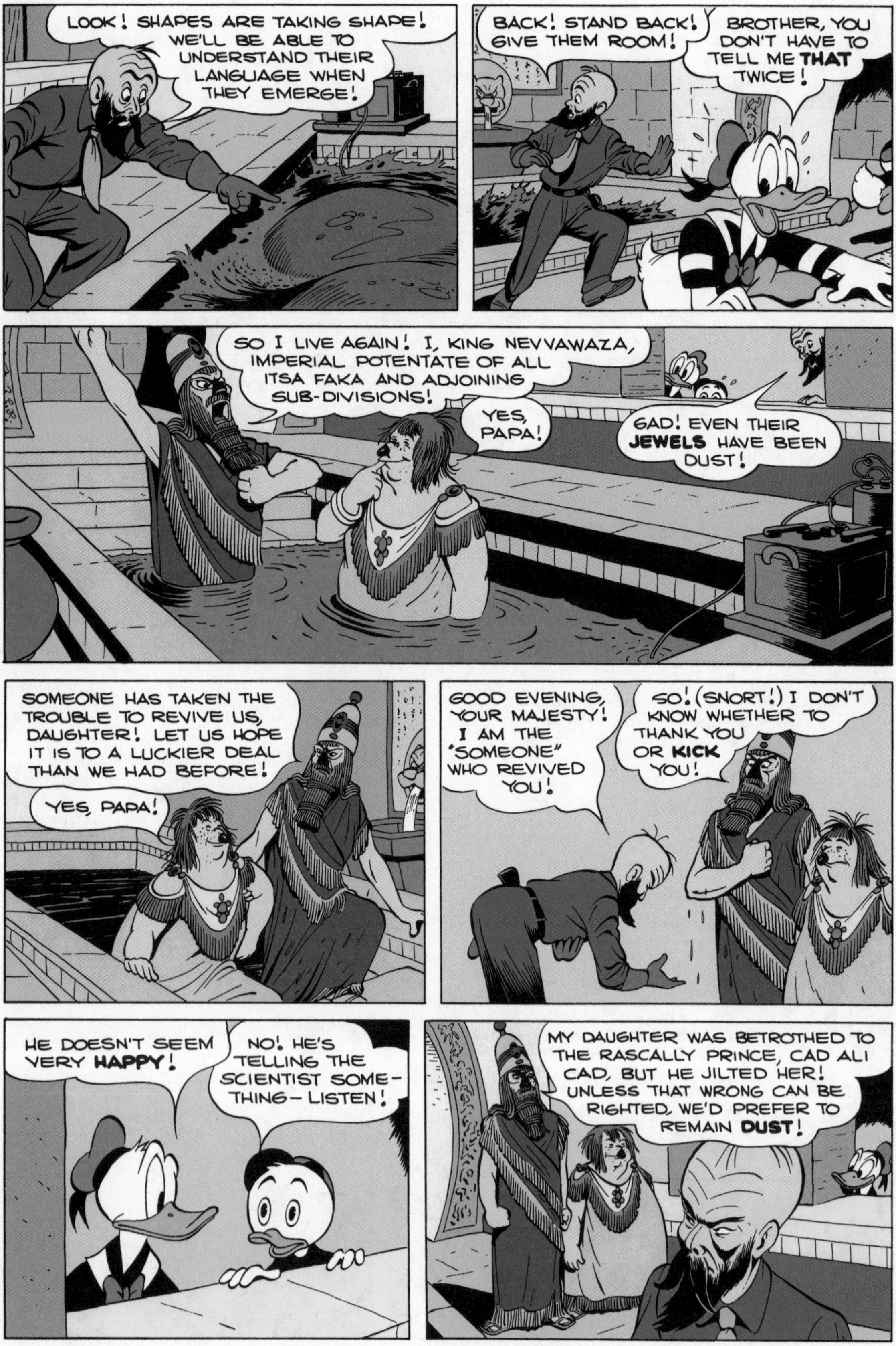
LOOK! SHAPES ARE TAKING SHAPE! WE'LL BE ABLE TO UNDERSTAND THEIR LANGUAGE WHEN THEY EMERGE!
BACK! STAND BACK! GIVE THEM ROOM!
BROTHER, YOU DON'T HAVE TO TELL ME THAT TWICE!
SO I LIVE AGAIN! I, KING NEVVAWAZA, IMPERIAL POTENTATE OF ALL ITSA FAKA AND ADJOINING SUB-DIVISIONS!
YES, PAPA!
GAD! EVEN THEIR JEWELS HAVE BEEN DUST!
SOMEONE HAS TAKEN THE TROUBLE TO REVIVE US, DAUGHTER! LET US HOPE IT IS TO A LUCKIER DEAL THAN WE HAD BEFORE!
YES, PAPA!
GOOD EVENING, YOUR MAJESTY! I AM THE "SOMEONE" WHO REVIVED YOU!
SO! (SNORT!) I DON'T KNOW WHETHER TO THANK YOU OR KICK YOU!
HE DOESN'T SEEM VERY HAPPY!
NO! HE'S TELLING THE SCIENTIST SOME-THING– LISTEN!
MY DAUGHTER WAS BETROTHED TO THE RASCALLY PRINCE, CAD ALI CAD, BUT HE JILTED HER! UNLESS THAT WRONG CAN BE RIGHTED, WE'D PREFER TO REMAIN DUST!

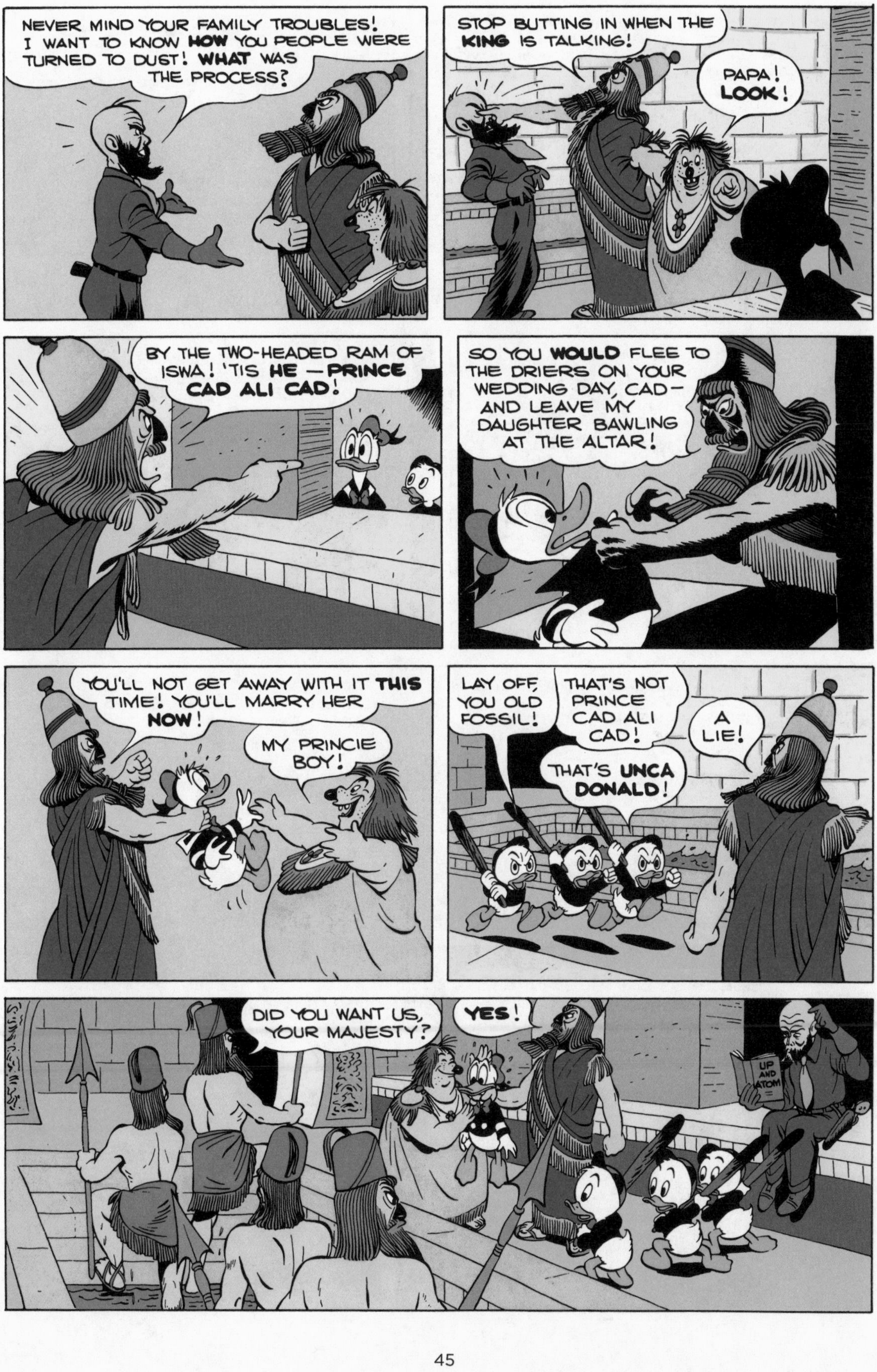
NEVER MIND YOUR FAMILY TROUBLES! I WANT TO KNOW **HOW** YOU PEOPLE WERE TURNED TO DUST! **WHAT** WAS THE PROCESS?
STOP BUTTING IN WHEN THE **KING** IS TALKING!
PAPA! **LOOK**!
BY THE TWO-HEADED RAM OF ISWA! 'TIS **HE — PRINCE CAD ALI CAD**!
SO YOU **WOULD** FLEE TO THE DRIERS ON YOUR WEDDING DAY, CAD — AND LEAVE MY DAUGHTER BAWLING AT THE ALTAR!
YOU'LL NOT GET AWAY WITH IT **THIS** TIME! YOU'LL MARRY HER **NOW**!
MY PRINCIE BOY!
LAY OFF, YOU OLD FOSSIL!
THAT'S NOT PRINCE CAD ALI CAD!
THAT'S **UNCA DONALD**!
A LIE!
DID YOU WANT US, YOUR MAJESTY?
YES!
UP AND ATOM

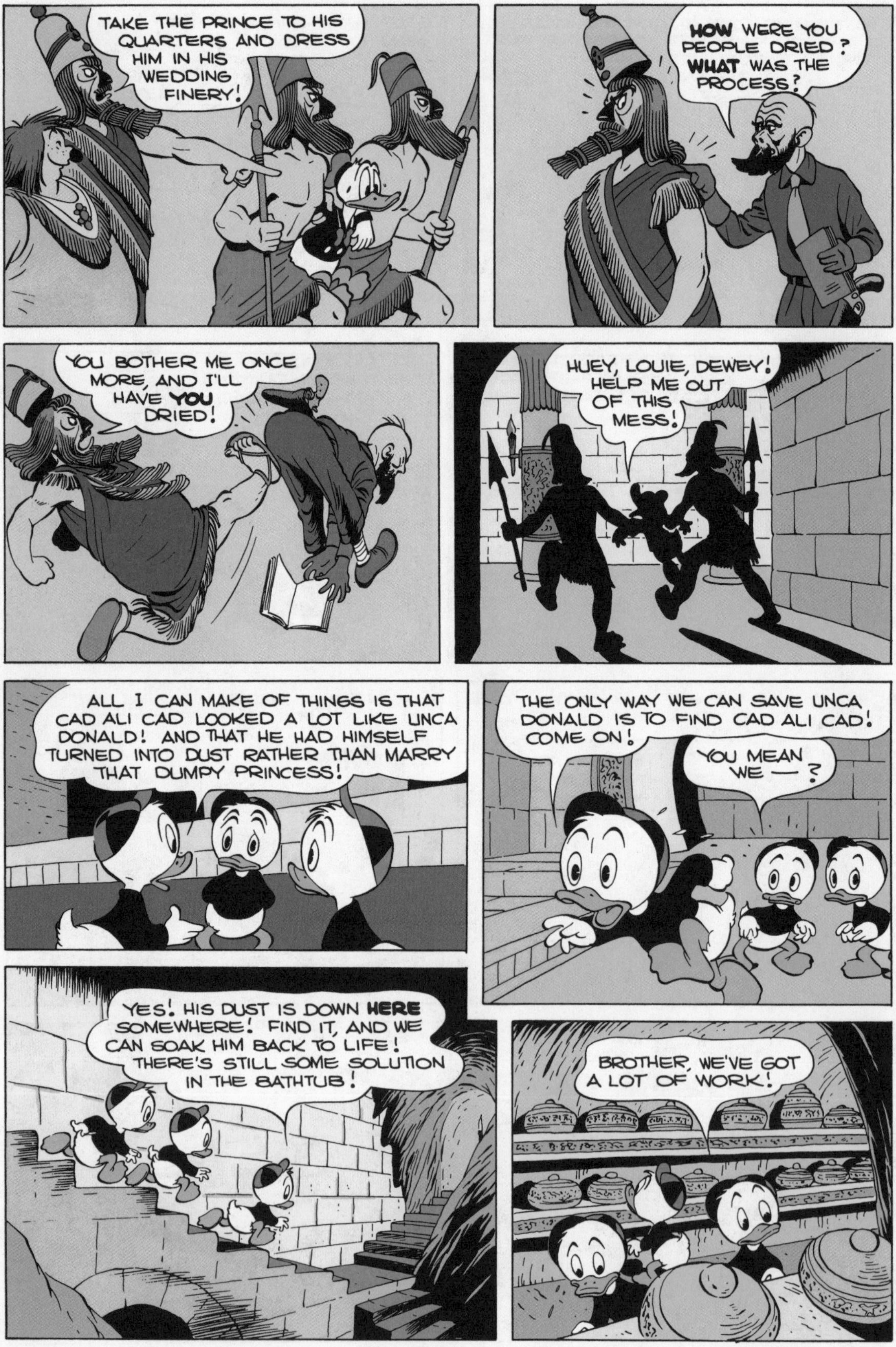
TAKE THE PRINCE TO HIS QUARTERS AND DRESS HIM IN HIS WEDDING FINERY!
HOW WERE YOU PEOPLE DRIED? WHAT WAS THE PROCESS?
YOU BOTHER ME ONCE MORE, AND I'LL HAVE YOU DRIED!
HUEY, LOUIE, DEWEY! HELP ME OUT OF THIS MESS!
ALL I CAN MAKE OF THINGS IS THAT CAD ALI CAD LOOKED A LOT LIKE UNCA DONALD! AND THAT HE HAD HIMSELF TURNED INTO DUST RATHER THAN MARRY THAT DUMPY PRINCESS!
THE ONLY WAY WE CAN SAVE UNCA DONALD IS TO FIND CAD ALI CAD! COME ON!
YOU MEAN WE — ?
YES! HIS DUST IS DOWN HERE SOMEWHERE! FIND IT, AND WE CAN SOAK HIM BACK TO LIFE! THERE'S STILL SOME SOLUTION IN THE BATHTUB!
BROTHER, WE'VE GOT A LOT OF WORK!

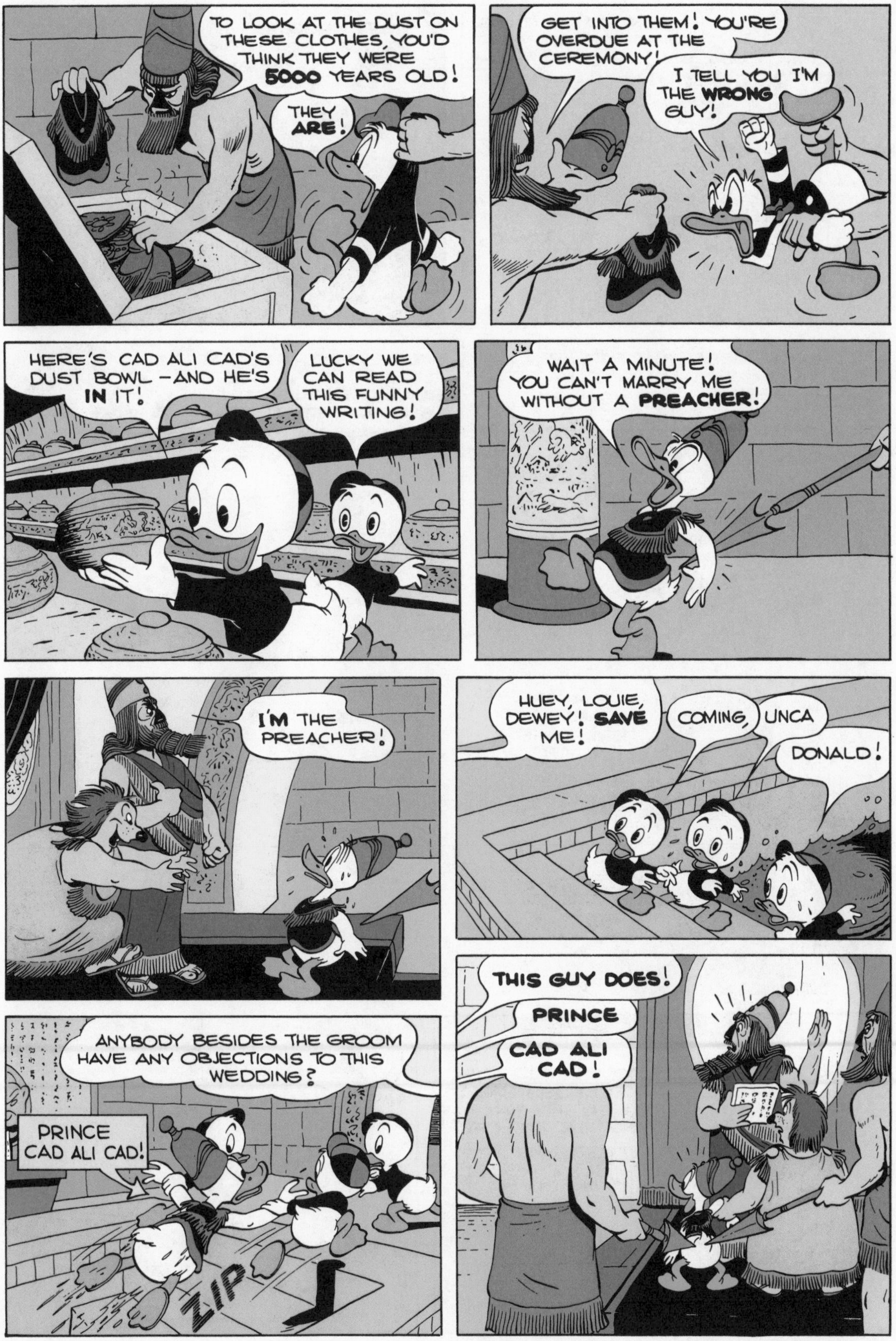
TO LOOK AT THE DUST ON THESE CLOTHES, YOU'D THINK THEY WERE **5000** YEARS OLD!
THEY **ARE**!
GET INTO THEM! YOU'RE OVERDUE AT THE CEREMONY!
I TELL YOU I'M THE **WRONG** GUY!
HERE'S CAD ALI CAD'S DUST BOWL —AND HE'S **IN** IT!
LUCKY WE CAN READ THIS FUNNY WRITING!
WAIT A MINUTE! YOU CAN'T MARRY ME WITHOUT A **PREACHER**!
I'M THE PREACHER!
HUEY, LOUIE, DEWEY! **SAVE** ME!
COMING, UNCA
DONALD!
ANYBODY BESIDES THE GROOM HAVE ANY OBJECTIONS TO THIS WEDDING?
PRINCE CAD ALI CAD!
ZIP
THIS GUY DOES!
PRINCE
CAD ALI CAD!

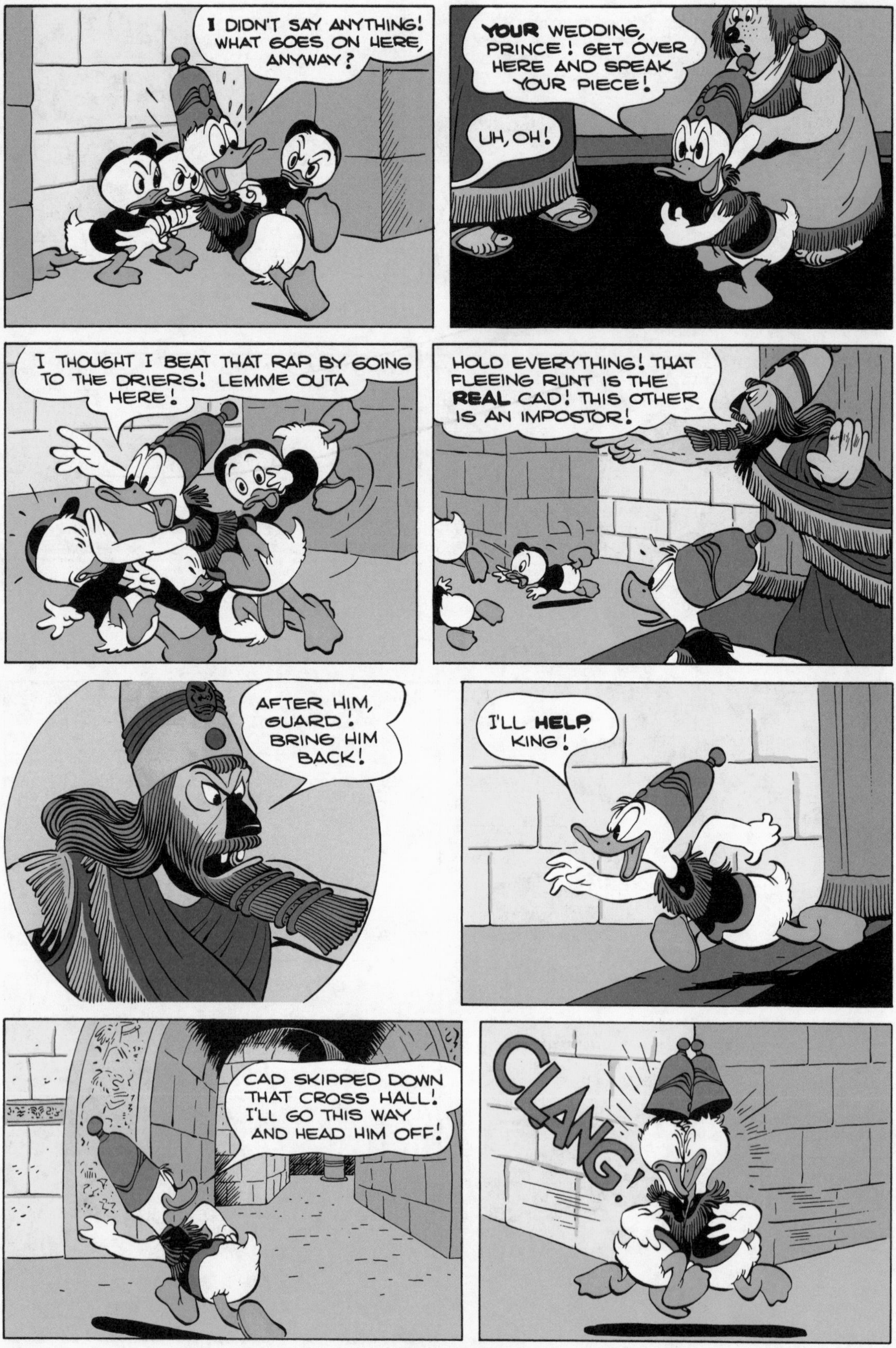
I DIDN'T SAY ANYTHING! WHAT GOES ON HERE, ANYWAY?
YOUR WEDDING, PRINCE! GET OVER HERE AND SPEAK YOUR PIECE!
UH, OH!
I THOUGHT I BEAT THAT RAP BY GOING TO THE DRIERS! LEMME OUTA HERE!
HOLD EVERYTHING! THAT FLEEING RUNT IS THE REAL CAD! THIS OTHER IS AN IMPOSTOR!
AFTER HIM, GUARD! BRING HIM BACK!
I'LL HELP, KING!
CAD SKIPPED DOWN THAT CROSS HALL! I'LL GO THIS WAY AND HEAD HIM OFF!
CLANG!

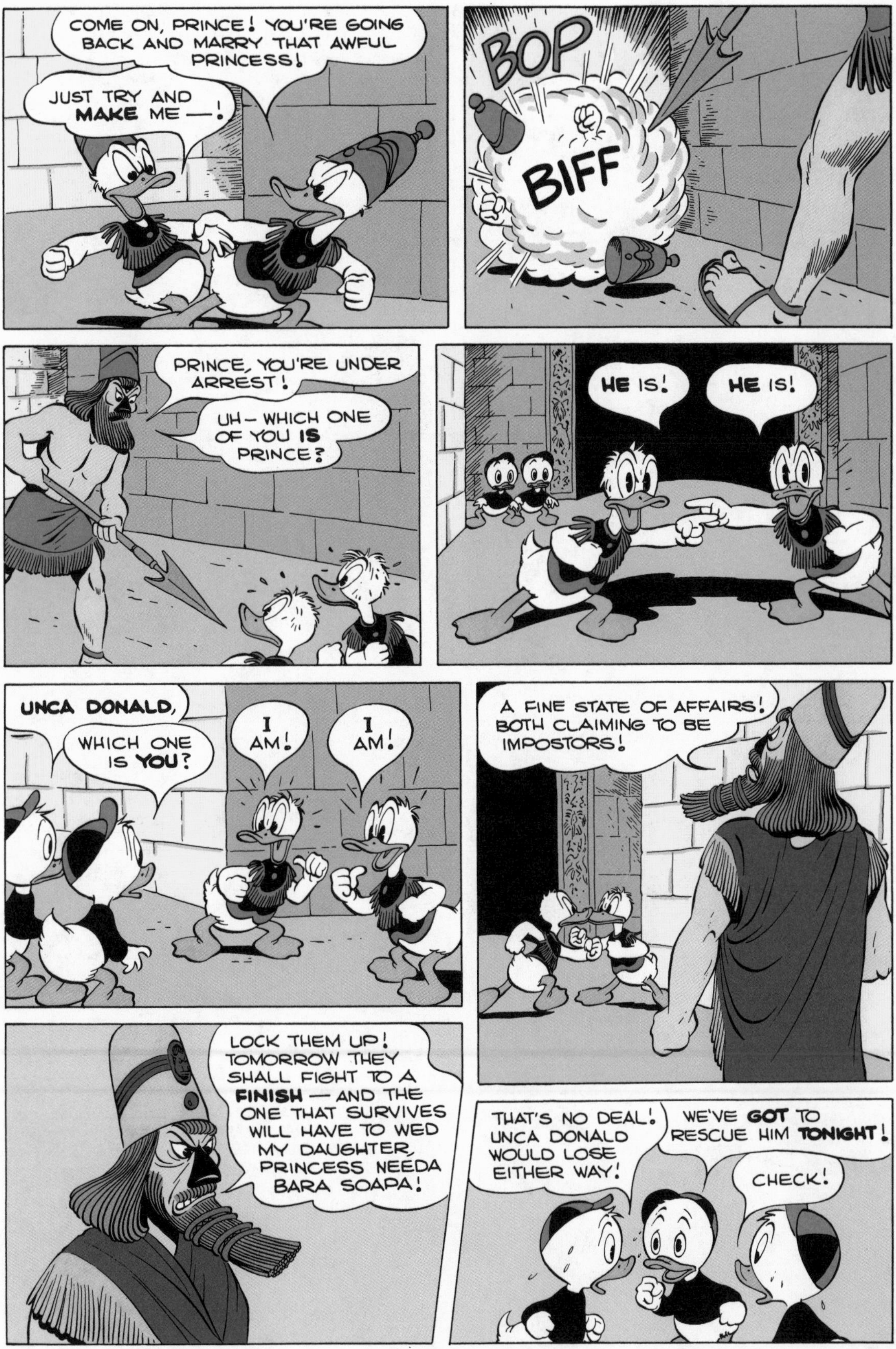

COME ON, PRINCE! YOU'RE GOING BACK AND MARRY THAT AWFUL PRINCESS!
JUST TRY AND **MAKE** ME —!
BOP
BIFF
PRINCE, YOU'RE UNDER ARREST!
UH— WHICH ONE OF YOU **IS** PRINCE?
HE IS!
HE IS!
UNCA DONALD,
WHICH ONE IS **YOU**?
I AM!
I AM!
A FINE STATE OF AFFAIRS! BOTH CLAIMING TO BE IMPOSTORS!
LOCK THEM UP! TOMORROW THEY SHALL FIGHT TO A **FINISH** — AND THE ONE THAT SURVIVES WILL HAVE TO WED MY DAUGHTER, PRINCESS NEEDA BARA SOAPA!
THAT'S NO DEAL! UNCA DONALD WOULD LOSE EITHER WAY!
WE'VE **GOT** TO RESCUE HIM **TONIGHT**!
CHECK!

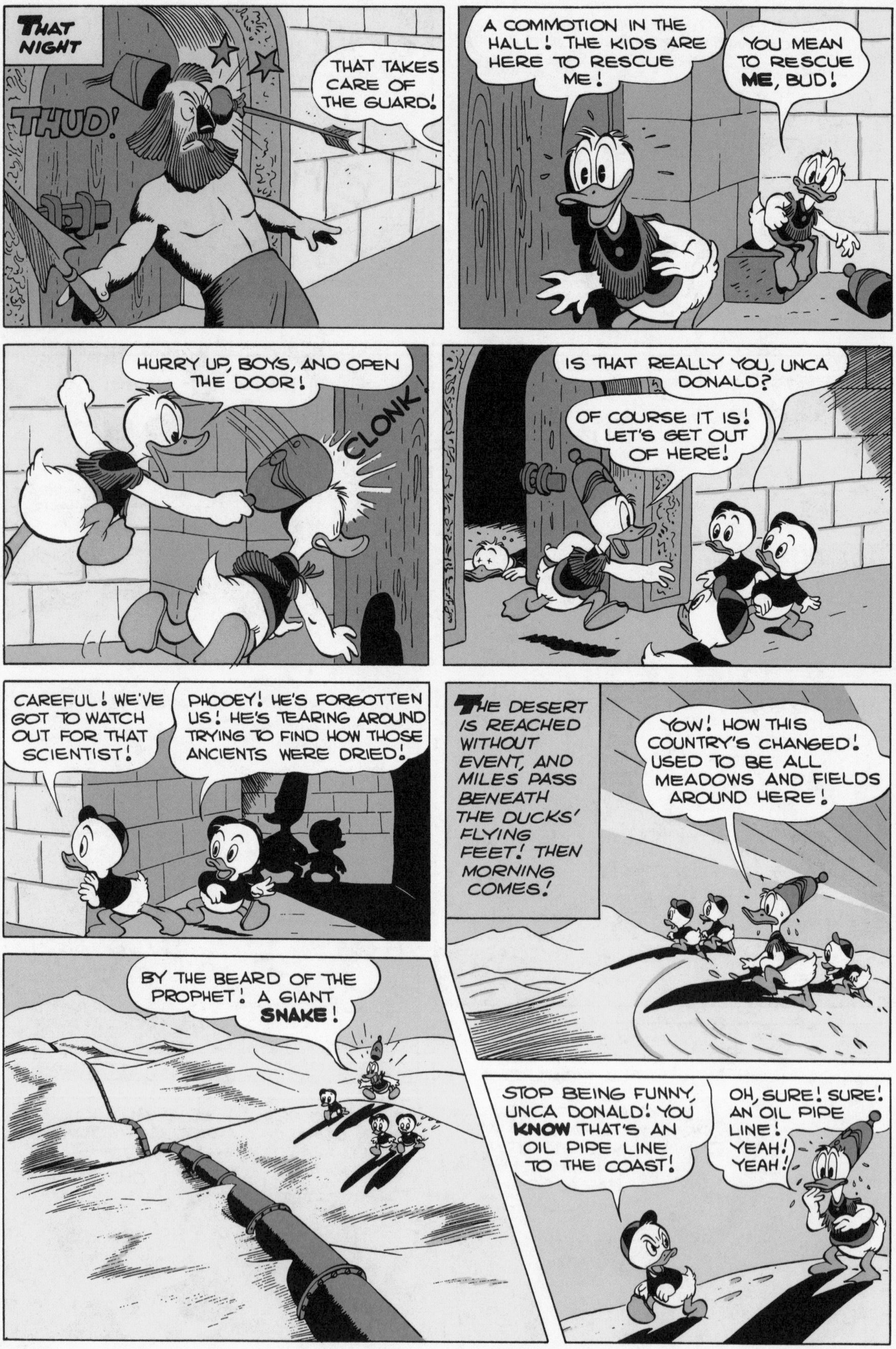
THAT NIGHT
THUD!
THAT TAKES CARE OF THE GUARD!
A COMMOTION IN THE HALL! THE KIDS ARE HERE TO RESCUE ME!
YOU MEAN TO RESCUE ME, BUD!
HURRY UP, BOYS, AND OPEN THE DOOR!
CLONK!
IS THAT REALLY YOU, UNCA DONALD?
OF COURSE IT IS! LET'S GET OUT OF HERE!
CAREFUL! WE'VE GOT TO WATCH OUT FOR THAT SCIENTIST!
PHOOEY! HE'S FORGOTTEN US! HE'S TEARING AROUND TRYING TO FIND HOW THOSE ANCIENTS WERE DRIED!
THE DESERT IS REACHED WITHOUT EVENT, AND MILES PASS BENEATH THE DUCKS' FLYING FEET! THEN MORNING COMES!
YOW! HOW THIS COUNTRY'S CHANGED! USED TO BE ALL MEADOWS AND FIELDS AROUND HERE!
BY THE BEARD OF THE PROPHET! A GIANT SNAKE!
STOP BEING FUNNY, UNCA DONALD! YOU KNOW THAT'S AN OIL PIPE LINE TO THE COAST!
OH, SURE! SURE! AN OIL PIPE LINE! YEAH! YEAH!

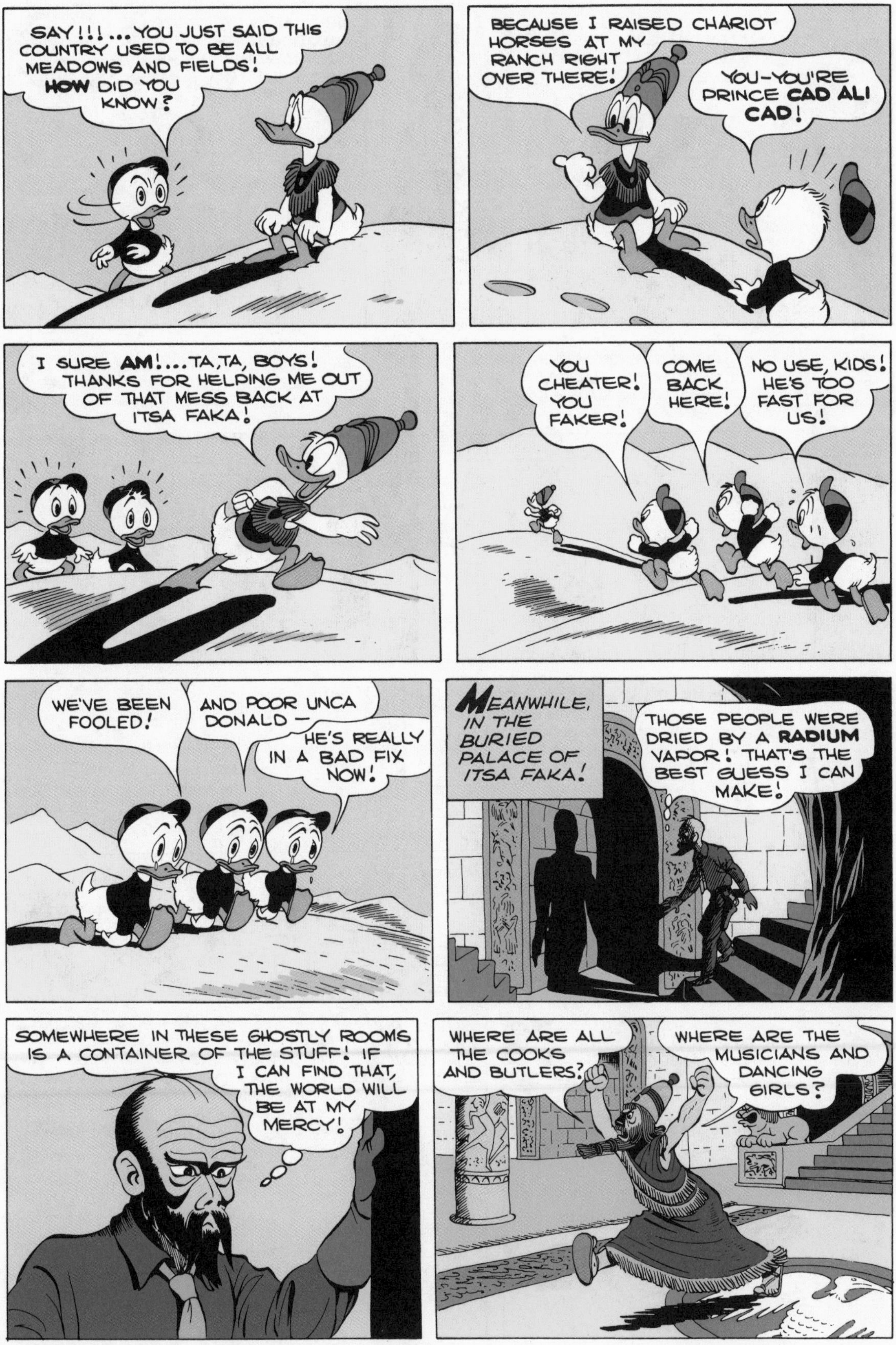
SAY!!!... YOU JUST SAID THIS COUNTRY USED TO BE ALL MEADOWS AND FIELDS! **HOW** DID YOU KNOW?
BECAUSE I RAISED CHARIOT HORSES AT MY RANCH RIGHT OVER THERE!
YOU-YOU'RE PRINCE **CAD ALI CAD**!
I SURE **AM**!... TA, TA, BOYS! THANKS FOR HELPING ME OUT OF THAT MESS BACK AT ITSA FAKA!
YOU CHEATER! YOU FAKER!
COME BACK HERE!
NO USE, KIDS! HE'S TOO FAST FOR US!
WE'VE BEEN FOOLED!
AND POOR UNCA DONALD —
HE'S REALLY IN A BAD FIX NOW!
MEANWHILE, IN THE BURIED PALACE OF ITSA FAKA!
THOSE PEOPLE WERE DRIED BY A **RADIUM** VAPOR! THAT'S THE BEST GUESS I CAN MAKE!
SOMEWHERE IN THESE GHOSTLY ROOMS IS A CONTAINER OF THE STUFF! IF I CAN FIND THAT, THE WORLD WILL BE AT MY MERCY!
WHERE ARE ALL THE COOKS AND BUTLERS?
WHERE ARE THE MUSICIANS AND DANCING GIRLS?

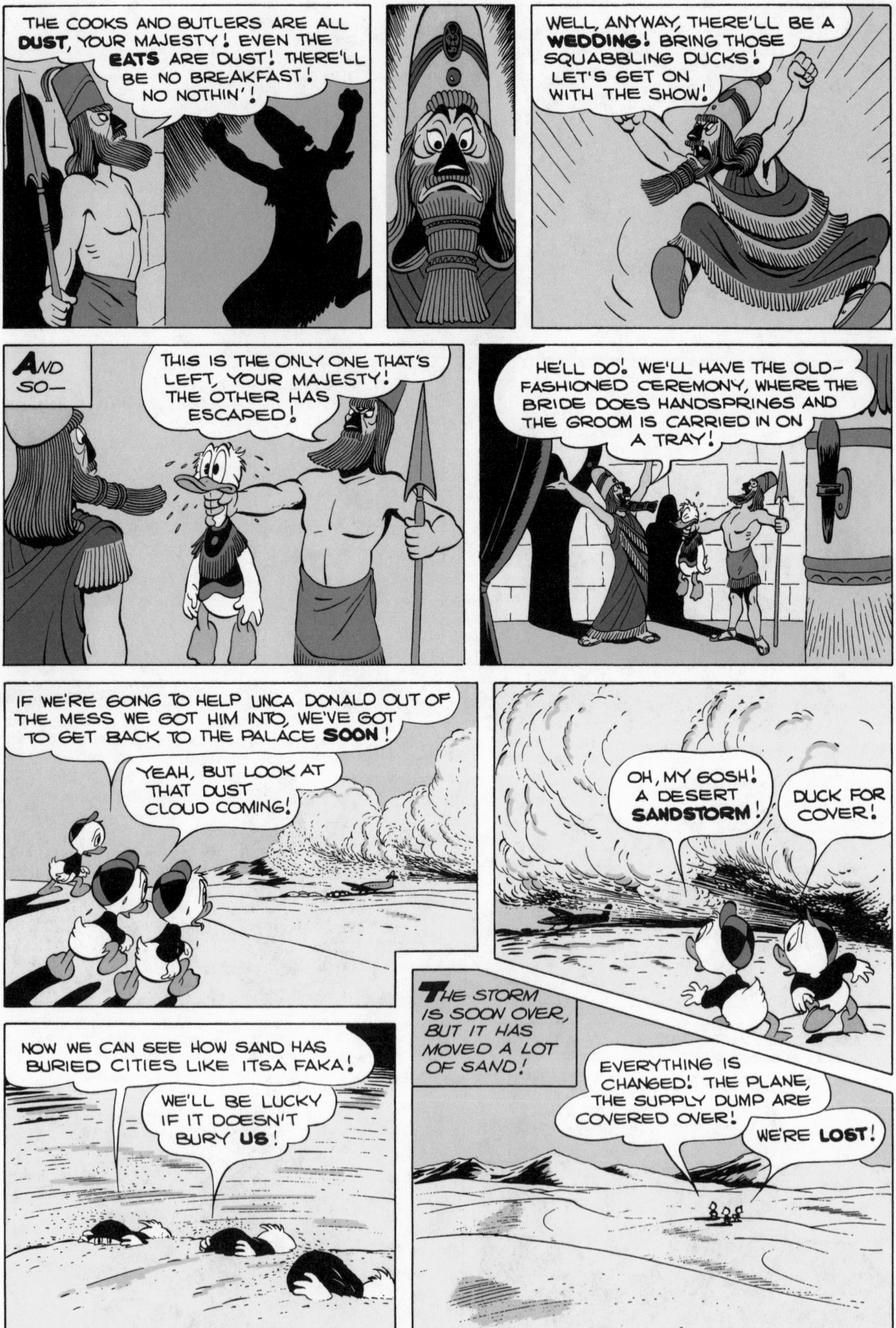
THE COOKS AND BUTLERS ARE ALL DUST, YOUR MAJESTY! EVEN THE EATS ARE DUST! THERE'LL BE NO BREAKFAST! NO NOTHIN'!
WELL, ANYWAY, THERE'LL BE A WEDDING! BRING THOSE SQUABBLING DUCKS! LET'S GET ON WITH THE SHOW!
AND SO—
THIS IS THE ONLY ONE THAT'S LEFT, YOUR MAJESTY! THE OTHER HAS ESCAPED!
HE'LL DO! WE'LL HAVE THE OLD-FASHIONED CEREMONY, WHERE THE BRIDE DOES HANDSPRINGS AND THE GROOM IS CARRIED IN ON A TRAY!
IF WE'RE GOING TO HELP UNCA DONALD OUT OF THE MESS WE GOT HIM INTO, WE'VE GOT TO GET BACK TO THE PALACE SOON!
YEAH, BUT LOOK AT THAT DUST CLOUD COMING!
OH, MY GOSH! A DESERT SANDSTORM!
DUCK FOR COVER!
NOW WE CAN SEE HOW SAND HAS BURIED CITIES LIKE ITSA FAKA!
WE'LL BE LUCKY IF IT DOESN'T BURY US!
THE STORM IS SOON OVER, BUT IT HAS MOVED A LOT OF SAND!
EVERYTHING IS CHANGED! THE PLANE, THE SUPPLY DUMP ARE COVERED OVER!
WE'RE LOST!

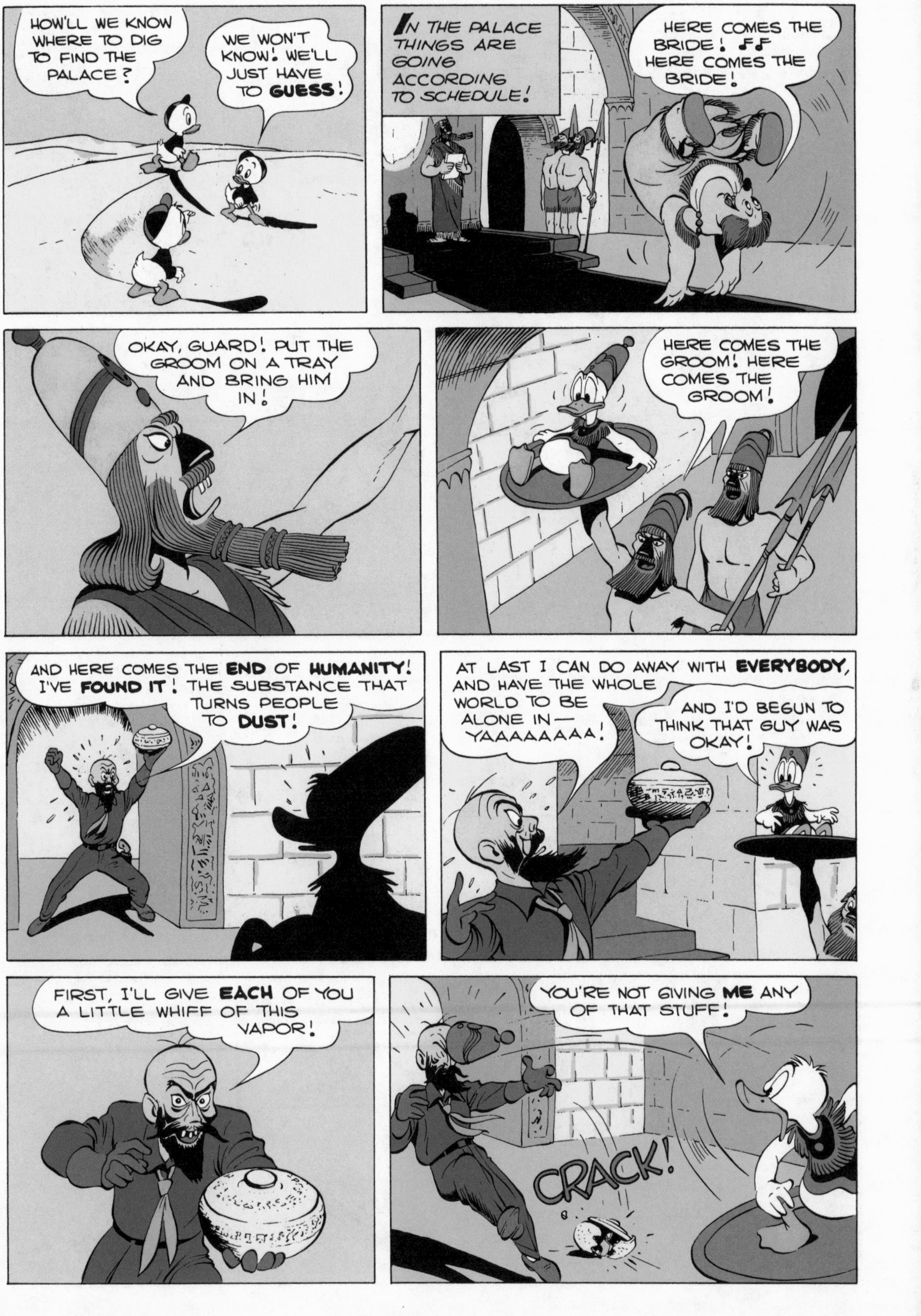
HOW'LL WE KNOW WHERE TO DIG TO FIND THE PALACE?
WE WON'T KNOW! WE'LL JUST HAVE TO GUESS!
IN THE PALACE THINGS ARE GOING ACCORDING TO SCHEDULE!
HERE COMES THE BRIDE! HERE COMES THE BRIDE!
OKAY, GUARD! PUT THE GROOM ON A TRAY AND BRING HIM IN!
HERE COMES THE GROOM! HERE COMES THE GROOM!
AND HERE COMES THE END OF HUMANITY! I'VE FOUND IT! THE SUBSTANCE THAT TURNS PEOPLE TO DUST!
AT LAST I CAN DO AWAY WITH EVERYBODY, AND HAVE THE WHOLE WORLD TO BE ALONE IN— YAAAAAAAA!
AND I'D BEGUN TO THINK THAT GUY WAS OKAY!
FIRST, I'LL GIVE EACH OF YOU A LITTLE WHIFF OF THIS VAPOR!
YOU'RE NOT GIVING ME ANY OF THAT STUFF!
CRACK!

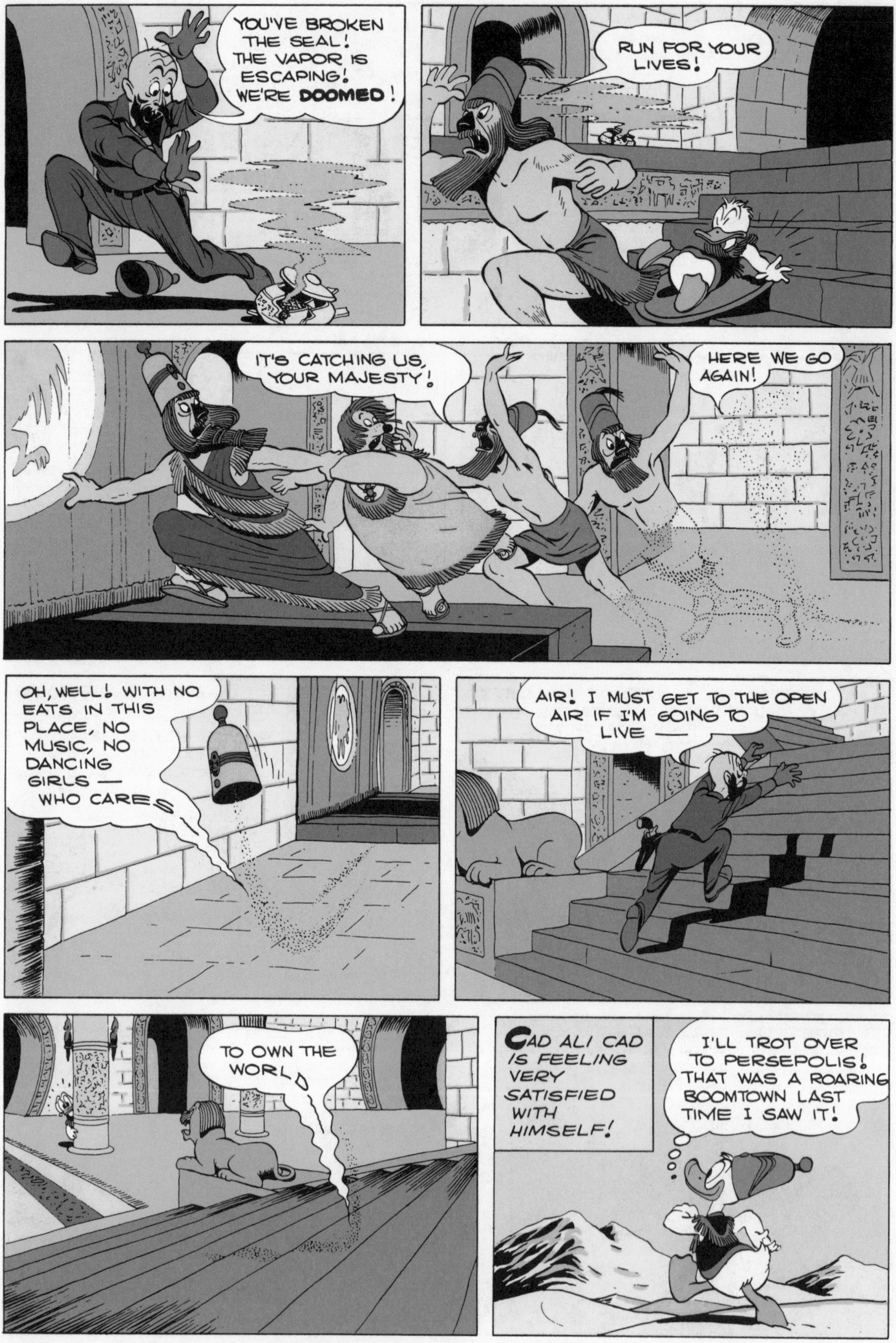
YOU'VE BROKEN THE SEAL! THE VAPOR IS ESCAPING! WE'RE **DOOMED**!
RUN FOR YOUR LIVES!
IT'S CATCHING US, YOUR MAJESTY!
HERE WE GO AGAIN!
OH, WELL! WITH NO EATS IN THIS PLACE, NO MUSIC, NO DANCING GIRLS — WHO CARES
AIR! I MUST GET TO THE OPEN AIR IF I'M GOING TO LIVE —
TO OWN THE WORLD
CAD ALI CAD IS FEELING VERY SATISFIED WITH HIMSELF!
I'LL TROT OVER TO PERSEPOLIS! THAT WAS A ROARING BOOMTOWN LAST TIME I SAW IT!

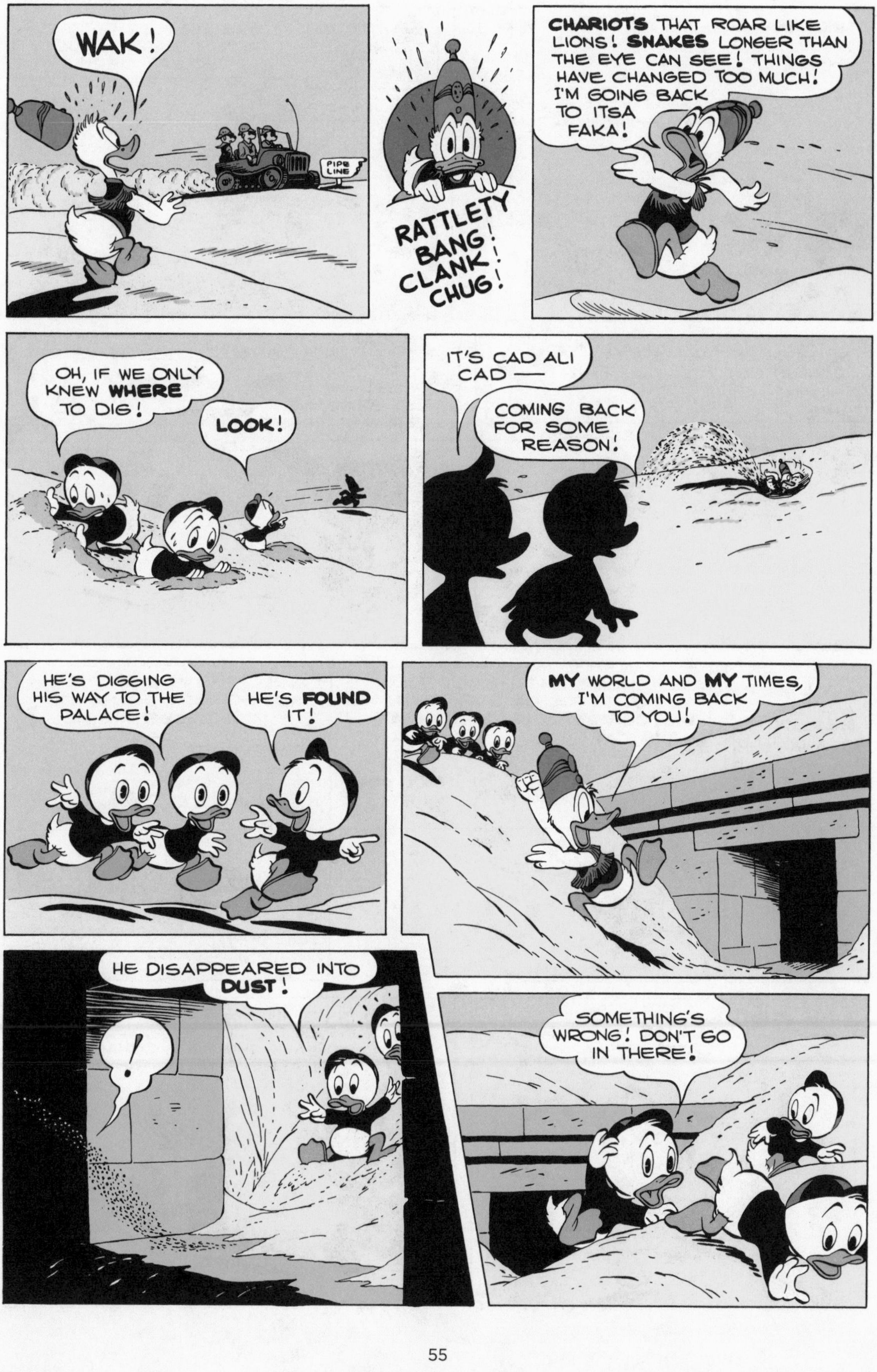
WAK!
PIPE LINE
RATTLETY BANG! CLANK! CHUG!
CHARIOTS THAT ROAR LIKE LIONS! SNAKES LONGER THAN THE EYE CAN SEE! THINGS HAVE CHANGED TOO MUCH! I'M GOING BACK TO ITSA FAKA!
OH, IF WE ONLY KNEW WHERE TO DIG!
LOOK!
IT'S CAD ALI CAD —
COMING BACK FOR SOME REASON!
HE'S DIGGING HIS WAY TO THE PALACE!
HE'S FOUND IT!
MY WORLD AND MY TIMES, I'M COMING BACK TO YOU!
HE DISAPPEARED INTO DUST!
!
SOMETHING'S WRONG! DON'T GO IN THERE!

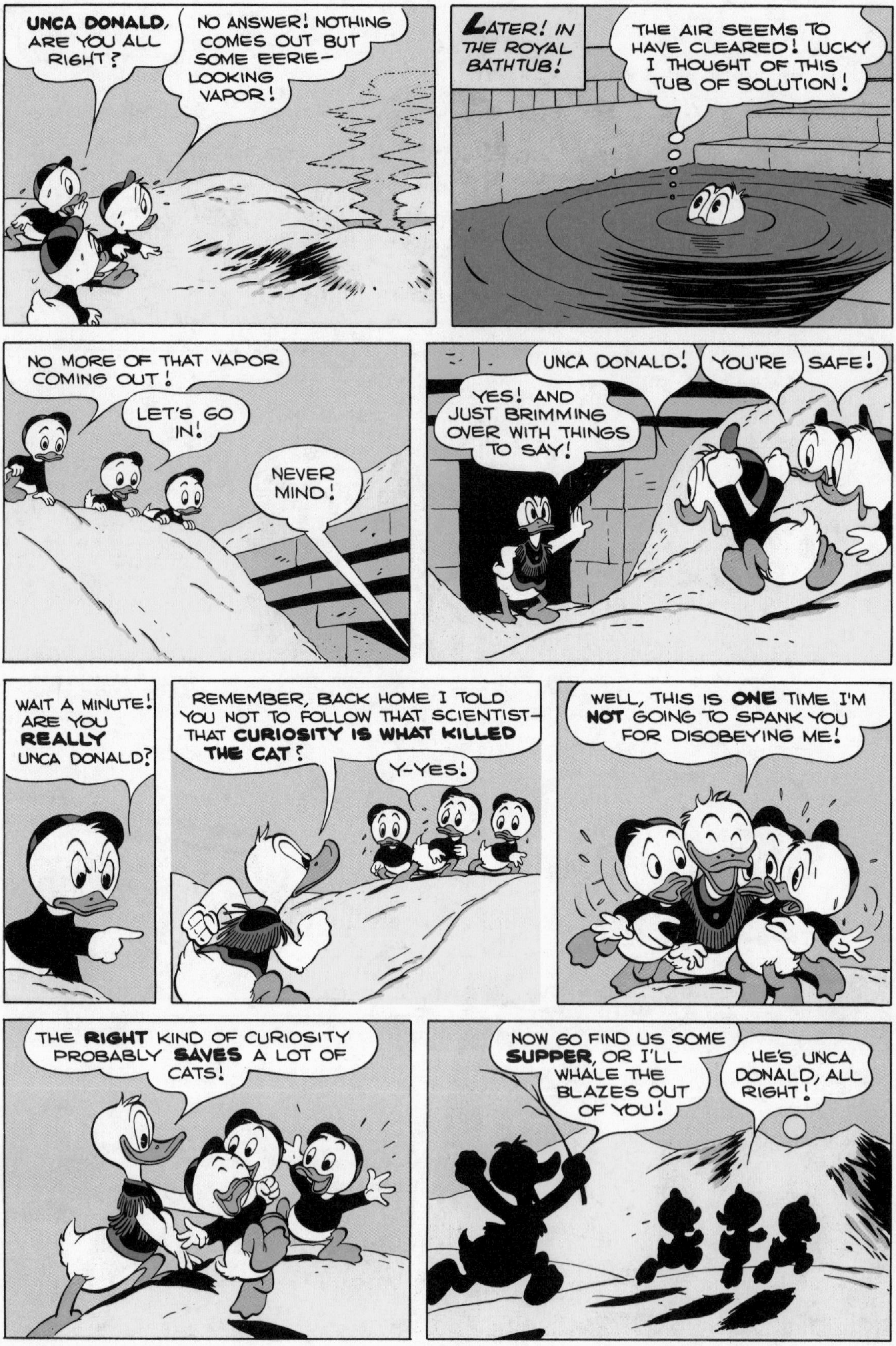
UNCA DONALD, ARE YOU ALL RIGHT?
NO ANSWER! NOTHING COMES OUT BUT SOME EERIE-LOOKING VAPOR!
LATER! IN THE ROYAL BATHTUB!
THE AIR SEEMS TO HAVE CLEARED! LUCKY I THOUGHT OF THIS TUB OF SOLUTION!
NO MORE OF THAT VAPOR COMING OUT!
LET'S GO IN!
NEVER MIND!
UNCA DONALD!
YOU'RE
SAFE!
YES! AND JUST BRIMMING OVER WITH THINGS TO SAY!
WAIT A MINUTE! ARE YOU REALLY UNCA DONALD?
REMEMBER, BACK HOME I TOLD YOU NOT TO FOLLOW THAT SCIENTIST-THAT CURIOSITY IS WHAT KILLED THE CAT?
Y-YES!
WELL, THIS IS ONE TIME I'M NOT GOING TO SPANK YOU FOR DISOBEYING ME!
THE RIGHT KIND OF CURIOSITY PROBABLY SAVES A LOT OF CATS!
NOW GO FIND US SOME SUPPER, OR I'LL WHALE THE BLAZES OUT OF YOU!
HE'S UNCA DONALD, ALL RIGHT!

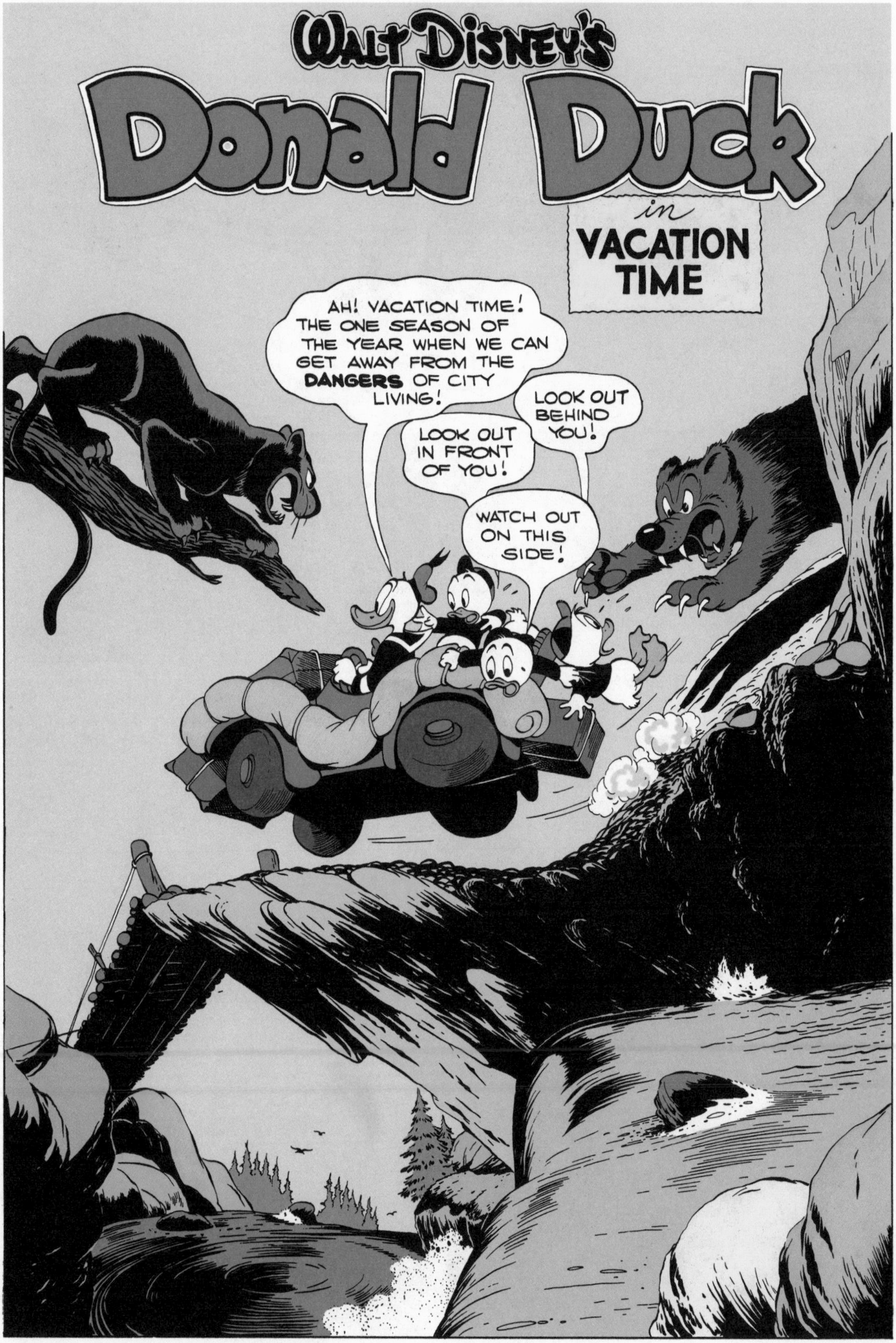
WALT DISNEY'S
Donald Duck
in
VACATION TIME
AH! VACATION TIME! THE ONE SEASON OF THE YEAR WHEN WE CAN GET AWAY FROM THE DANGERS OF CITY LIVING!
LOOK OUT IN FRONT OF YOU!
LOOK OUT BEHIND YOU!
WATCH OUT ON THIS SIDE!

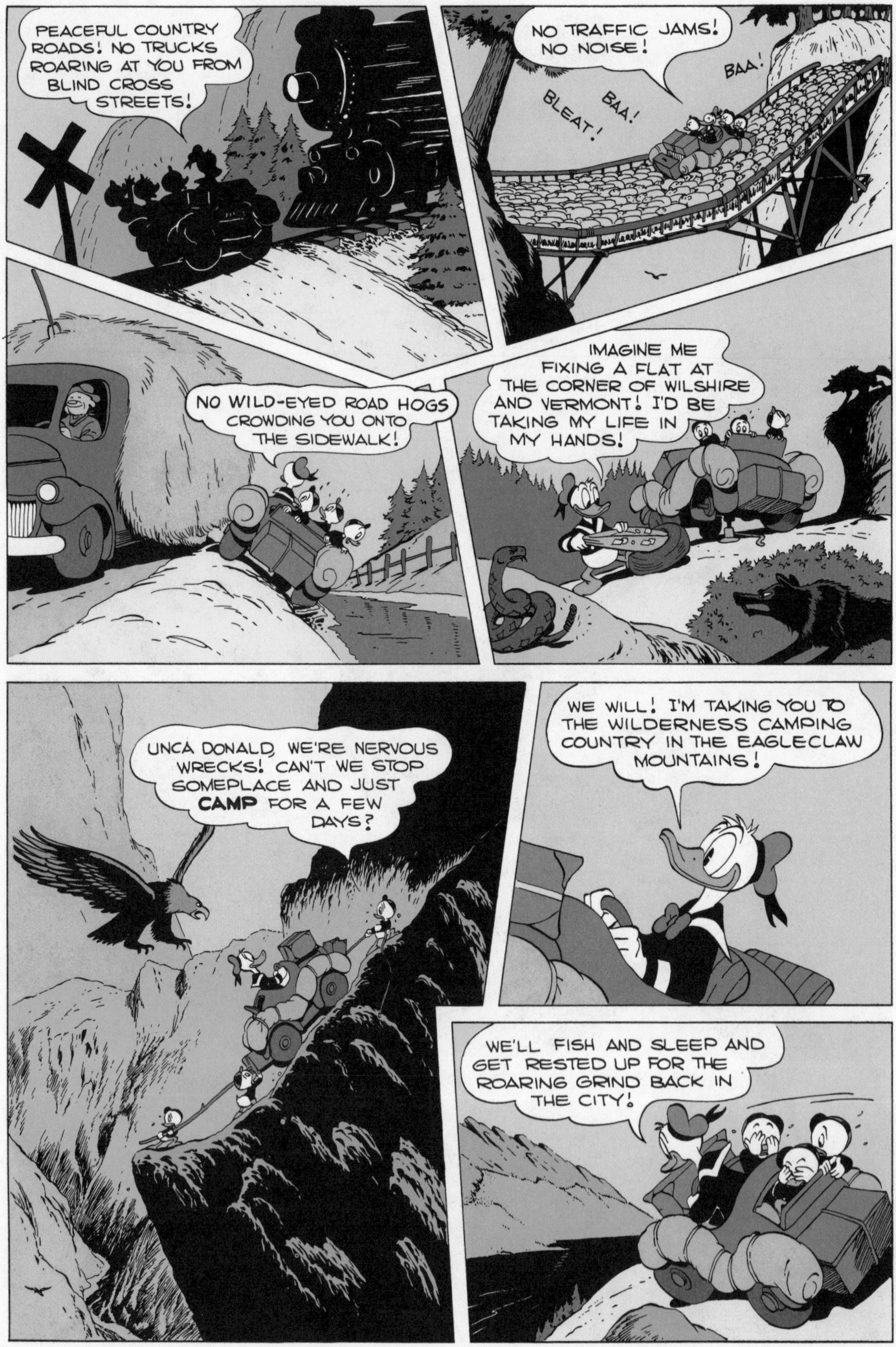
PEACEFUL COUNTRY ROADS! NO TRUCKS ROARING AT YOU FROM BLIND CROSS STREETS!
NO TRAFFIC JAMS! NO NOISE!
BAA!
BAA!
BLEAT!
NO WILD-EYED ROAD HOGS CROWDING YOU ONTO THE SIDEWALK!
IMAGINE ME FIXING A FLAT AT THE CORNER OF WILSHIRE AND VERMONT! I'D BE TAKING MY LIFE IN MY HANDS!
UNCA DONALD, WE'RE NERVOUS WRECKS! CAN'T WE STOP SOMEPLACE AND JUST CAMP FOR A FEW DAYS?
WE WILL! I'M TAKING YOU TO THE WILDERNESS CAMPING COUNTRY IN THE EAGLECLAW MOUNTAINS!
WE'LL FISH AND SLEEP AND GET RESTED UP FOR THE ROARING GRIND BACK IN THE CITY!

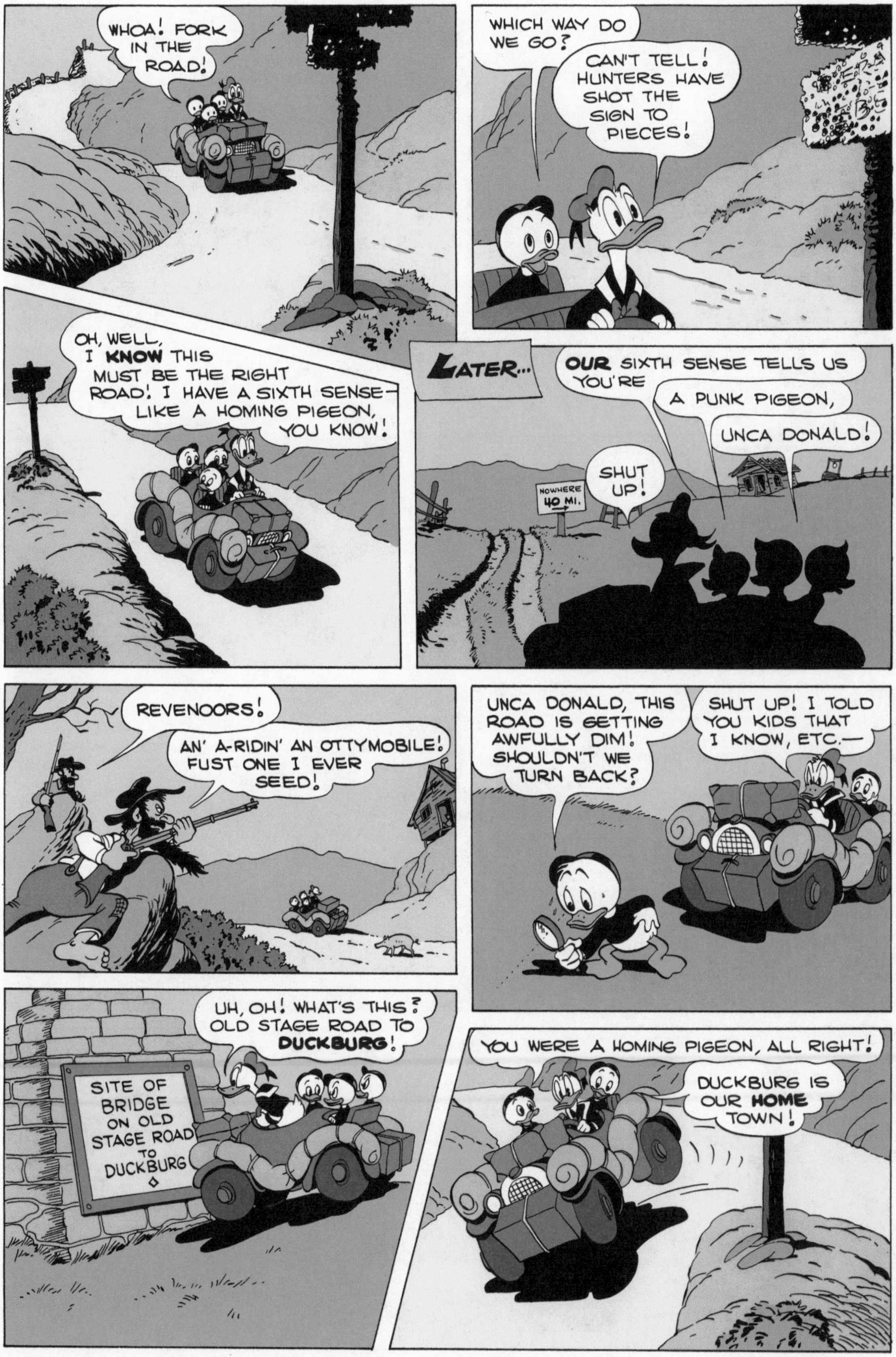

WHOA! FORK IN THE ROAD!
WHICH WAY DO WE GO?
CAN'T TELL! HUNTERS HAVE SHOT THE SIGN TO PIECES!
OH, WELL, I **KNOW** THIS MUST BE THE RIGHT ROAD! I HAVE A SIXTH SENSE— LIKE A HOMING PIGEON, YOU KNOW!
LATER...
OUR SIXTH SENSE TELLS US YOU'RE
A PUNK PIGEON,
UNCA DONALD!
SHUT UP!
NOWHERE 40 MI.
REVENOORS!
AN' A-RIDIN' AN OTTYMOBILE! FUST ONE I EVER SEED!
UNCA DONALD, THIS ROAD IS GETTING AWFULLY DIM! SHOULDN'T WE TURN BACK?
SHUT UP! I TOLD YOU KIDS THAT I KNOW, ETC.—
UH, OH! WHAT'S THIS? OLD STAGE ROAD TO **DUCKBURG**!
SITE OF BRIDGE ON OLD STAGE ROAD TO DUCKBURG
YOU WERE A HOMING PIGEON, ALL RIGHT!
DUCKBURG IS OUR **HOME** TOWN!

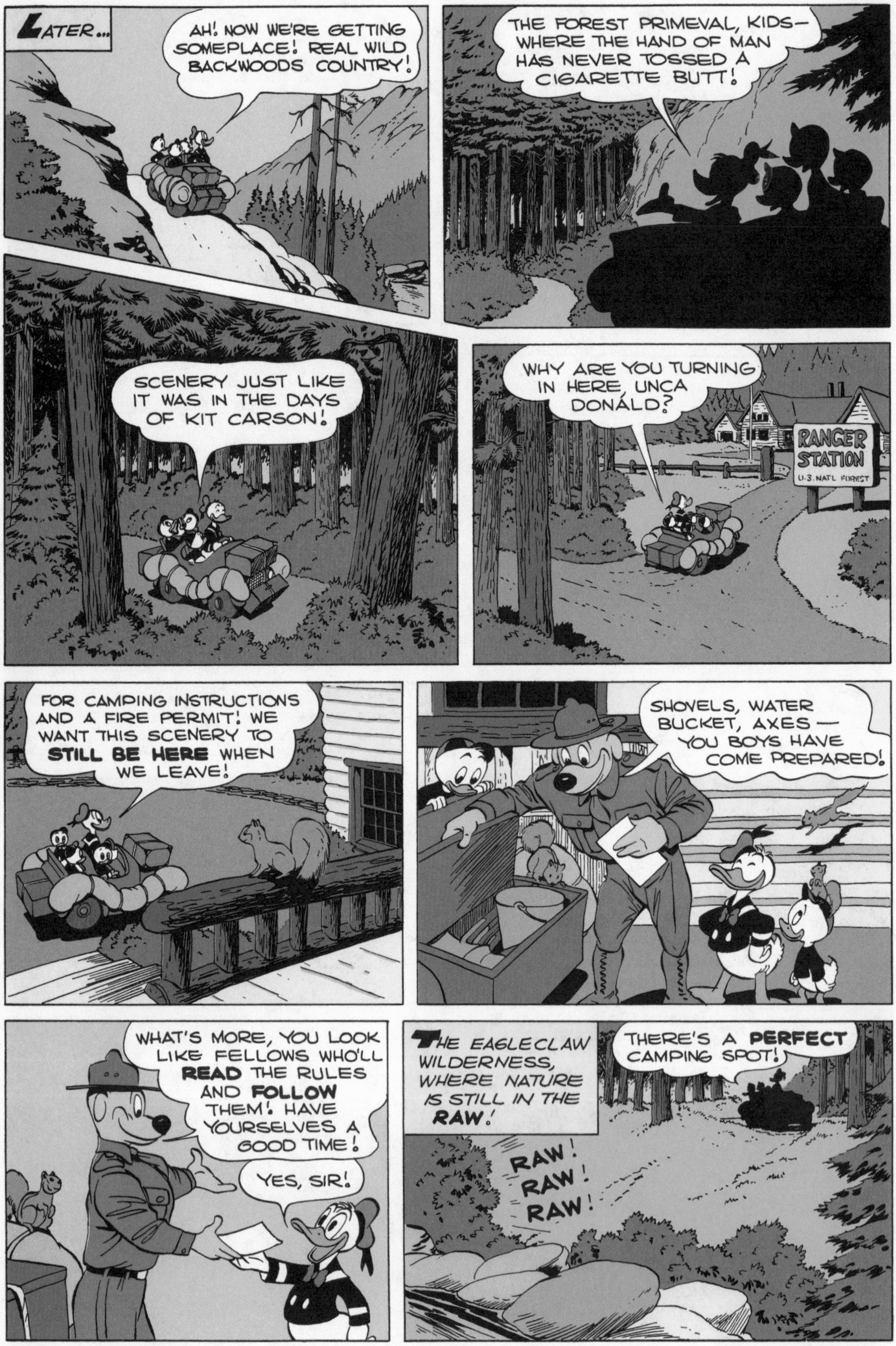
LATER...
AH! NOW WE'RE GETTING SOMEPLACE! REAL WILD BACKWOODS COUNTRY!
THE FOREST PRIMEVAL, KIDS— WHERE THE HAND OF MAN HAS NEVER TOSSED A CIGARETTE BUTT!
SCENERY JUST LIKE IT WAS IN THE DAYS OF KIT CARSON!
WHY ARE YOU TURNING IN HERE, UNCA DONALD?
RANGER STATION
U.S. NAT'L FOREST
FOR CAMPING INSTRUCTIONS AND A FIRE PERMIT! WE WANT THIS SCENERY TO STILL BE HERE WHEN WE LEAVE!
SHOVELS, WATER BUCKET, AXES— YOU BOYS HAVE COME PREPARED!
WHAT'S MORE, YOU LOOK LIKE FELLOWS WHO'LL READ THE RULES AND FOLLOW THEM! HAVE YOURSELVES A GOOD TIME!
YES, SIR!
THE EAGLECLAW WILDERNESS, WHERE NATURE IS STILL IN THE RAW!
THERE'S A PERFECT CAMPING SPOT!
RAW! RAW! RAW!

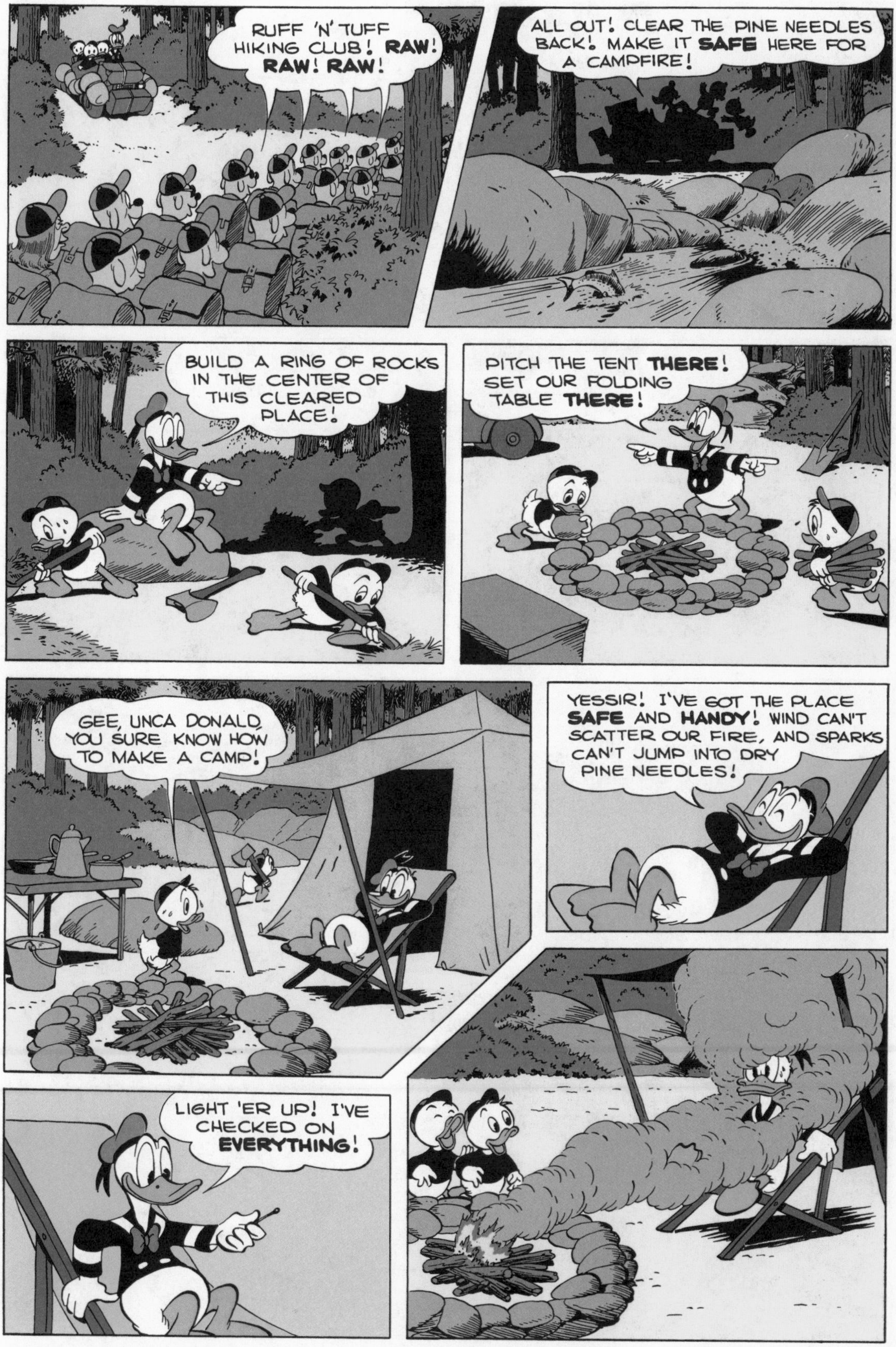
RUFF 'N' TUFF HIKING CLUB! RAW! RAW! RAW!
ALL OUT! CLEAR THE PINE NEEDLES BACK! MAKE IT SAFE HERE FOR A CAMPFIRE!
BUILD A RING OF ROCKS IN THE CENTER OF THIS CLEARED PLACE!
PITCH THE TENT THERE! SET OUR FOLDING TABLE THERE!
GEE, UNCA DONALD, YOU SURE KNOW HOW TO MAKE A CAMP!
YESSIR! I'VE GOT THE PLACE SAFE AND HANDY! WIND CAN'T SCATTER OUR FIRE, AND SPARKS CAN'T JUMP INTO DRY PINE NEEDLES!
LIGHT 'ER UP! I'VE CHECKED ON EVERYTHING!

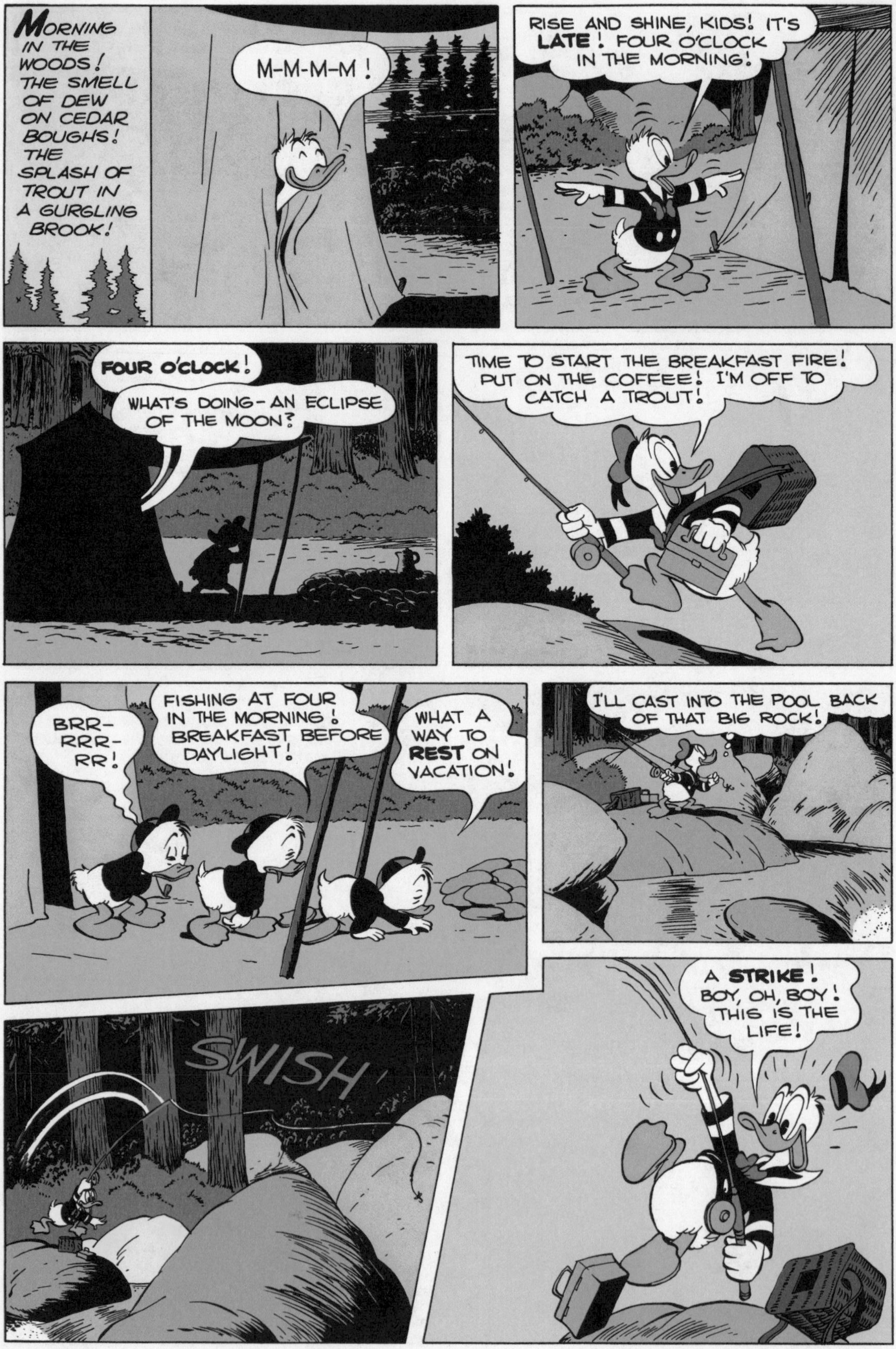
MORNING IN THE WOODS! THE SMELL OF DEW ON CEDAR BOUGHS! THE SPLASH OF TROUT IN A GURGLING BROOK!
M-M-M-M!
RISE AND SHINE, KIDS! IT'S LATE! FOUR O'CLOCK IN THE MORNING!
FOUR O'CLOCK!
WHAT'S DOING- AN ECLIPSE OF THE MOON?
TIME TO START THE BREAKFAST FIRE! PUT ON THE COFFEE! I'M OFF TO CATCH A TROUT!
BRR-RRR-RR!
FISHING AT FOUR IN THE MORNING! BREAKFAST BEFORE DAYLIGHT!
WHAT A WAY TO REST ON VACATION!
I'LL CAST INTO THE POOL BACK OF THAT BIG ROCK!
SWISH
A STRIKE! BOY, OH, BOY! THIS IS THE LIFE!

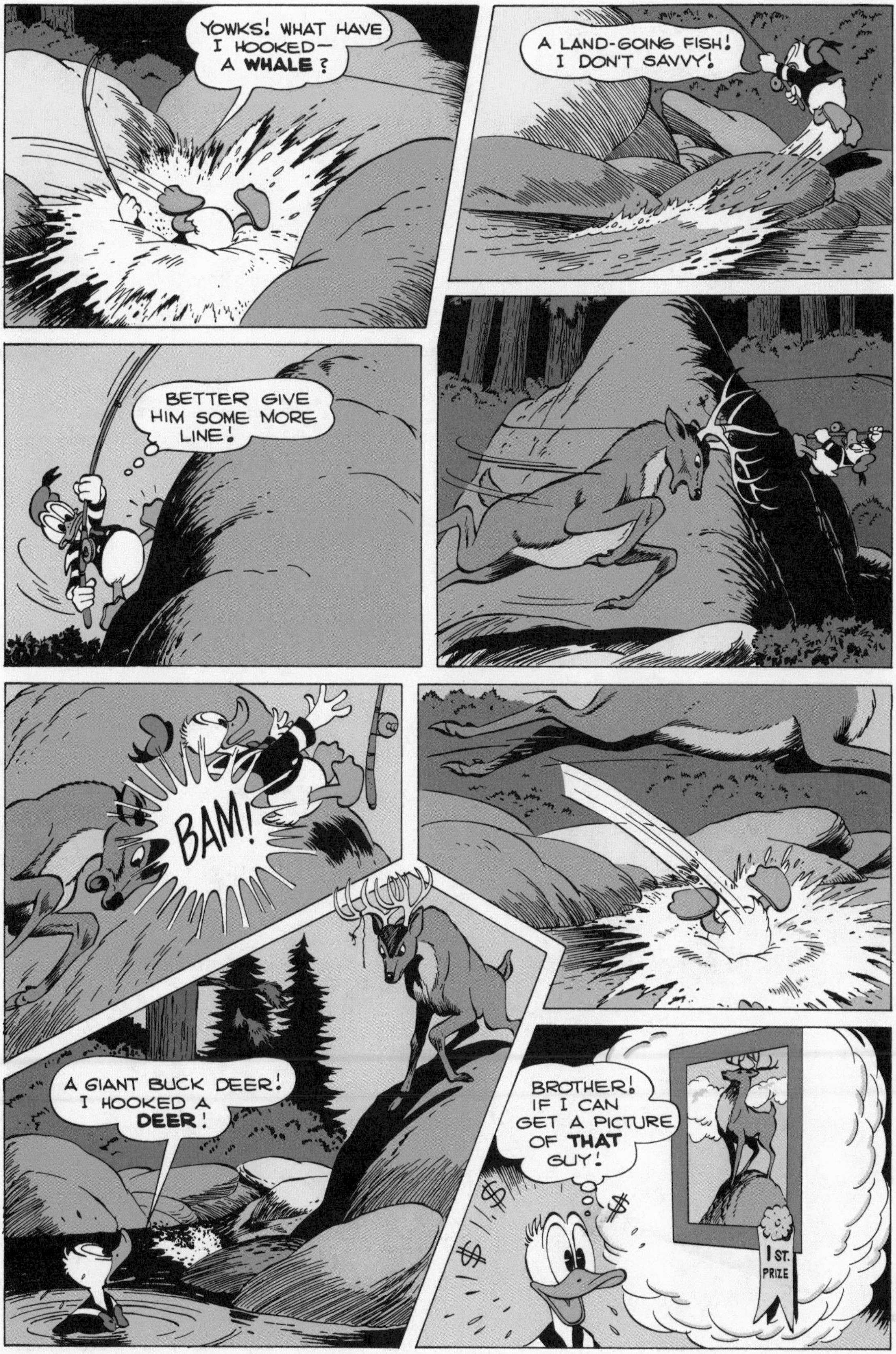
YOWKS! WHAT HAVE I HOOKED— A WHALE?
A LAND-GOING FISH! I DON'T SAVVY!
BETTER GIVE HIM SOME MORE LINE!
BAM!
A GIANT BUCK DEER! I HOOKED A DEER!
BROTHER! IF I CAN GET A PICTURE OF THAT GUY!
1 ST. PRIZE

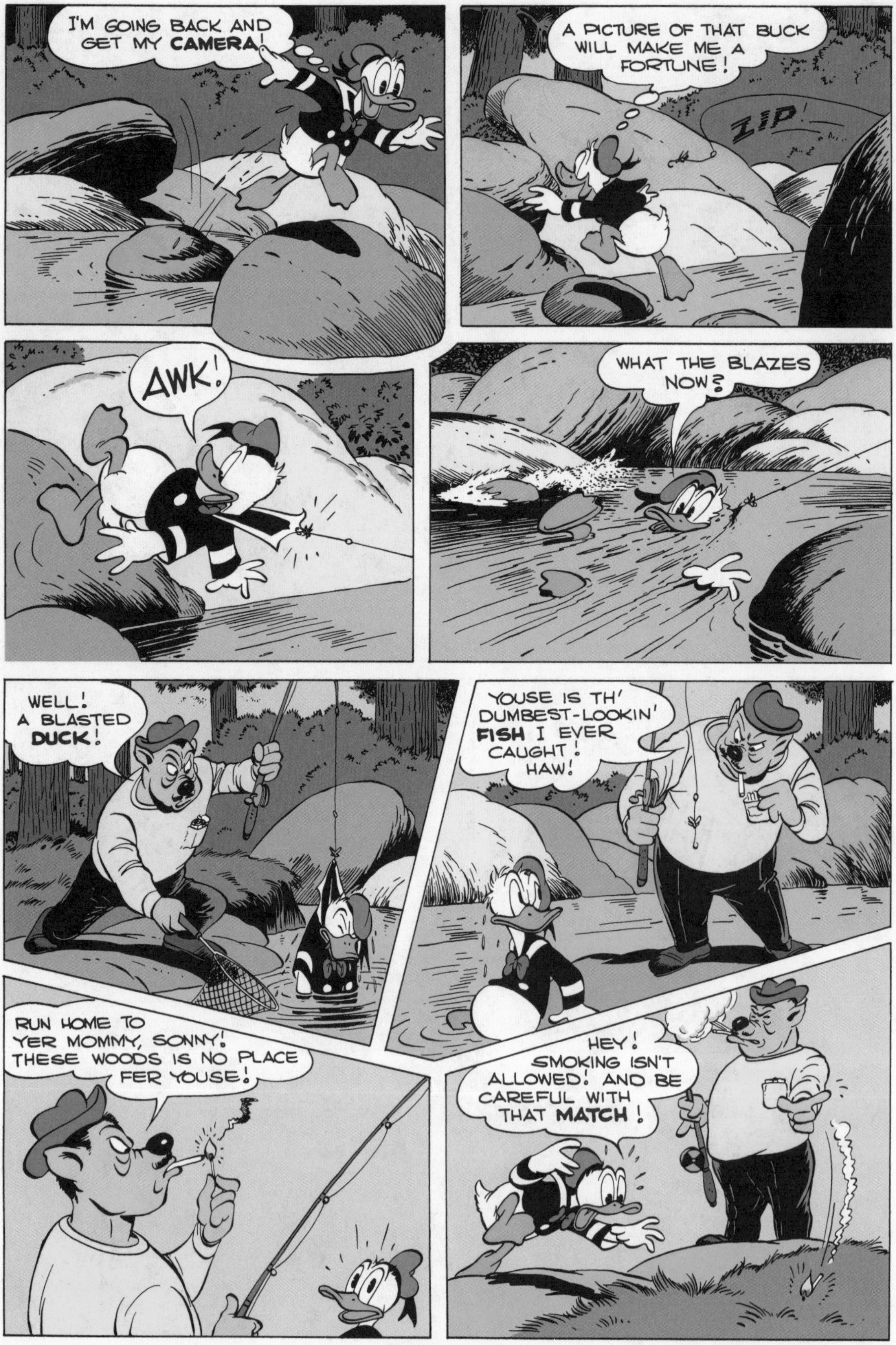
I'M GOING BACK AND GET MY **CAMERA**!
A PICTURE OF THAT BUCK WILL MAKE ME A FORTUNE!
ZIP!
AWK!
WHAT THE BLAZES NOW?
WELL! A BLASTED **DUCK**!
YOUSE IS TH' DUMBEST-LOOKIN' **FISH** I EVER CAUGHT! HAW!
RUN HOME TO YER MOMMY, SONNY! THESE WOODS IS NO PLACE FER YOUSE!
HEY! SMOKING ISN'T ALLOWED! AND BE CAREFUL WITH THAT **MATCH**!

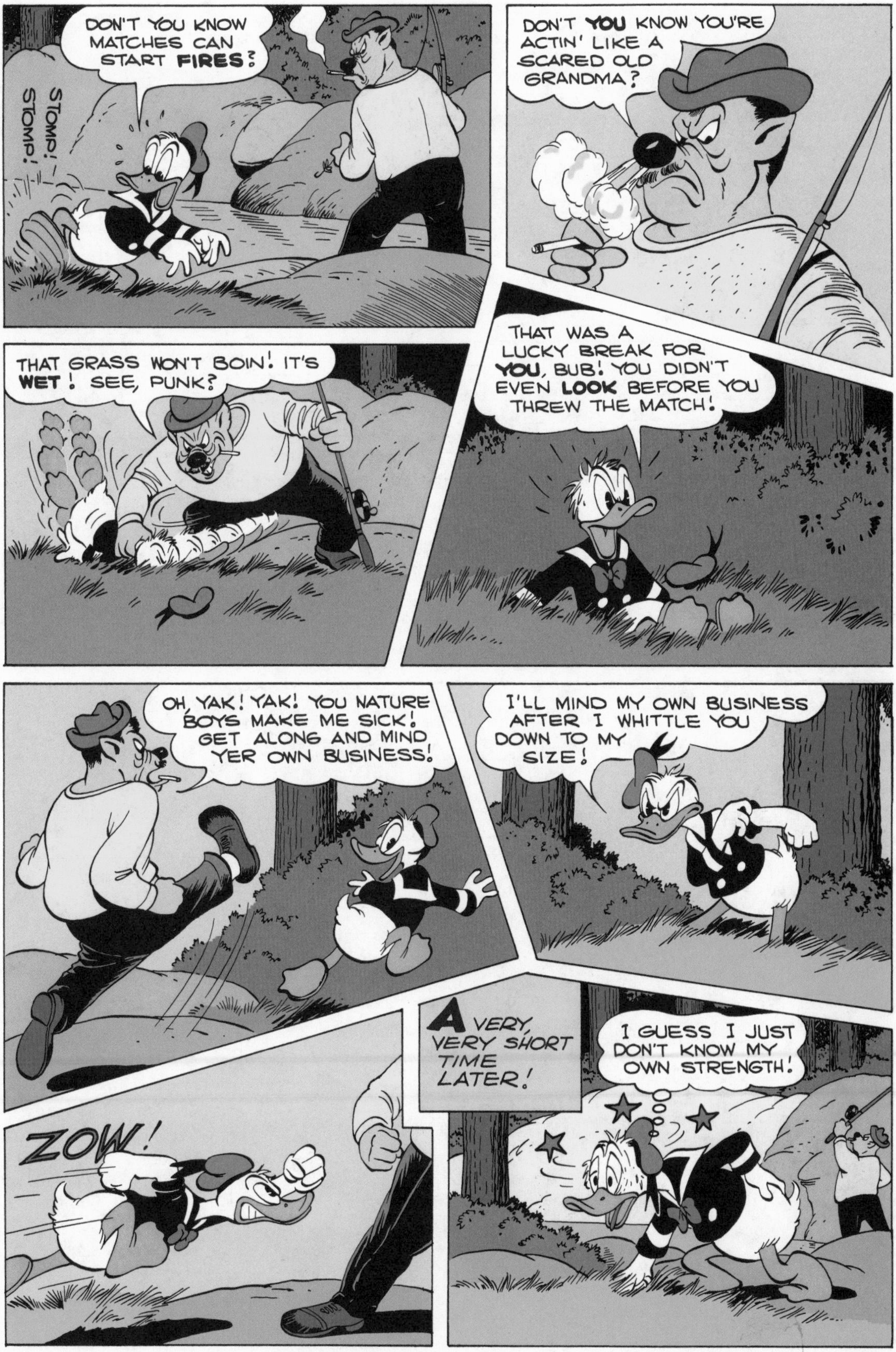
DON'T YOU KNOW MATCHES CAN START FIRES?
STOMP! STOMP!
DON'T YOU KNOW YOU'RE ACTIN' LIKE A SCARED OLD GRANDMA?
THAT GRASS WON'T BOIN! IT'S WET! SEE, PUNK?
THAT WAS A LUCKY BREAK FOR YOU, BUB! YOU DIDN'T EVEN LOOK BEFORE YOU THREW THE MATCH!
OH, YAK! YAK! YOU NATURE BOYS MAKE ME SICK! GET ALONG AND MIND YER OWN BUSINESS!
I'LL MIND MY OWN BUSINESS AFTER I WHITTLE YOU DOWN TO MY SIZE!
ZOW!
A VERY, VERY SHORT TIME LATER!
I GUESS I JUST DON'T KNOW MY OWN STRENGTH!

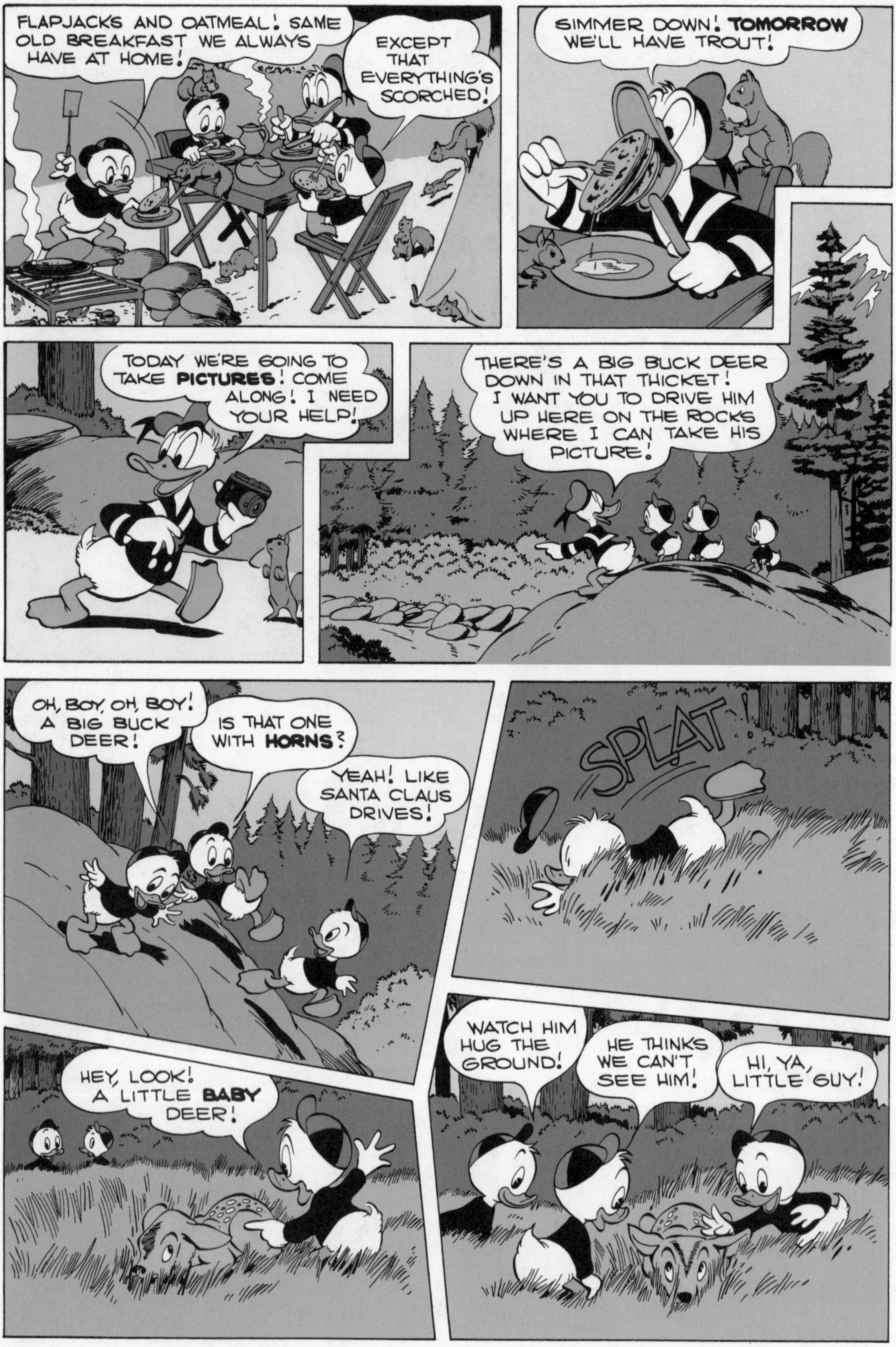
FLAPJACKS AND OATMEAL! SAME OLD BREAKFAST WE ALWAYS HAVE AT HOME!
EXCEPT THAT EVERYTHING'S SCORCHED!
SIMMER DOWN! TOMORROW WE'LL HAVE TROUT!
TODAY WE'RE GOING TO TAKE PICTURES! COME ALONG! I NEED YOUR HELP!
THERE'S A BIG BUCK DEER DOWN IN THAT THICKET! I WANT YOU TO DRIVE HIM UP HERE ON THE ROCKS WHERE I CAN TAKE HIS PICTURE!
OH, BOY, OH, BOY! A BIG BUCK DEER!
IS THAT ONE WITH HORNS?
YEAH! LIKE SANTA CLAUS DRIVES!
SPLAT!
HEY, LOOK! A LITTLE BABY DEER!
WATCH HIM HUG THE GROUND!
HE THINKS WE CAN'T SEE HIM!
HI, YA, LITTLE GUY!

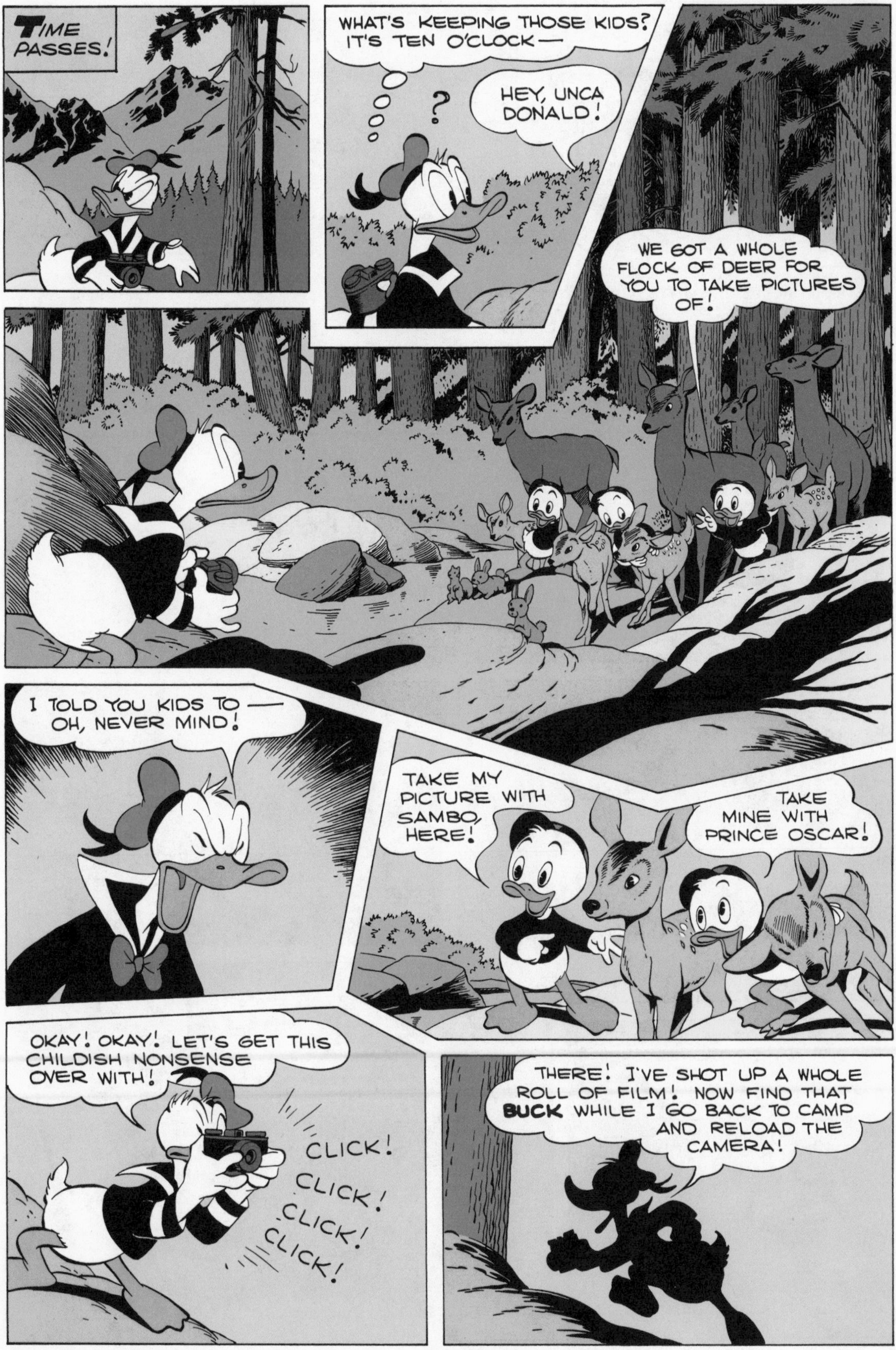
TIME PASSES!
WHAT'S KEEPING THOSE KIDS? IT'S TEN O'CLOCK—
?
HEY, UNCA DONALD!
WE GOT A WHOLE FLOCK OF DEER FOR YOU TO TAKE PICTURES OF!
I TOLD YOU KIDS TO— OH, NEVER MIND!
TAKE MY PICTURE WITH SAMBO, HERE!
TAKE MINE WITH PRINCE OSCAR!
OKAY! OKAY! LET'S GET THIS CHILDISH NONSENSE OVER WITH!
CLICK! CLICK! CLICK! CLICK!
THERE! I'VE SHOT UP A WHOLE ROLL OF FILM! NOW FIND THAT BUCK WHILE I GO BACK TO CAMP AND RELOAD THE CAMERA!

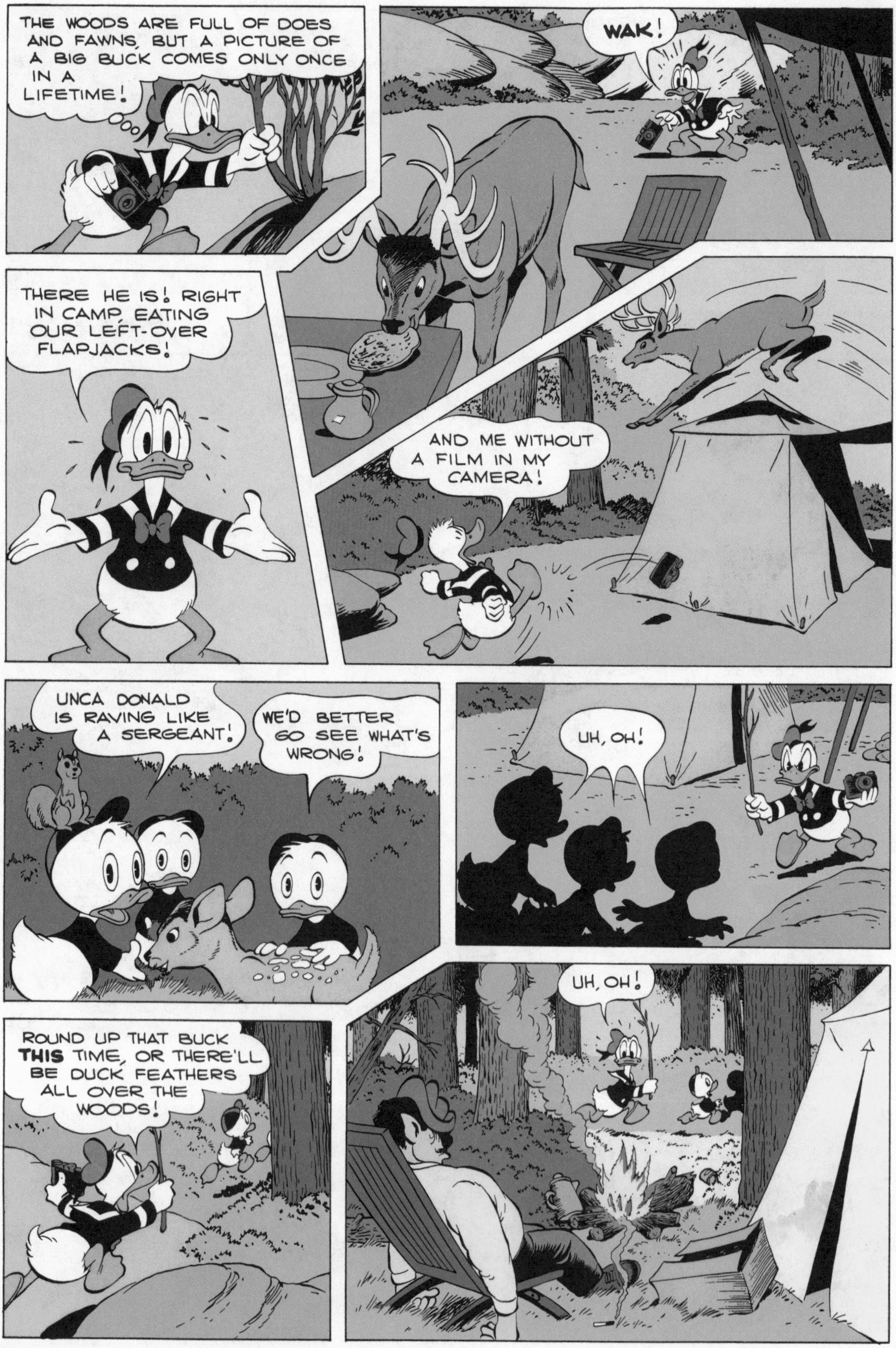
THE WOODS ARE FULL OF DOES AND FAWNS, BUT A PICTURE OF A BIG BUCK COMES ONLY ONCE IN A LIFETIME!
WAK!
THERE HE IS! RIGHT IN CAMP, EATING OUR LEFT-OVER FLAPJACKS!
AND ME WITHOUT A FILM IN MY CAMERA!
UNCA DONALD IS RAVING LIKE A SERGEANT!
WE'D BETTER GO SEE WHAT'S WRONG!
UH, OH!
ROUND UP THAT BUCK **THIS** TIME, OR THERE'LL BE DUCK FEATHERS ALL OVER THE WOODS!
UH, OH!

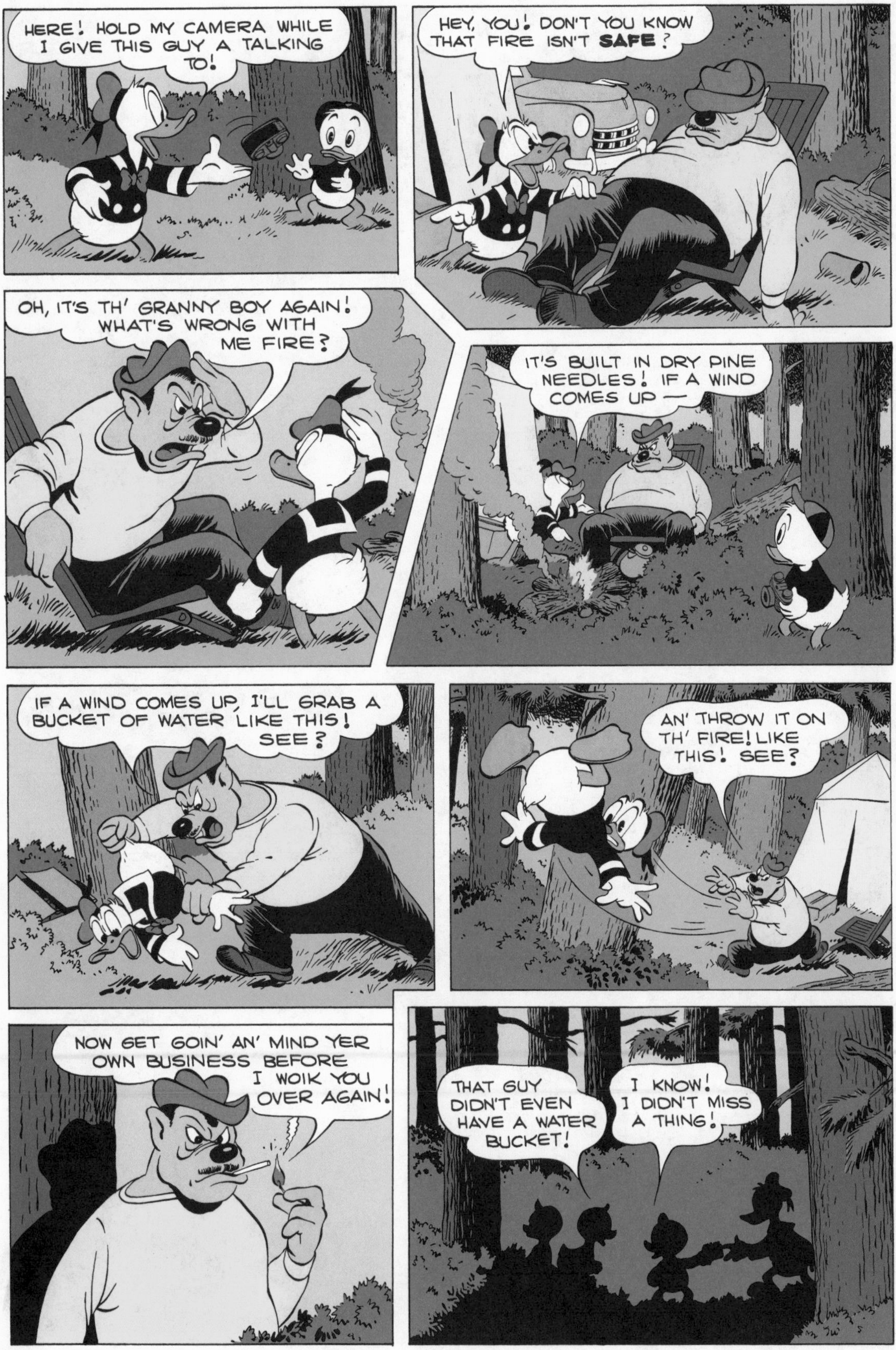
HERE! HOLD MY CAMERA WHILE I GIVE THIS GUY A TALKING TO!
HEY, YOU! DON'T YOU KNOW THAT FIRE ISN'T SAFE?
OH, IT'S TH' GRANNY BOY AGAIN! WHAT'S WRONG WITH ME FIRE?
IT'S BUILT IN DRY PINE NEEDLES! IF A WIND COMES UP —
IF A WIND COMES UP, I'LL GRAB A BUCKET OF WATER LIKE THIS! SEE?
AN' THROW IT ON TH' FIRE! LIKE THIS! SEE?
NOW GET GOIN' AN' MIND YER OWN BUSINESS BEFORE I WOIK YOU OVER AGAIN!
THAT GUY DIDN'T EVEN HAVE A WATER BUCKET!
I KNOW! I DIDN'T MISS A THING!

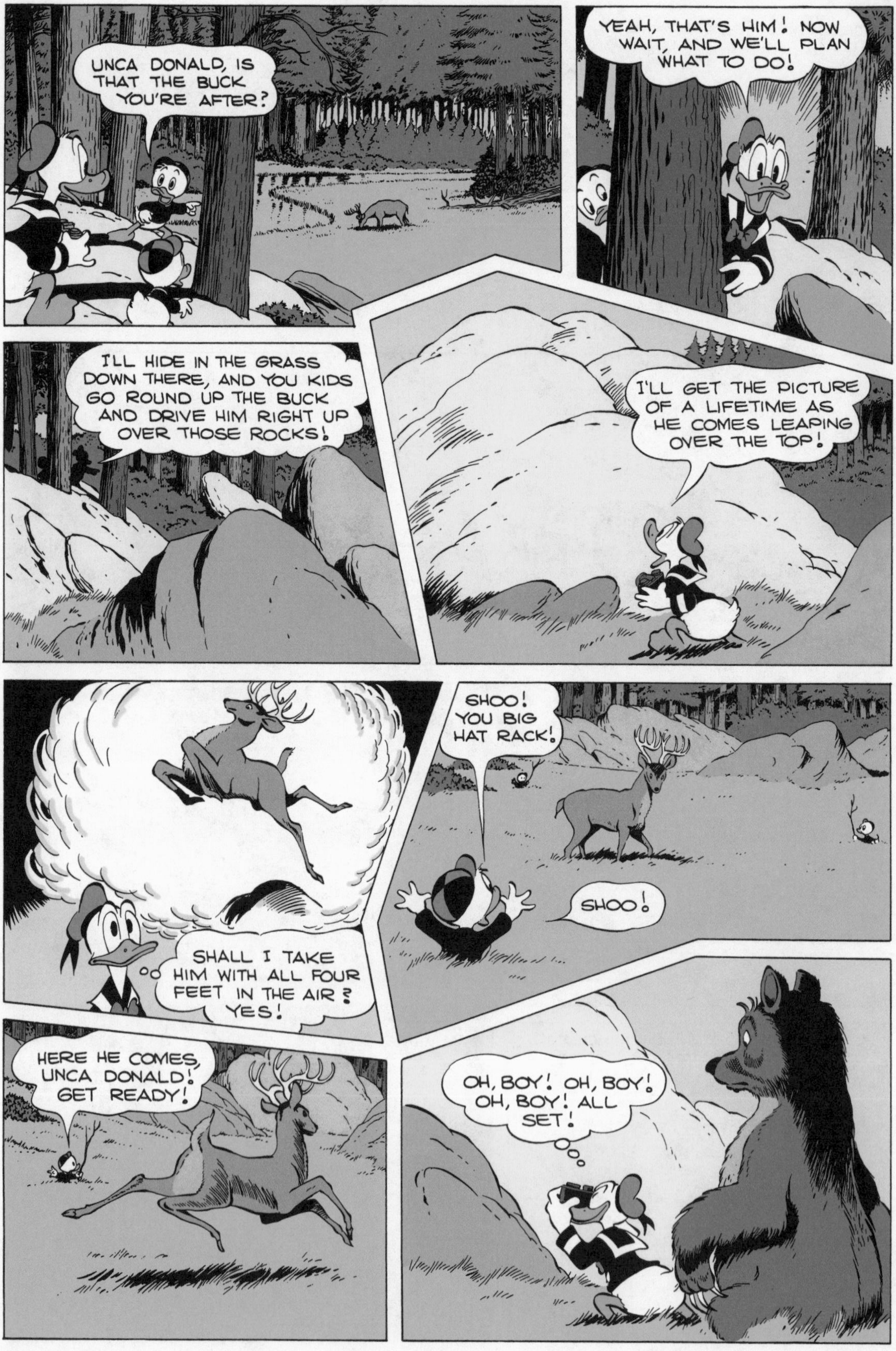
UNCA DONALD, IS THAT THE BUCK YOU'RE AFTER?
YEAH, THAT'S HIM! NOW WAIT, AND WE'LL PLAN WHAT TO DO!
I'LL HIDE IN THE GRASS DOWN THERE, AND YOU KIDS GO ROUND UP THE BUCK AND DRIVE HIM RIGHT UP OVER THOSE ROCKS!
I'LL GET THE PICTURE OF A LIFETIME AS HE COMES LEAPING OVER THE TOP!
SHALL I TAKE HIM WITH ALL FOUR FEET IN THE AIR? YES!
SHOO! YOU BIG HAT RACK!
SHOO!
HERE HE COMES, UNCA DONALD! GET READY!
OH, BOY! OH, BOY! OH, BOY! ALL SET!

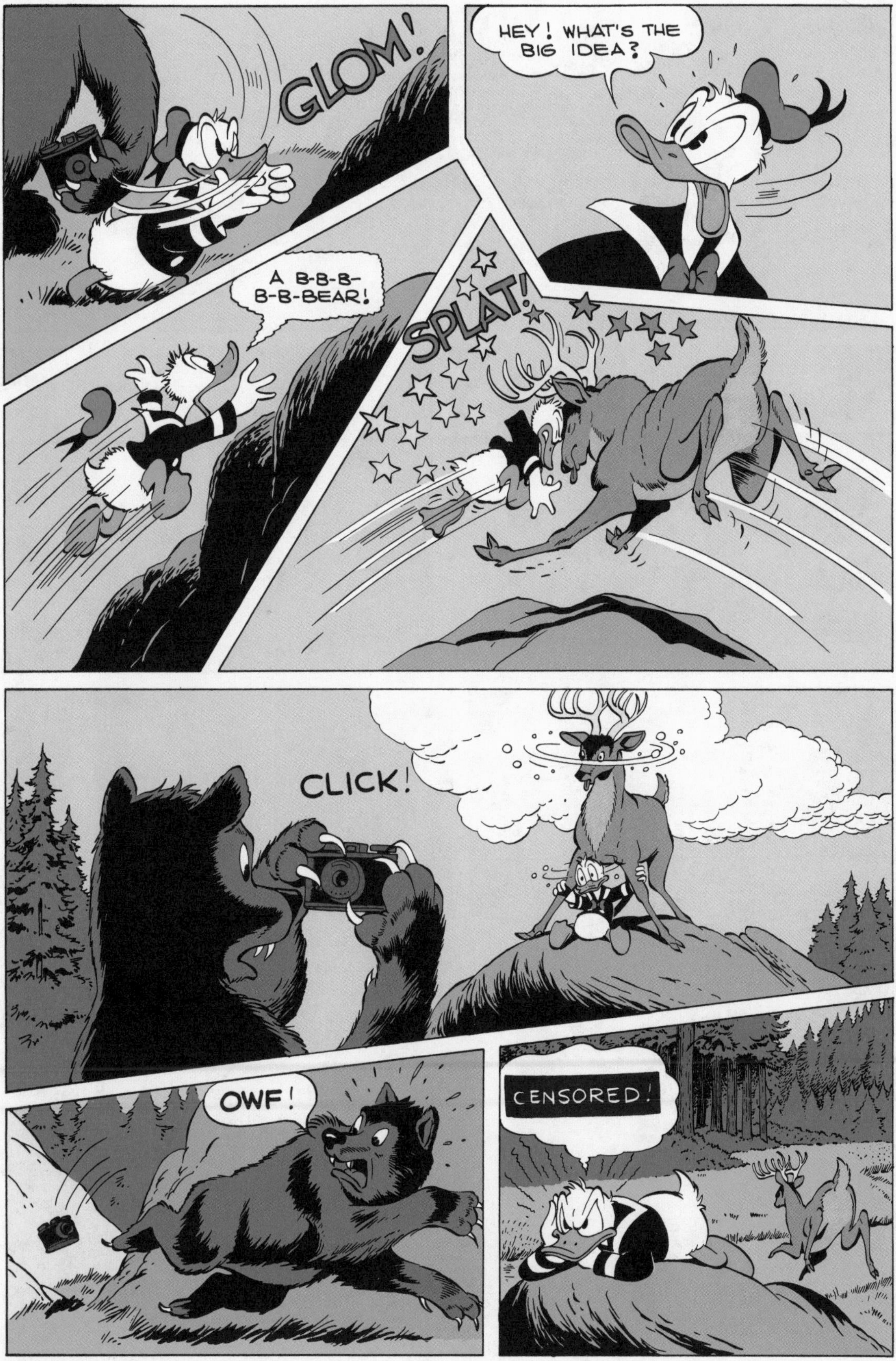
GLOM!
HEY! WHAT'S THE BIG IDEA?
A B-B-B-B-B-BEAR!
SPLAT!
CLICK!
OWF!
CENSORED!

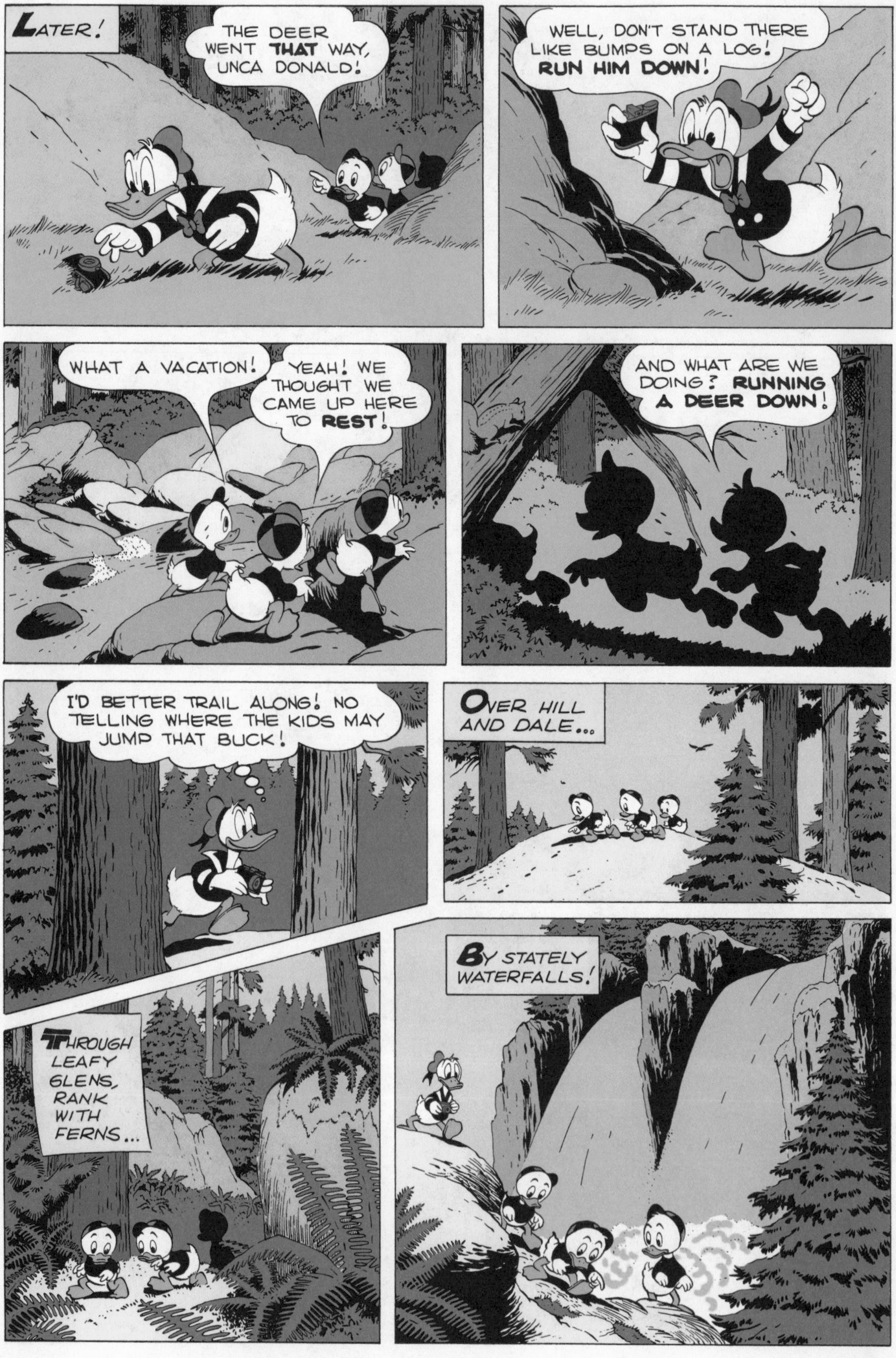
LATER!
THE DEER WENT THAT WAY, UNCA DONALD!
WELL, DON'T STAND THERE LIKE BUMPS ON A LOG! RUN HIM DOWN!
WHAT A VACATION!
YEAH! WE THOUGHT WE CAME UP HERE TO REST!
AND WHAT ARE WE DOING? RUNNING A DEER DOWN!
I'D BETTER TRAIL ALONG! NO TELLING WHERE THE KIDS MAY JUMP THAT BUCK!
OVER HILL AND DALE...
THROUGH LEAFY GLENS, RANK WITH FERNS...
BY STATELY WATERFALLS!

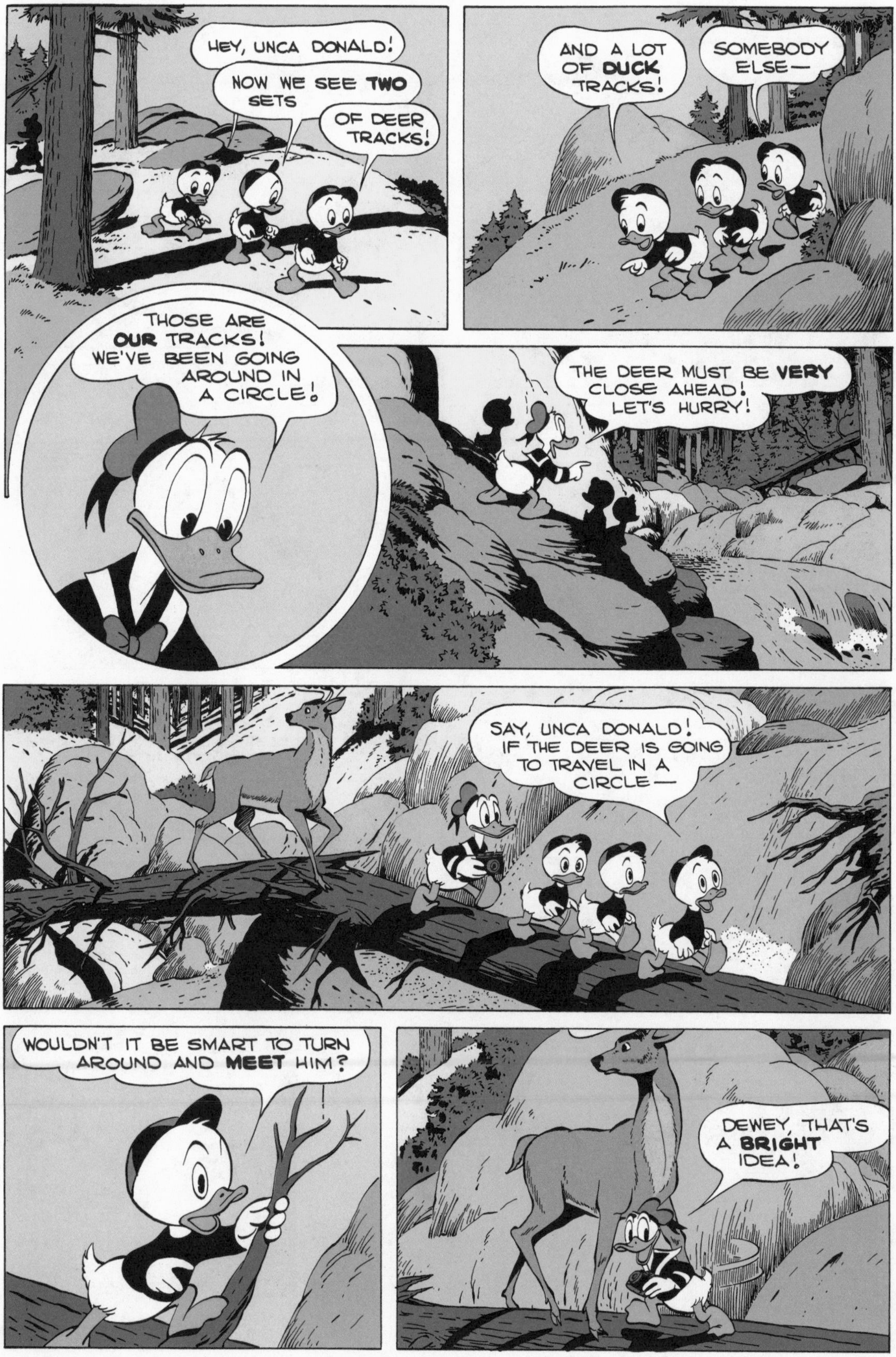
HEY, UNCA DONALD!
NOW WE SEE TWO SETS
OF DEER TRACKS!
AND A LOT OF DUCK TRACKS!
SOMEBODY ELSE—
THOSE ARE OUR TRACKS! WE'VE BEEN GOING AROUND IN A CIRCLE!
THE DEER MUST BE VERY CLOSE AHEAD! LET'S HURRY!
SAY, UNCA DONALD! IF THE DEER IS GOING TO TRAVEL IN A CIRCLE—
WOULDN'T IT BE SMART TO TURN AROUND AND MEET HIM?
DEWEY, THAT'S A BRIGHT IDEA!

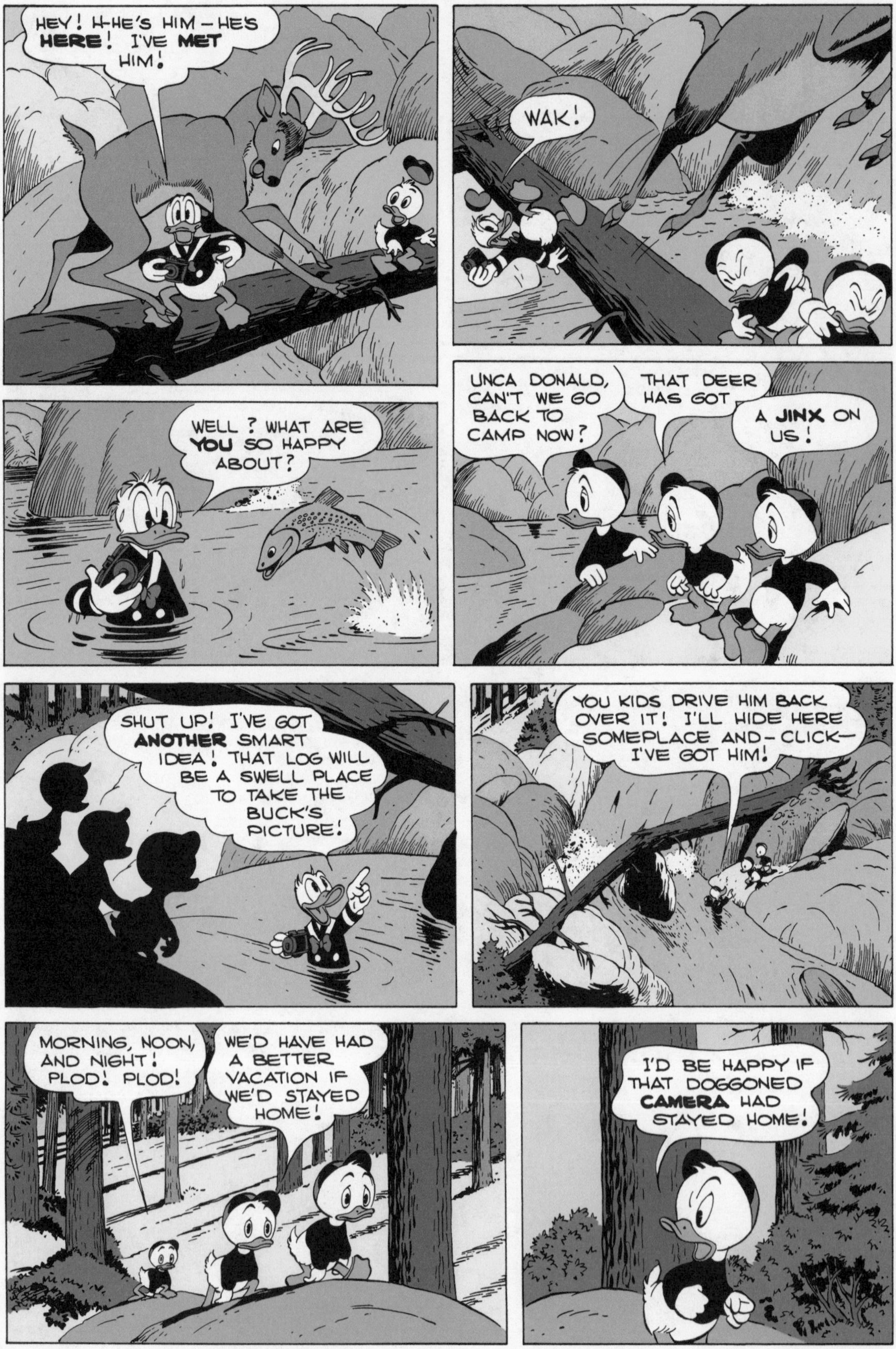
HEY! H-HE'S HIM—HE'S HERE! I'VE MET HIM!
WAK!
WELL? WHAT ARE YOU SO HAPPY ABOUT?
UNCA DONALD, CAN'T WE GO BACK TO CAMP NOW?
THAT DEER HAS GOT
A JINX ON US!
SHUT UP! I'VE GOT ANOTHER SMART IDEA! THAT LOG WILL BE A SWELL PLACE TO TAKE THE BUCK'S PICTURE!
YOU KIDS DRIVE HIM BACK OVER IT! I'LL HIDE HERE SOMEPLACE AND—CLICK—I'VE GOT HIM!
MORNING, NOON, AND NIGHT! PLOD! PLOD!
WE'D HAVE HAD A BETTER VACATION IF WE'D STAYED HOME!
I'D BE HAPPY IF THAT DOGGONED CAMERA HAD STAYED HOME!

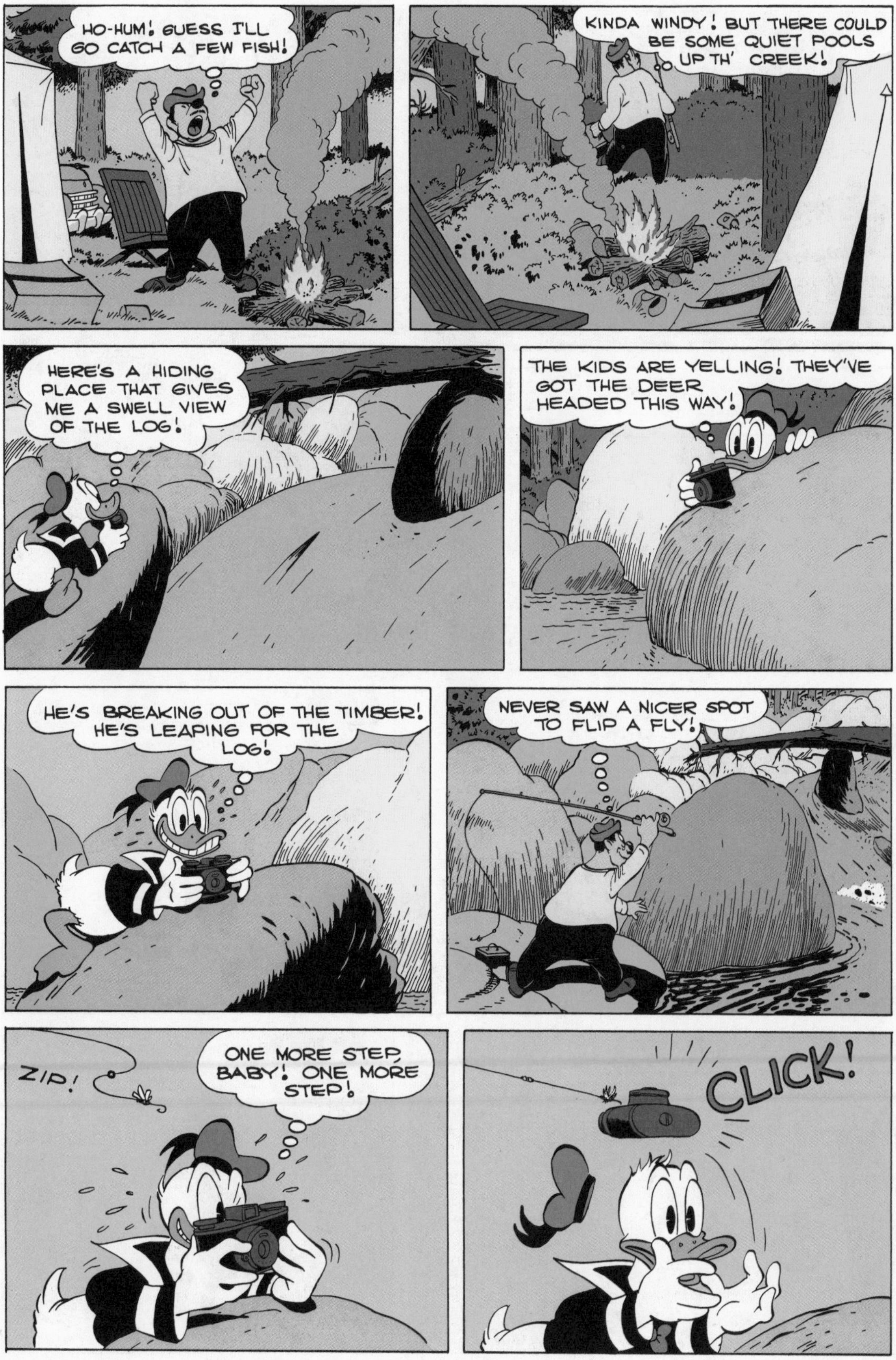

HO-HUM! GUESS I'LL GO CATCH A FEW FISH!
KINDA WINDY! BUT THERE COULD BE SOME QUIET POOLS UP TH' CREEK!
HERE'S A HIDING PLACE THAT GIVES ME A SWELL VIEW OF THE LOG!
THE KIDS ARE YELLING! THEY'VE GOT THE DEER HEADED THIS WAY!
HE'S BREAKING OUT OF THE TIMBER! HE'S LEAPING FOR THE LOG!
NEVER SAW A NICER SPOT TO FLIP A FLY!
ZIP!
ONE MORE STEP, BABY! ONE MORE STEP!
CLICK!

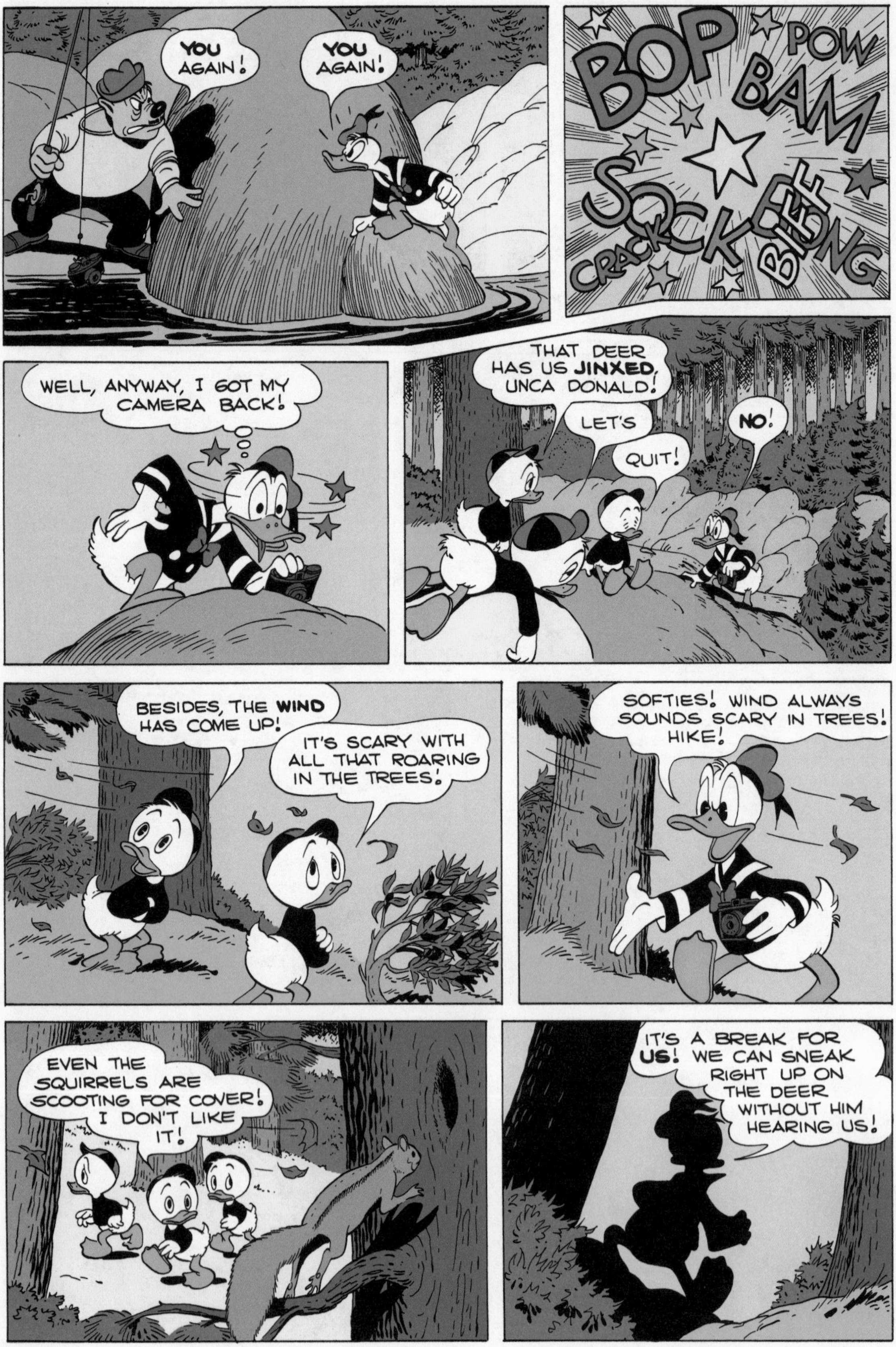
YOU AGAIN!
YOU AGAIN!
BOP
POW
BAM
SOCK
CRACK
BIFF
BONG
WELL, ANYWAY, I GOT MY CAMERA BACK!
THAT DEER HAS US JINXED, UNCA DONALD!
LET'S
QUIT!
NO!
BESIDES, THE WIND HAS COME UP!
IT'S SCARY WITH ALL THAT ROARING IN THE TREES!
SOFTIES! WIND ALWAYS SOUNDS SCARY IN TREES! HIKE!
EVEN THE SQUIRRELS ARE SCOOTING FOR COVER! I DON'T LIKE IT!
IT'S A BREAK FOR US! WE CAN SNEAK RIGHT UP ON THE DEER WITHOUT HIM HEARING US!

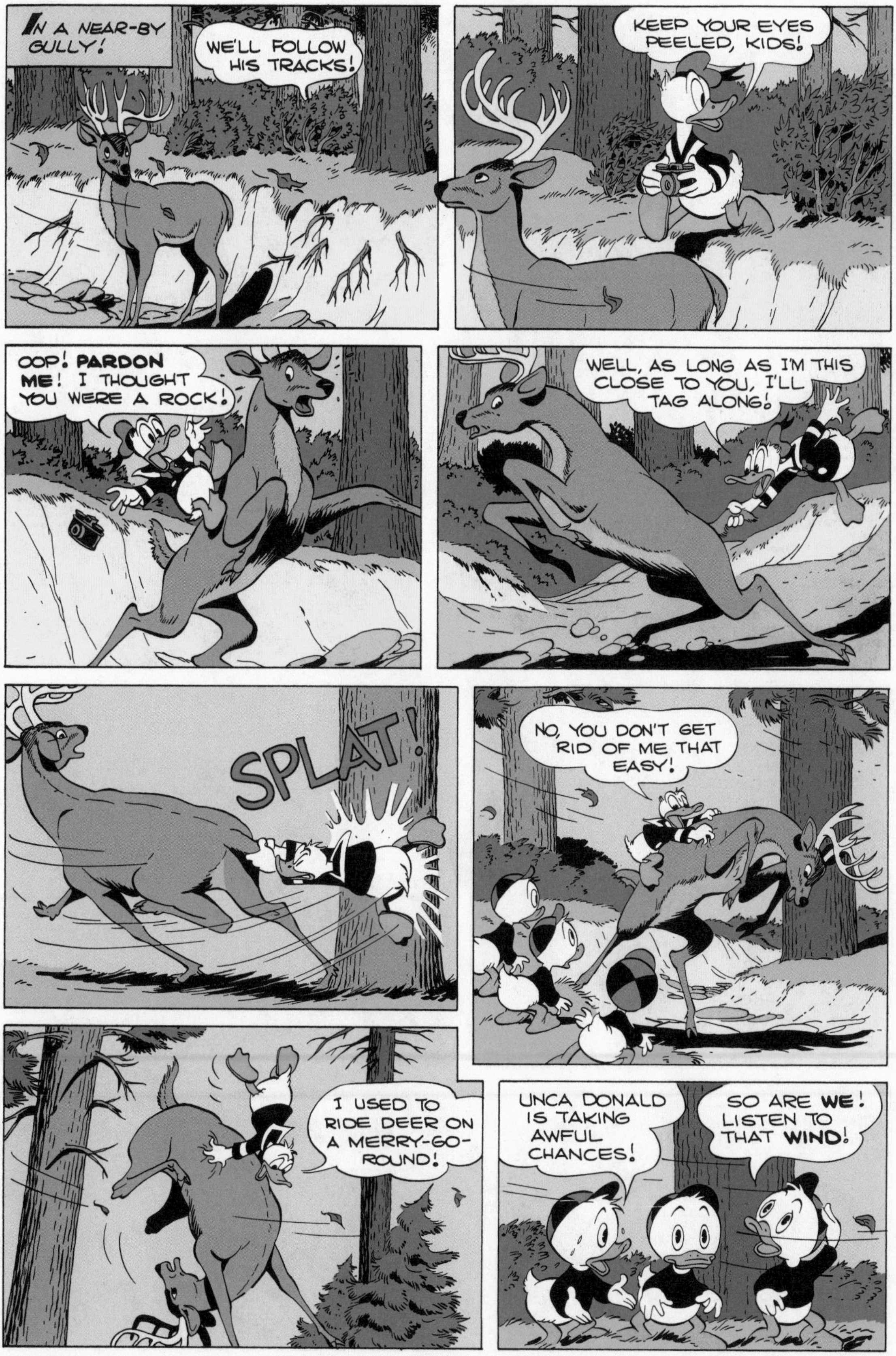

IN A NEAR-BY GULLY!
WE'LL FOLLOW HIS TRACKS!
KEEP YOUR EYES PEELED, KIDS!
OOP! PARDON ME! I THOUGHT YOU WERE A ROCK!
WELL, AS LONG AS I'M THIS CLOSE TO YOU, I'LL TAG ALONG!
SPLAT!
NO, YOU DON'T GET RID OF ME THAT EASY!
I USED TO RIDE DEER ON A MERRY-GO-ROUND!
UNCA DONALD IS TAKING AWFUL CHANCES!
SO ARE WE! LISTEN TO THAT WIND!

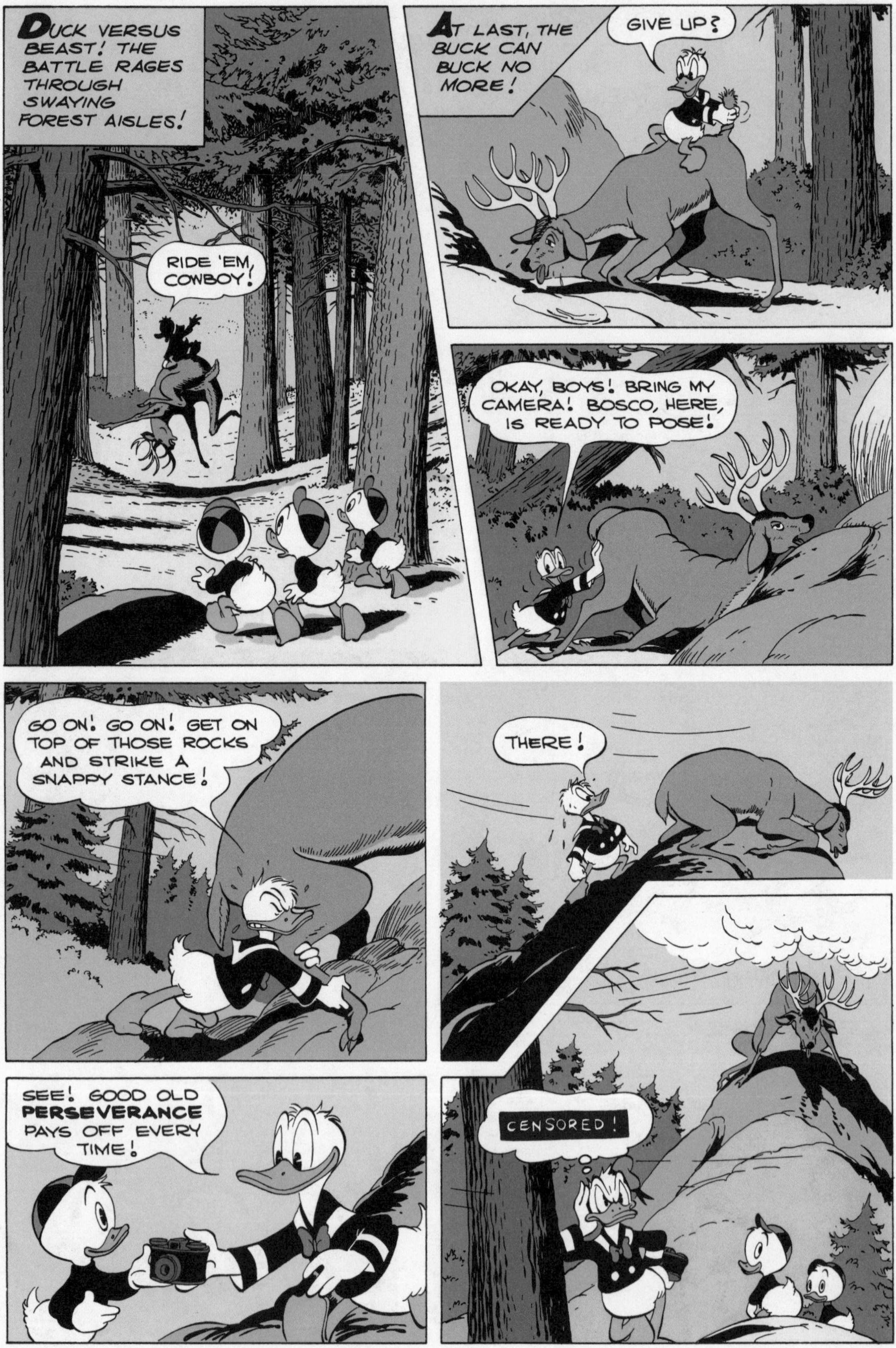
DUCK VERSUS BEAST! THE BATTLE RAGES THROUGH SWAYING FOREST AISLES!
RIDE 'EM, COWBOY!
AT LAST, THE BUCK CAN BUCK NO MORE!
GIVE UP?
OKAY, BOYS! BRING MY CAMERA! BOSCO, HERE, IS READY TO POSE!
GO ON! GO ON! GET ON TOP OF THOSE ROCKS AND STRIKE A SNAPPY STANCE!
THERE!
SEE! GOOD OLD **PERSEVERANCE** PAYS OFF EVERY TIME!
CENSORED!

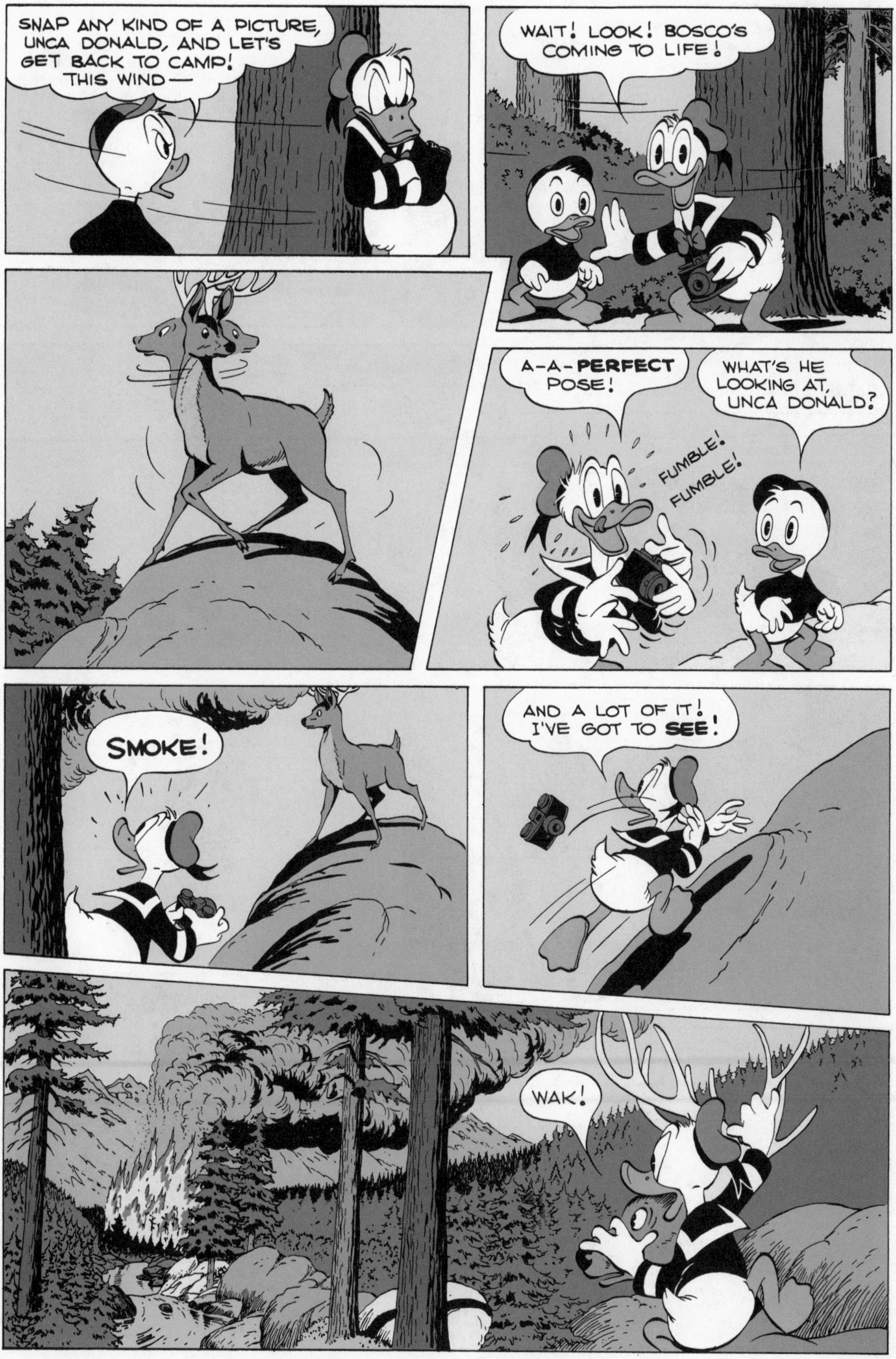
SNAP ANY KIND OF A PICTURE, UNCA DONALD, AND LET'S GET BACK TO CAMP! THIS WIND—
WAIT! LOOK! BOSCO'S COMING TO LIFE!
A-A-**PERFECT** POSE!
FUMBLE! FUMBLE!
WHAT'S HE LOOKING AT, UNCA DONALD?
SMOKE!
AND A LOT OF IT! I'VE GOT TO **SEE**!
WAK!

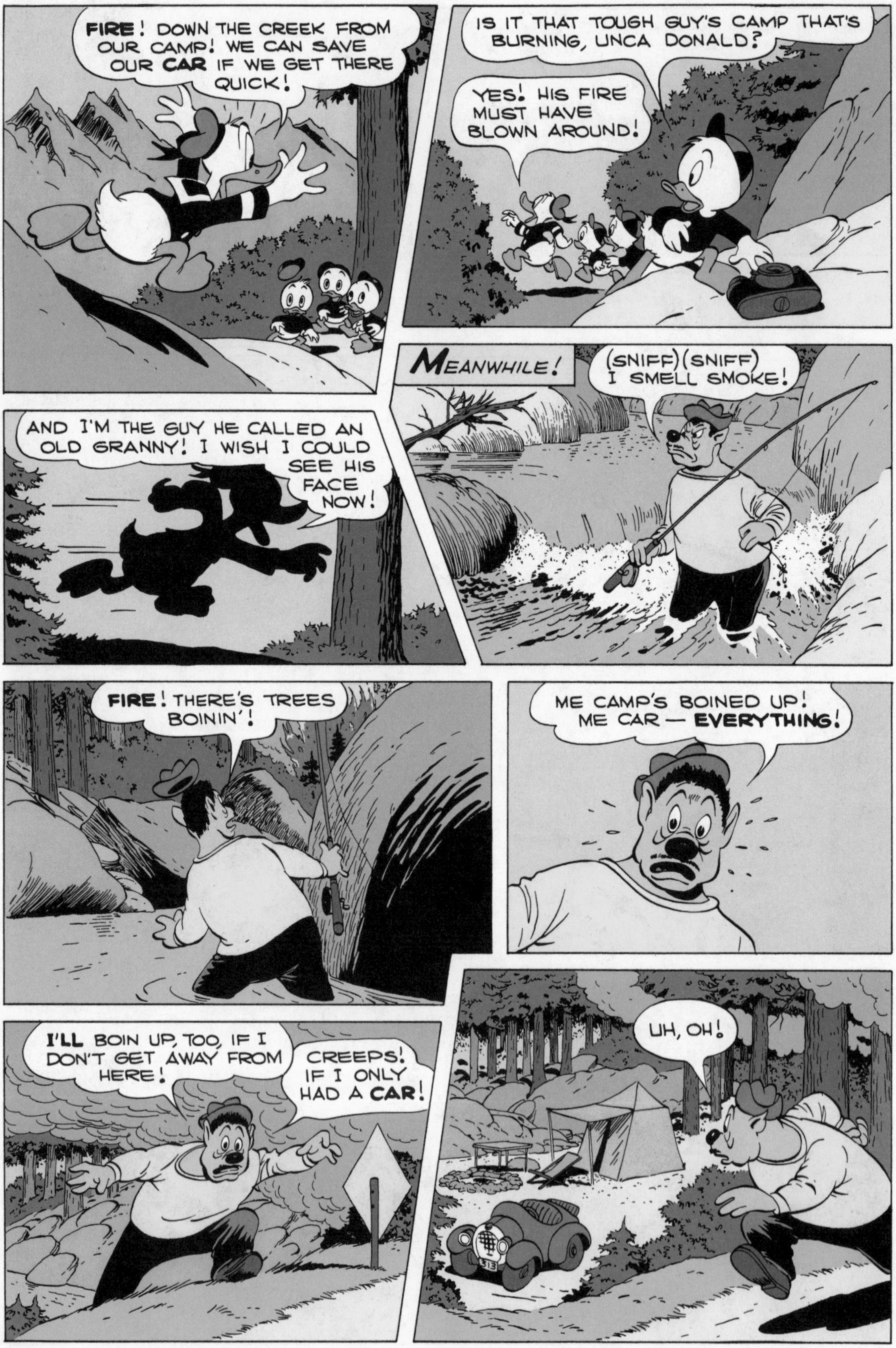
FIRE! DOWN THE CREEK FROM OUR CAMP! WE CAN SAVE OUR CAR IF WE GET THERE QUICK!
IS IT THAT TOUGH GUY'S CAMP THAT'S BURNING, UNCA DONALD?
YES! HIS FIRE MUST HAVE BLOWN AROUND!
AND I'M THE GUY HE CALLED AN OLD GRANNY! I WISH I COULD SEE HIS FACE NOW!
MEANWHILE!
(SNIFF) (SNIFF) I SMELL SMOKE!
FIRE! THERE'S TREES BOININ'!
ME CAMP'S BOINED UP! ME CAR — EVERYTHING!
I'LL BOIN UP, TOO, IF I DON'T GET AWAY FROM HERE!
CREEPS! IF I ONLY HAD A CAR!
UH, OH!
313

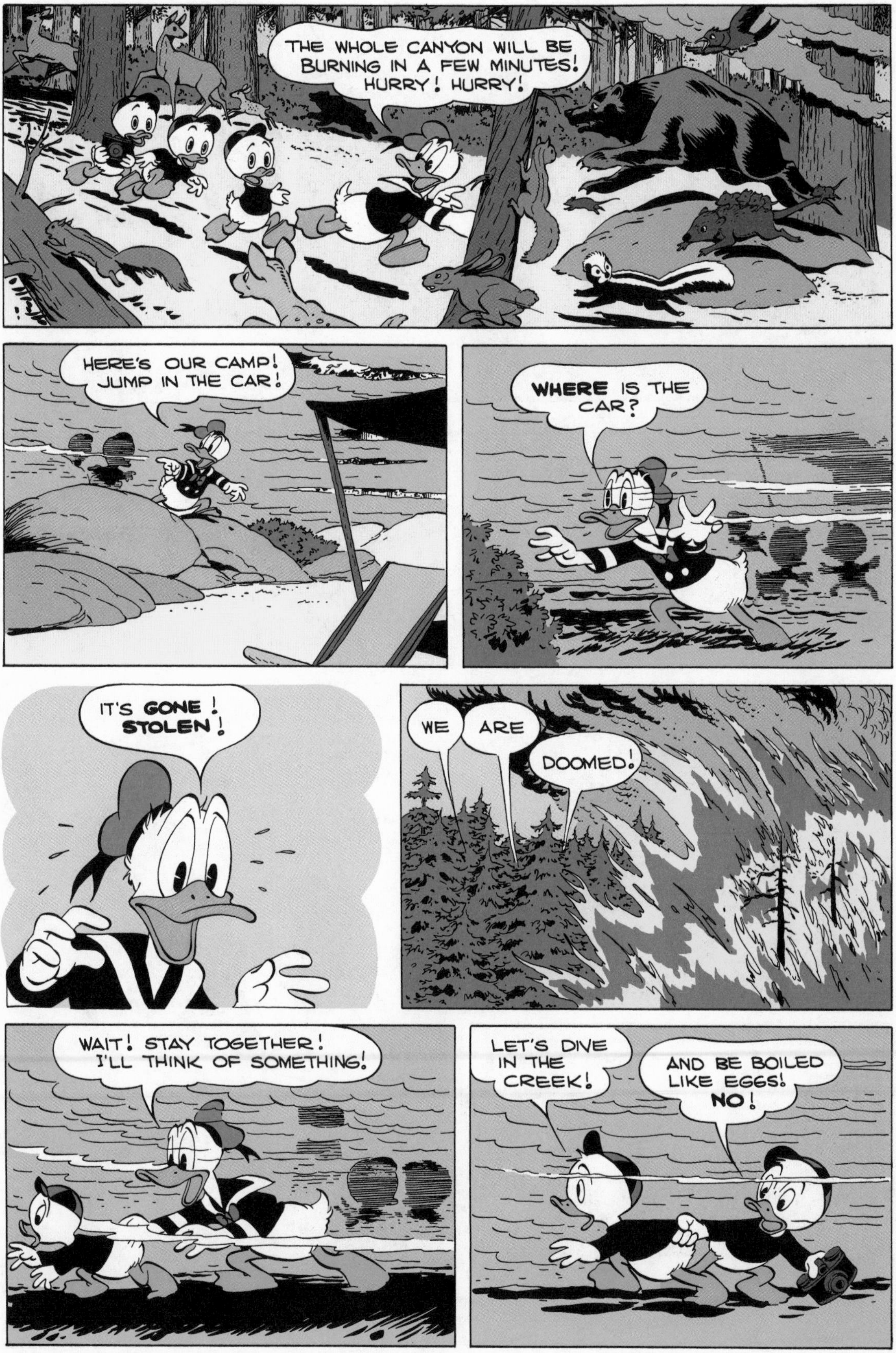
THE WHOLE CANYON WILL BE BURNING IN A FEW MINUTES! HURRY! HURRY!
HERE'S OUR CAMP! JUMP IN THE CAR!
WHERE IS THE CAR?
IT'S GONE! STOLEN!
WE
ARE
DOOMED!
WAIT! STAY TOGETHER! I'LL THINK OF SOMETHING!
LET'S DIVE IN THE CREEK!
AND BE BOILED LIKE EGGS! NO!

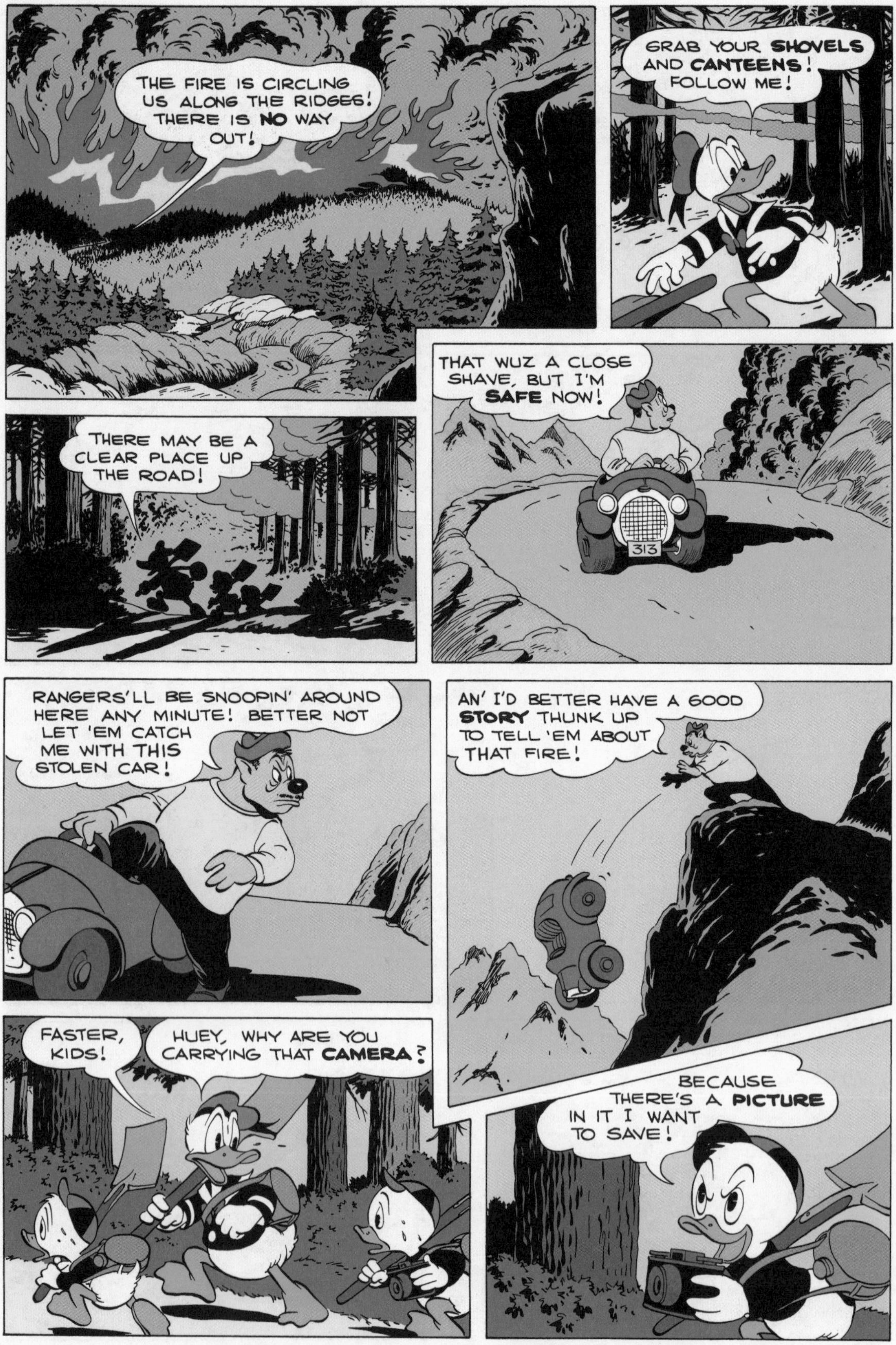
THE FIRE IS CIRCLING US ALONG THE RIDGES! THERE IS NO WAY OUT!
GRAB YOUR SHOVELS AND CANTEENS! FOLLOW ME!
THERE MAY BE A CLEAR PLACE UP THE ROAD!
THAT WUZ A CLOSE SHAVE, BUT I'M SAFE NOW!
313
RANGERS'LL BE SNOOPIN' AROUND HERE ANY MINUTE! BETTER NOT LET 'EM CATCH ME WITH THIS STOLEN CAR!
AN' I'D BETTER HAVE A GOOD STORY THUNK UP TO TELL 'EM ABOUT THAT FIRE!
FASTER, KIDS!
HUEY, WHY ARE YOU CARRYING THAT CAMERA?
BECAUSE THERE'S A PICTURE IN IT I WANT TO SAVE!

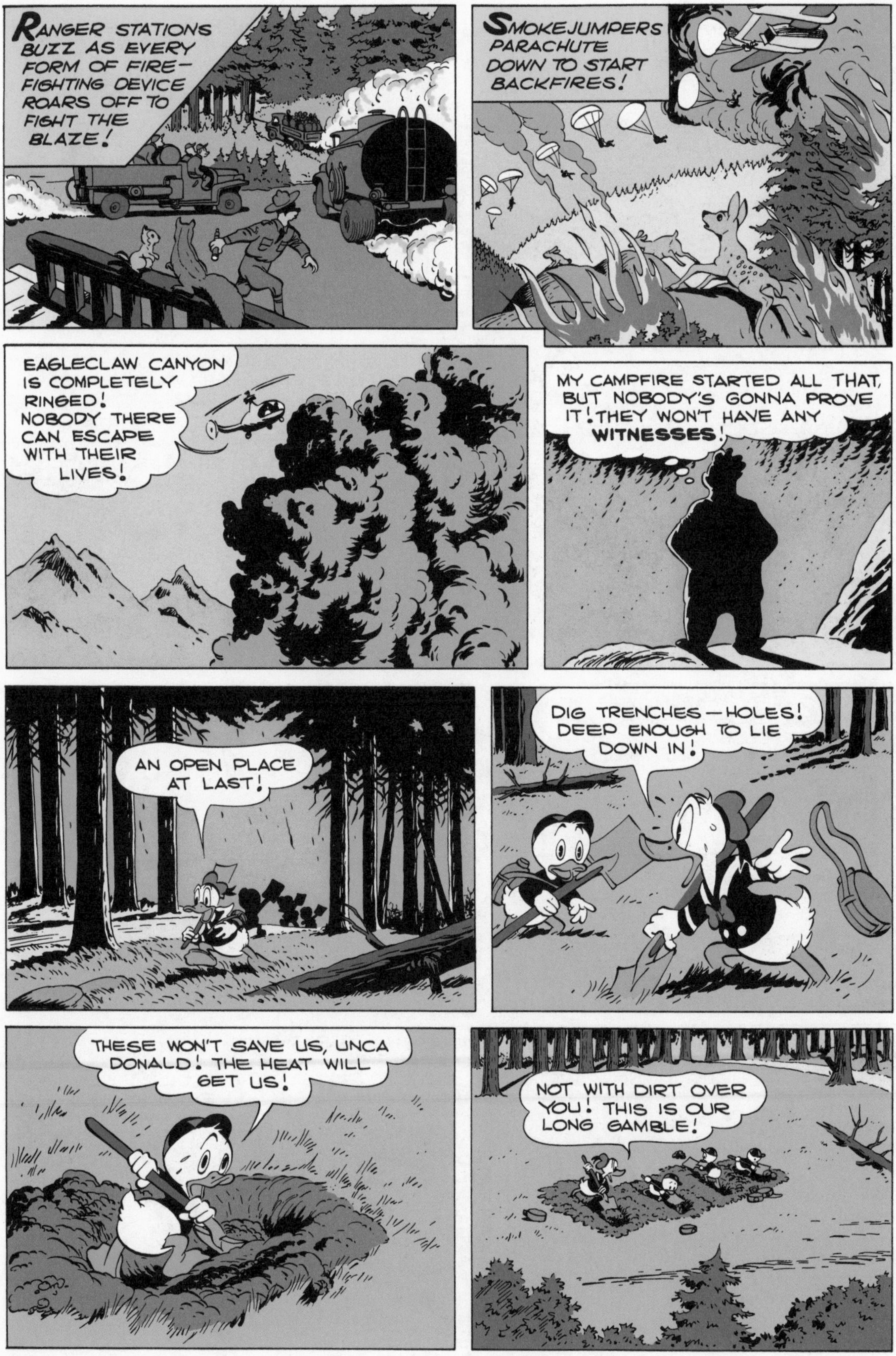
RANGER STATIONS BUZZ AS EVERY FORM OF FIRE-FIGHTING DEVICE ROARS OFF TO FIGHT THE BLAZE!
SMOKEJUMPERS PARACHUTE DOWN TO START BACKFIRES!
EAGLECLAW CANYON IS COMPLETELY RINGED! NOBODY THERE CAN ESCAPE WITH THEIR LIVES!
MY CAMPFIRE STARTED ALL THAT, BUT NOBODY'S GONNA PROVE IT! THEY WON'T HAVE ANY WITNESSES!
AN OPEN PLACE AT LAST!
DIG TRENCHES—HOLES! DEEP ENOUGH TO LIE DOWN IN!
THESE WON'T SAVE US, UNCA DONALD! THE HEAT WILL GET US!
NOT WITH DIRT OVER YOU! THIS IS OUR LONG GAMBLE!

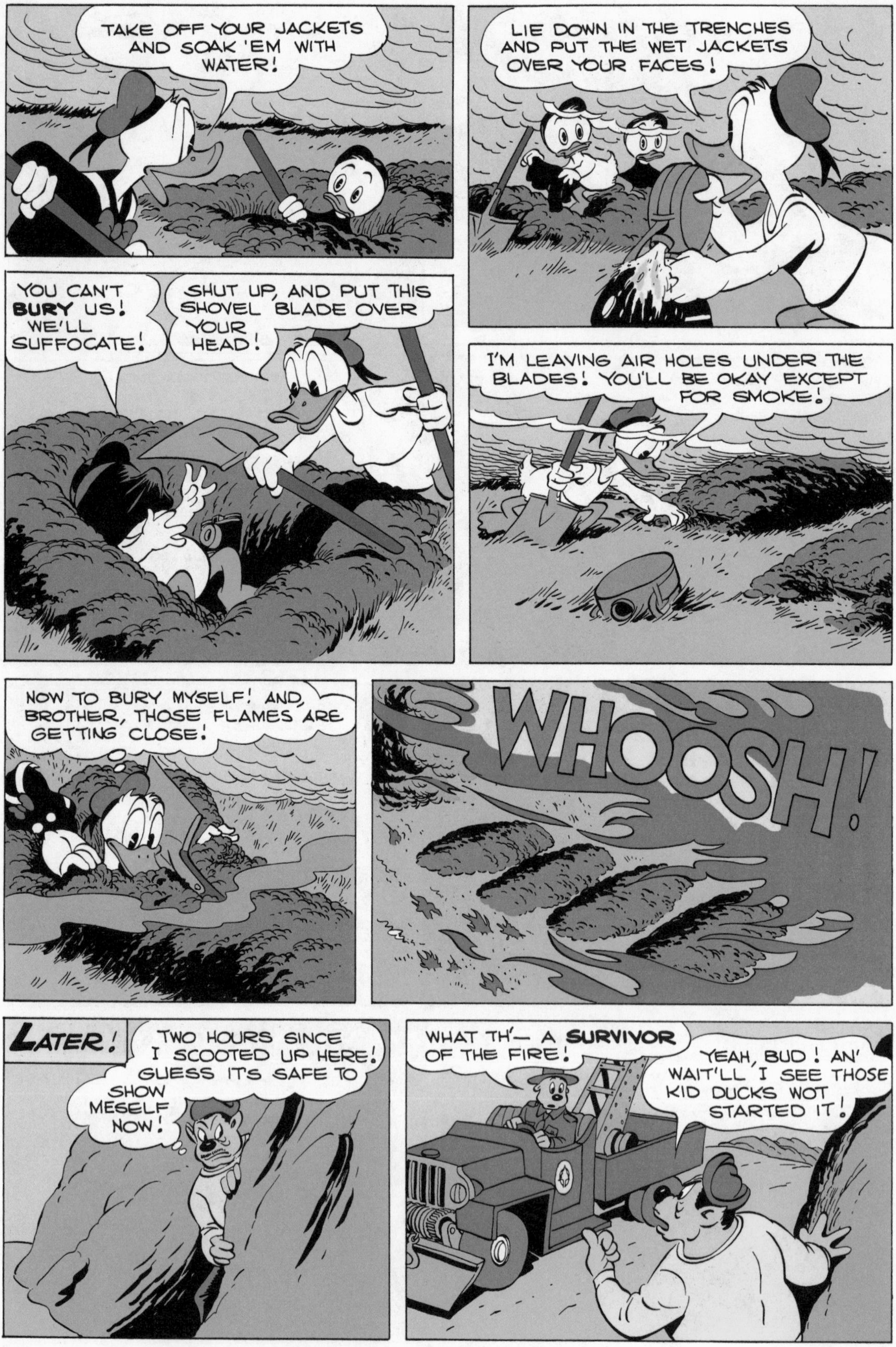
TAKE OFF YOUR JACKETS AND SOAK 'EM WITH WATER!
LIE DOWN IN THE TRENCHES AND PUT THE WET JACKETS OVER YOUR FACES!
YOU CAN'T BURY US! WE'LL SUFFOCATE!
SHUT UP, AND PUT THIS SHOVEL BLADE OVER YOUR HEAD!
I'M LEAVING AIR HOLES UNDER THE BLADES! YOU'LL BE OKAY EXCEPT FOR SMOKE!
NOW TO BURY MYSELF! AND, BROTHER, THOSE FLAMES ARE GETTING CLOSE!
WHOOSH!
LATER!
TWO HOURS SINCE I SCOOTED UP HERE! GUESS IT'S SAFE TO SHOW MESELF NOW!
WHAT TH'— A SURVIVOR OF THE FIRE!
YEAH, BUD! AN' WAIT'LL I SEE THOSE KID DUCKS WOT STARTED IT!

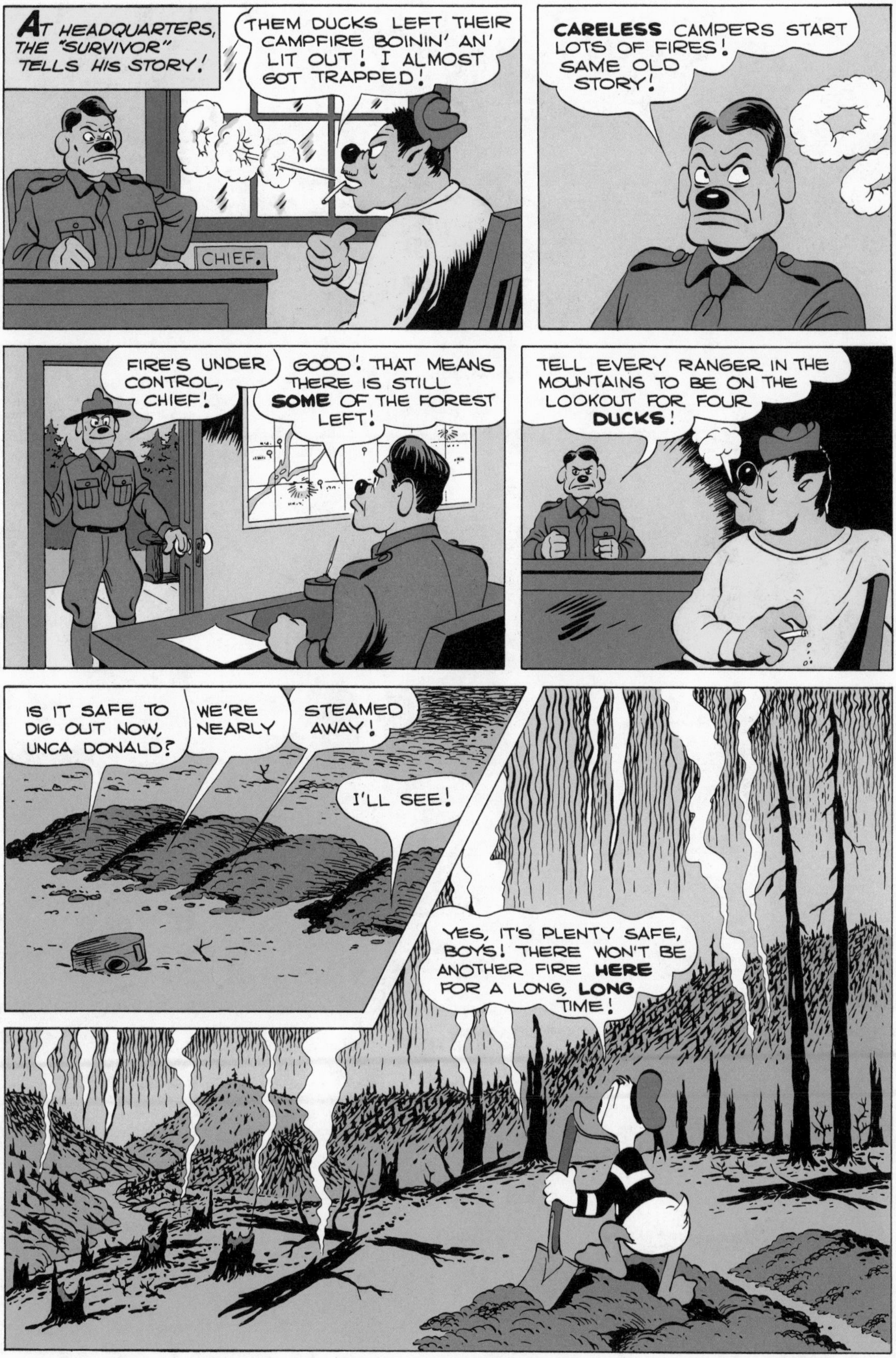
AT HEADQUARTERS, THE "SURVIVOR" TELLS HIS STORY!
THEM DUCKS LEFT THEIR CAMPFIRE BOININ' AN' LIT OUT! I ALMOST GOT TRAPPED!
CHIEF.
CARELESS CAMPERS START LOTS OF FIRES! SAME OLD STORY!
FIRE'S UNDER CONTROL, CHIEF!
GOOD! THAT MEANS THERE IS STILL SOME OF THE FOREST LEFT!
TELL EVERY RANGER IN THE MOUNTAINS TO BE ON THE LOOKOUT FOR FOUR DUCKS!
IS IT SAFE TO DIG OUT NOW, UNCA DONALD?
WE'RE NEARLY
STEAMED AWAY!
I'LL SEE!
YES, IT'S PLENTY SAFE, BOYS! THERE WON'T BE ANOTHER FIRE HERE FOR A LONG, LONG TIME!

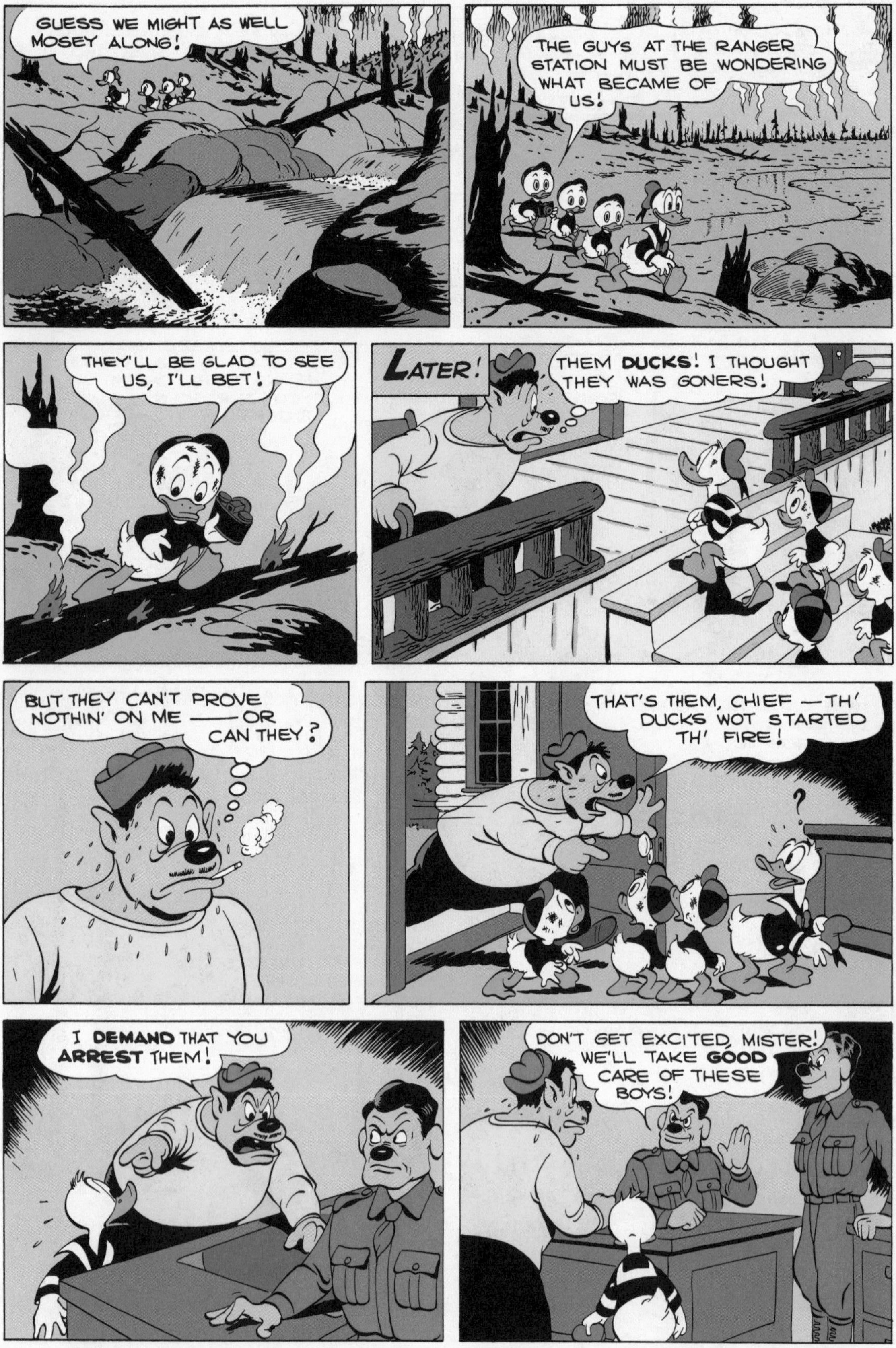
GUESS WE MIGHT AS WELL MOSEY ALONG!
THE GUYS AT THE RANGER STATION MUST BE WONDERING WHAT BECAME OF US!
THEY'LL BE GLAD TO SEE US, I'LL BET!
LATER!
THEM DUCKS! I THOUGHT THEY WAS GONERS!
BUT THEY CAN'T PROVE NOTHIN' ON ME —— OR CAN THEY?
THAT'S THEM, CHIEF — TH' DUCKS WOT STARTED TH' FIRE!
?
I DEMAND THAT YOU ARREST THEM!
DON'T GET EXCITED, MISTER! WE'LL TAKE GOOD CARE OF THESE BOYS!

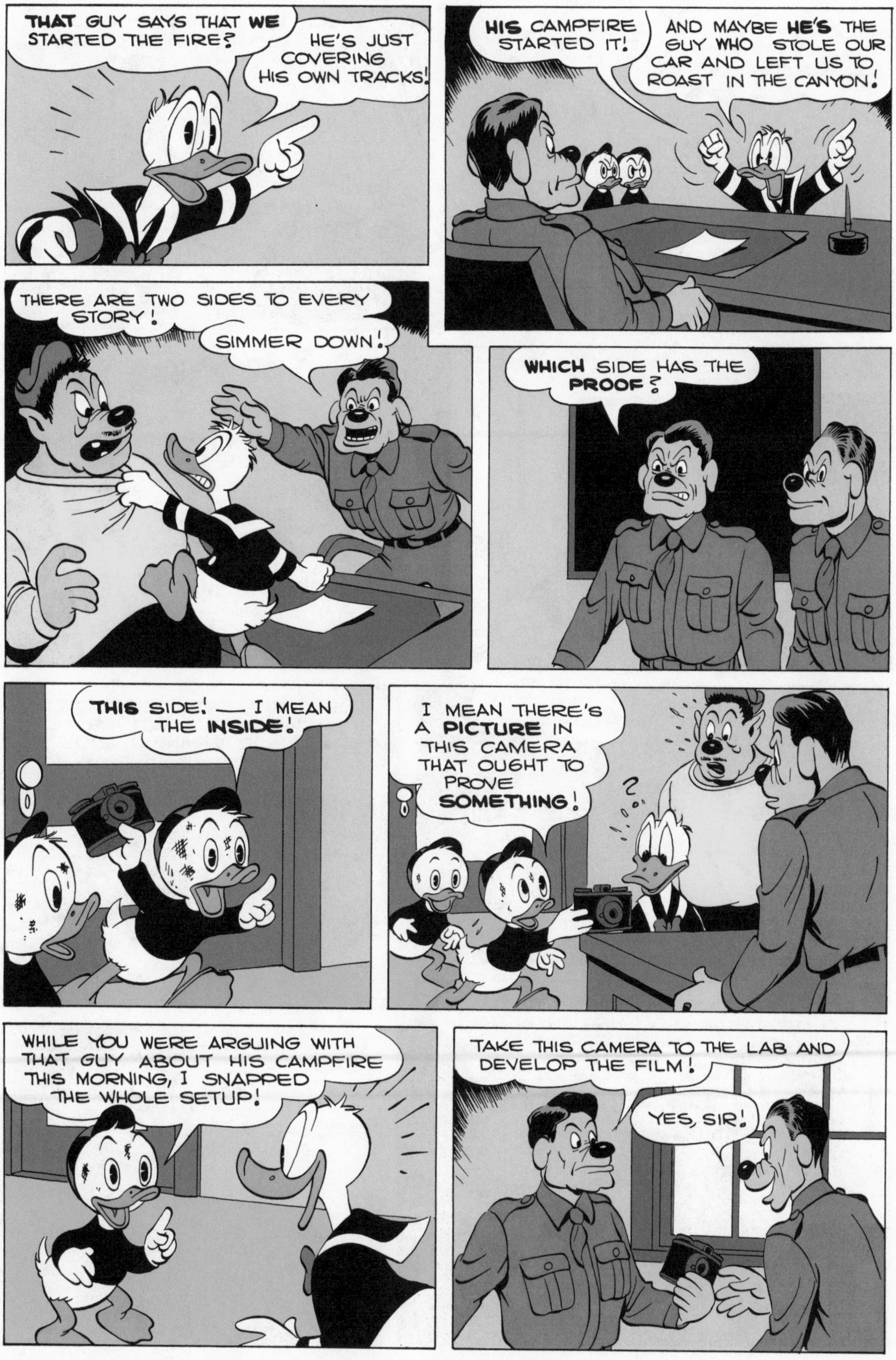
THAT GUY SAYS THAT WE STARTED THE FIRE?
HE'S JUST COVERING HIS OWN TRACKS!
HIS CAMPFIRE STARTED IT!
AND MAYBE HE'S THE GUY WHO STOLE OUR CAR AND LEFT US TO ROAST IN THE CANYON!
THERE ARE TWO SIDES TO EVERY STORY!
SIMMER DOWN!
WHICH SIDE HAS THE PROOF?
THIS SIDE! — I MEAN THE INSIDE!
I MEAN THERE'S A PICTURE IN THIS CAMERA THAT OUGHT TO PROVE SOMETHING!
WHILE YOU WERE ARGUING WITH THAT GUY ABOUT HIS CAMPFIRE THIS MORNING, I SNAPPED THE WHOLE SETUP!
TAKE THIS CAMERA TO THE LAB AND DEVELOP THE FILM!
YES, SIR!

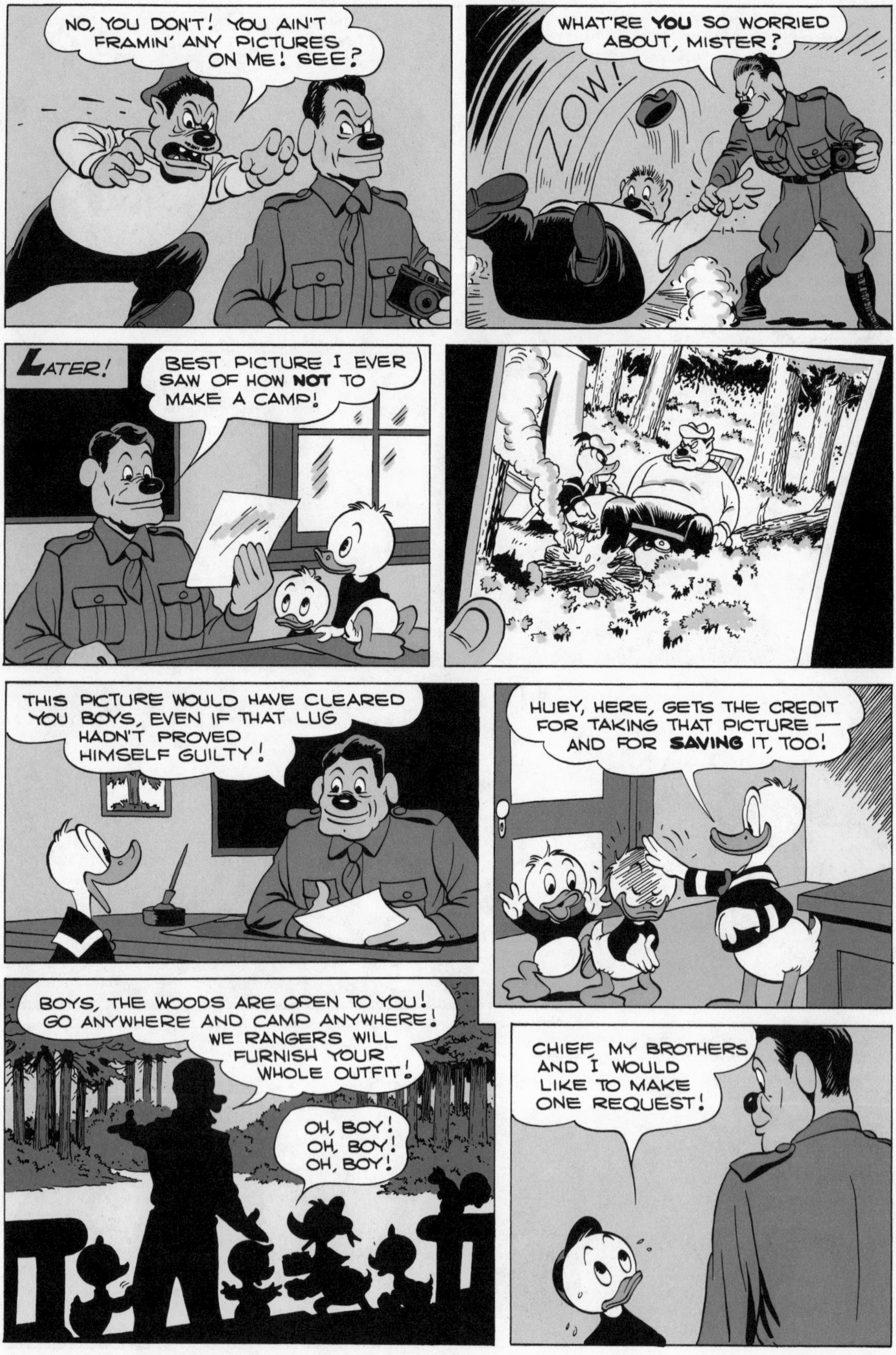
NO, YOU DON'T! YOU AIN'T FRAMIN' ANY PICTURES ON ME! SEE?
WHAT'RE YOU SO WORRIED ABOUT, MISTER?
ZOW!
LATER!
BEST PICTURE I EVER SAW OF HOW NOT TO MAKE A CAMP!
THIS PICTURE WOULD HAVE CLEARED YOU BOYS, EVEN IF THAT LUG HADN'T PROVED HIMSELF GUILTY!
HUEY, HERE, GETS THE CREDIT FOR TAKING THAT PICTURE — AND FOR SAVING IT, TOO!
BOYS, THE WOODS ARE OPEN TO YOU! GO ANYWHERE AND CAMP ANYWHERE! WE RANGERS WILL FURNISH YOUR WHOLE OUTFIT!
OH, BOY! OH, BOY! OH, BOY!
CHIEF, MY BROTHERS AND I WOULD LIKE TO MAKE ONE REQUEST!

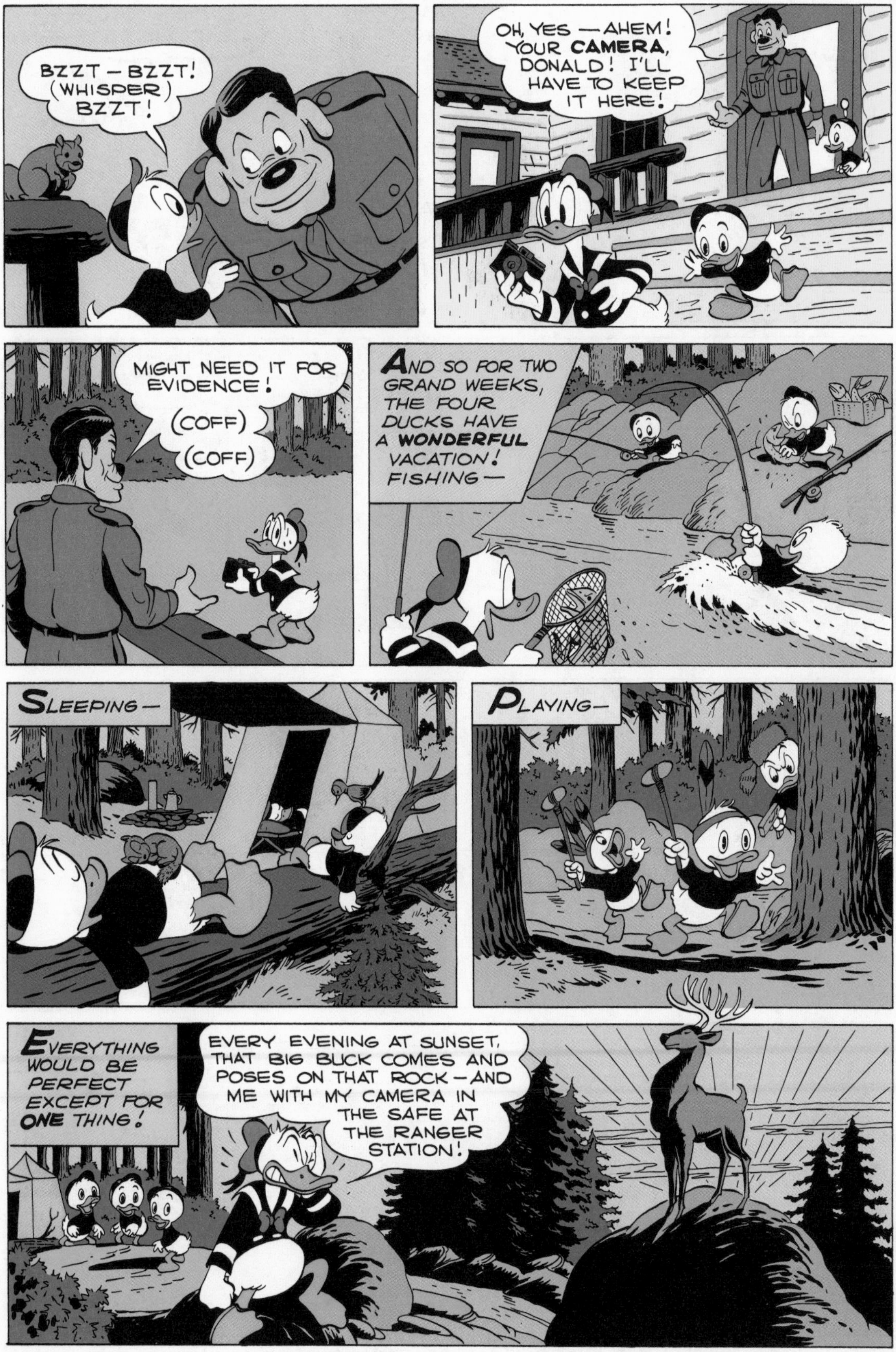

BZZT — BZZT! (WHISPER) BZZT!
OH, YES — AHEM! YOUR **CAMERA**, DONALD! I'LL HAVE TO KEEP IT HERE!
MIGHT NEED IT FOR EVIDENCE!
(COFF) (COFF)
AND SO FOR TWO GRAND WEEKS, THE FOUR DUCKS HAVE A **WONDERFUL** VACATION! FISHING —
SLEEPING —
PLAYING —
EVERYTHING WOULD BE PERFECT EXCEPT FOR **ONE** THING!
EVERY EVENING AT SUNSET, THAT BIG BUCK COMES AND POSES ON THAT ROCK — AND ME WITH MY CAMERA IN THE SAFE AT THE RANGER STATION!

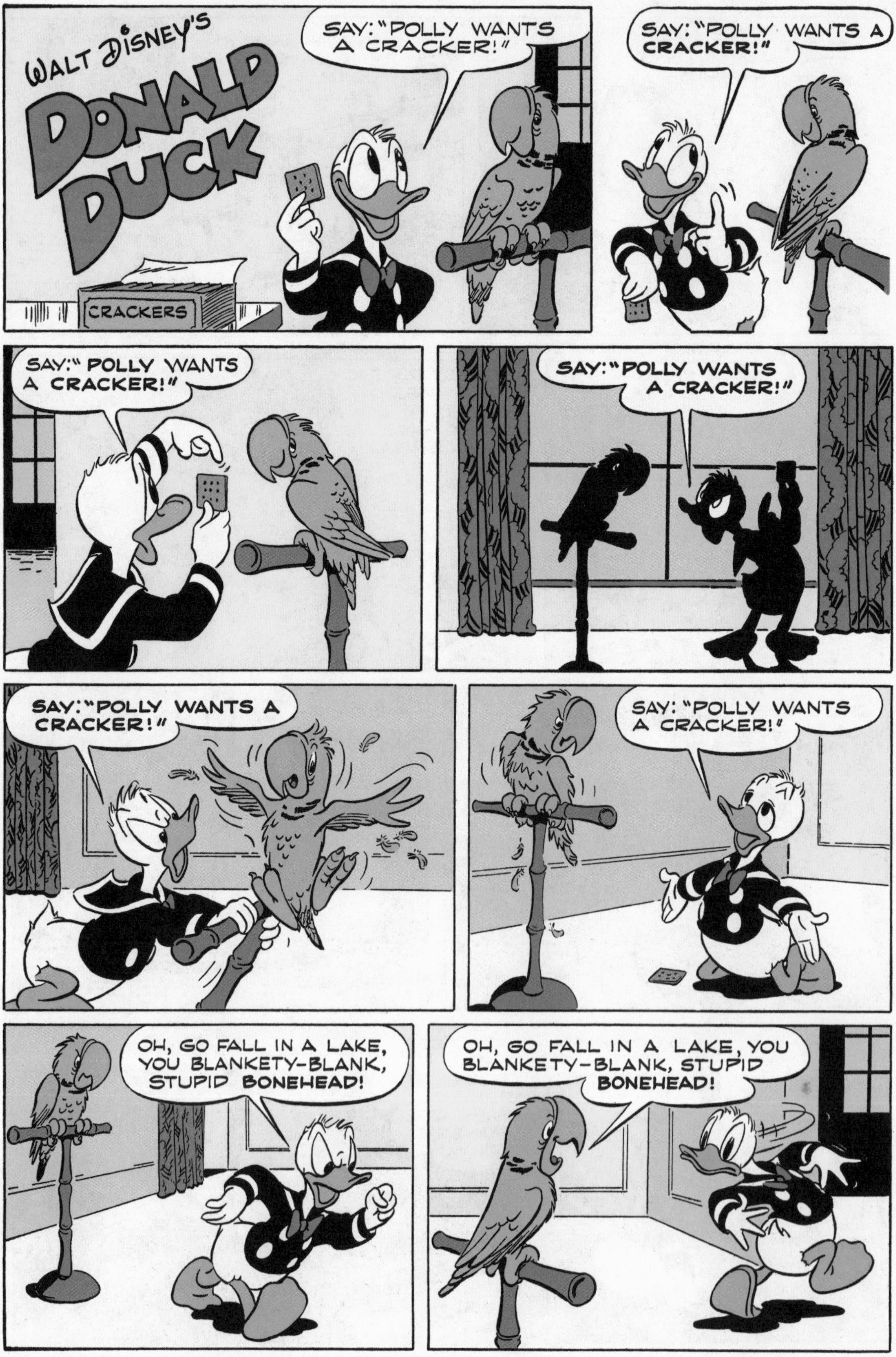
WALT DISNEY'S
DONALD DUCK
CRACKERS
SAY: "POLLY WANTS A CRACKER!"
SAY: "POLLY WANTS A CRACKER!"
SAY: "POLLY WANTS A CRACKER!"
SAY: "POLLY WANTS A CRACKER!"
SAY: "POLLY WANTS A CRACKER!"
SAY: "POLLY WANTS A CRACKER!"
OH, GO FALL IN A LAKE, YOU BLANKETY-BLANK, STUPID BONEHEAD!
OH, GO FALL IN A LAKE, YOU BLANKETY-BLANK, STUPID BONEHEAD!

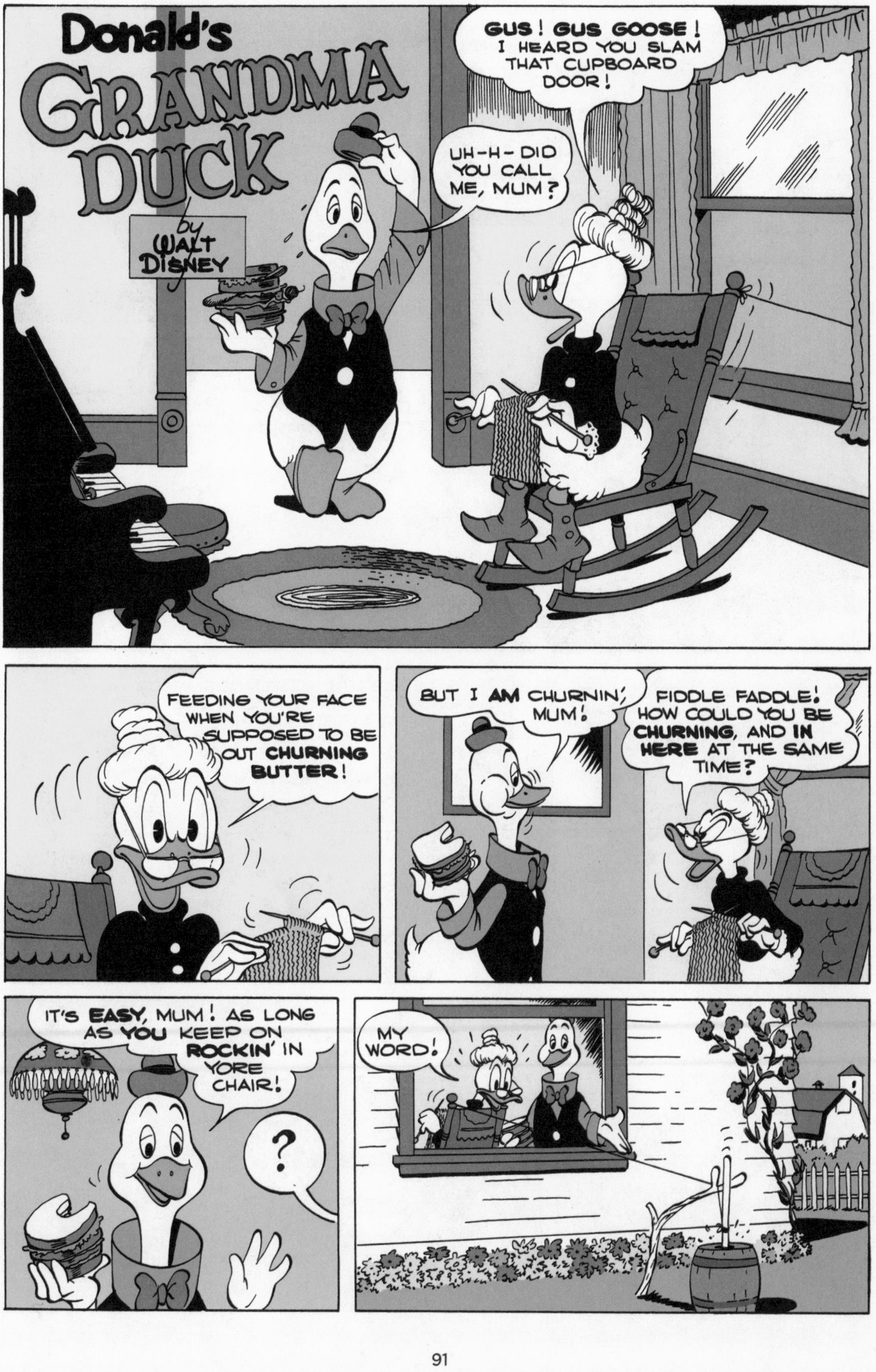

Donald's
GRANDMA DUCK
by WALT DISNEY
GUS! GUS GOOSE! I HEARD YOU SLAM THAT CUPBOARD DOOR!
UH-H- DID YOU CALL ME, MUM?
FEEDING YOUR FACE WHEN YOU'RE SUPPOSED TO BE OUT CHURNING BUTTER!
BUT I AM CHURNIN', MUM!
FIDDLE FADDLE! HOW COULD YOU BE CHURNING, AND IN HERE AT THE SAME TIME?
IT'S EASY, MUM! AS LONG AS YOU KEEP ON ROCKIN' IN YORE CHAIR!
?
MY WORD!

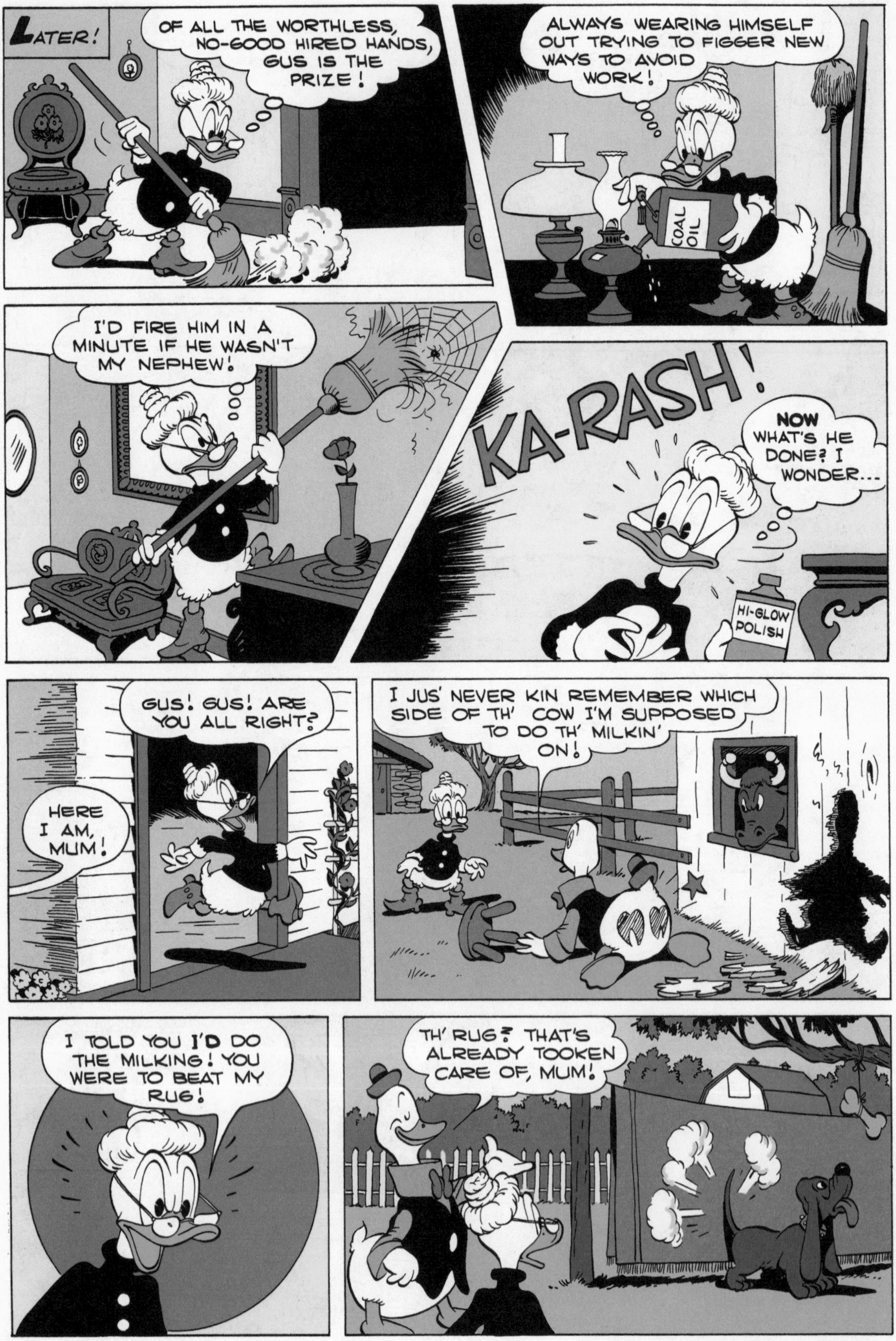
LATER!
OF ALL THE WORTHLESS, NO-GOOD HIRED HANDS, GUS IS THE PRIZE!
ALWAYS WEARING HIMSELF OUT TRYING TO FIGGER NEW WAYS TO AVOID WORK!
COAL OIL
I'D FIRE HIM IN A MINUTE IF HE WASN'T MY NEPHEW!
KA-RASH!
NOW WHAT'S HE DONE? I WONDER...
HI-GLOW POLISH
GUS! GUS! ARE YOU ALL RIGHT?
HERE I AM, MUM!
I JUS' NEVER KIN REMEMBER WHICH SIDE OF TH' COW I'M SUPPOSED TO DO TH' MILKIN' ON!
I TOLD YOU I'D DO THE MILKING! YOU WERE TO BEAT MY RUG!
TH' RUG? THAT'S ALREADY TOOKEN CARE OF, MUM!

UH-H – WHERE YA HEADED NOW, GRANDMA DUCK?

I'M GOING OUT TO SEE IF I GOT ANY **MAIL** TODAY!

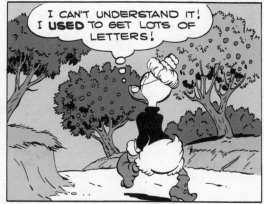

I CAN'T UNDERSTAND IT! I **USED** TO GET LOTS OF LETTERS!

BUT FOR THE PAST MONTH, GUS TELLS ME THERE HASN'T BEEN SO MUCH AS A POST CARD!

COME BACK, GRANDMA DUCK!

LET **ME** DO IT FOR YOU!

NO NEED OF YOU EXERTIN' YORESELF! I'LL LOOK IN TH' MAILBOX!

OUT OF MY WAY, GUS!

THERE'S SOMETHING **MIGHTY** PECULIAR ABOUT THIS, AND I AIM TO FIND OUT WHAT IT IS!

GRANDMA DUCK

LAND SAKES ALIVE!!! A **BIRD'S** NEST!

YES, MUM! NOW YA KNOWS!

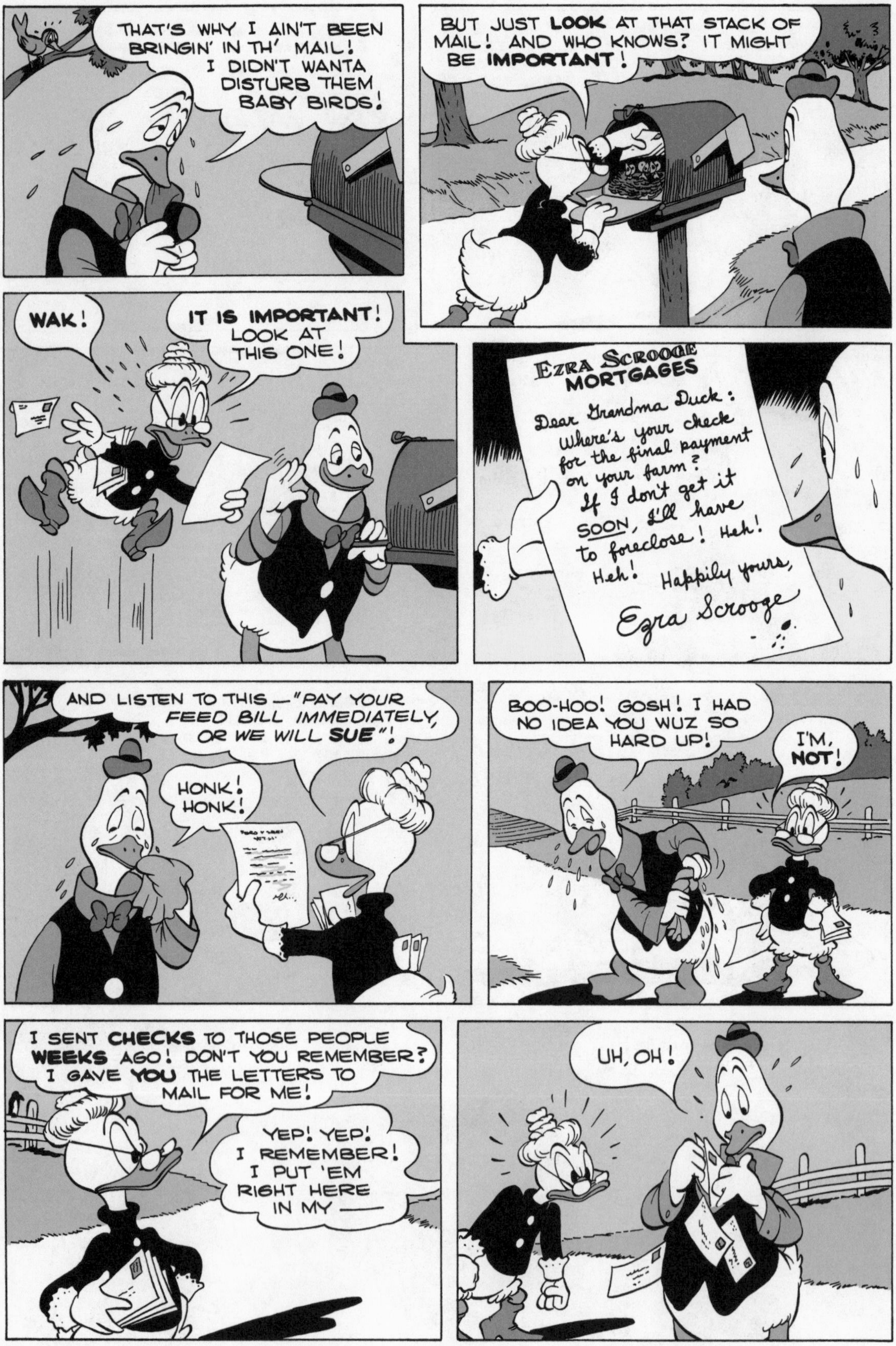
THAT'S WHY I AIN'T BEEN BRINGIN' IN TH' MAIL! I DIDN'T WANTA DISTURB THEM BABY BIRDS!
BUT JUST LOOK AT THAT STACK OF MAIL! AND WHO KNOWS? IT MIGHT BE IMPORTANT!
WAK!
IT IS IMPORTANT! LOOK AT THIS ONE!
EZRA SCROOGE MORTGAGES
Dear Grandma Duck: Where's your check for the final payment on your farm? If I don't get it SOON, I'll have to foreclose! Heh! Heh! Happily yours, Ezra Scrooge
AND LISTEN TO THIS — "PAY YOUR FEED BILL IMMEDIATELY, OR WE WILL SUE"!
HONK! HONK!
BOO-HOO! GOSH! I HAD NO IDEA YOU WUZ SO HARD UP!
I'M, NOT!
I SENT CHECKS TO THOSE PEOPLE WEEKS AGO! DON'T YOU REMEMBER? I GAVE YOU THE LETTERS TO MAIL FOR ME!
YEP! YEP! I REMEMBER! I PUT 'EM RIGHT HERE IN MY —
UH, OH!

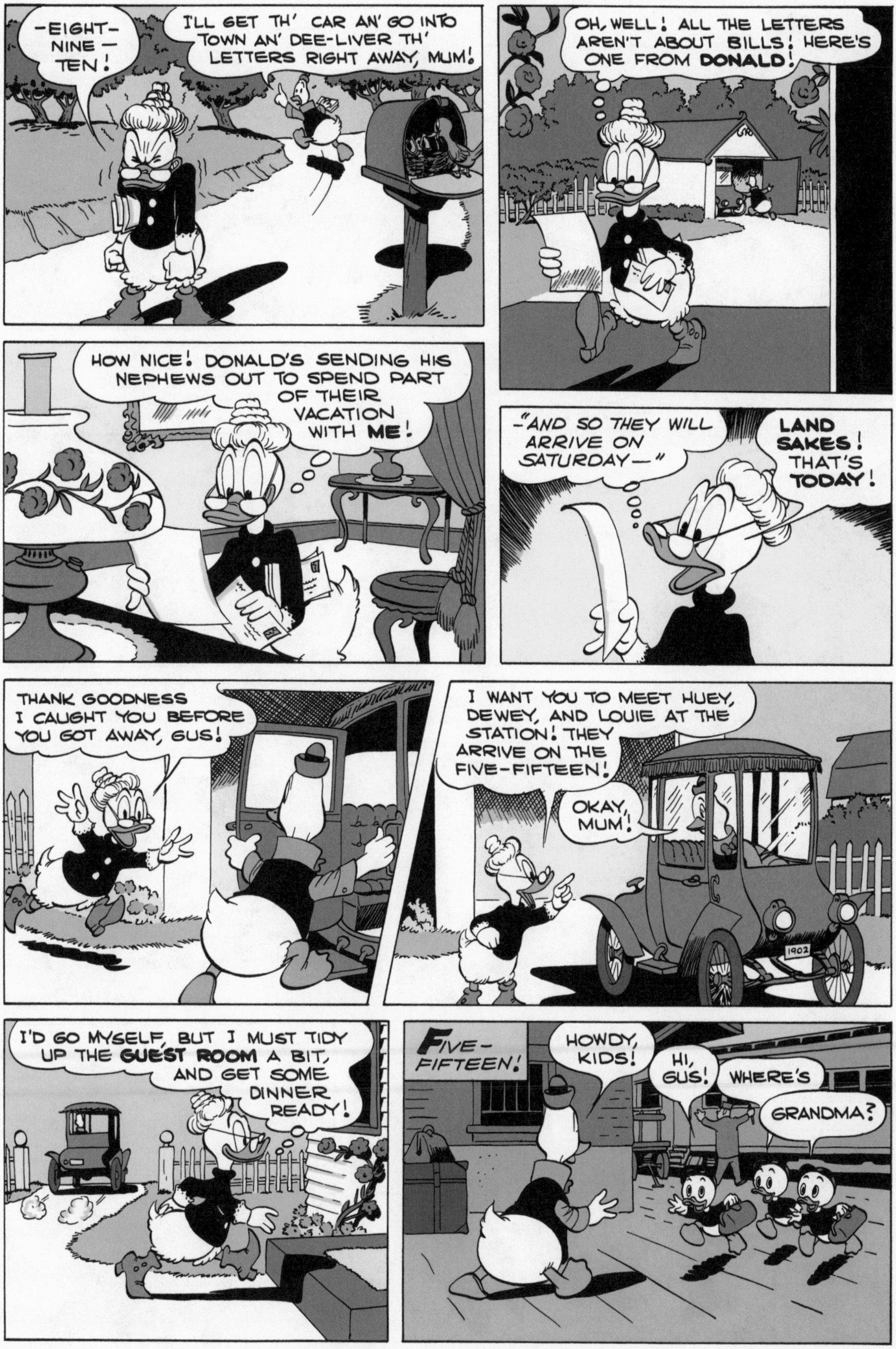

-EIGHT-
NINE —
TEN!
I'LL GET TH' CAR AN' GO INTO TOWN AN' DEE-LIVER TH' LETTERS RIGHT AWAY, MUM!
OH, WELL! ALL THE LETTERS AREN'T ABOUT BILLS! HERE'S ONE FROM DONALD!
HOW NICE! DONALD'S SENDING HIS NEPHEWS OUT TO SPEND PART OF THEIR VACATION WITH ME!
-"AND SO THEY WILL ARRIVE ON SATURDAY—"
LAND SAKES! THAT'S TODAY!
THANK GOODNESS I CAUGHT YOU BEFORE YOU GOT AWAY, GUS!
I WANT YOU TO MEET HUEY, DEWEY, AND LOUIE AT THE STATION! THEY ARRIVE ON THE FIVE-FIFTEEN!
OKAY, MUM!
1902
I'D GO MYSELF, BUT I MUST TIDY UP THE GUEST ROOM A BIT, AND GET SOME DINNER READY!
FIVE-FIFTEEN!
HOWDY, KIDS!
HI, GUS!
WHERE'S
GRANDMA?

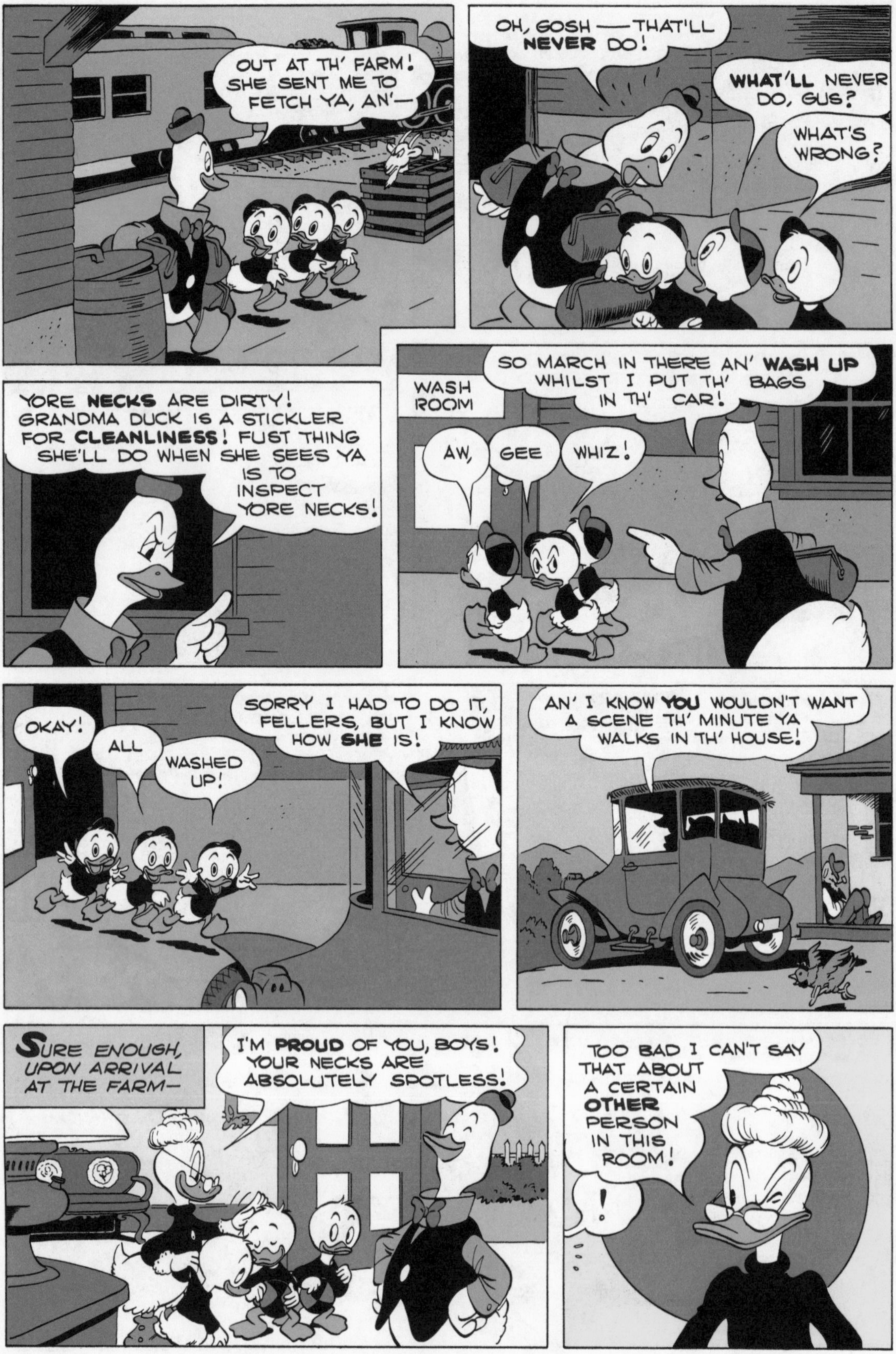
OUT AT TH' FARM! SHE SENT ME TO FETCH YA, AN'—
OH, GOSH —THAT'LL NEVER DO!
WHAT'LL NEVER DO, GUS?
WHAT'S WRONG?
YORE NECKS ARE DIRTY! GRANDMA DUCK IS A STICKLER FOR CLEANLINESS! FUST THING SHE'LL DO WHEN SHE SEES YA IS TO INSPECT YORE NECKS!
WASH ROOM
SO MARCH IN THERE AN' WASH UP WHILST I PUT TH' BAGS IN TH' CAR!
AW,
GEE
WHIZ!
OKAY!
ALL
WASHED UP!
SORRY I HAD TO DO IT, FELLERS, BUT I KNOW HOW SHE IS!
AN' I KNOW YOU WOULDN'T WANT A SCENE TH' MINUTE YA WALKS IN TH' HOUSE!
SURE ENOUGH, UPON ARRIVAL AT THE FARM—
I'M PROUD OF YOU, BOYS! YOUR NECKS ARE ABSOLUTELY SPOTLESS!
TOO BAD I CAN'T SAY THAT ABOUT A CERTAIN OTHER PERSON IN THIS ROOM!
!

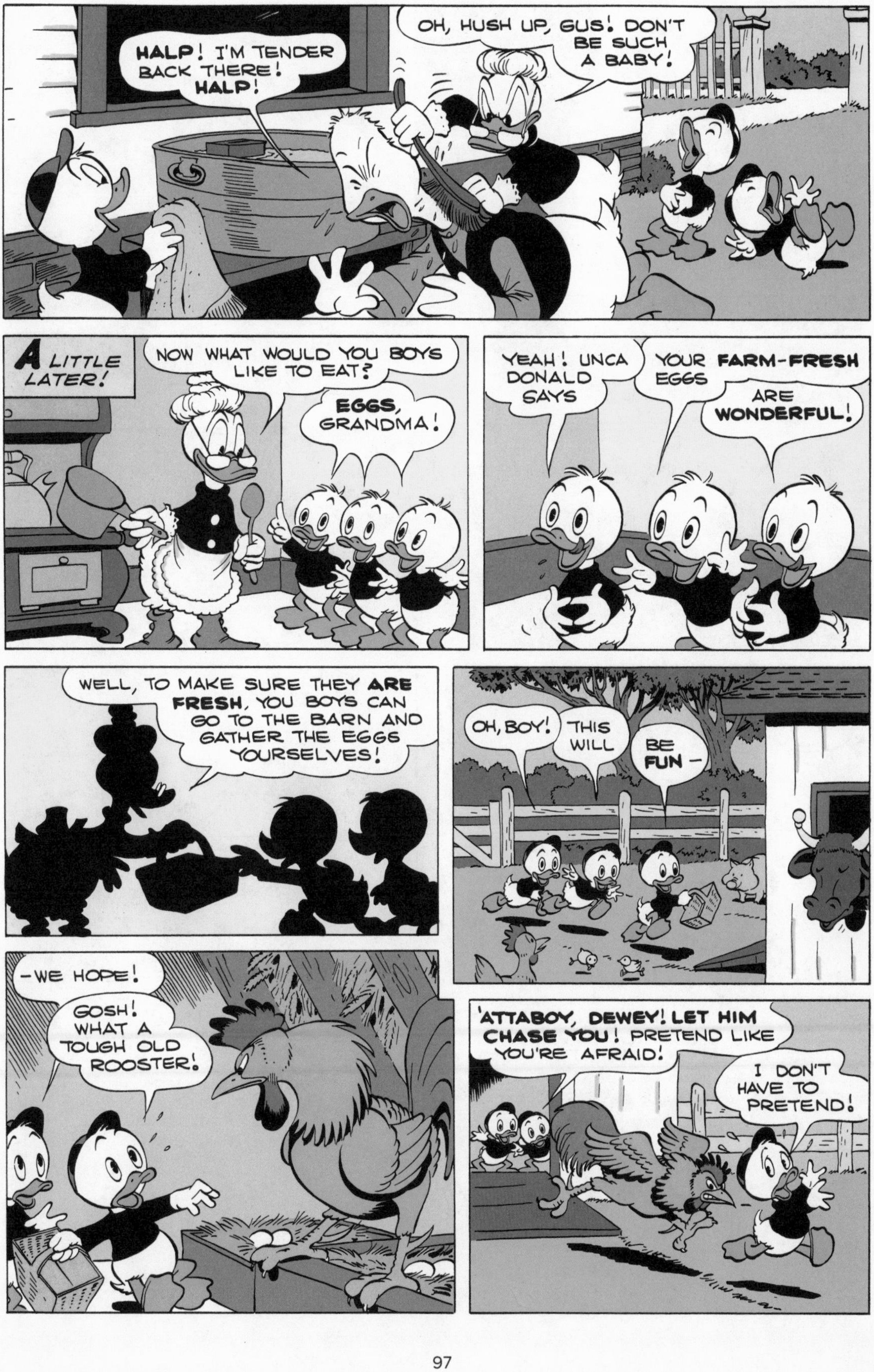
HALP! I'M TENDER BACK THERE! HALP!
OH, HUSH UP, GUS! DON'T BE SUCH A BABY!
A LITTLE LATER!
NOW WHAT WOULD YOU BOYS LIKE TO EAT?
EGGS, GRANDMA!
YEAH! UNCA DONALD SAYS
YOUR FARM-FRESH EGGS
ARE WONDERFUL!
WELL, TO MAKE SURE THEY ARE FRESH, YOU BOYS CAN GO TO THE BARN AND GATHER THE EGGS YOURSELVES!
OH, BOY!
THIS WILL
BE FUN —
—WE HOPE!
GOSH! WHAT A TOUGH OLD ROOSTER!
'ATTABOY, DEWEY! LET HIM CHASE YOU! PRETEND LIKE YOU'RE AFRAID!
I DON'T HAVE TO PRETEND!

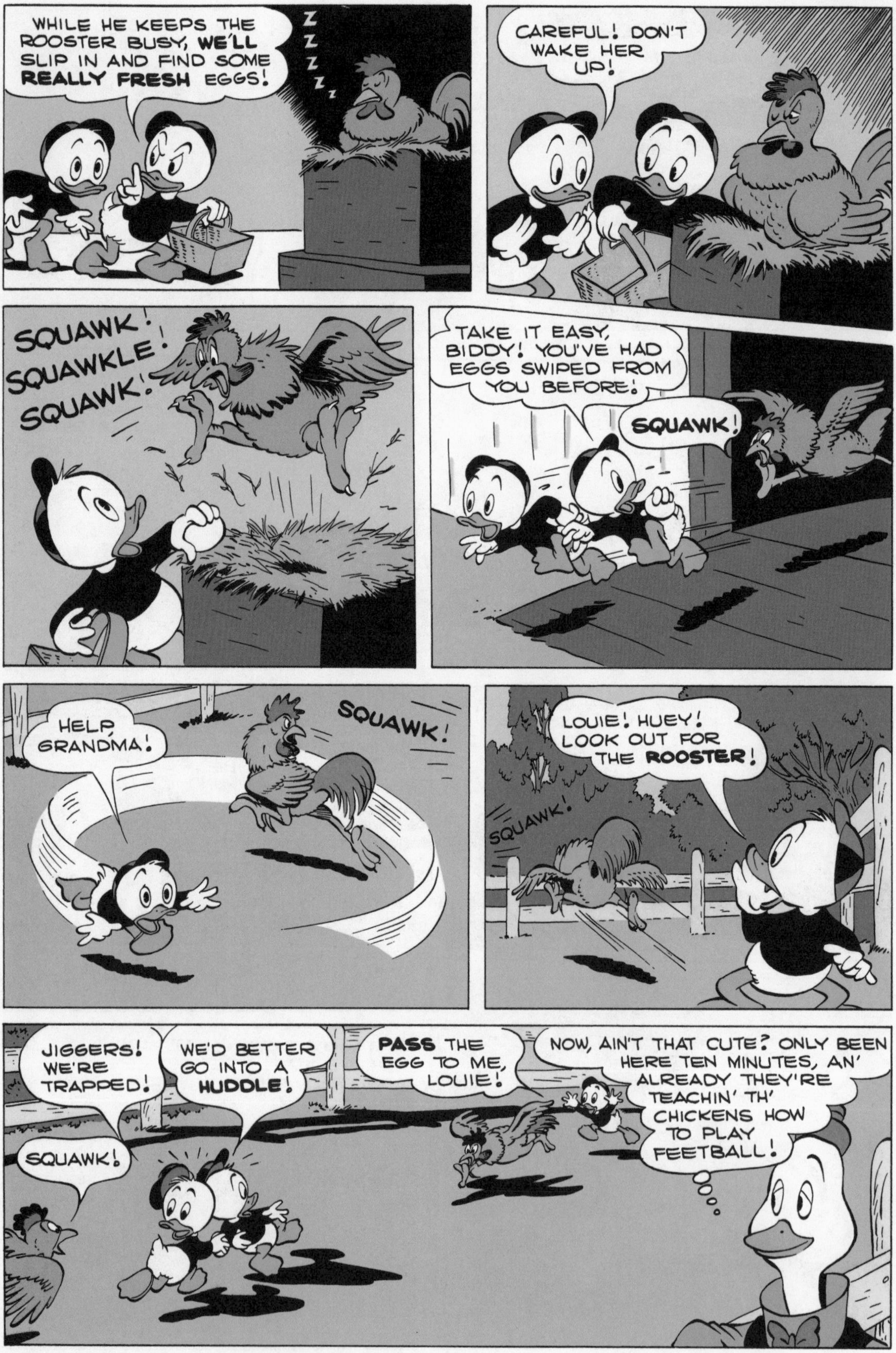
WHILE HE KEEPS THE ROOSTER BUSY, WE'LL SLIP IN AND FIND SOME REALLY FRESH EGGS!
Z Z Z Z Z
CAREFUL! DON'T WAKE HER UP!
SQUAWK! SQUAWKLE! SQUAWK!
TAKE IT EASY, BIDDY! YOU'VE HAD EGGS SWIPED FROM YOU BEFORE!
SQUAWK!
HELP, GRANDMA!
SQUAWK!
LOUIE! HUEY! LOOK OUT FOR THE ROOSTER!
SQUAWK!
JIGGERS! WE'RE TRAPPED!
WE'D BETTER GO INTO A HUDDLE!
SQUAWK!
PASS THE EGG TO ME, LOUIE!
NOW, AIN'T THAT CUTE? ONLY BEEN HERE TEN MINUTES, AN' ALREADY THEY'RE TEACHIN' TH' CHICKENS HOW TO PLAY FEETBALL!

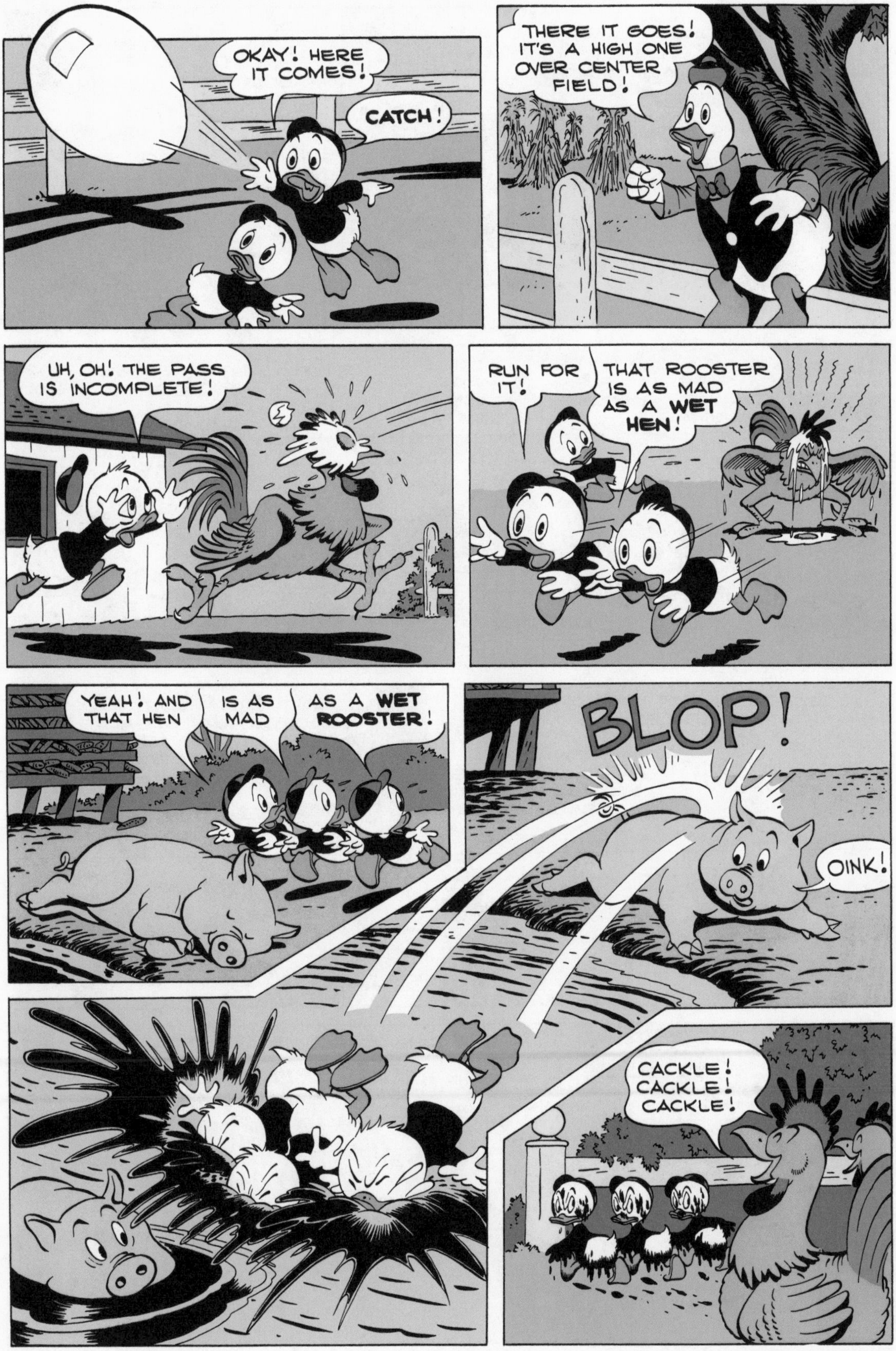
OKAY! HERE IT COMES!
CATCH!
THERE IT GOES! IT'S A HIGH ONE OVER CENTER FIELD!
UH, OH! THE PASS IS INCOMPLETE!
RUN FOR IT!
THAT ROOSTER IS AS MAD AS A **WET HEN**!
YEAH! AND THAT HEN
IS AS MAD
AS A **WET ROOSTER**!
BLOP!
OINK!
CACKLE! CACKLE! CACKLE!

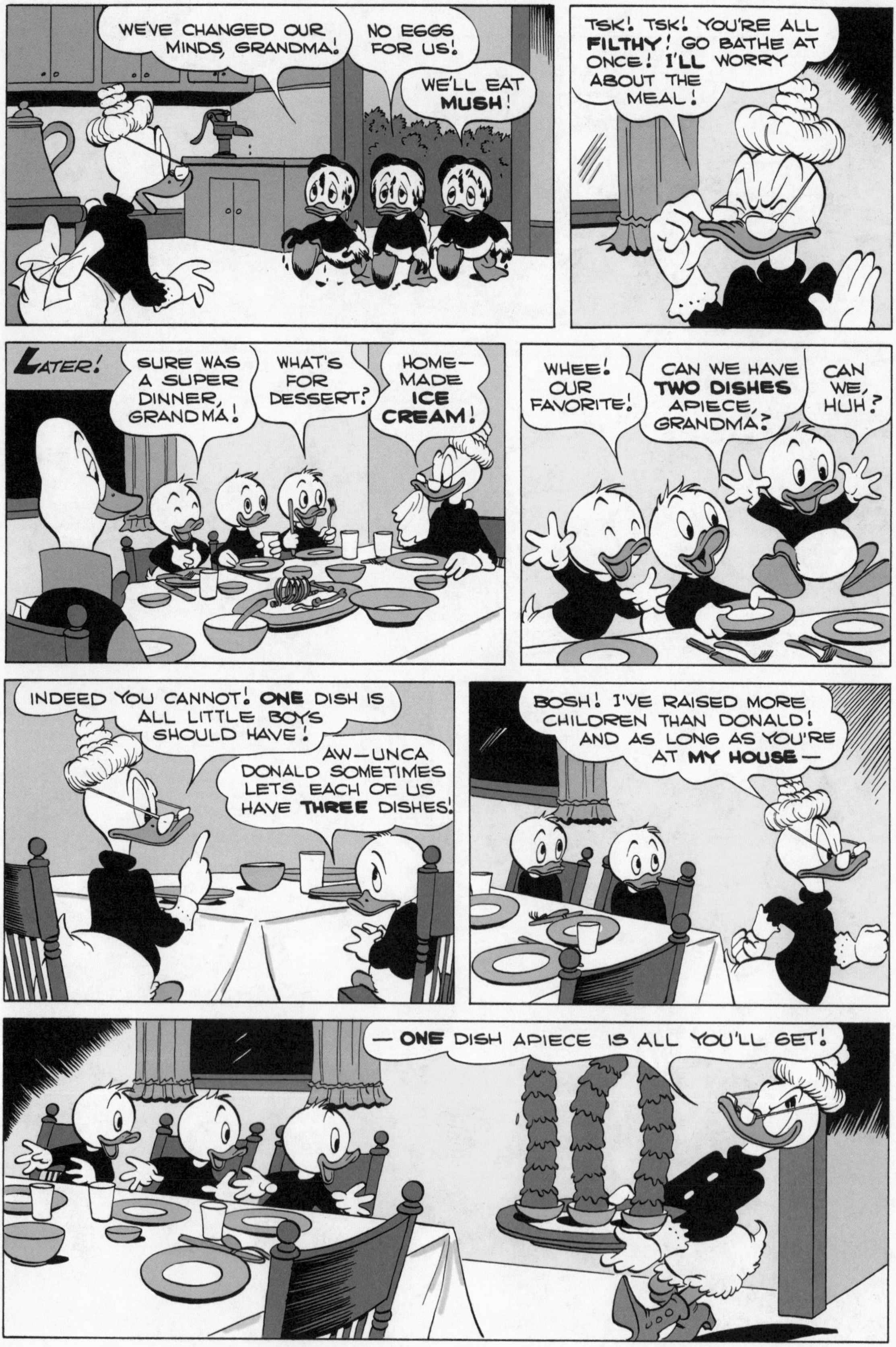
WE'VE CHANGED OUR MINDS, GRANDMA!
NO EGGS FOR US!
WE'LL EAT MUSH!
TSK! TSK! YOU'RE ALL FILTHY! GO BATHE AT ONCE! I'LL WORRY ABOUT THE MEAL!
LATER!
SURE WAS A SUPER DINNER, GRANDMA!
WHAT'S FOR DESSERT?
HOME-MADE ICE CREAM!
WHEE! OUR FAVORITE!
CAN WE HAVE TWO DISHES APIECE, GRANDMA?
CAN WE, HUH?
INDEED YOU CANNOT! ONE DISH IS ALL LITTLE BOYS SHOULD HAVE!
AW—UNCA DONALD SOMETIMES LETS EACH OF US HAVE THREE DISHES!
BOSH! I'VE RAISED MORE CHILDREN THAN DONALD! AND AS LONG AS YOU'RE AT MY HOUSE—
—ONE DISH APIECE IS ALL YOU'LL GET!

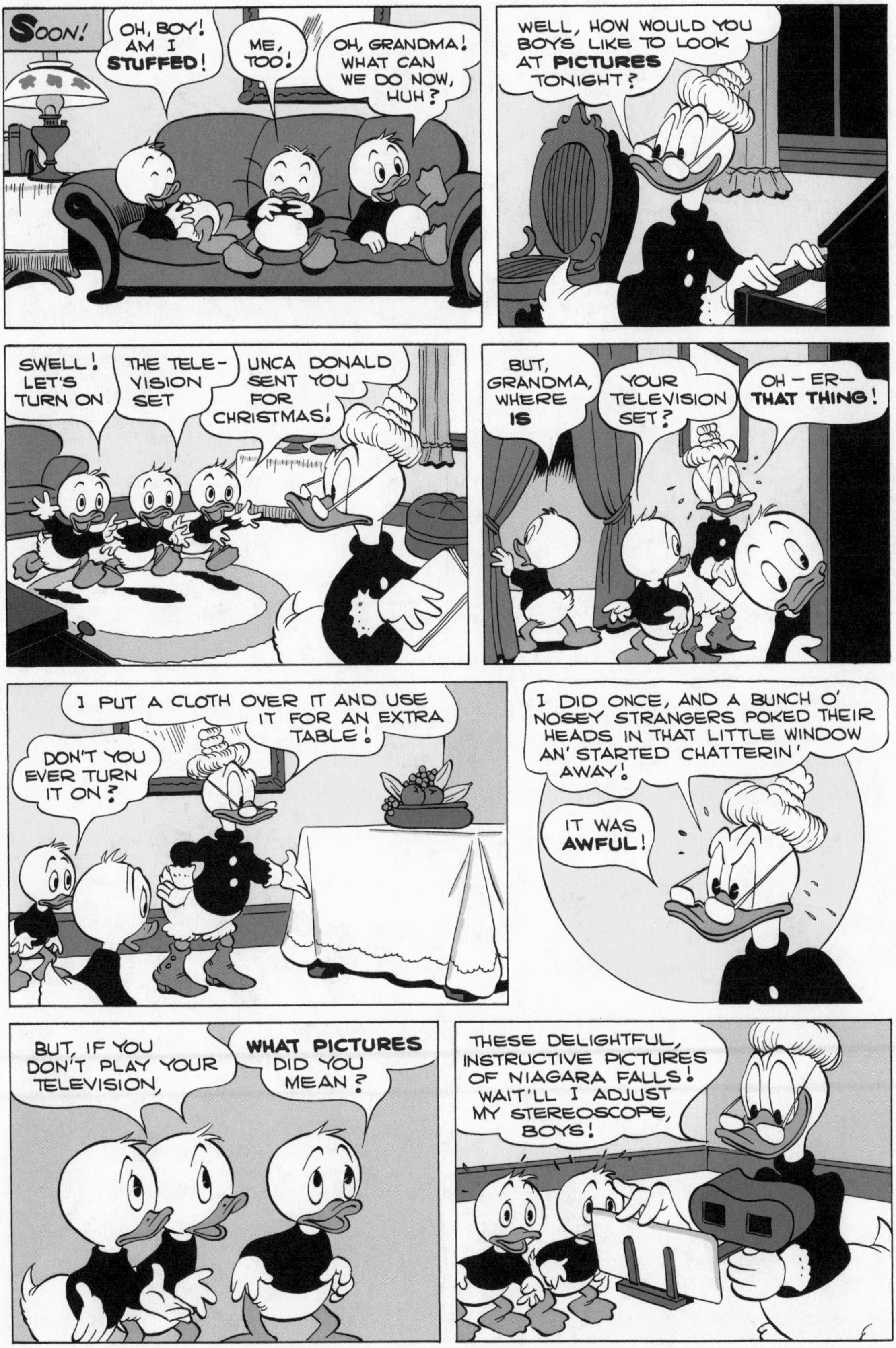
SOON!
OH, BOY! AM I STUFFED!
ME, TOO!
OH, GRANDMA! WHAT CAN WE DO NOW, HUH?
WELL, HOW WOULD YOU BOYS LIKE TO LOOK AT PICTURES TONIGHT?
SWELL! LET'S TURN ON
THE TELE-VISION SET
UNCA DONALD SENT YOU FOR CHRISTMAS!
BUT, GRANDMA, WHERE IS
YOUR TELEVISION SET?
OH — ER— THAT THING!
I PUT A CLOTH OVER IT AND USE IT FOR AN EXTRA TABLE!
DON'T YOU EVER TURN IT ON?
I DID ONCE, AND A BUNCH O' NOSEY STRANGERS POKED THEIR HEADS IN THAT LITTLE WINDOW AN' STARTED CHATTERIN' AWAY!
IT WAS AWFUL!
BUT, IF YOU DON'T PLAY YOUR TELEVISION,
WHAT PICTURES DID YOU MEAN?
THESE DELIGHTFUL, INSTRUCTIVE PICTURES OF NIAGARA FALLS! WAIT'LL I ADJUST MY STEREOSCOPE, BOYS!

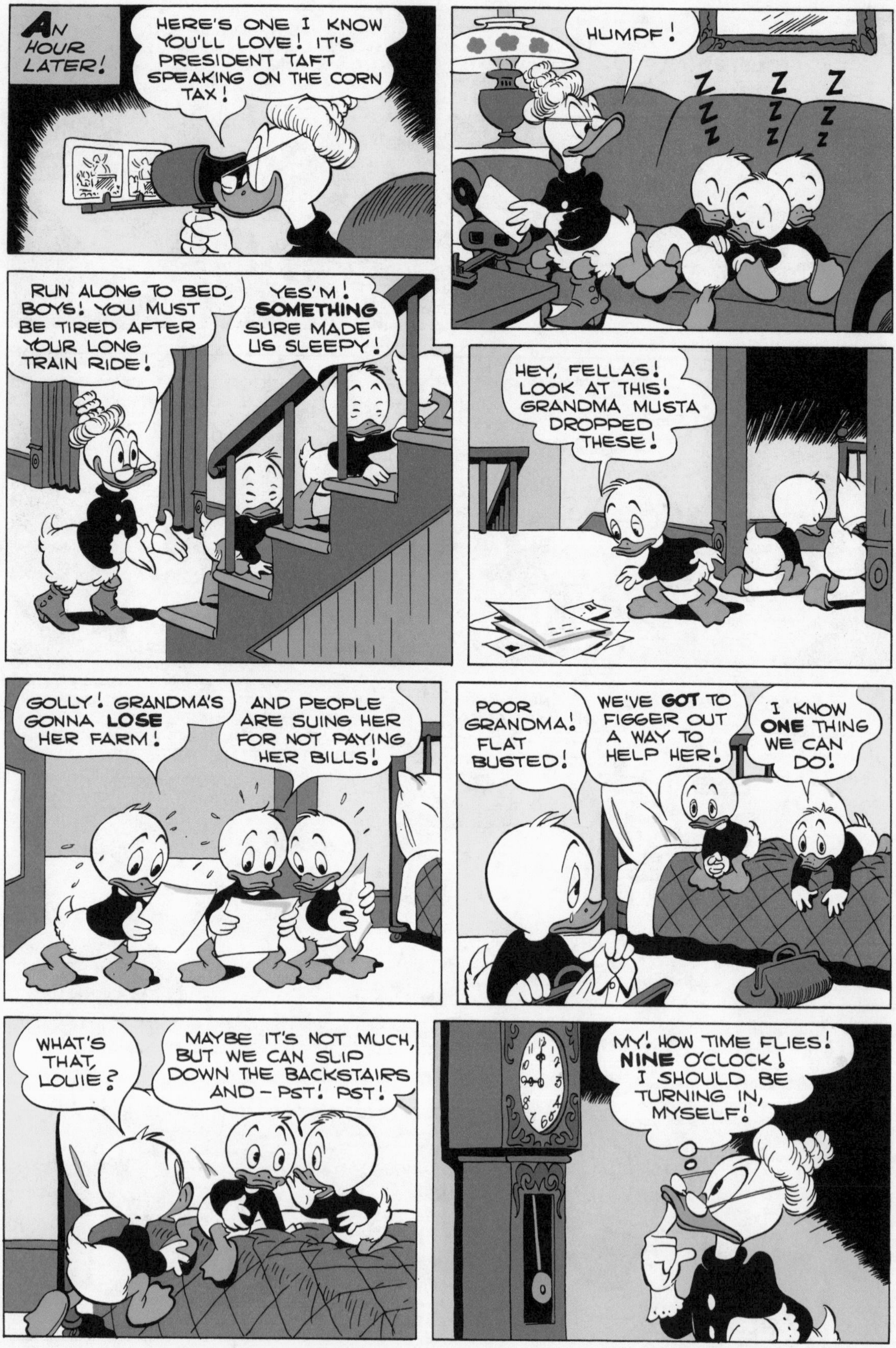
AN HOUR LATER!
HERE'S ONE I KNOW YOU'LL LOVE! IT'S PRESIDENT TAFT SPEAKING ON THE CORN TAX!
HUMPF!
Z Z Z
Z Z Z
Z Z Z
RUN ALONG TO BED, BOYS! YOU MUST BE TIRED AFTER YOUR LONG TRAIN RIDE!
YES'M! SOMETHING SURE MADE US SLEEPY!
HEY, FELLAS! LOOK AT THIS! GRANDMA MUSTA DROPPED THESE!
GOLLY! GRANDMA'S GONNA LOSE HER FARM!
AND PEOPLE ARE SUING HER FOR NOT PAYING HER BILLS!
POOR GRANDMA! FLAT BUSTED!
WE'VE GOT TO FIGGER OUT A WAY TO HELP HER!
I KNOW ONE THING WE CAN DO!
WHAT'S THAT, LOUIE?
MAYBE IT'S NOT MUCH, BUT WE CAN SLIP DOWN THE BACKSTAIRS AND - PST! PST!
MY! HOW TIME FLIES! NINE O'CLOCK! I SHOULD BE TURNING IN, MYSELF!

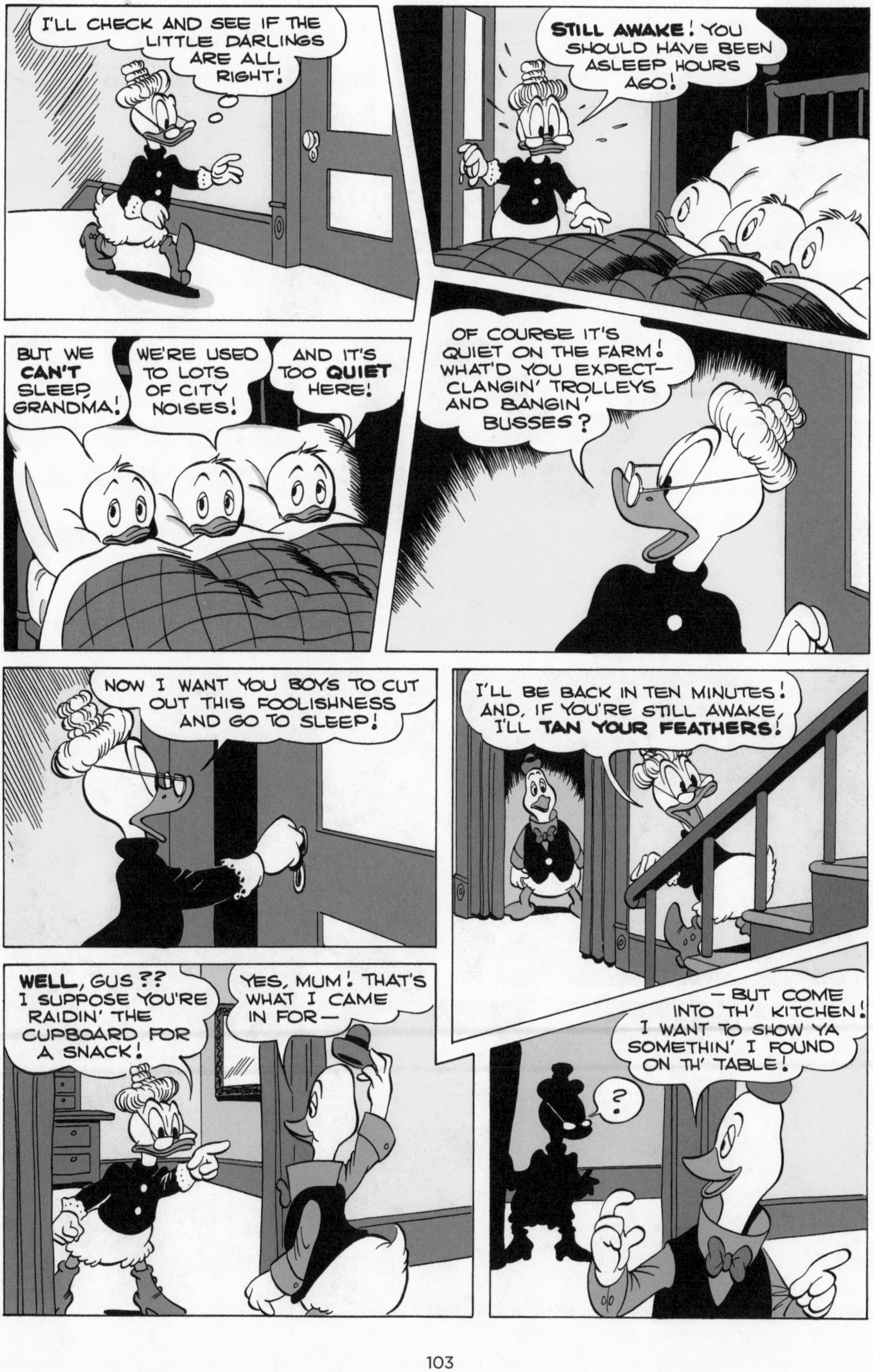
I'LL CHECK AND SEE IF THE LITTLE DARLINGS ARE ALL RIGHT!
STILL AWAKE! YOU SHOULD HAVE BEEN ASLEEP HOURS AGO!
BUT WE CAN'T SLEEP, GRANDMA!
WE'RE USED TO LOTS OF CITY NOISES!
AND IT'S TOO QUIET HERE!
OF COURSE IT'S QUIET ON THE FARM! WHAT'D YOU EXPECT— CLANGIN' TROLLEYS AND BANGIN' BUSSES?
NOW I WANT YOU BOYS TO CUT OUT THIS FOOLISHNESS AND GO TO SLEEP!
I'LL BE BACK IN TEN MINUTES! AND, IF YOU'RE STILL AWAKE, I'LL TAN YOUR FEATHERS!
WELL, GUS?? I SUPPOSE YOU'RE RAIDIN' THE CUPBOARD FOR A SNACK!
YES, MUM! THAT'S WHAT I CAME IN FOR—
—BUT COME INTO TH' KITCHEN! I WANT TO SHOW YA SOMETHIN' I FOUND ON TH' TABLE!
?

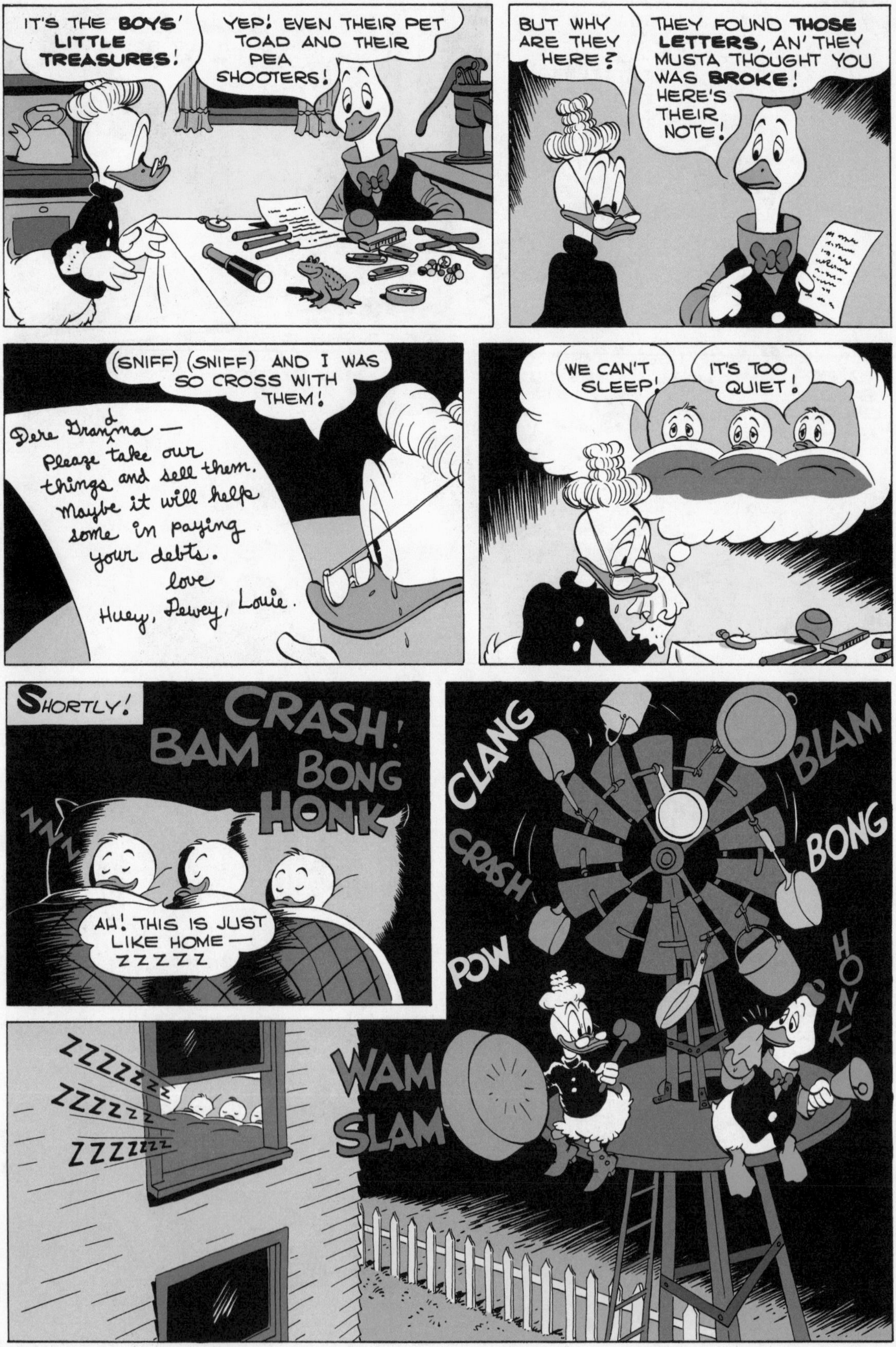
IT'S THE BOYS' LITTLE TREASURES!
YEP! EVEN THEIR PET TOAD AND THEIR PEA SHOOTERS!
BUT WHY ARE THEY HERE?
THEY FOUND THOSE LETTERS, AN' THEY MUSTA THOUGHT YOU WAS BROKE! HERE'S THEIR NOTE!
(SNIFF) (SNIFF) AND I WAS SO CROSS WITH THEM!
Dere Grandma — Pleaze take our things and sell them. Maybe it will help some in paying your debts. love Huey, Dewey, Louie.
WE CAN'T SLEEP!
IT'S TOO QUIET!
SHORTLY!
CRASH!
BAM
BONG
HONK
ZZZ
AH! THIS IS JUST LIKE HOME — ZZZZZ
CLANG
BLAM
CRASH
BONG
POW
HONK
WAM
SLAM
ZZZZZZZ
ZZZZZZ
ZZZZZZZ

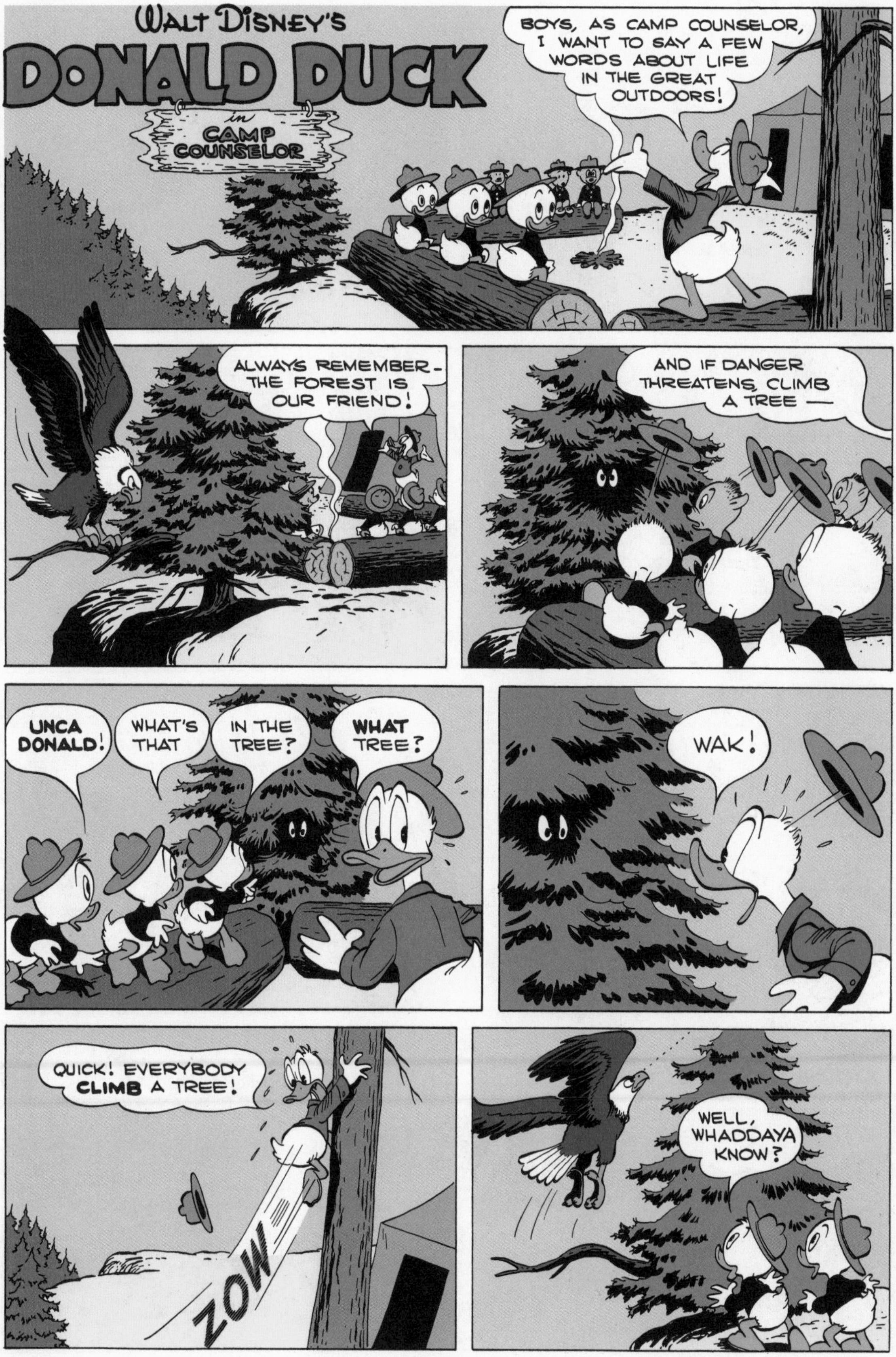
WALT DISNEY'S
DONALD DUCK
in
CAMP COUNSELOR
BOYS, AS CAMP COUNSELOR, I WANT TO SAY A FEW WORDS ABOUT LIFE IN THE GREAT OUTDOORS!
ALWAYS REMEMBER- THE FOREST IS OUR FRIEND!
AND IF DANGER THREATENS, CLIMB A TREE —
UNCA DONALD!
WHAT'S THAT
IN THE TREE?
WHAT TREE?
WAK!
QUICK! EVERYBODY CLIMB A TREE!
ZOW
WELL, WHADDAYA KNOW?

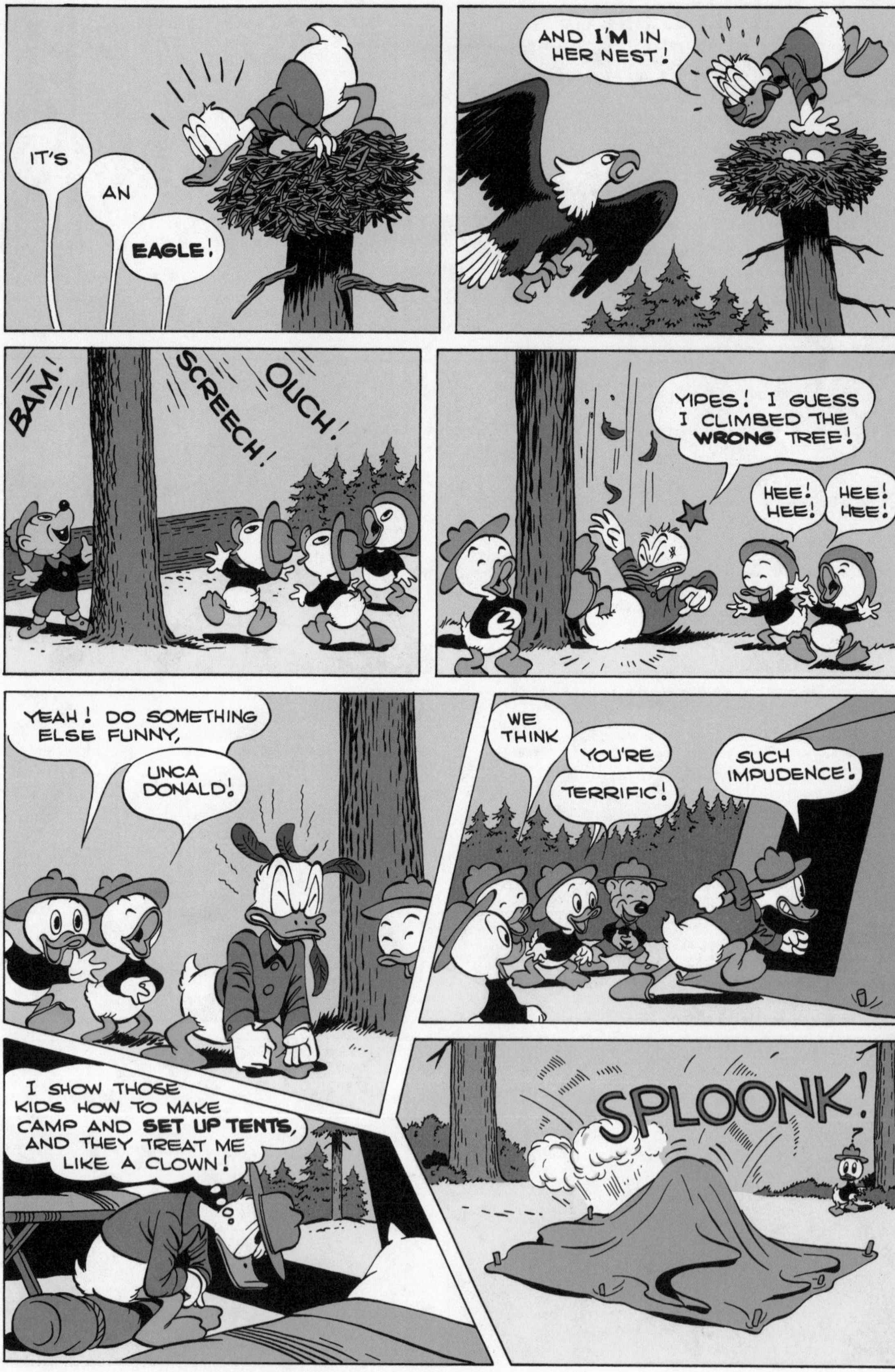

IT'S
AN
EAGLE!
AND I'M IN HER NEST!
BAM!
SCREECH!
OUCH!
YIPES! I GUESS I CLIMBED THE WRONG TREE!
HEE! HEE!
HEE! HEE!
YEAH! DO SOMETHING ELSE FUNNY,
UNCA DONALD!
WE THINK
YOU'RE
TERRIFIC!
SUCH IMPUDENCE!
I SHOW THOSE KIDS HOW TO MAKE CAMP AND SET UP TENTS, AND THEY TREAT ME LIKE A CLOWN!
SPLOONK!

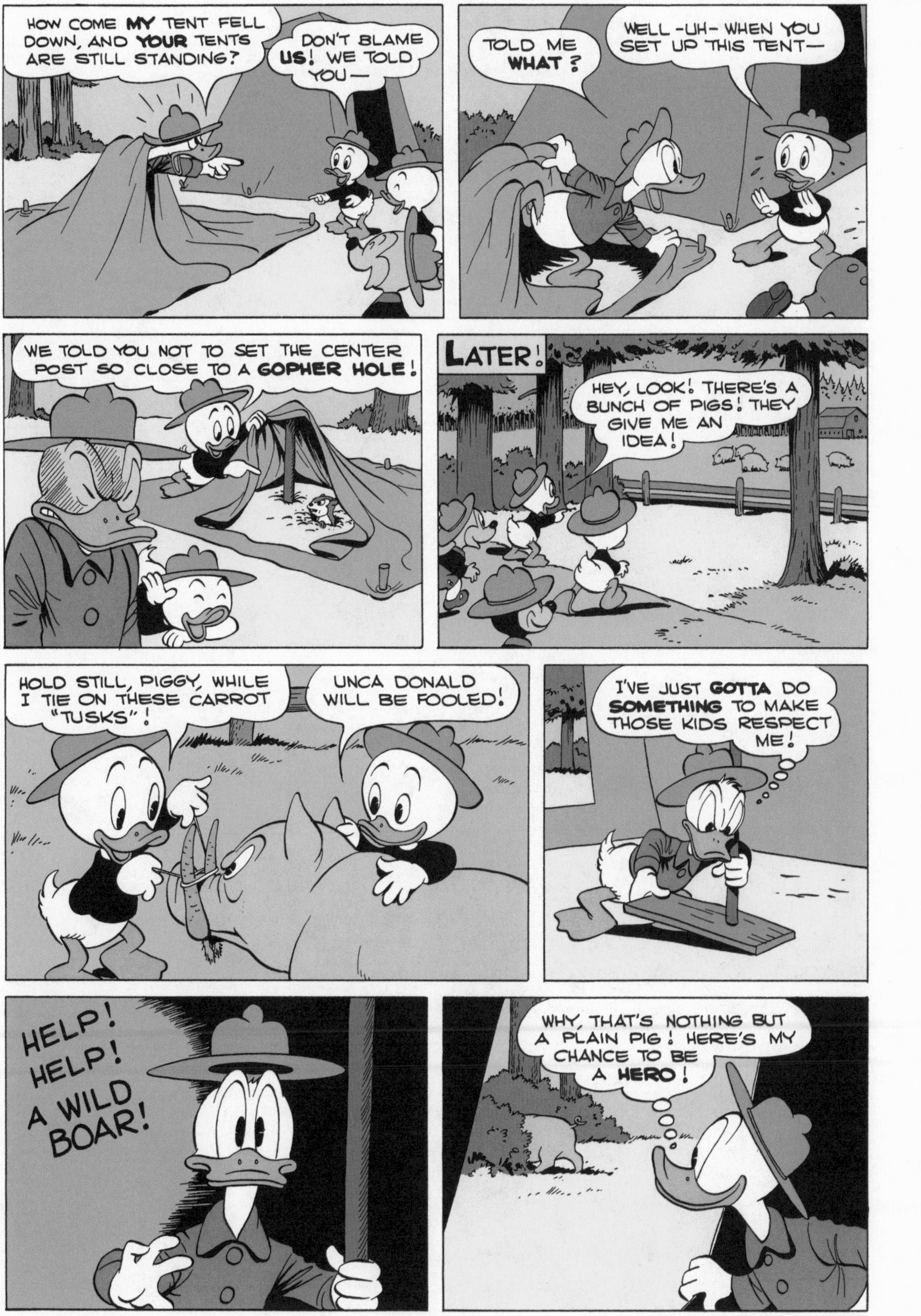

HOW COME MY TENT FELL DOWN, AND YOUR TENTS ARE STILL STANDING?
DON'T BLAME US! WE TOLD YOU—
TOLD ME WHAT?
WELL -UH- WHEN YOU SET UP THIS TENT—
WE TOLD YOU NOT TO SET THE CENTER POST SO CLOSE TO A GOPHER HOLE!
LATER!
HEY, LOOK! THERE'S A BUNCH OF PIGS! THEY GIVE ME AN IDEA!
HOLD STILL, PIGGY, WHILE I TIE ON THESE CARROT "TUSKS"!
UNCA DONALD WILL BE FOOLED!
I'VE JUST GOTTA DO SOMETHING TO MAKE THOSE KIDS RESPECT ME!
HELP! HELP! A WILD BOAR!
WHY, THAT'S NOTHING BUT A PLAIN PIG! HERE'S MY CHANCE TO BE A HERO!

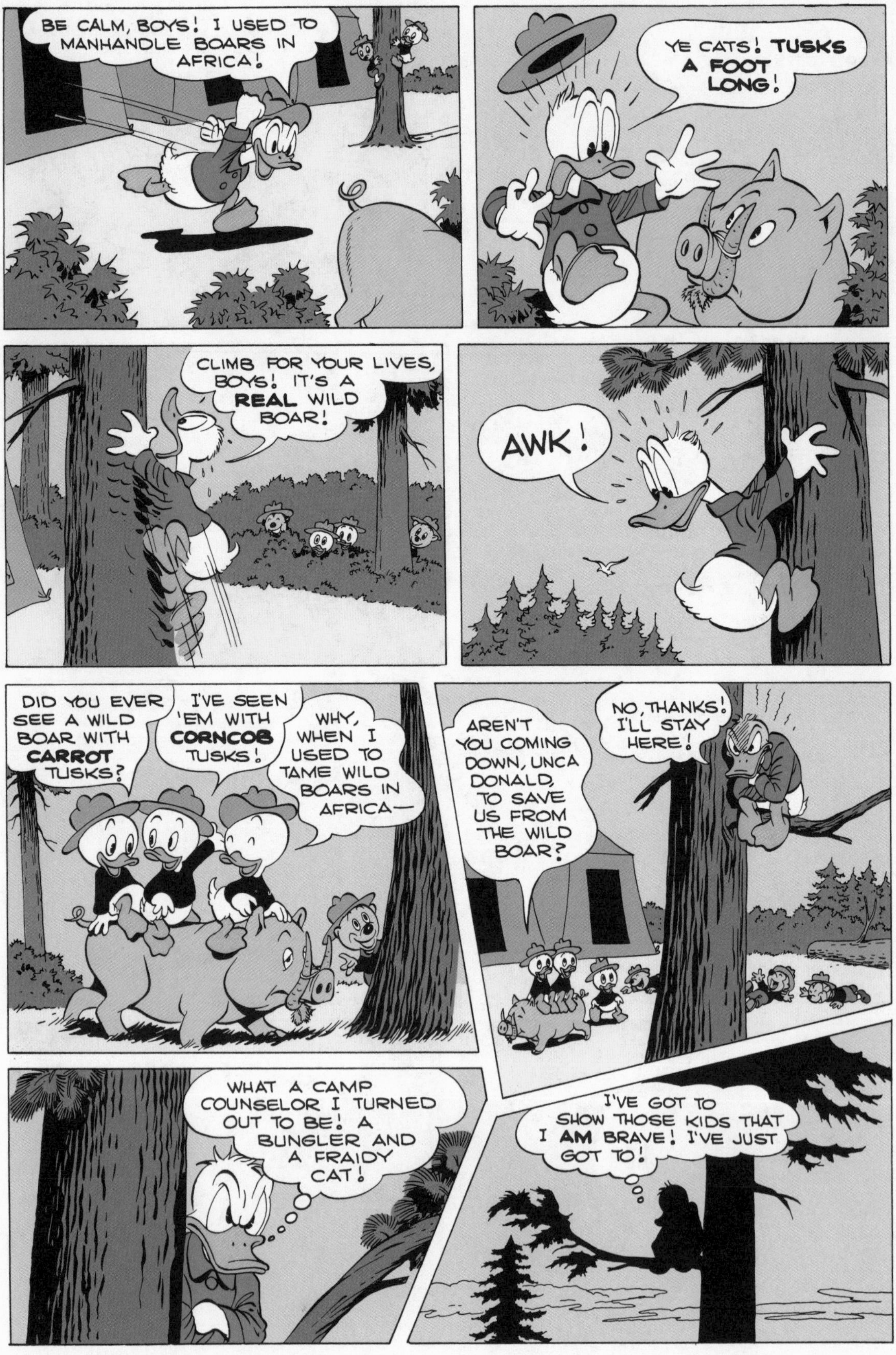
BE CALM, BOYS! I USED TO MANHANDLE BOARS IN AFRICA!
YE CATS! TUSKS A FOOT LONG!
CLIMB FOR YOUR LIVES, BOYS! IT'S A REAL WILD BOAR!
AWK!
DID YOU EVER SEE A WILD BOAR WITH CARROT TUSKS?
I'VE SEEN 'EM WITH CORNCOB TUSKS!
WHY, WHEN I USED TO TAME WILD BOARS IN AFRICA—
AREN'T YOU COMING DOWN, UNCA DONALD, TO SAVE US FROM THE WILD BOAR?
NO, THANKS! I'LL STAY HERE!
WHAT A CAMP COUNSELOR I TURNED OUT TO BE! A BUNGLER AND A FRAIDY CAT!
I'VE GOT TO SHOW THOSE KIDS THAT I AM BRAVE! I'VE JUST GOT TO!

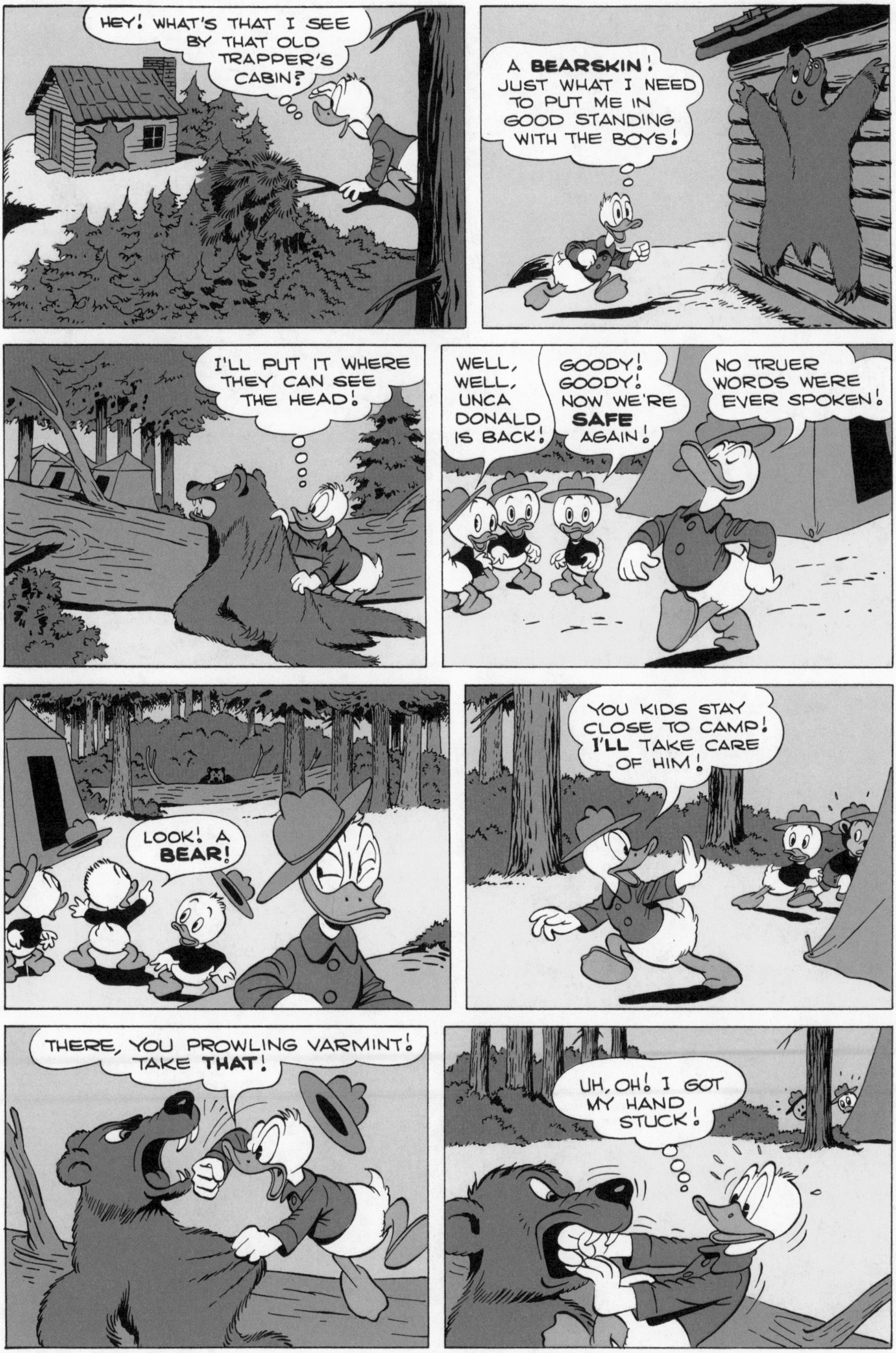
HEY! WHAT'S THAT I SEE BY THAT OLD TRAPPER'S CABIN?
A **BEARSKIN**! JUST WHAT I NEED TO PUT ME IN GOOD STANDING WITH THE BOYS!
I'LL PUT IT WHERE THEY CAN SEE THE HEAD!
WELL, WELL, UNCA DONALD IS BACK!
GOODY! GOODY! NOW WE'RE **SAFE** AGAIN!
NO TRUER WORDS WERE EVER SPOKEN!
LOOK! A **BEAR**!
YOU KIDS STAY CLOSE TO CAMP! **I'LL** TAKE CARE OF HIM!
THERE, YOU PROWLING VARMINT! TAKE **THAT**!
UH, OH! I GOT MY HAND STUCK!

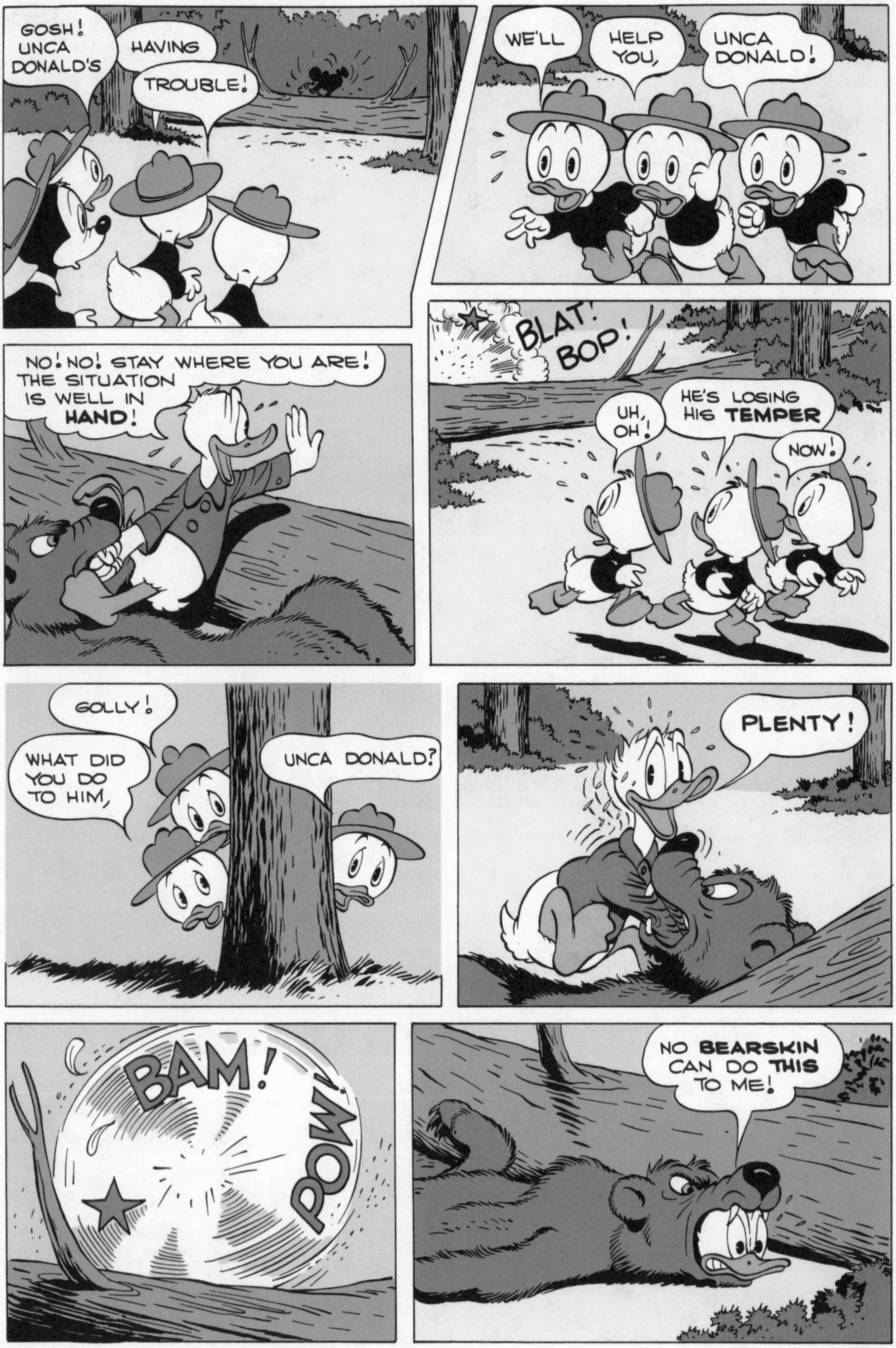
GOSH! UNCA DONALD'S
HAVING
TROUBLE!
WE'LL
HELP YOU,
UNCA DONALD!
NO! NO! STAY WHERE YOU ARE! THE SITUATION IS WELL IN **HAND**!
BLAT!
BOP!
UH, OH!
HE'S LOSING HIS **TEMPER**
NOW!
GOLLY!
WHAT DID YOU DO TO HIM,
UNCA DONALD?
PLENTY!
BAM!
POW!
NO **BEARSKIN** CAN DO **THIS** TO ME!

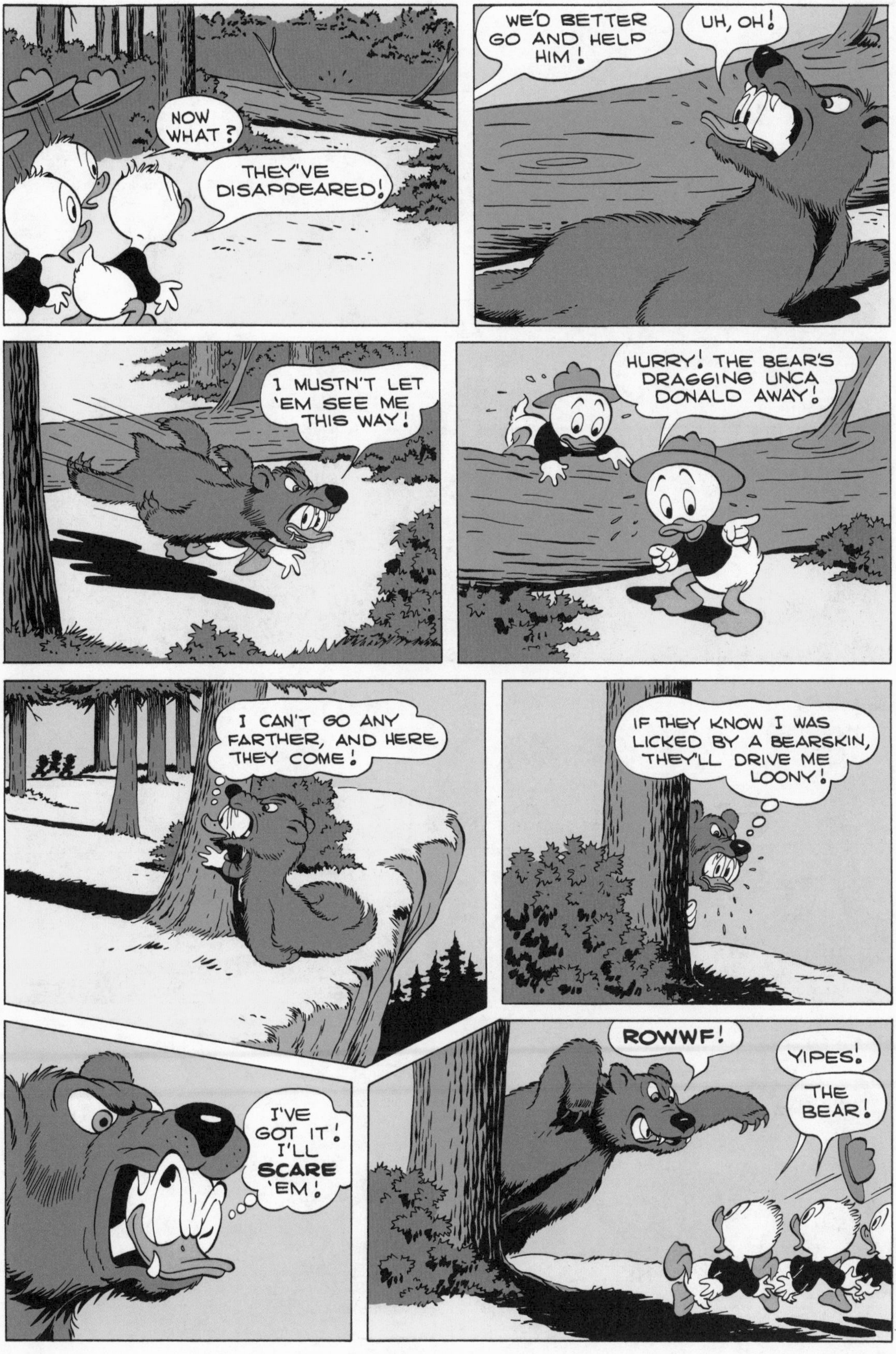
NOW WHAT?
THEY'VE DISAPPEARED!
WE'D BETTER GO AND HELP HIM!
UH, OH!
I MUSTN'T LET 'EM SEE ME THIS WAY!
HURRY! THE BEAR'S DRAGGING UNCA DONALD AWAY!
I CAN'T GO ANY FARTHER, AND HERE THEY COME!
IF THEY KNOW I WAS LICKED BY A BEARSKIN, THEY'LL DRIVE ME LOONY!
I'VE GOT IT! I'LL SCARE 'EM!
ROWWF!
YIPES!
THE BEAR!

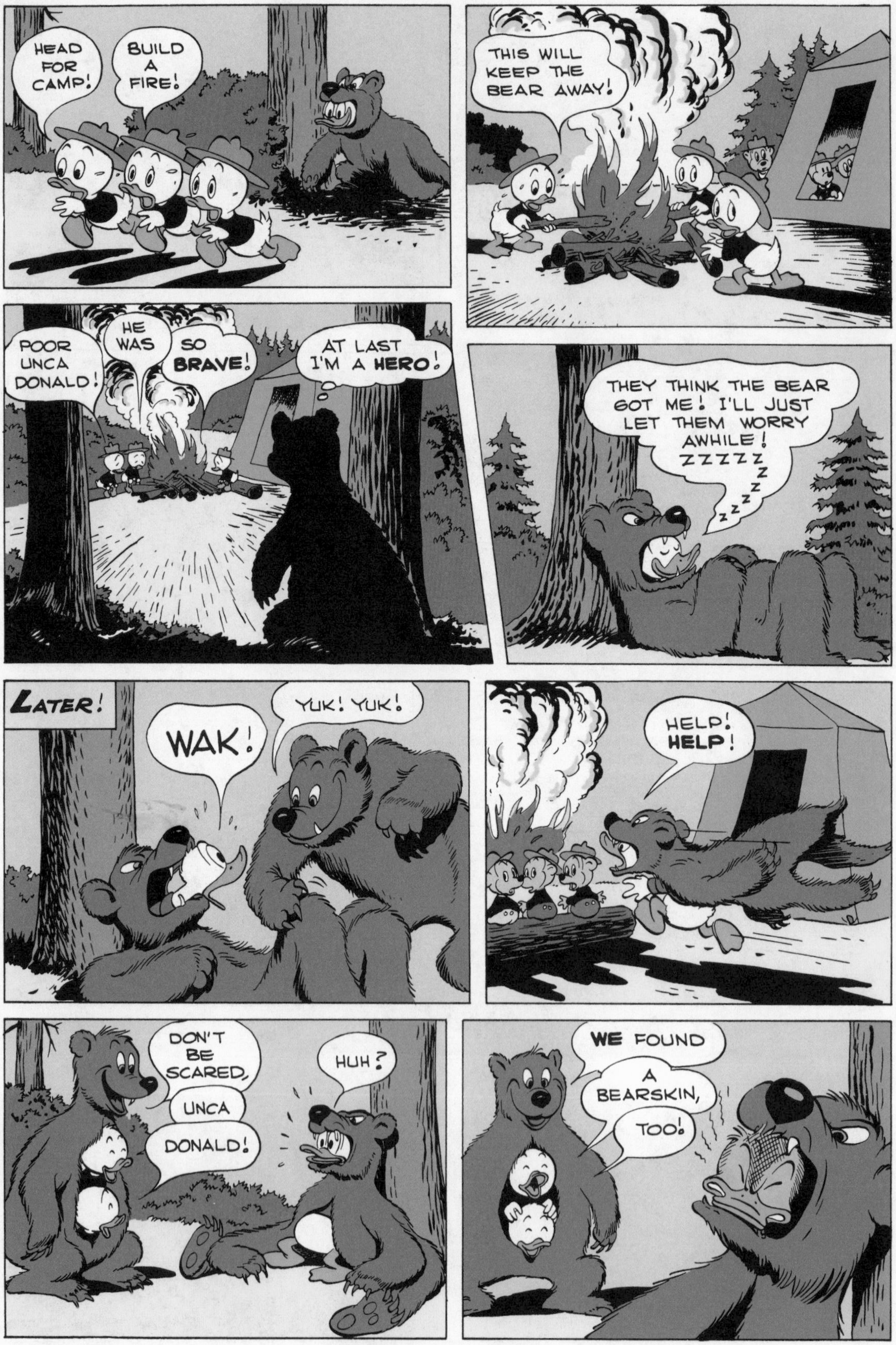
HEAD FOR CAMP!
BUILD A FIRE!
THIS WILL KEEP THE BEAR AWAY!
POOR UNCA DONALD!
HE WAS
SO BRAVE!
AT LAST I'M A HERO!
THEY THINK THE BEAR GOT ME! I'LL JUST LET THEM WORRY AWHILE! ZZZZZ
ZZZZZ
LATER!
WAK!
YUK! YUK!
HELP! HELP!
DON'T BE SCARED,
UNCA
DONALD!
HUH?
WE FOUND
A BEARSKIN,
TOO!

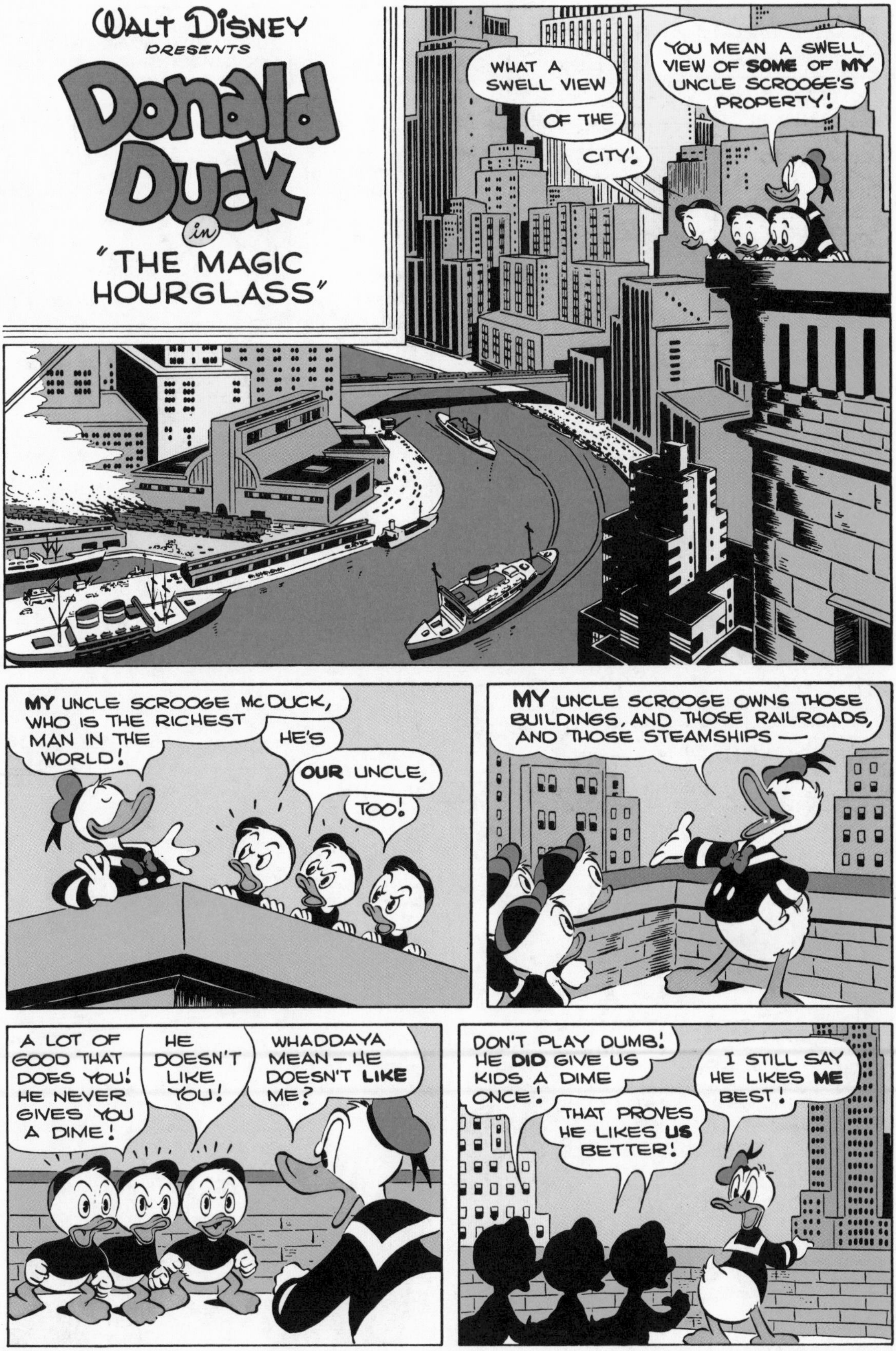
WALT DISNEY
PRESENTS
Donald Duck
in
"THE MAGIC HOURGLASS"
WHAT A SWELL VIEW
OF THE
CITY!
YOU MEAN A SWELL VIEW OF SOME OF MY UNCLE SCROOGE'S PROPERTY!
MY UNCLE SCROOGE McDUCK, WHO IS THE RICHEST MAN IN THE WORLD!
HE'S
OUR UNCLE,
TOO!
MY UNCLE SCROOGE OWNS THOSE BUILDINGS, AND THOSE RAILROADS, AND THOSE STEAMSHIPS —
A LOT OF GOOD THAT DOES YOU! HE NEVER GIVES YOU A DIME!
HE DOESN'T LIKE YOU!
WHADDAYA MEAN — HE DOESN'T LIKE ME?
DON'T PLAY DUMB! HE DID GIVE US KIDS A DIME ONCE!
THAT PROVES HE LIKES US BETTER!
I STILL SAY HE LIKES ME BEST!

WHILE DONALD AND HIS NEPHEWS ARGUE, DESTINY IS HATCHING A LITTLE SCHEME TO PROVE JUST **WHO** UNCLE SCROOGE DOES LIKE BEST!

DESTINY

IT ALL STARTS WITH BREAKFAST IN THE OLD MISER'S FRUGAL KITCHEN!

WHEN I EAT EGGS I WANT THEM COOKED **EXACTLY** RIGHT!

THAT'S WHY I'VE ALWAYS USED THIS **WONDERFUL** OLD HOURGLASS TO TIME MY HEN FRUIT!

NOT ONCE HAS IT FAILED TO TELL THE TIME **EXACTLY**! NOT ONCE IN ALL THE YEARS SINCE I BOUGHT IT IN A THIEVES' MARKET IN MOROCCO!

AH, ME! I WAS THEN ONLY A POOR CABIN BOY ON A CATTLE BOAT... ... BUT, HO! THE SAND HAS REACHED THE THREE-MINUTE MARK!

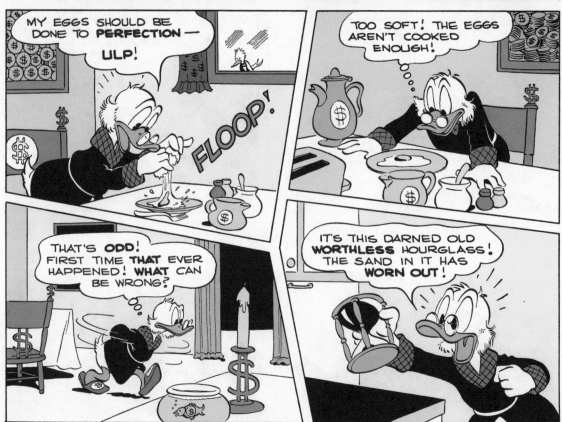

MY EGGS SHOULD BE DONE TO **PERFECTION** — ULP!

FLOOP!

TOO SOFT! THE EGGS AREN'T COOKED ENOUGH!

THAT'S **ODD**! FIRST TIME **THAT** EVER HAPPENED! **WHAT** CAN BE WRONG?

IT'S THIS DARNED OLD **WORTHLESS** HOURGLASS! THE SAND IN IT HAS **WORN OUT**!

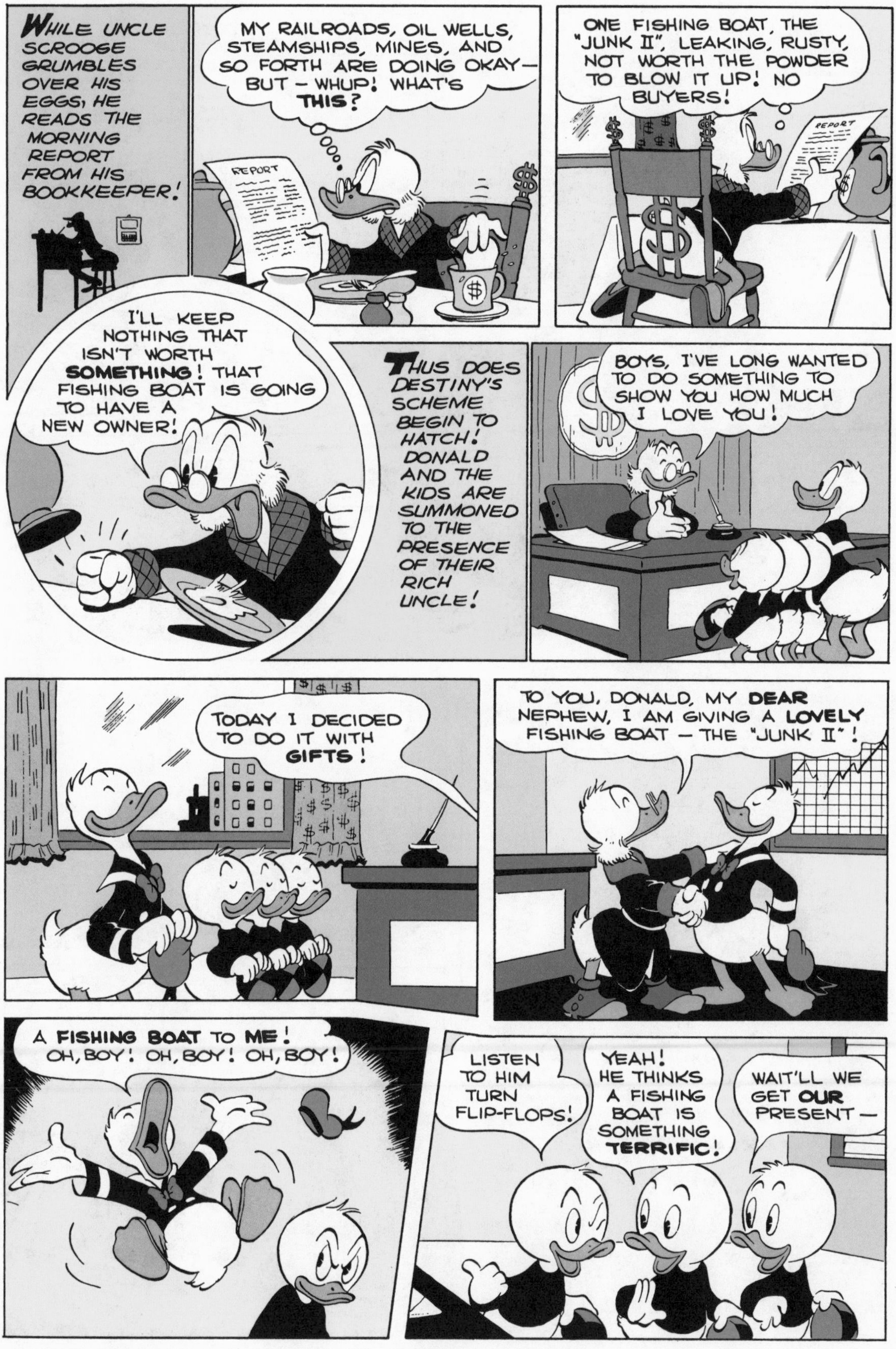
WHILE UNCLE SCROOGE GRUMBLES OVER HIS EGGS, HE READS THE MORNING REPORT FROM HIS BOOKKEEPER!
MY RAILROADS, OIL WELLS, STEAMSHIPS, MINES, AND SO FORTH ARE DOING OKAY— BUT – WHUP! WHAT'S THIS?
REPORT
ONE FISHING BOAT, THE "JUNK II", LEAKING, RUSTY, NOT WORTH THE POWDER TO BLOW IT UP! NO BUYERS!
REPORT
I'LL KEEP NOTHING THAT ISN'T WORTH SOMETHING! THAT FISHING BOAT IS GOING TO HAVE A NEW OWNER!
THUS DOES DESTINY'S SCHEME BEGIN TO HATCH! DONALD AND THE KIDS ARE SUMMONED TO THE PRESENCE OF THEIR RICH UNCLE!
BOYS, I'VE LONG WANTED TO DO SOMETHING TO SHOW YOU HOW MUCH I LOVE YOU!
TODAY I DECIDED TO DO IT WITH GIFTS!
TO YOU, DONALD, MY DEAR NEPHEW, I AM GIVING A LOVELY FISHING BOAT – THE "JUNK II"!
A FISHING BOAT TO ME! OH, BOY! OH, BOY! OH, BOY!
LISTEN TO HIM TURN FLIP-FLOPS!
YEAH! HE THINKS A FISHING BOAT IS SOMETHING TERRIFIC!
WAIT'LL WE GET OUR PRESENT—

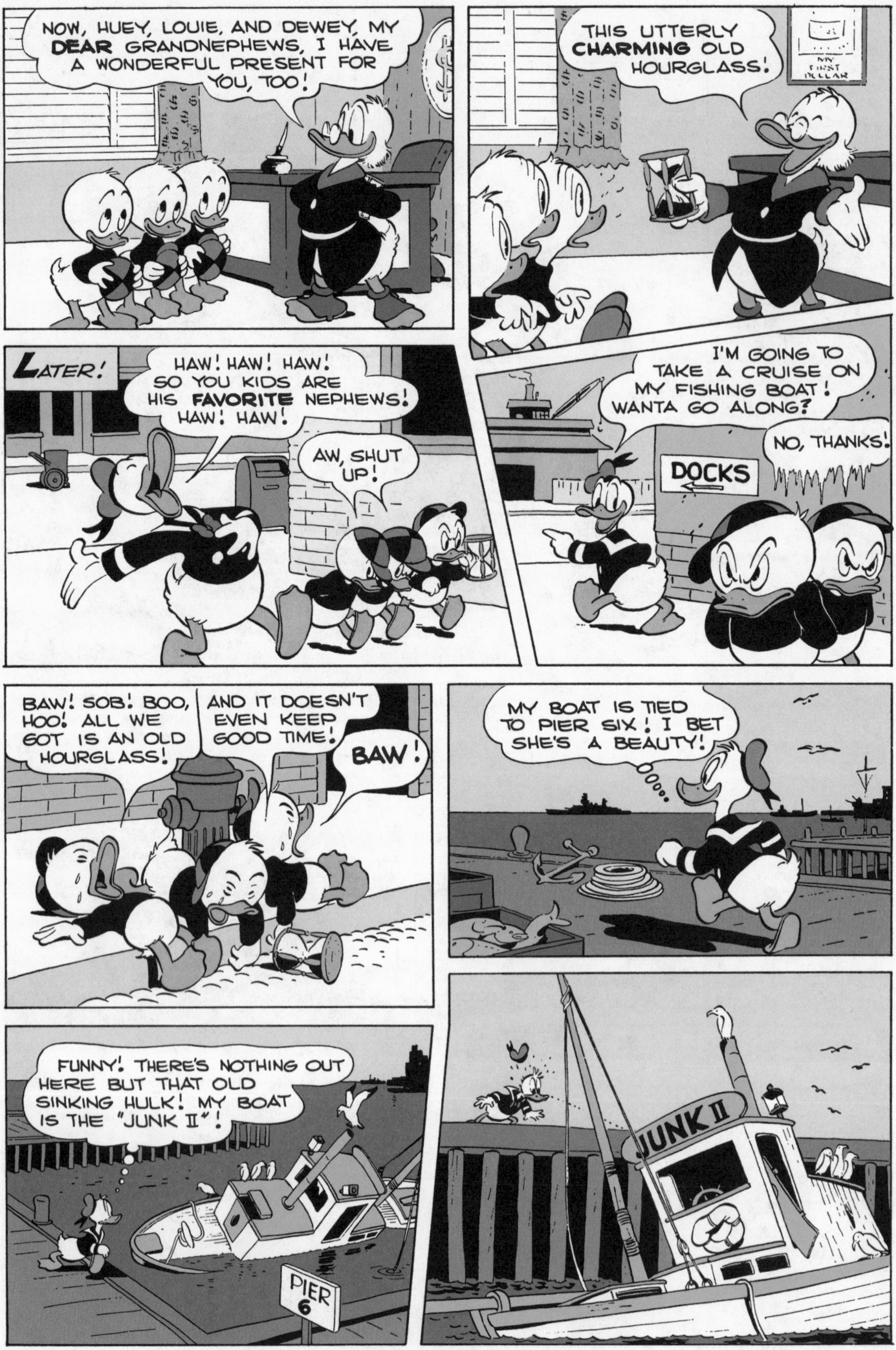
NOW, HUEY, LOUIE, AND DEWEY, MY DEAR GRANDNEPHEWS, I HAVE A WONDERFUL PRESENT FOR YOU, TOO!
THIS UTTERLY CHARMING OLD HOURGLASS!
MY FIRST DOLLAR
LATER!
HAW! HAW! HAW! SO YOU KIDS ARE HIS FAVORITE NEPHEWS! HAW! HAW!
AW, SHUT UP!
I'M GOING TO TAKE A CRUISE ON MY FISHING BOAT! WANTA GO ALONG?
NO, THANKS!
DOCKS
BAW! SOB! BOO, HOO! ALL WE GOT IS AN OLD HOURGLASS!
AND IT DOESN'T EVEN KEEP GOOD TIME!
BAW!
MY BOAT IS TIED TO PIER SIX! I BET SHE'S A BEAUTY!
FUNNY! THERE'S NOTHING OUT HERE BUT THAT OLD SINKING HULK! MY BOAT IS THE "JUNK II"!
PIER 6
JUNK II

THAT OLD MISER! THAT OLD SKINFLINT! I MIGHTA KNOWN HE'D NEVER GIVE AWAY ANYTHING WORTH HAVING!

BUT, ANYWAY, IT'S MORE THAN THE KIDS GOT! THAT HOURGLASS — HAW!

ARE YOU THE NEW OWNER OF THIS BOAT?

YEAH! WANTA **BUY** IT?

NO! I WANTA COLLECT THIS BILL FOR TWO YEARS' DOCK RENT, AND THIS OTHER BILL FOR OBSTRUCTING NAVIGATION!

ATLAS DOCK Co

$100.00

THERE GOES MY LAST DOLLAR! THOSE KIDS AND THEIR HOUR-GLASS — SOME PEOPLE HAVE ALL THE LUCK!

I'M CRIED OUT!

LET'S TAKE THIS THING TO A JUNK-MAN!

MAYBE WE CAN SELL IT FOR A WHOLE BIG **DIME**!

A DIME FOR **THIS**! DON'T MAKE ME LAUGH!

I BUY JUNK!

AND DON'T TRY TO TELL ME IT'S A **MAGIC** HOURGLASS JUST BECAUSE OF WHAT'S WRITTEN ON THE TOP OF IT!

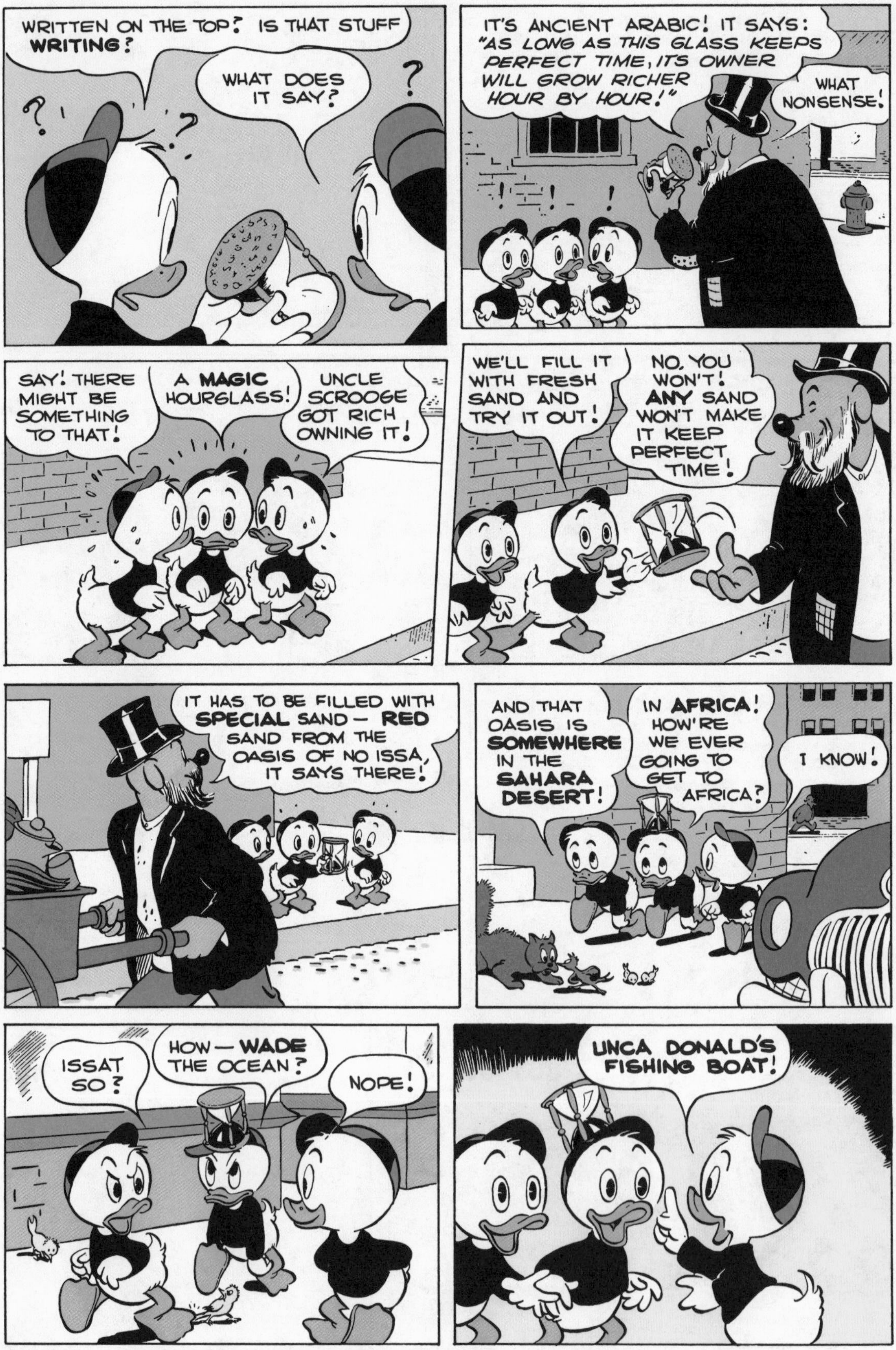
WRITTEN ON THE TOP? IS THAT STUFF WRITING?
WHAT DOES IT SAY?
IT'S ANCIENT ARABIC! IT SAYS: "AS LONG AS THIS GLASS KEEPS PERFECT TIME, ITS OWNER WILL GROW RICHER HOUR BY HOUR!"
WHAT NONSENSE!
SAY! THERE MIGHT BE SOMETHING TO THAT!
A MAGIC HOURGLASS!
UNCLE SCROOGE GOT RICH OWNING IT!
WE'LL FILL IT WITH FRESH SAND AND TRY IT OUT!
NO, YOU WON'T! ANY SAND WON'T MAKE IT KEEP PERFECT TIME!
IT HAS TO BE FILLED WITH SPECIAL SAND — RED SAND FROM THE OASIS OF NO ISSA, IT SAYS THERE!
AND THAT OASIS IS SOMEWHERE IN THE SAHARA DESERT!
IN AFRICA! HOW'RE WE EVER GOING TO GET TO AFRICA?
I KNOW!
ISSAT SO?
HOW — WADE THE OCEAN?
NOPE!
UNCA DONALD'S FISHING BOAT!

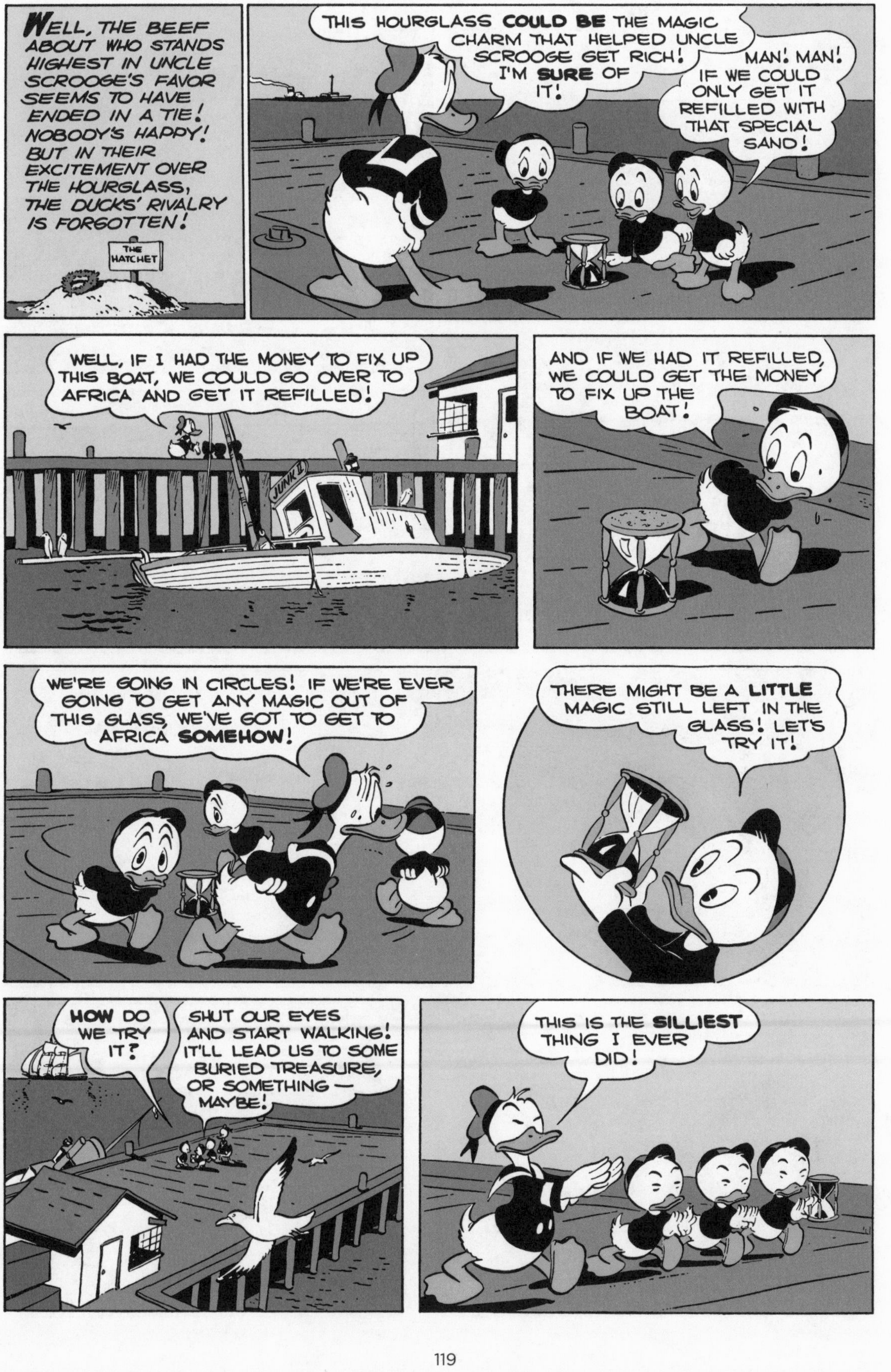
WELL, THE BEEF ABOUT WHO STANDS HIGHEST IN UNCLE SCROOGE'S FAVOR SEEMS TO HAVE ENDED IN A TIE! NOBODY'S HAPPY! BUT IN THEIR EXCITEMENT OVER THE HOURGLASS, THE DUCKS' RIVALRY IS FORGOTTEN!
THE HATCHET
THIS HOURGLASS COULD BE THE MAGIC CHARM THAT HELPED UNCLE SCROOGE GET RICH! I'M SURE OF IT!
MAN! MAN! IF WE COULD ONLY GET IT REFILLED WITH THAT SPECIAL SAND!
WELL, IF I HAD THE MONEY TO FIX UP THIS BOAT, WE COULD GO OVER TO AFRICA AND GET IT REFILLED!
JUNK II
AND IF WE HAD IT REFILLED, WE COULD GET THE MONEY TO FIX UP THE BOAT!
WE'RE GOING IN CIRCLES! IF WE'RE EVER GOING TO GET ANY MAGIC OUT OF THIS GLASS, WE'VE GOT TO GET TO AFRICA SOMEHOW!
THERE MIGHT BE A LITTLE MAGIC STILL LEFT IN THE GLASS! LET'S TRY IT!
HOW DO WE TRY IT?
SHUT OUR EYES AND START WALKING! IT'LL LEAD US TO SOME BURIED TREASURE, OR SOMETHING — MAYBE!
THIS IS THE SILLIEST THING I EVER DID!

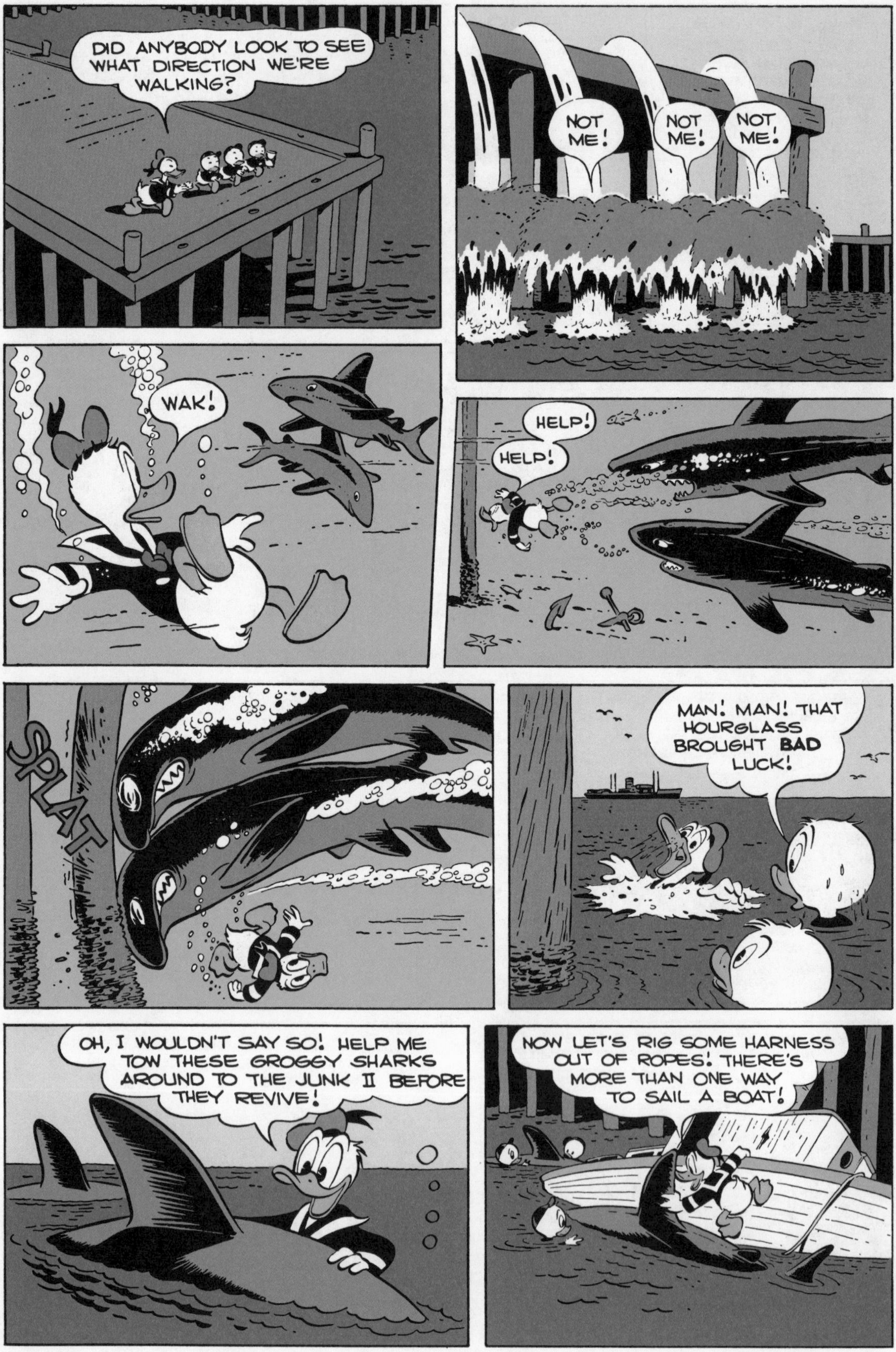
DID ANYBODY LOOK TO SEE WHAT DIRECTION WE'RE WALKING?
NOT ME!
NOT ME!
NOT ME!
WAK!
HELP!
HELP!
SPLAT
MAN! MAN! THAT HOURGLASS BROUGHT BAD LUCK!
OH, I WOULDN'T SAY SO! HELP ME TOW THESE GROGGY SHARKS AROUND TO THE JUNK II BEFORE THEY REVIVE!
NOW LET'S RIG SOME HARNESS OUT OF ROPES! THERE'S MORE THAN ONE WAY TO SAIL A BOAT!

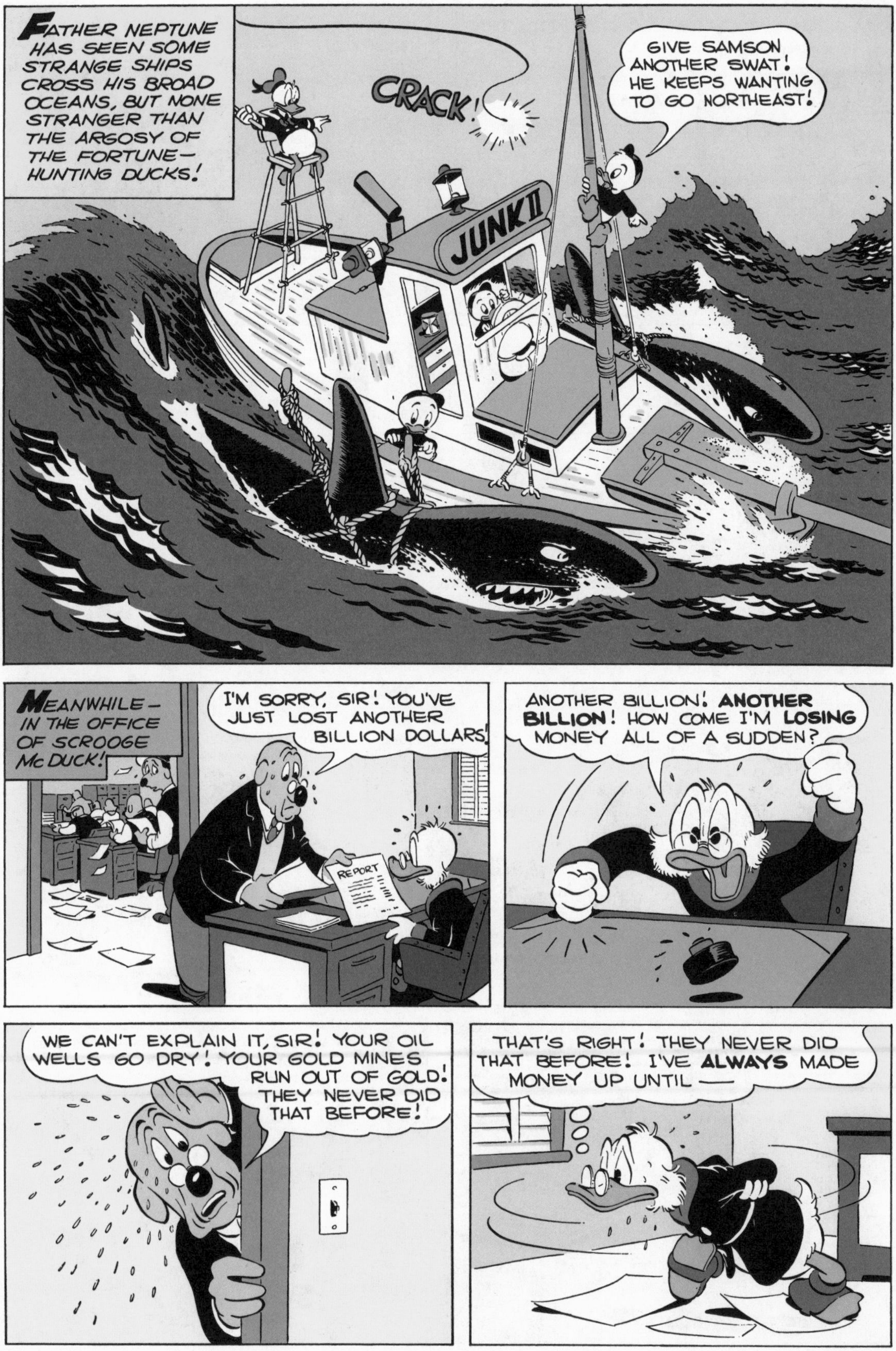
FATHER NEPTUNE HAS SEEN SOME STRANGE SHIPS CROSS HIS BROAD OCEANS, BUT NONE STRANGER THAN THE ARGOSY OF THE FORTUNE-HUNTING DUCKS!
CRACK!
GIVE SAMSON ANOTHER SWAT! HE KEEPS WANTING TO GO NORTHEAST!
JUNK II
MEANWHILE— IN THE OFFICE OF SCROOGE McDUCK!
I'M SORRY, SIR! YOU'VE JUST LOST ANOTHER BILLION DOLLARS!
REPORT
ANOTHER BILLION! ANOTHER BILLION! HOW COME I'M LOSING MONEY ALL OF A SUDDEN?
WE CAN'T EXPLAIN IT, SIR! YOUR OIL WELLS GO DRY! YOUR GOLD MINES RUN OUT OF GOLD! THEY NEVER DID THAT BEFORE!
THAT'S RIGHT! THEY NEVER DID THAT BEFORE! I'VE ALWAYS MADE MONEY UP UNTIL—

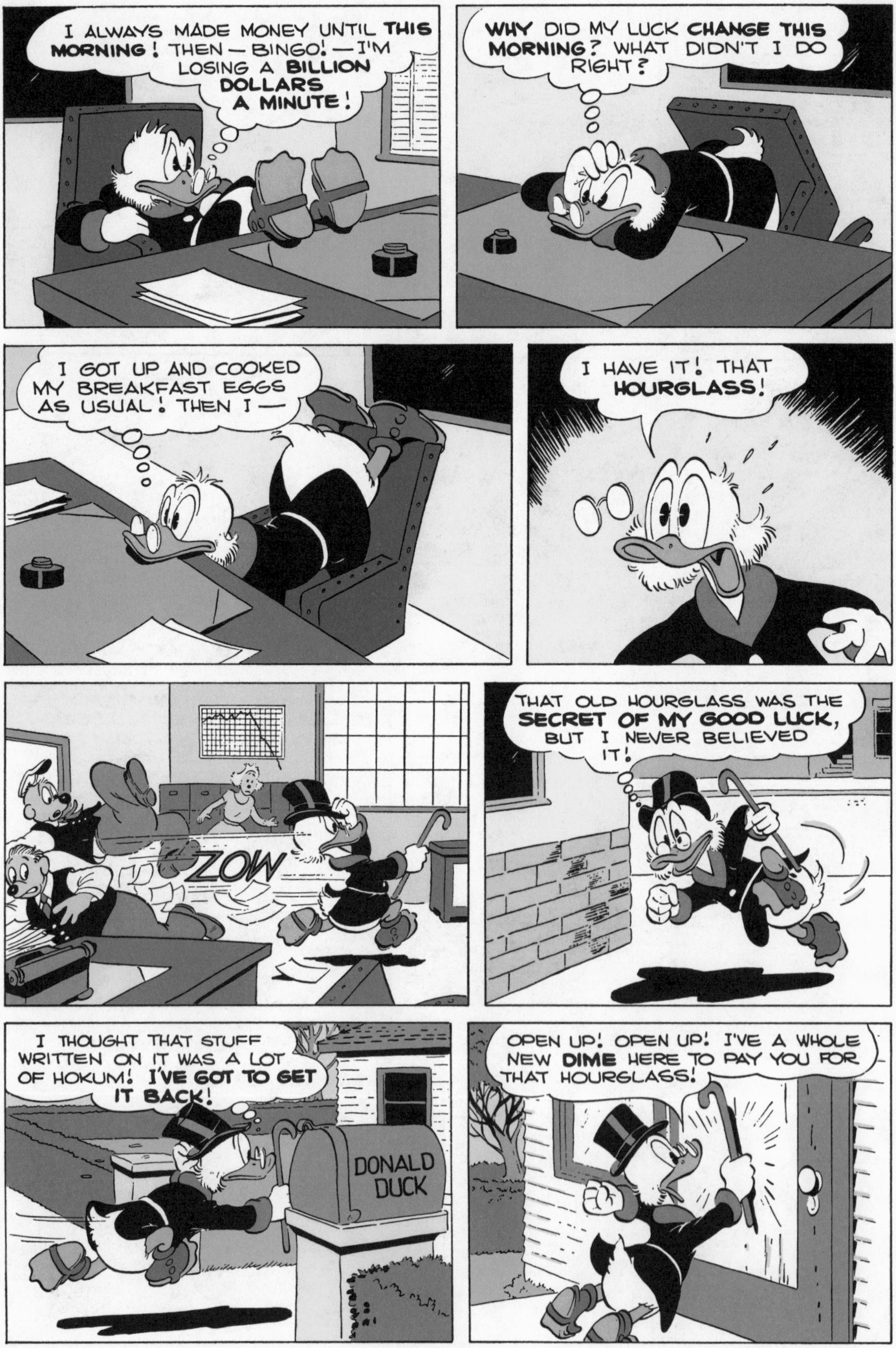
I ALWAYS MADE MONEY UNTIL THIS MORNING! THEN—BINGO!—I'M LOSING A BILLION DOLLARS A MINUTE!
WHY DID MY LUCK CHANGE THIS MORNING? WHAT DIDN'T I DO RIGHT?
I GOT UP AND COOKED MY BREAKFAST EGGS AS USUAL! THEN I—
I HAVE IT! THAT HOURGLASS!
ZOW
THAT OLD HOURGLASS WAS THE SECRET OF MY GOOD LUCK, BUT I NEVER BELIEVED IT!
I THOUGHT THAT STUFF WRITTEN ON IT WAS A LOT OF HOKUM! I'VE GOT TO GET IT BACK!
DONALD DUCK
OPEN UP! OPEN UP! I'VE A WHOLE NEW DIME HERE TO PAY YOU FOR THAT HOURGLASS!

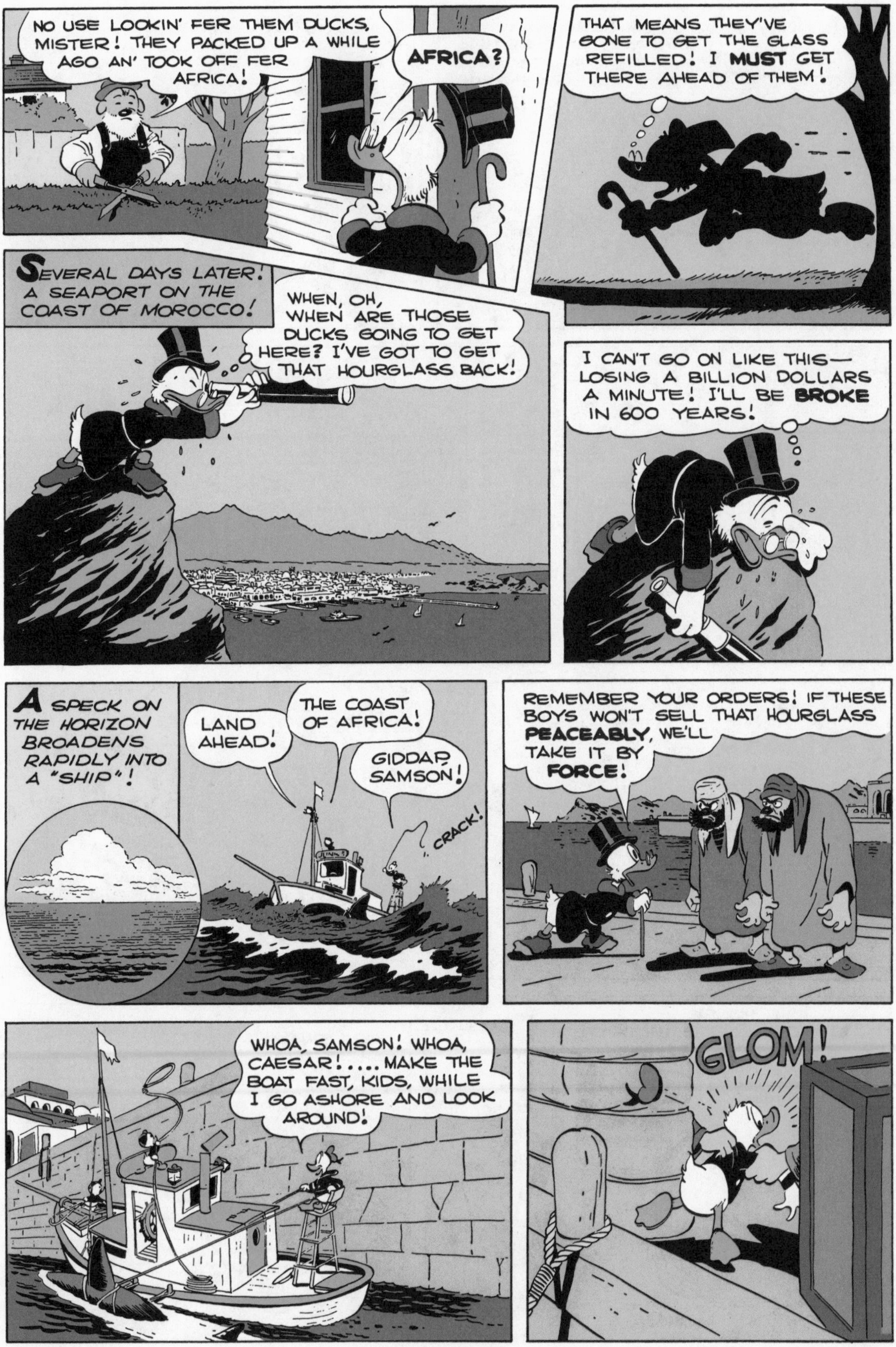
NO USE LOOKIN' FER THEM DUCKS, MISTER! THEY PACKED UP A WHILE AGO AN' TOOK OFF FER AFRICA!
AFRICA?
THAT MEANS THEY'VE GONE TO GET THE GLASS REFILLED! I MUST GET THERE AHEAD OF THEM!
SEVERAL DAYS LATER! A SEAPORT ON THE COAST OF MOROCCO!
WHEN, OH, WHEN ARE THOSE DUCKS GOING TO GET HERE? I'VE GOT TO GET THAT HOURGLASS BACK!
I CAN'T GO ON LIKE THIS— LOSING A BILLION DOLLARS A MINUTE! I'LL BE BROKE IN 600 YEARS!
A SPECK ON THE HORIZON BROADENS RAPIDLY INTO A "SHIP"!
LAND AHEAD!
THE COAST OF AFRICA!
GIDDAP, SAMSON!
CRACK!
REMEMBER YOUR ORDERS! IF THESE BOYS WON'T SELL THAT HOURGLASS PEACEABLY, WE'LL TAKE IT BY FORCE!
WHOA, SAMSON! WHOA, CAESAR!.... MAKE THE BOAT FAST, KIDS, WHILE I GO ASHORE AND LOOK AROUND!
GLOM!

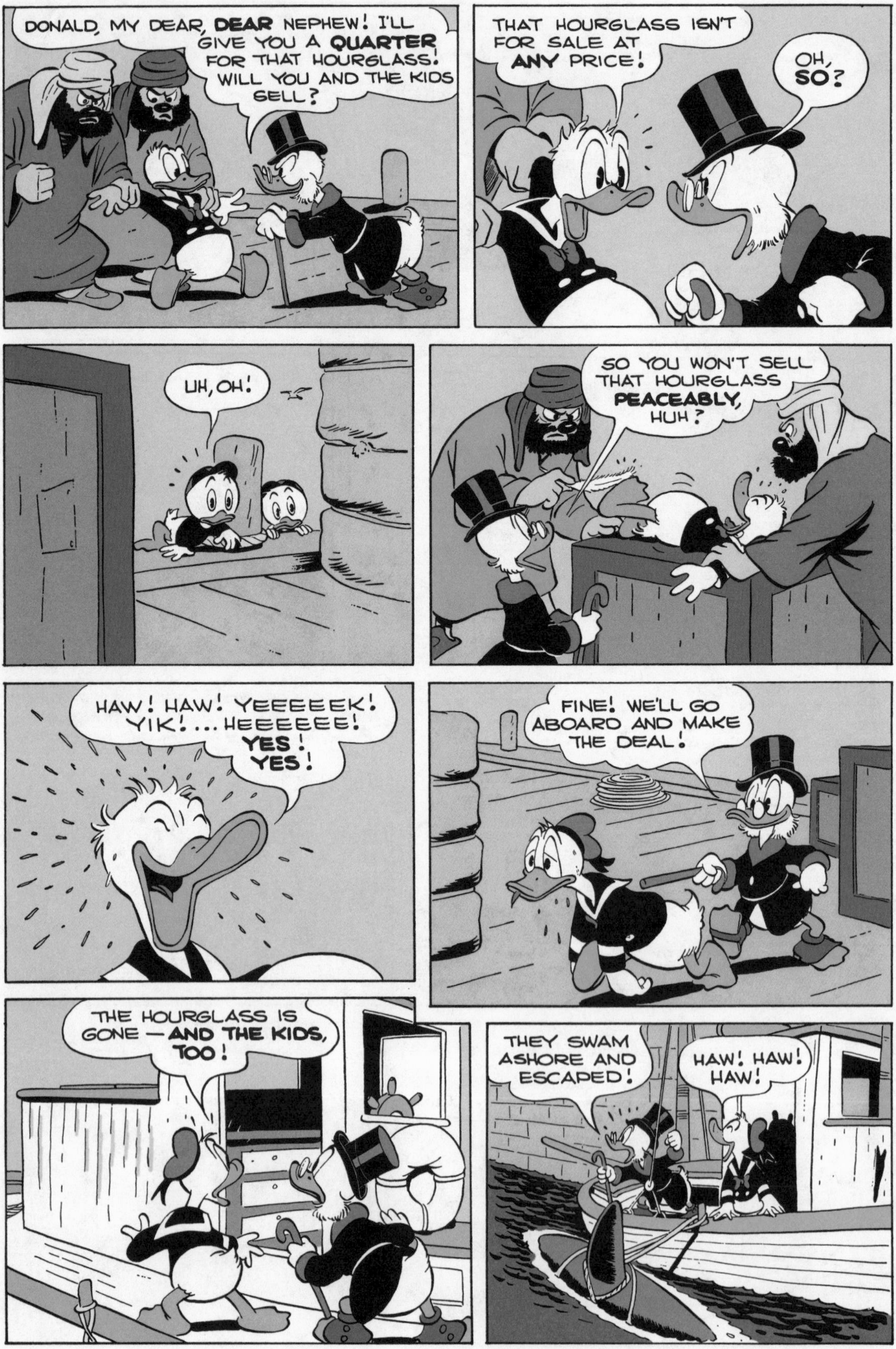
DONALD, MY DEAR, DEAR NEPHEW! I'LL GIVE YOU A QUARTER FOR THAT HOURGLASS! WILL YOU AND THE KIDS SELL?
THAT HOURGLASS ISN'T FOR SALE AT ANY PRICE!
OH, SO?
UH, OH!
SO YOU WON'T SELL THAT HOURGLASS PEACEABLY, HUH?
HAW! HAW! YEEEEEK! YIK! ... HEEEEEEE! YES! YES!
FINE! WE'LL GO ABOARD AND MAKE THE DEAL!
THE HOURGLASS IS GONE — AND THE KIDS, TOO!
THEY SWAM ASHORE AND ESCAPED!
HAW! HAW! HAW!

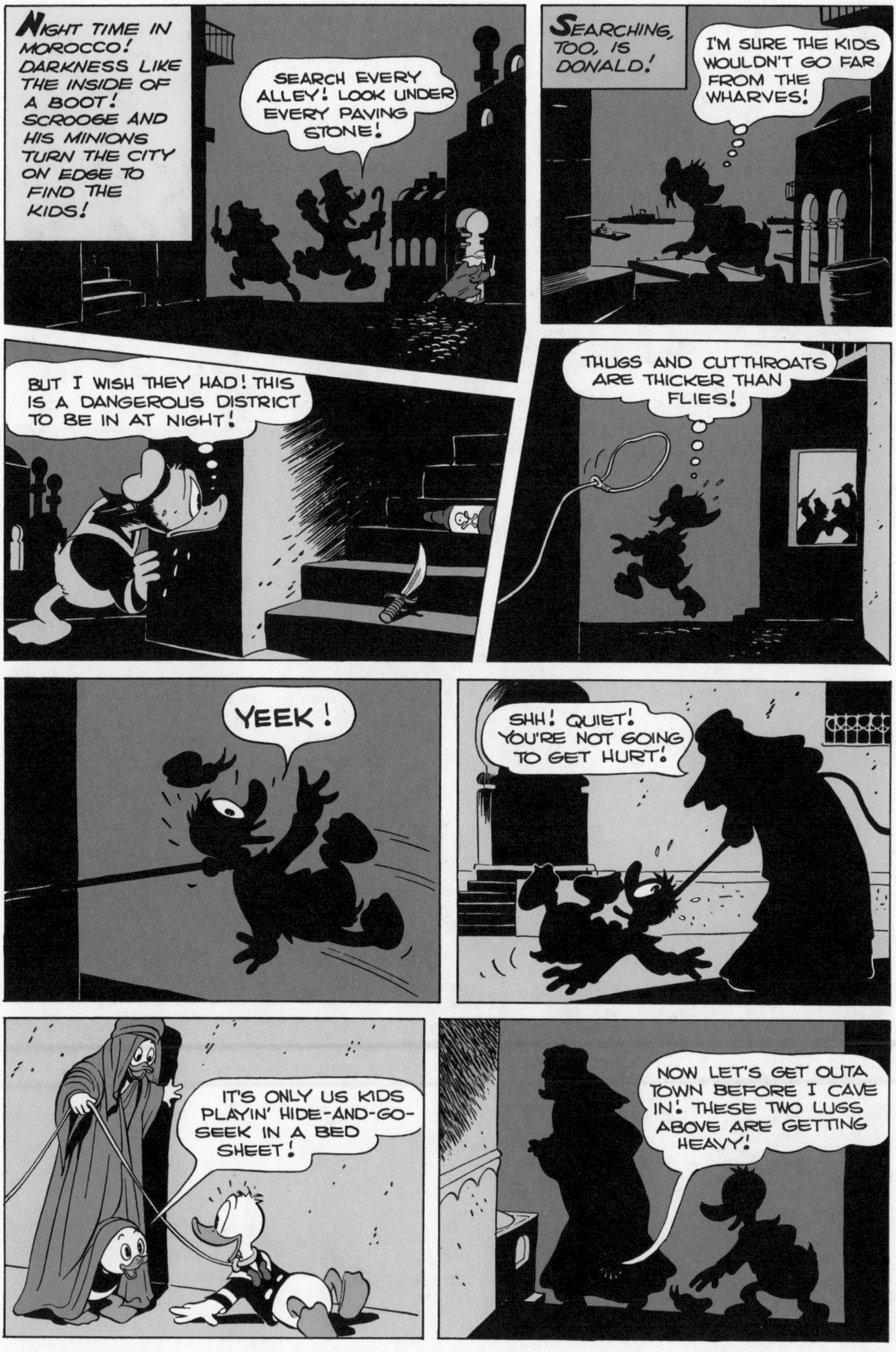

NIGHT TIME IN MOROCCO! DARKNESS LIKE THE INSIDE OF A BOOT! SCROOGE AND HIS MINIONS TURN THE CITY ON EDGE TO FIND THE KIDS!
SEARCH EVERY ALLEY! LOOK UNDER EVERY PAVING STONE!
SEARCHING, TOO, IS DONALD!
I'M SURE THE KIDS WOULDN'T GO FAR FROM THE WHARVES!
BUT I WISH THEY HAD! THIS IS A DANGEROUS DISTRICT TO BE IN AT NIGHT!
THUGS AND CUTTHROATS ARE THICKER THAN FLIES!
YEEK!
SHH! QUIET! YOU'RE NOT GOING TO GET HURT!
IT'S ONLY US KIDS PLAYIN' HIDE-AND-GO-SEEK IN A BED SHEET!
NOW LET'S GET OUTA TOWN BEFORE I CAVE IN! THESE TWO LUGS ABOVE ARE GETTING HEAVY!

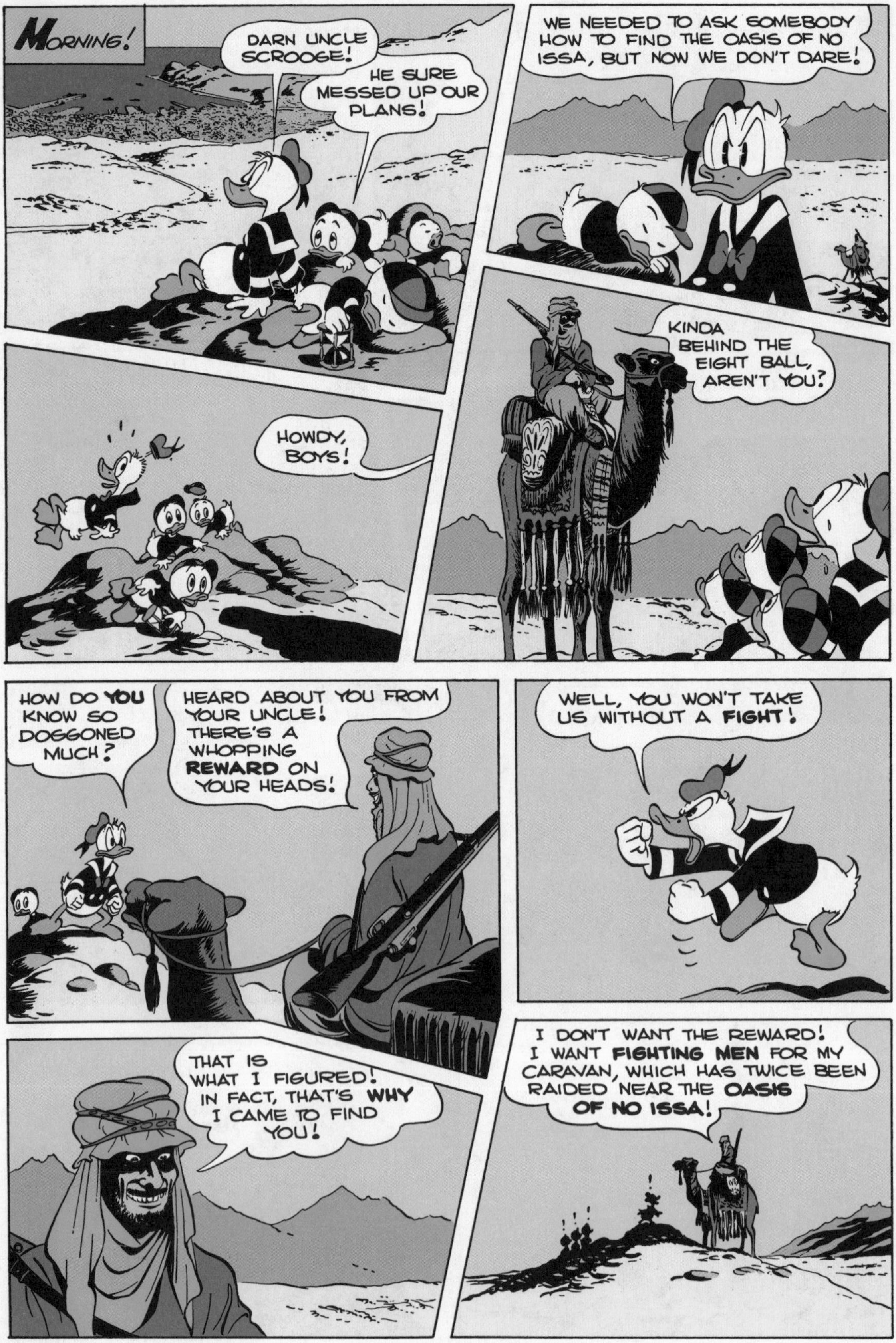
MORNING!
DARN UNCLE SCROOGE!
HE SURE MESSED UP OUR PLANS!
WE NEEDED TO ASK SOMEBODY HOW TO FIND THE OASIS OF NO ISSA, BUT NOW WE DON'T DARE!
HOWDY, BOYS!
KINDA BEHIND THE EIGHT BALL, AREN'T YOU?
HOW DO YOU KNOW SO DOGGONED MUCH?
HEARD ABOUT YOU FROM YOUR UNCLE! THERE'S A WHOPPING REWARD ON YOUR HEADS!
WELL, YOU WON'T TAKE US WITHOUT A FIGHT!
THAT IS WHAT I FIGURED! IN FACT, THAT'S WHY I CAME TO FIND YOU!
I DON'T WANT THE REWARD! I WANT FIGHTING MEN FOR MY CARAVAN, WHICH HAS TWICE BEEN RAIDED NEAR THE OASIS OF NO ISSA!

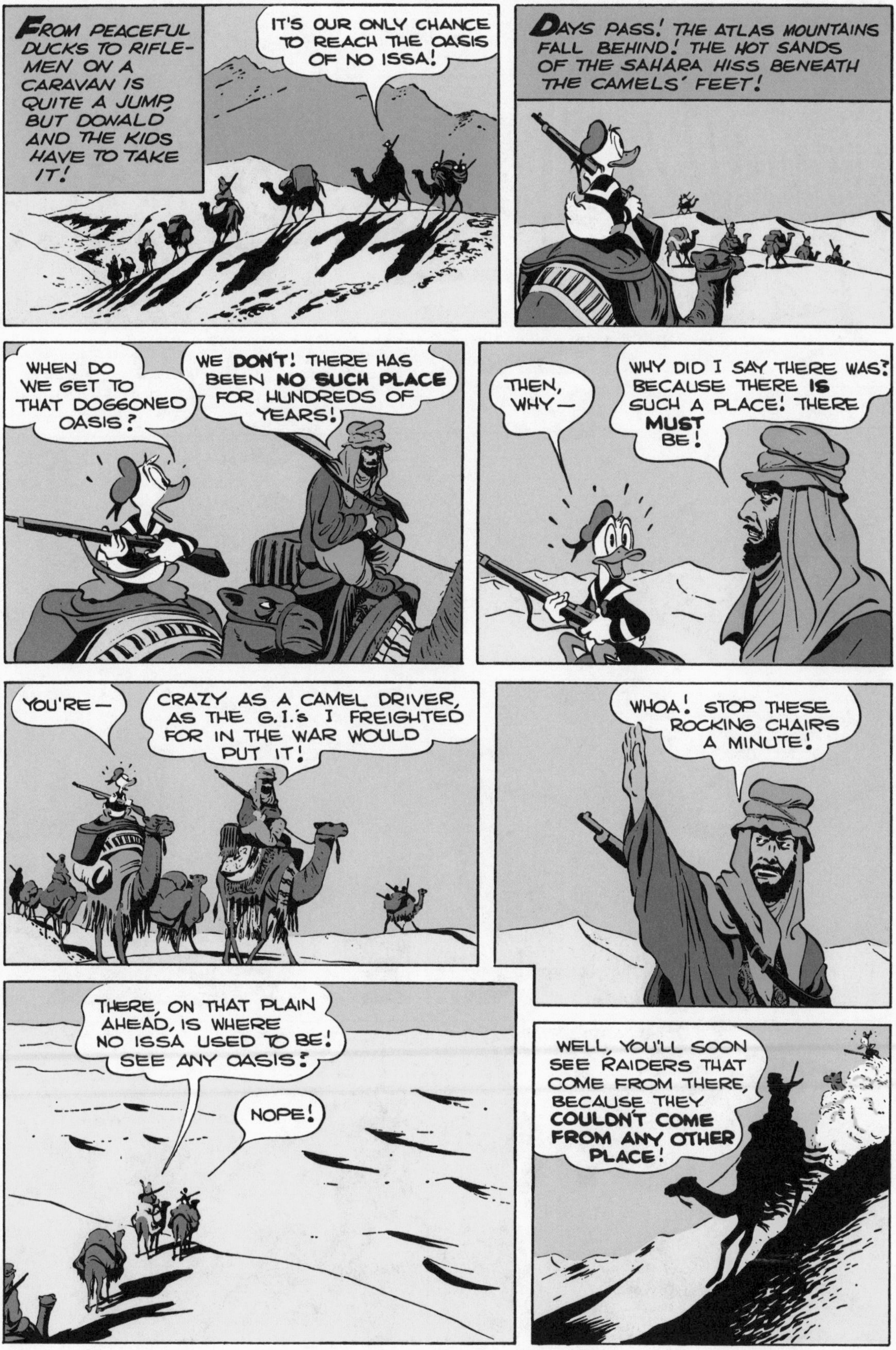
FROM PEACEFUL DUCKS TO RIFLEMEN ON A CARAVAN IS QUITE A JUMP, BUT DONALD AND THE KIDS HAVE TO TAKE IT!
IT'S OUR ONLY CHANCE TO REACH THE OASIS OF NO ISSA!
DAYS PASS! THE ATLAS MOUNTAINS FALL BEHIND! THE HOT SANDS OF THE SAHARA HISS BENEATH THE CAMELS' FEET!
WHEN DO WE GET TO THAT DOGGONED OASIS?
WE **DON'T**! THERE HAS BEEN **NO SUCH PLACE** FOR HUNDREDS OF YEARS!
THEN, WHY—
WHY DID I SAY THERE WAS? BECAUSE THERE **IS** SUCH A PLACE! THERE **MUST** BE!
YOU'RE—
CRAZY AS A CAMEL DRIVER, AS THE G.I.'s I FREIGHTED FOR IN THE WAR WOULD PUT IT!
WHOA! STOP THESE ROCKING CHAIRS A MINUTE!
THERE, ON THAT PLAIN AHEAD, IS WHERE NO ISSA USED TO BE! SEE ANY OASIS?
NOPE!
WELL, YOU'LL SOON SEE RAIDERS THAT COME FROM THERE, BECAUSE THEY **COULDN'T COME FROM ANY OTHER PLACE**!

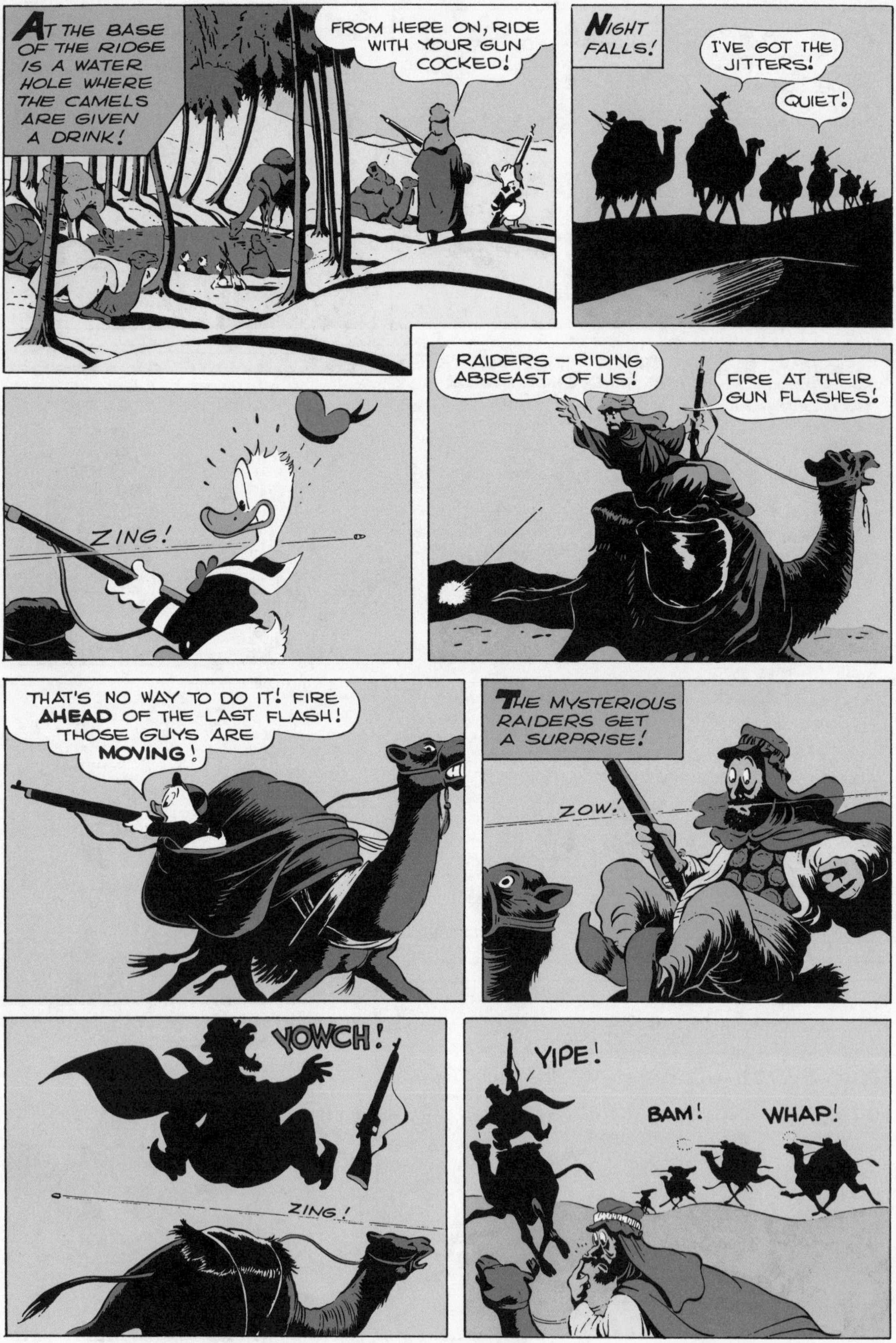
AT THE BASE OF THE RIDGE IS A WATER HOLE WHERE THE CAMELS ARE GIVEN A DRINK!
FROM HERE ON, RIDE WITH YOUR GUN COCKED!
NIGHT FALLS!
I'VE GOT THE JITTERS!
QUIET!
ZING!
RAIDERS — RIDING ABREAST OF US!
FIRE AT THEIR GUN FLASHES!
THAT'S NO WAY TO DO IT! FIRE AHEAD OF THE LAST FLASH! THOSE GUYS ARE MOVING!
THE MYSTERIOUS RAIDERS GET A SURPRISE!
ZOW!
YOWCH!
ZING!
YIPE!
BAM!
WHAP!

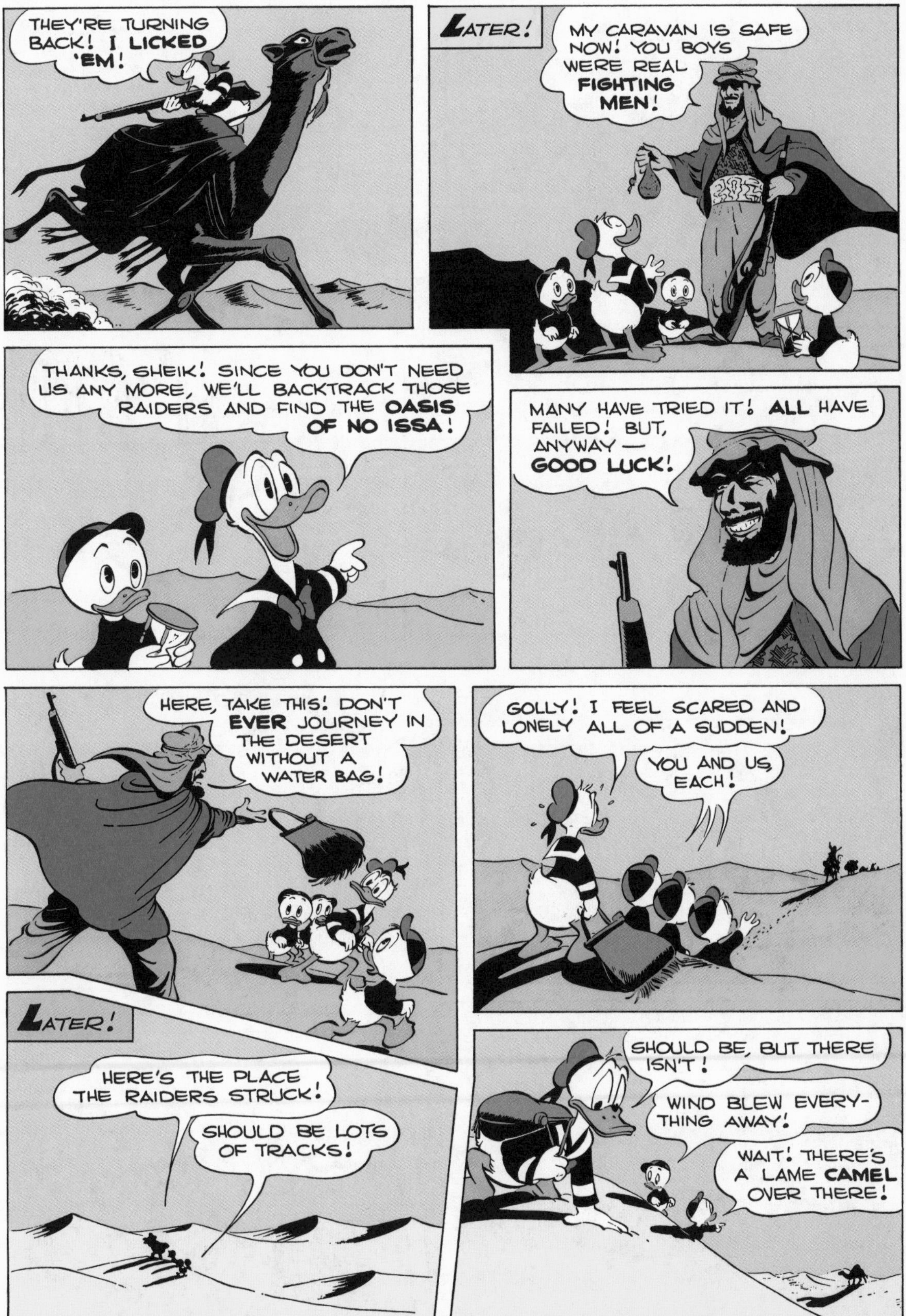
THEY'RE TURNING BACK! I LICKED 'EM!
LATER!
MY CARAVAN IS SAFE NOW! YOU BOYS WERE REAL FIGHTING MEN!
THANKS, SHEIK! SINCE YOU DON'T NEED US ANY MORE, WE'LL BACKTRACK THOSE RAIDERS AND FIND THE OASIS OF NO ISSA!
MANY HAVE TRIED IT! ALL HAVE FAILED! BUT, ANYWAY — GOOD LUCK!
HERE, TAKE THIS! DON'T EVER JOURNEY IN THE DESERT WITHOUT A WATER BAG!
GOLLY! I FEEL SCARED AND LONELY ALL OF A SUDDEN!
YOU AND US, EACH!
LATER!
HERE'S THE PLACE THE RAIDERS STRUCK!
SHOULD BE LOTS OF TRACKS!
SHOULD BE, BUT THERE ISN'T!
WIND BLEW EVERYTHING AWAY!
WAIT! THERE'S A LAME CAMEL OVER THERE!

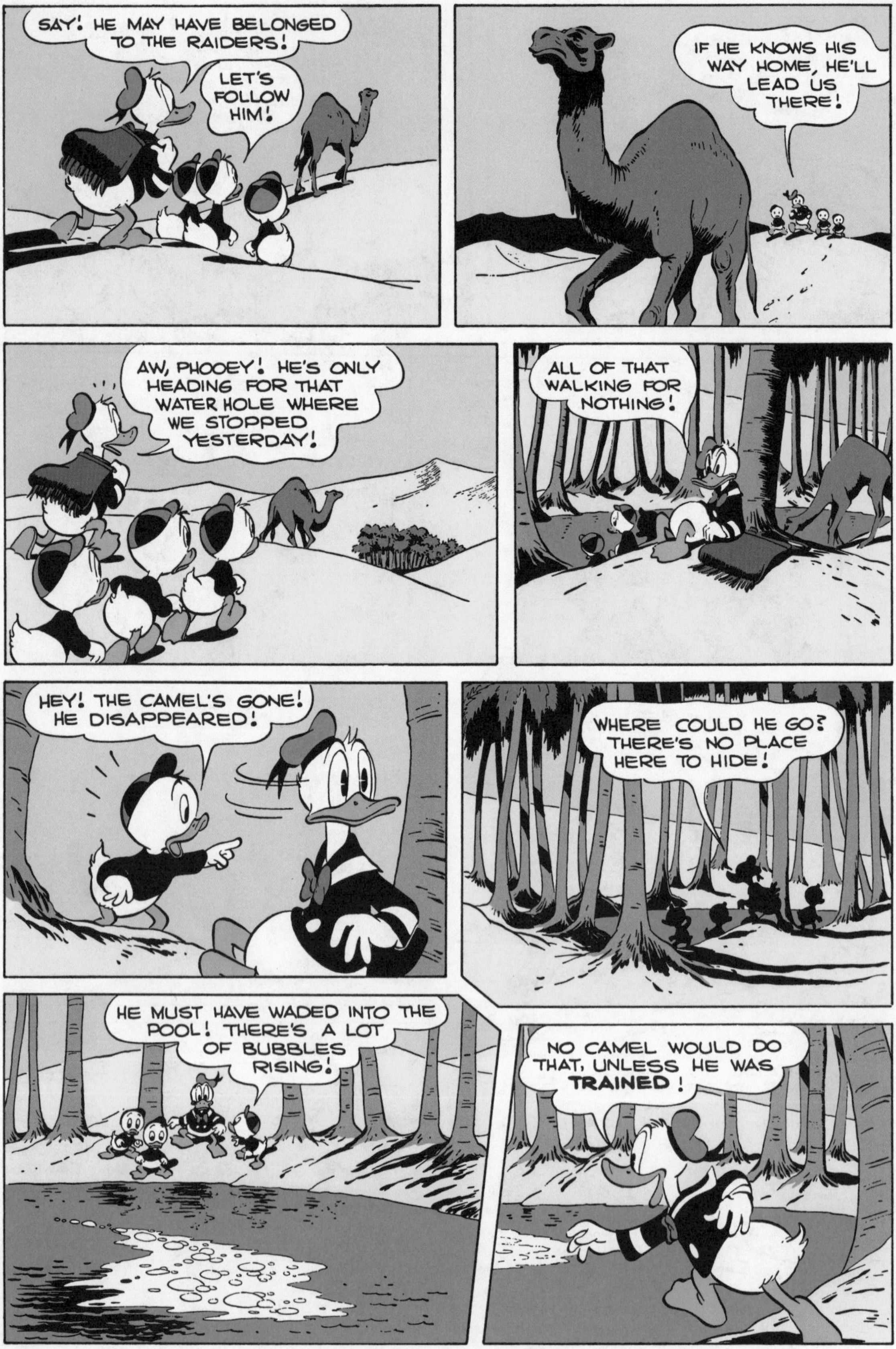
SAY! HE MAY HAVE BELONGED TO THE RAIDERS!
LET'S FOLLOW HIM!
IF HE KNOWS HIS WAY HOME, HE'LL LEAD US THERE!
AW, PHOOEY! HE'S ONLY HEADING FOR THAT WATER HOLE WHERE WE STOPPED YESTERDAY!
ALL OF THAT WALKING FOR NOTHING!
HEY! THE CAMEL'S GONE! HE DISAPPEARED!
WHERE COULD HE GO? THERE'S NO PLACE HERE TO HIDE!
HE MUST HAVE WADED INTO THE POOL! THERE'S A LOT OF BUBBLES RISING!
NO CAMEL WOULD DO THAT, UNLESS HE WAS **TRAINED**!

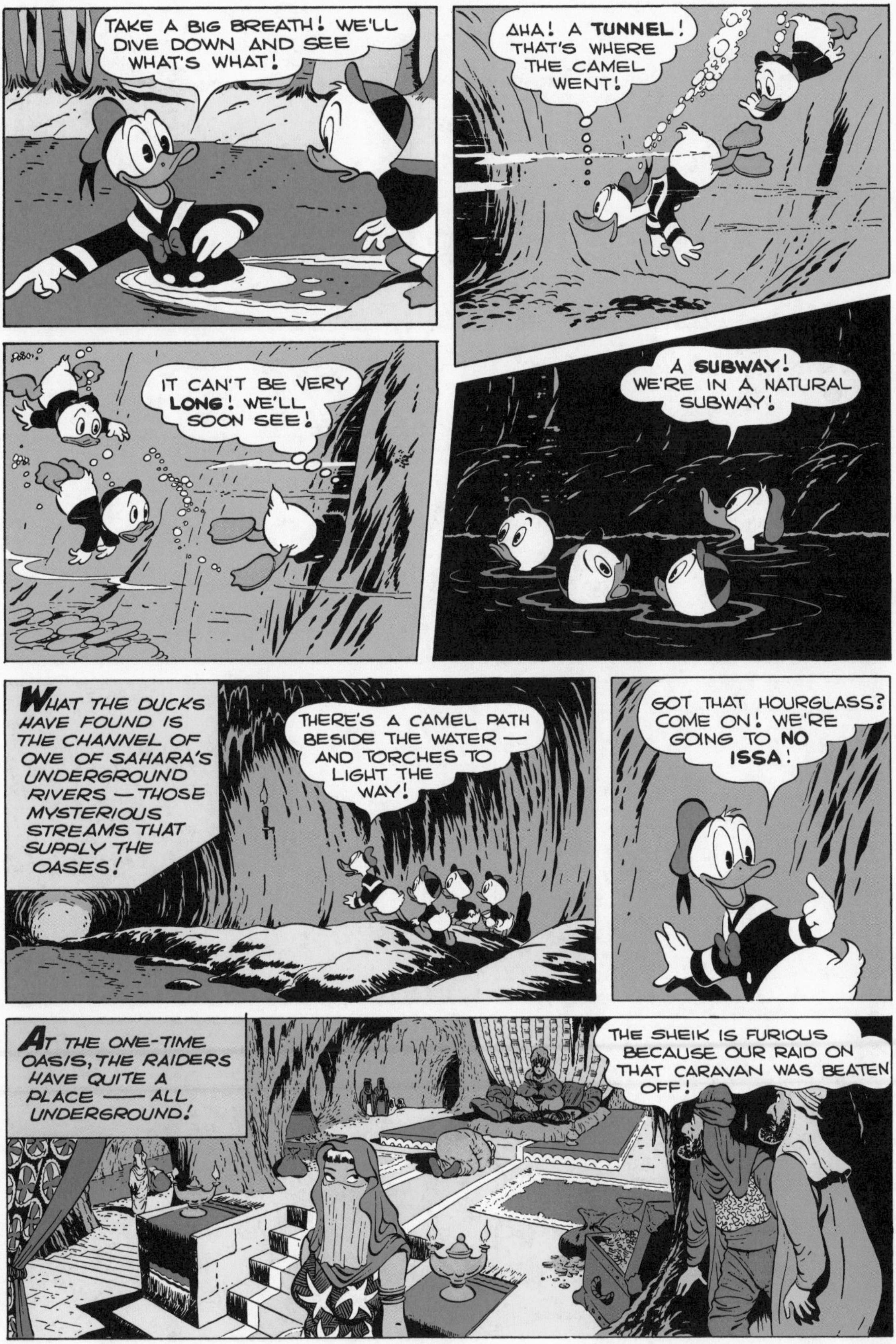
TAKE A BIG BREATH! WE'LL DIVE DOWN AND SEE WHAT'S WHAT!
AHA! A TUNNEL! THAT'S WHERE THE CAMEL WENT!
IT CAN'T BE VERY LONG! WE'LL SOON SEE!
A SUBWAY! WE'RE IN A NATURAL SUBWAY!
WHAT THE DUCKS HAVE FOUND IS THE CHANNEL OF ONE OF SAHARA'S UNDERGROUND RIVERS — THOSE MYSTERIOUS STREAMS THAT SUPPLY THE OASES!
THERE'S A CAMEL PATH BESIDE THE WATER — AND TORCHES TO LIGHT THE WAY!
GOT THAT HOURGLASS? COME ON! WE'RE GOING TO NO ISSA!
AT THE ONE-TIME OASIS, THE RAIDERS HAVE QUITE A PLACE — ALL UNDERGROUND!
THE SHEIK IS FURIOUS BECAUSE OUR RAID ON THAT CARAVAN WAS BEATEN OFF!

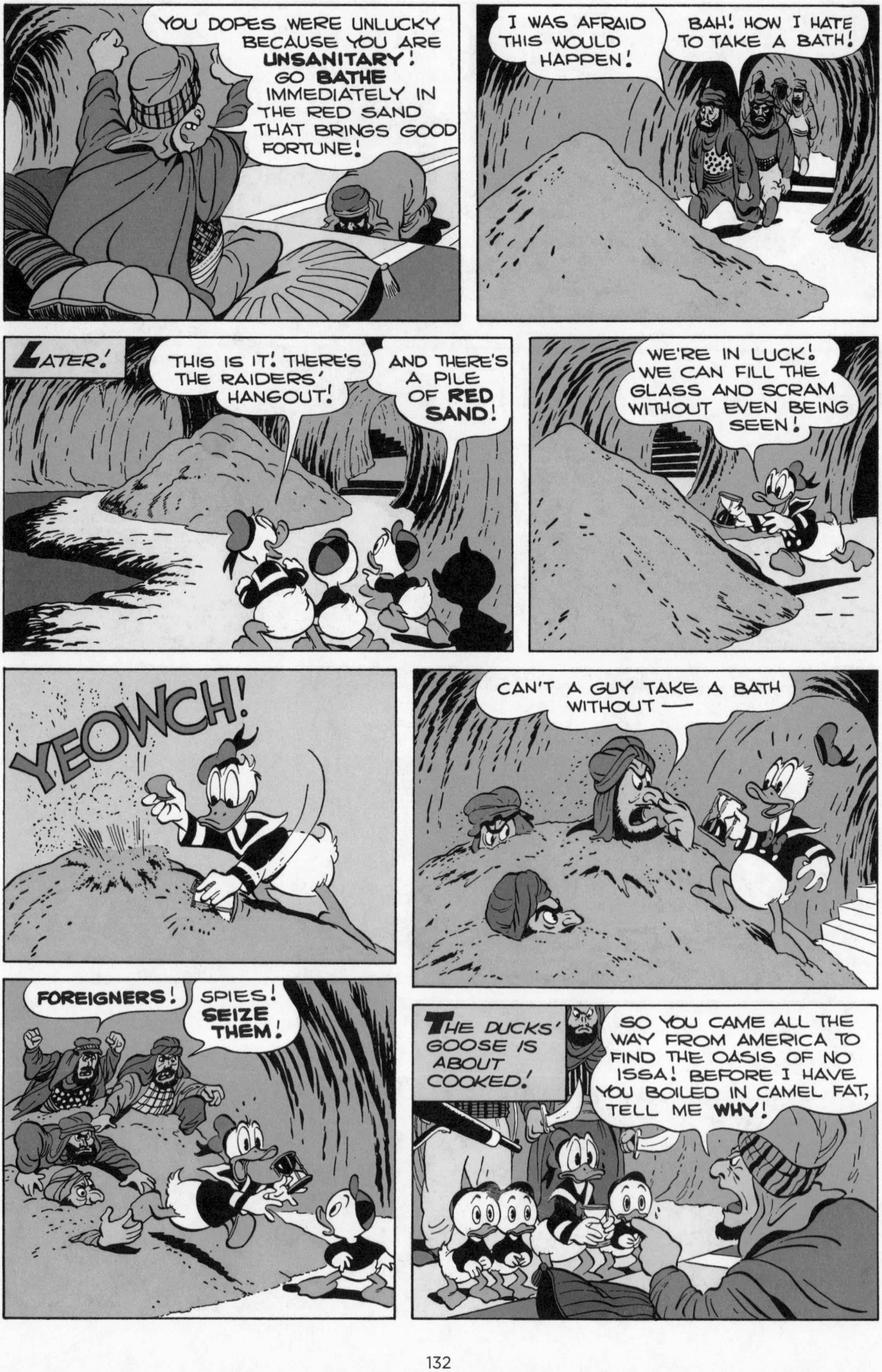
YOU DOPES WERE UNLUCKY BECAUSE YOU ARE UNSANITARY! GO BATHE IMMEDIATELY IN THE RED SAND THAT BRINGS GOOD FORTUNE!
I WAS AFRAID THIS WOULD HAPPEN!
BAH! HOW I HATE TO TAKE A BATH!
LATER!
THIS IS IT! THERE'S THE RAIDERS' HANGOUT!
AND THERE'S A PILE OF RED SAND!
WE'RE IN LUCK! WE CAN FILL THE GLASS AND SCRAM WITHOUT EVEN BEING SEEN!
YEOWCH!
CAN'T A GUY TAKE A BATH WITHOUT —
FOREIGNERS!
SPIES! SEIZE THEM!
THE DUCKS' GOOSE IS ABOUT COOKED!
SO YOU CAME ALL THE WAY FROM AMERICA TO FIND THE OASIS OF NO ISSA! BEFORE I HAVE YOU BOILED IN CAMEL FAT, TELL ME WHY!

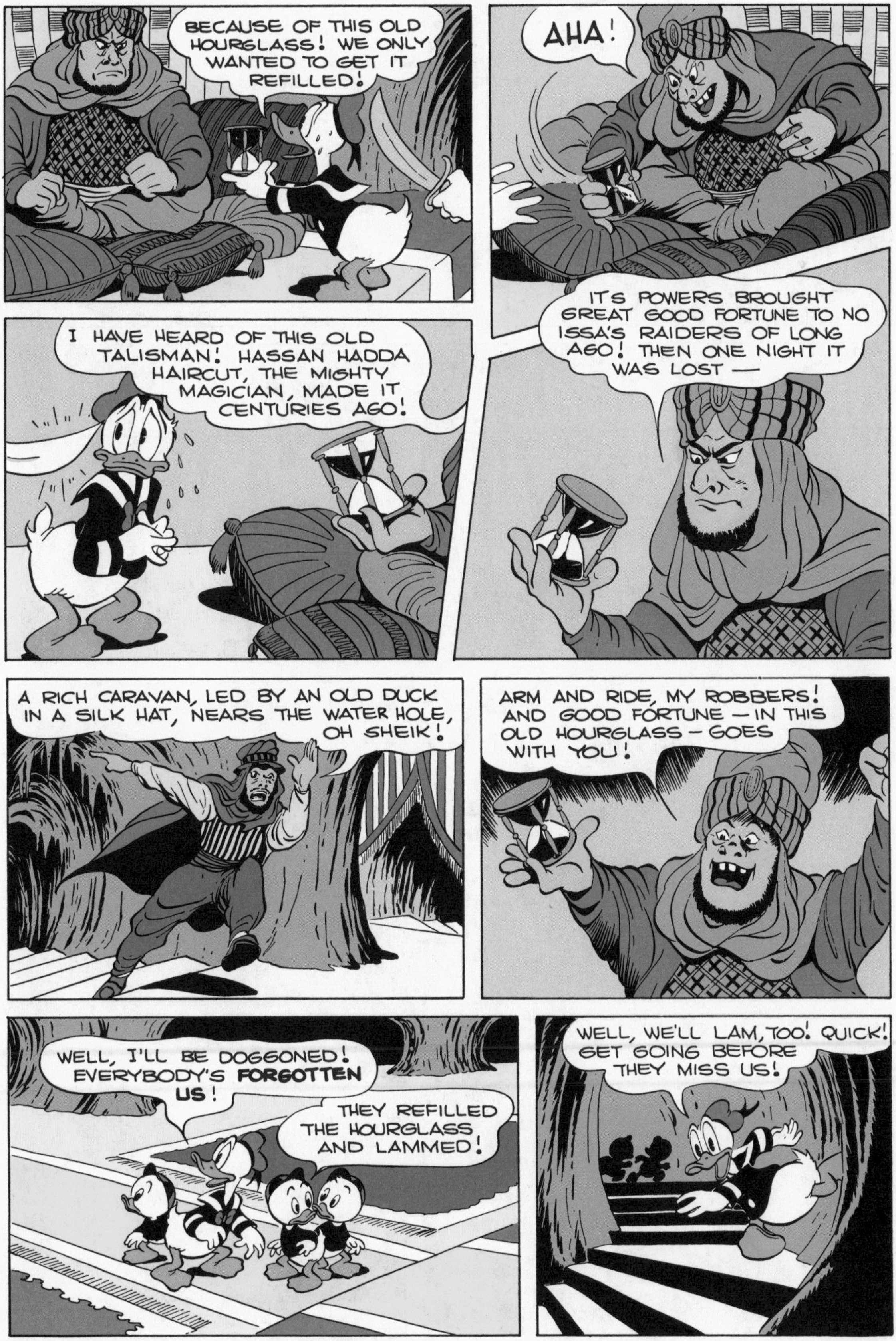
BECAUSE OF THIS OLD HOURGLASS! WE ONLY WANTED TO GET IT REFILLED!
AHA!
I HAVE HEARD OF THIS OLD TALISMAN! HASSAN HADDA HAIRCUT, THE MIGHTY MAGICIAN, MADE IT CENTURIES AGO!
IT'S POWERS BROUGHT GREAT GOOD FORTUNE TO NO ISSA'S RAIDERS OF LONG AGO! THEN ONE NIGHT IT WAS LOST —
A RICH CARAVAN, LED BY AN OLD DUCK IN A SILK HAT, NEARS THE WATER HOLE, OH SHEIK!
ARM AND RIDE, MY ROBBERS! AND GOOD FORTUNE — IN THIS OLD HOURGLASS — GOES WITH YOU!
WELL, I'LL BE DOGGONED! EVERYBODY'S **FORGOTTEN US**!
THEY REFILLED THE HOURGLASS AND LAMMED!
WELL, WE'LL LAM, TOO! QUICK! GET GOING BEFORE THEY MISS US!

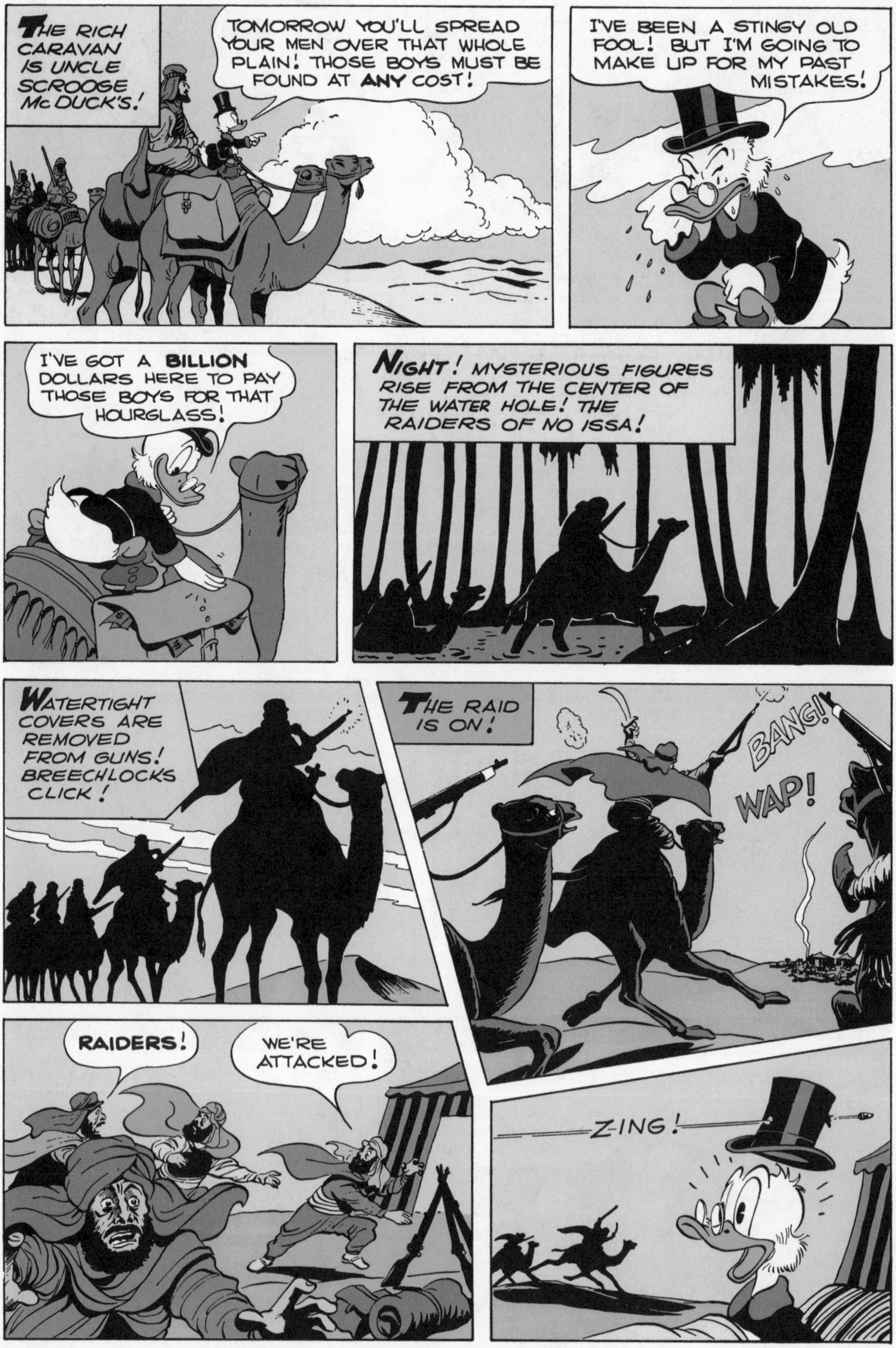
THE RICH CARAVAN IS UNCLE SCROOGE McDUCK'S!
TOMORROW YOU'LL SPREAD YOUR MEN OVER THAT WHOLE PLAIN! THOSE BOYS MUST BE FOUND AT ANY COST!
I'VE BEEN A STINGY OLD FOOL! BUT I'M GOING TO MAKE UP FOR MY PAST MISTAKES!
I'VE GOT A BILLION DOLLARS HERE TO PAY THOSE BOYS FOR THAT HOURGLASS!
NIGHT! MYSTERIOUS FIGURES RISE FROM THE CENTER OF THE WATER HOLE! THE RAIDERS OF NO ISSA!
WATERTIGHT COVERS ARE REMOVED FROM GUNS! BREECHLOCKS CLICK!
THE RAID IS ON!
BANG!
WAP!
RAIDERS!
WE'RE ATTACKED!
ZING!

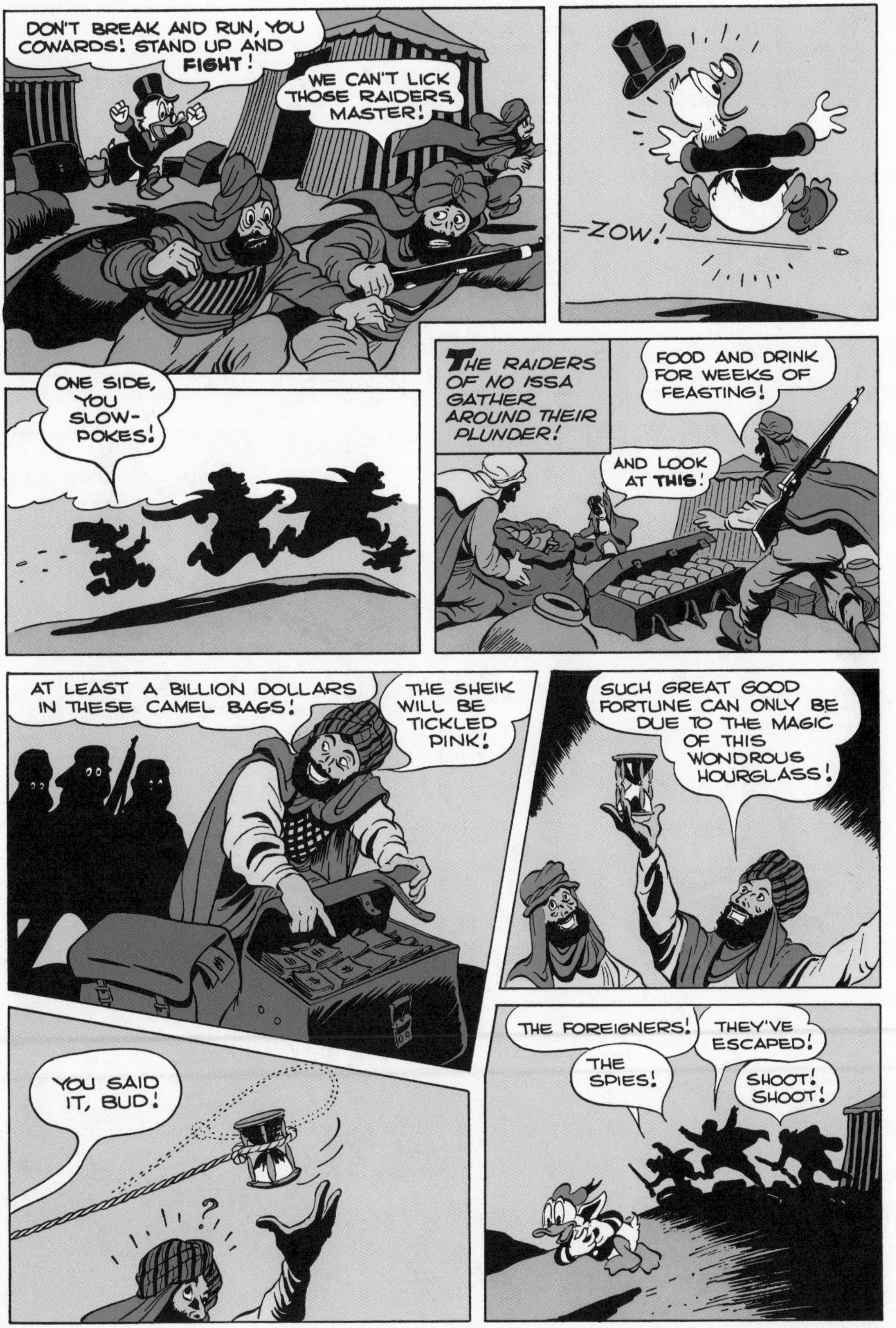
DON'T BREAK AND RUN, YOU COWARDS! STAND UP AND FIGHT!
WE CAN'T LICK THOSE RAIDERS, MASTER!
ZOW!
ONE SIDE, YOU SLOW-POKES!
THE RAIDERS OF NO ISSA GATHER AROUND THEIR PLUNDER!
FOOD AND DRINK FOR WEEKS OF FEASTING!
AND LOOK AT THIS!
AT LEAST A BILLION DOLLARS IN THESE CAMEL BAGS!
THE SHEIK WILL BE TICKLED PINK!
SUCH GREAT GOOD FORTUNE CAN ONLY BE DUE TO THE MAGIC OF THIS WONDROUS HOURGLASS!
YOU SAID IT, BUD!
THE FOREIGNERS!
THEY'VE ESCAPED!
THE SPIES!
SHOOT! SHOOT!

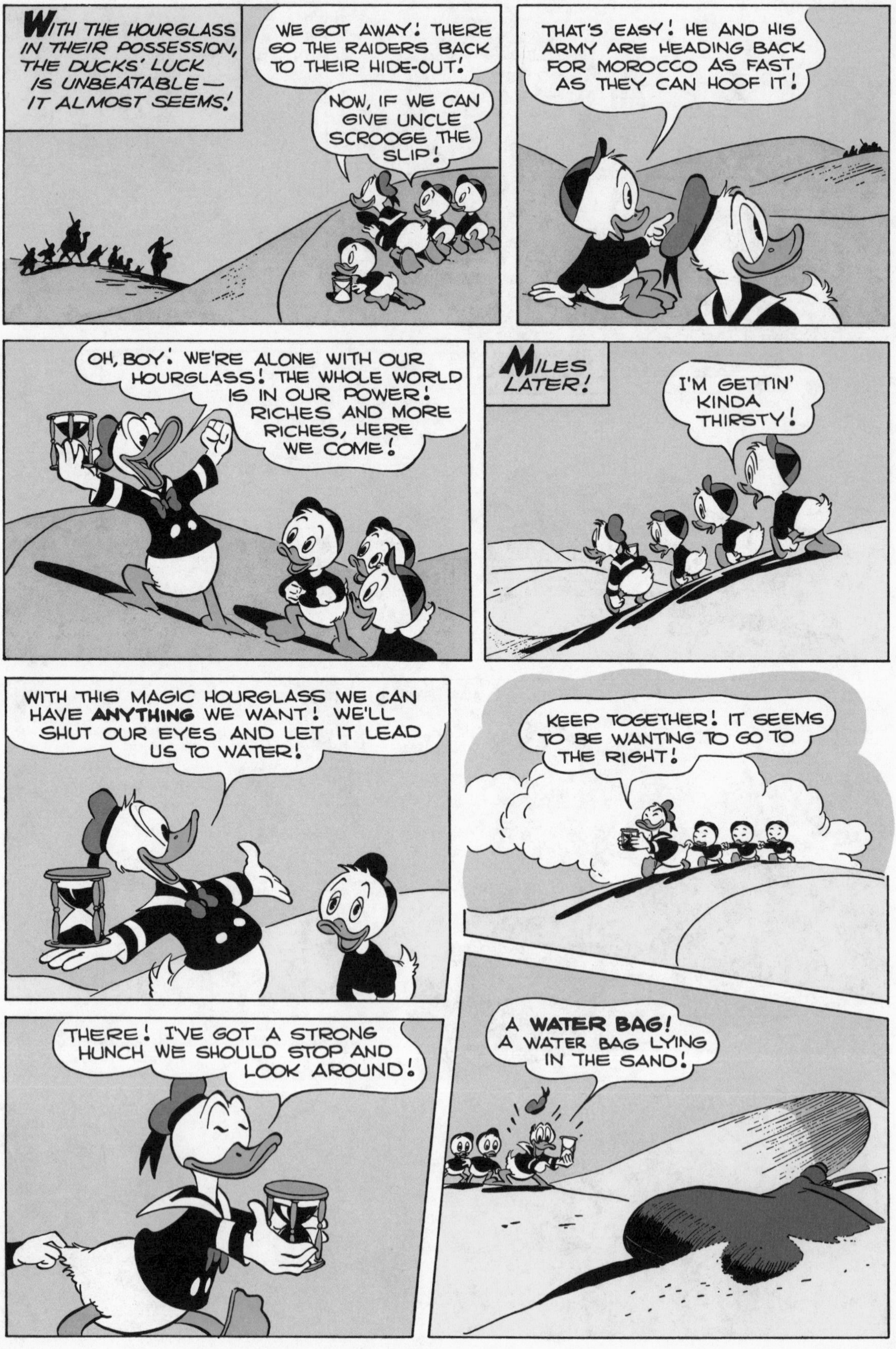
WITH THE HOURGLASS IN THEIR POSSESSION, THE DUCKS' LUCK IS UNBEATABLE— IT ALMOST SEEMS!
WE GOT AWAY! THERE GO THE RAIDERS BACK TO THEIR HIDE-OUT!
NOW, IF WE CAN GIVE UNCLE SCROOGE THE SLIP!
THAT'S EASY! HE AND HIS ARMY ARE HEADING BACK FOR MOROCCO AS FAST AS THEY CAN HOOF IT!
OH, BOY! WE'RE ALONE WITH OUR HOURGLASS! THE WHOLE WORLD IS IN OUR POWER! RICHES AND MORE RICHES, HERE WE COME!
MILES LATER!
I'M GETTIN' KINDA THIRSTY!
WITH THIS MAGIC HOURGLASS WE CAN HAVE **ANYTHING** WE WANT! WE'LL SHUT OUR EYES AND LET IT LEAD US TO WATER!
KEEP TOGETHER! IT SEEMS TO BE WANTING TO GO TO THE RIGHT!
THERE! I'VE GOT A STRONG HUNCH WE SHOULD STOP AND LOOK AROUND!
A **WATER BAG**! A WATER BAG LYING IN THE SAND!

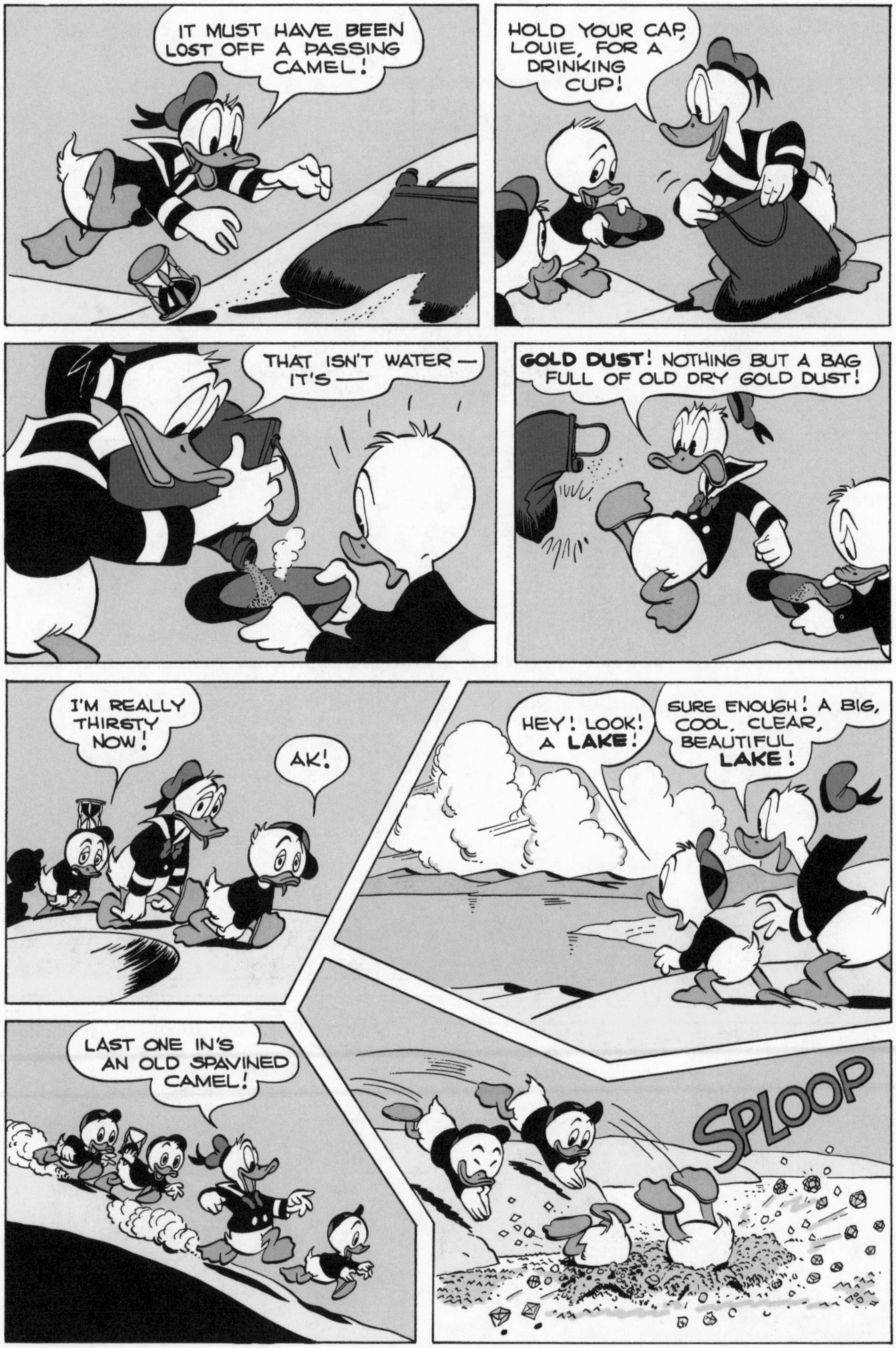
IT MUST HAVE BEEN LOST OFF A PASSING CAMEL!
HOLD YOUR CAP, LOUIE, FOR A DRINKING CUP!
THAT ISN'T WATER — IT'S —
GOLD DUST! NOTHING BUT A BAG FULL OF OLD DRY GOLD DUST!
I'M REALLY THIRSTY NOW!
AK!
HEY! LOOK! A LAKE!
SURE ENOUGH! A BIG, COOL, CLEAR, BEAUTIFUL LAKE!
LAST ONE IN'S AN OLD SPAVINED CAMEL!
SPLOOP

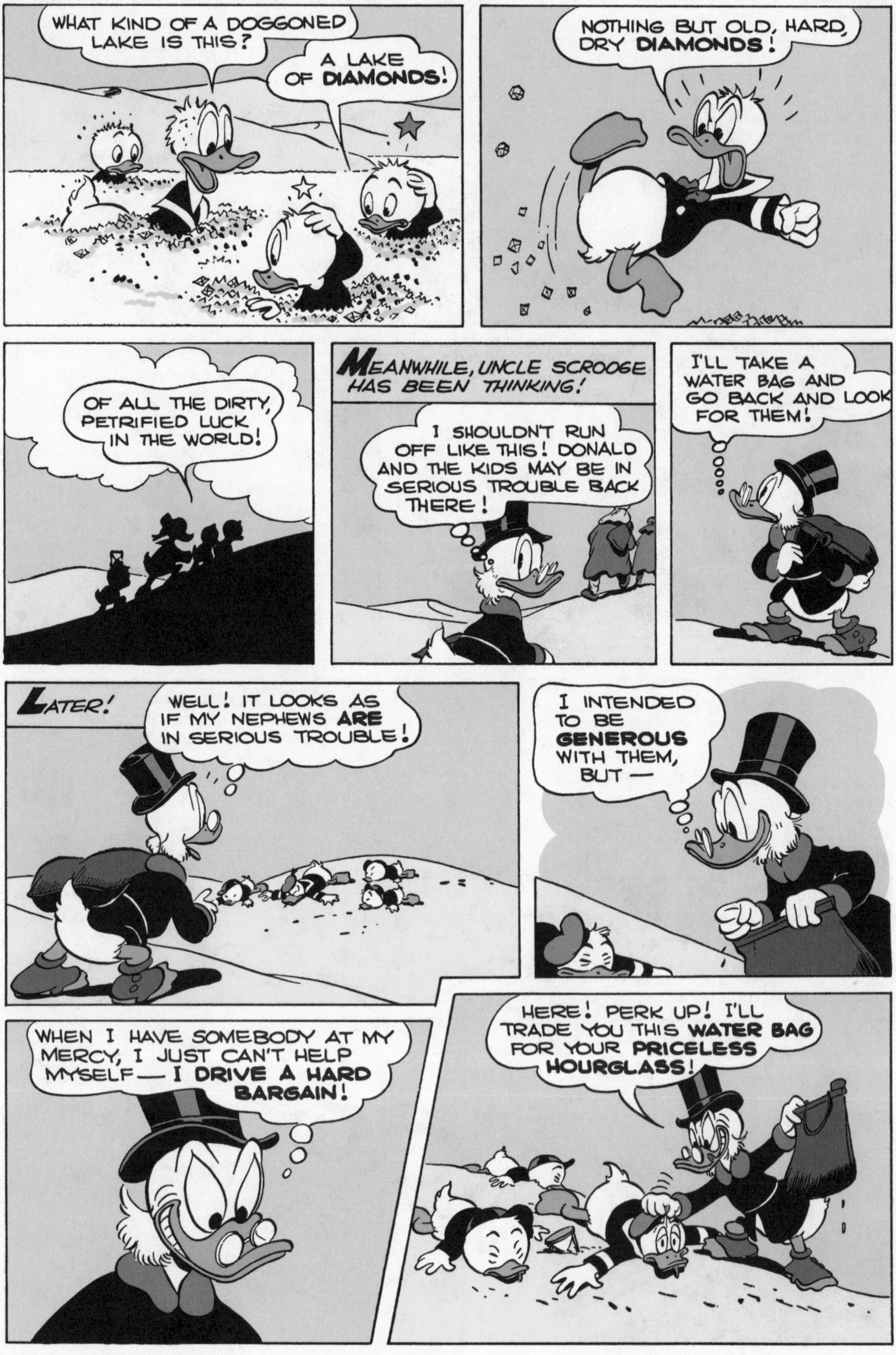
WHAT KIND OF A DOGGONED LAKE IS THIS?
A LAKE OF DIAMONDS!
NOTHING BUT OLD, HARD, DRY DIAMONDS!
OF ALL THE DIRTY, PETRIFIED LUCK IN THE WORLD!
MEANWHILE, UNCLE SCROOGE HAS BEEN THINKING!
I SHOULDN'T RUN OFF LIKE THIS! DONALD AND THE KIDS MAY BE IN SERIOUS TROUBLE BACK THERE!
I'LL TAKE A WATER BAG AND GO BACK AND LOOK FOR THEM!
LATER!
WELL! IT LOOKS AS IF MY NEPHEWS ARE IN SERIOUS TROUBLE!
I INTENDED TO BE GENEROUS WITH THEM, BUT —
WHEN I HAVE SOMEBODY AT MY MERCY, I JUST CAN'T HELP MYSELF — I DRIVE A HARD BARGAIN!
HERE! PERK UP! I'LL TRADE YOU THIS WATER BAG FOR YOUR PRICELESS HOURGLASS!

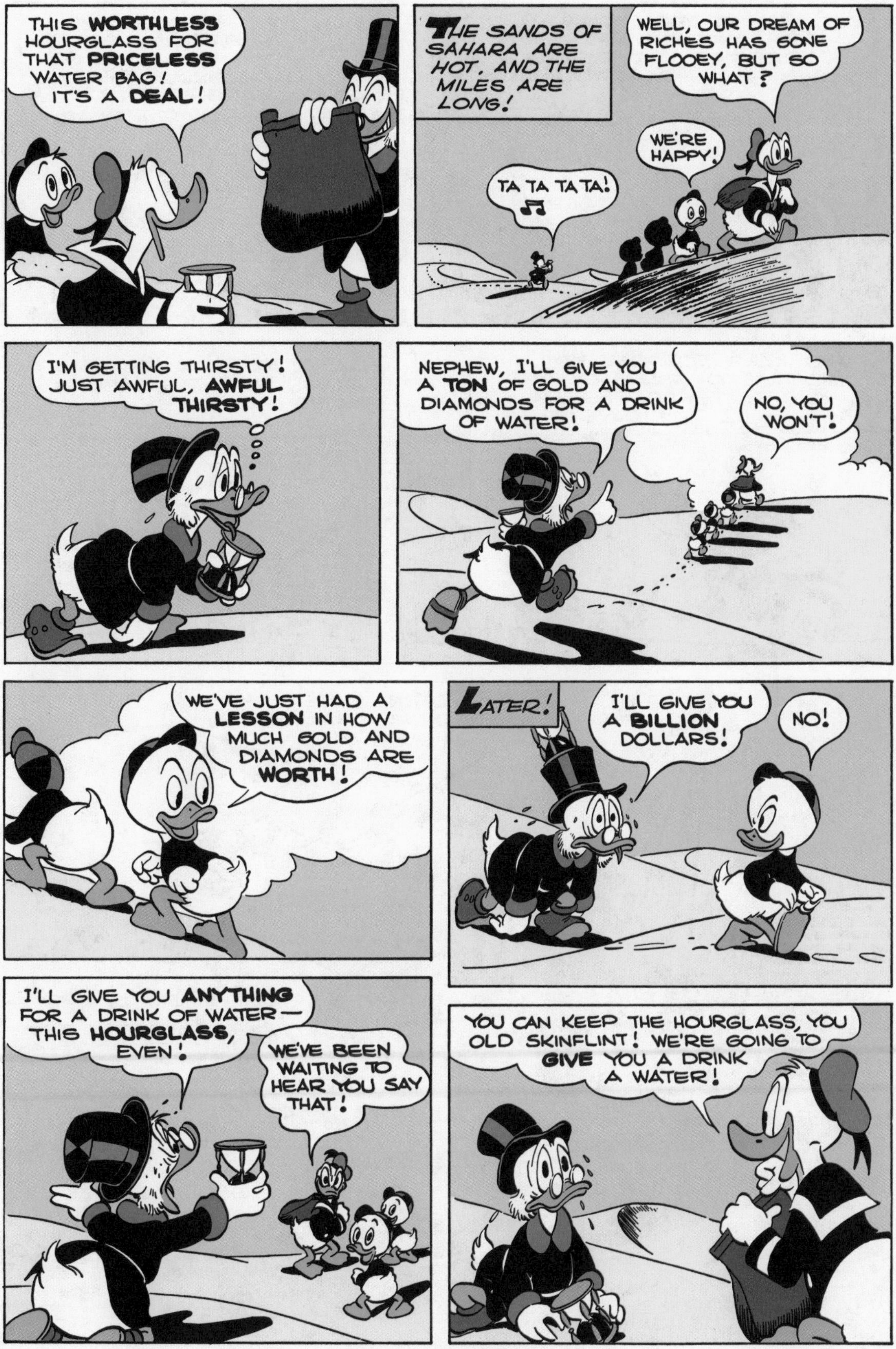
THIS WORTHLESS HOURGLASS FOR THAT PRICELESS WATER BAG! IT'S A DEAL!
THE SANDS OF SAHARA ARE HOT, AND THE MILES ARE LONG!
WELL, OUR DREAM OF RICHES HAS GONE FLOOEY, BUT SO WHAT?
WE'RE HAPPY!
TA TA TA TA!
I'M GETTING THIRSTY! JUST AWFUL, AWFUL THIRSTY!
NEPHEW, I'LL GIVE YOU A TON OF GOLD AND DIAMONDS FOR A DRINK OF WATER!
NO, YOU WON'T!
WE'VE JUST HAD A LESSON IN HOW MUCH GOLD AND DIAMONDS ARE WORTH!
LATER!
I'LL GIVE YOU A BILLION DOLLARS!
NO!
I'LL GIVE YOU ANYTHING FOR A DRINK OF WATER— THIS HOURGLASS, EVEN!
WE'VE BEEN WAITING TO HEAR YOU SAY THAT!
YOU CAN KEEP THE HOURGLASS, YOU OLD SKINFLINT! WE'RE GOING TO GIVE YOU A DRINK A WATER!

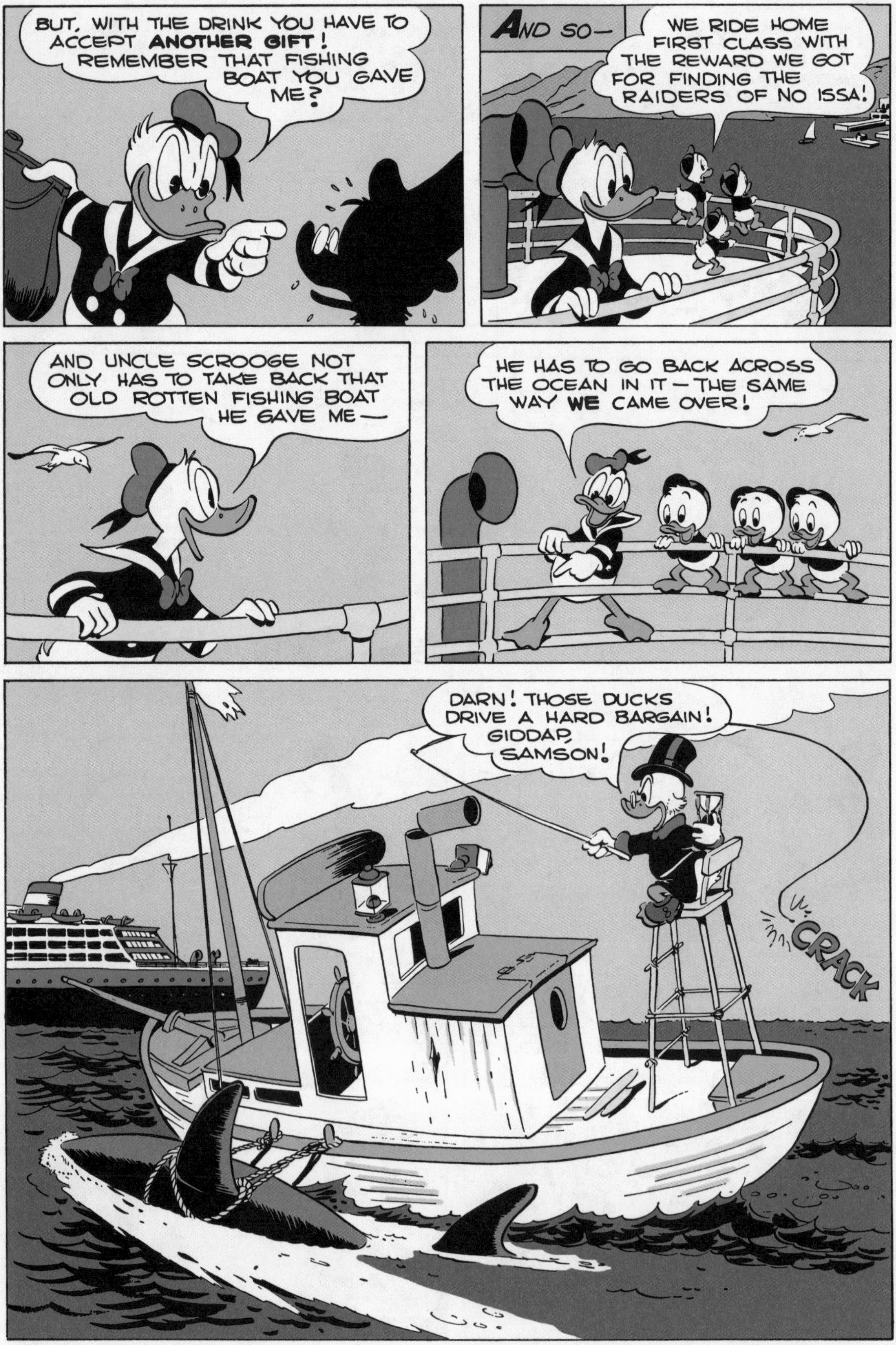
BUT, WITH THE DRINK YOU HAVE TO ACCEPT **ANOTHER GIFT**! REMEMBER THAT FISHING BOAT YOU GAVE ME?
AND SO—
WE RIDE HOME FIRST CLASS WITH THE REWARD WE GOT FOR FINDING THE RAIDERS OF NO ISSA!
AND UNCLE SCROOGE NOT ONLY HAS TO TAKE BACK THAT OLD ROTTEN FISHING BOAT HE GAVE ME—
HE HAS TO GO BACK ACROSS THE OCEAN IN IT—THE SAME WAY **WE** CAME OVER!
DARN! THOSE DUCKS DRIVE A HARD BARGAIN! GIDDAP, SAMSON!
CRACK

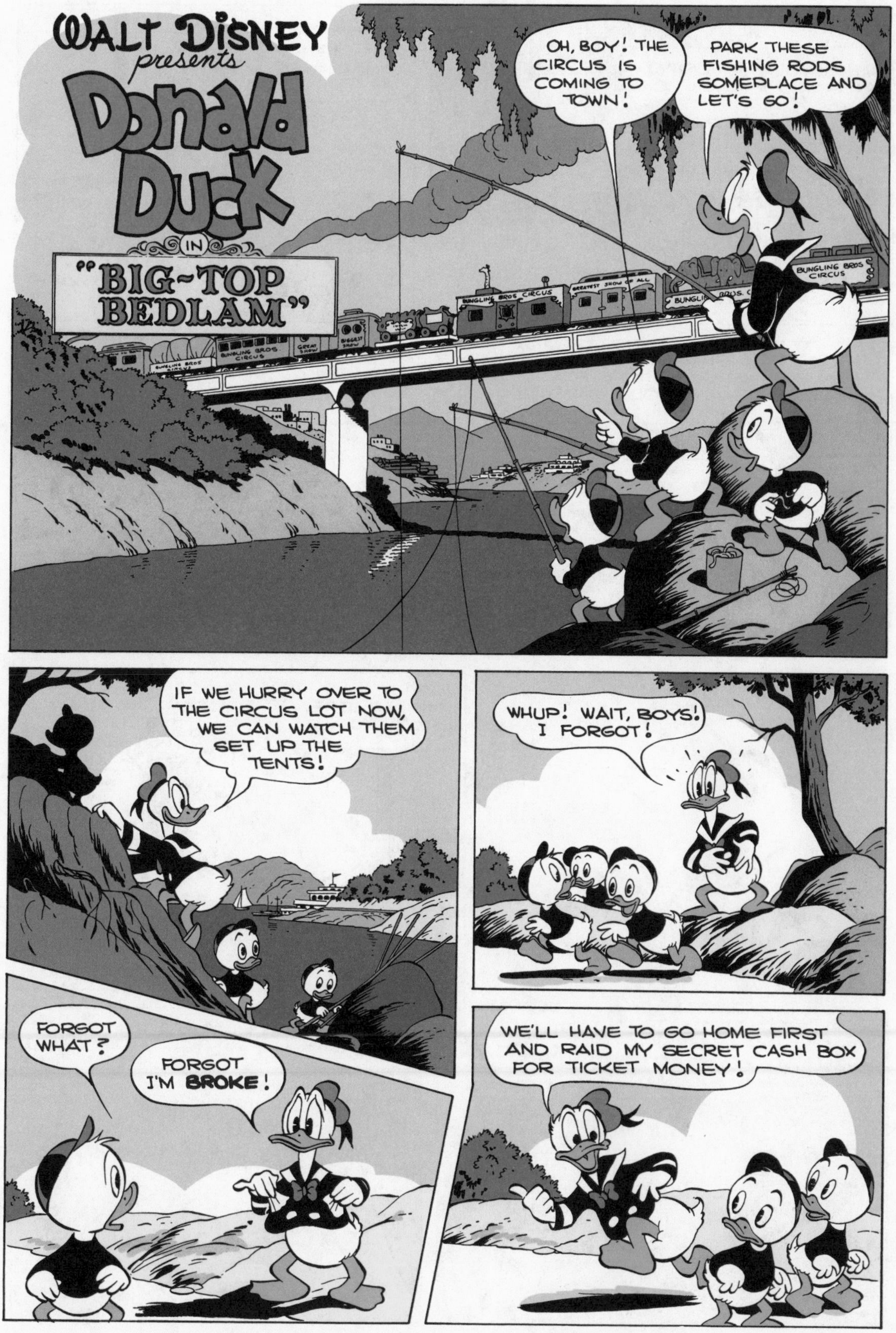
WALT DISNEY presents
Donald Duck
IN
"BIG-TOP BEDLAM"
OH, BOY! THE CIRCUS IS COMING TO TOWN!
PARK THESE FISHING RODS SOMEPLACE AND LET'S GO!
BUNGLING BROS CIRCUS
GREATEST SHOW OF ALL
IF WE HURRY OVER TO THE CIRCUS LOT NOW, WE CAN WATCH THEM SET UP THE TENTS!
WHUP! WAIT, BOYS! I FORGOT!
FORGOT WHAT?
FORGOT I'M **BROKE**!
WE'LL HAVE TO GO HOME FIRST AND RAID MY SECRET CASH BOX FOR TICKET MONEY!

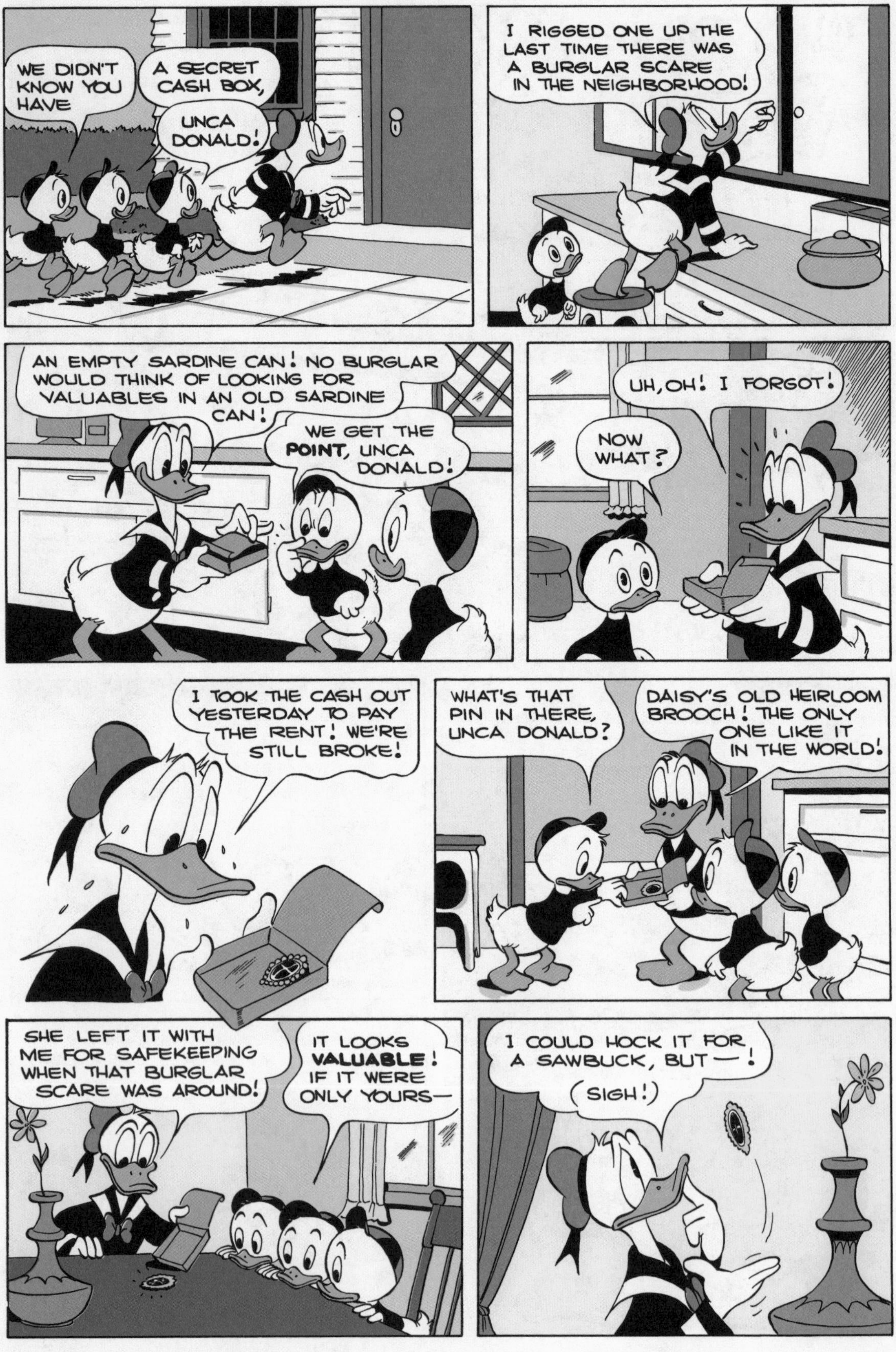
WE DIDN'T KNOW YOU HAVE
A SECRET CASH BOX,
UNCA DONALD!
I RIGGED ONE UP THE LAST TIME THERE WAS A BURGLAR SCARE IN THE NEIGHBORHOOD!
AN EMPTY SARDINE CAN! NO BURGLAR WOULD THINK OF LOOKING FOR VALUABLES IN AN OLD SARDINE CAN!
WE GET THE POINT, UNCA DONALD!
UH, OH! I FORGOT!
NOW WHAT?
I TOOK THE CASH OUT YESTERDAY TO PAY THE RENT! WE'RE STILL BROKE!
WHAT'S THAT PIN IN THERE, UNCA DONALD?
DAISY'S OLD HEIRLOOM BROOCH! THE ONLY ONE LIKE IT IN THE WORLD!
SHE LEFT IT WITH ME FOR SAFEKEEPING WHEN THAT BURGLAR SCARE WAS AROUND!
IT LOOKS VALUABLE! IF IT WERE ONLY YOURS—
I COULD HOCK IT FOR A SAWBUCK, BUT—!
(SIGH!)

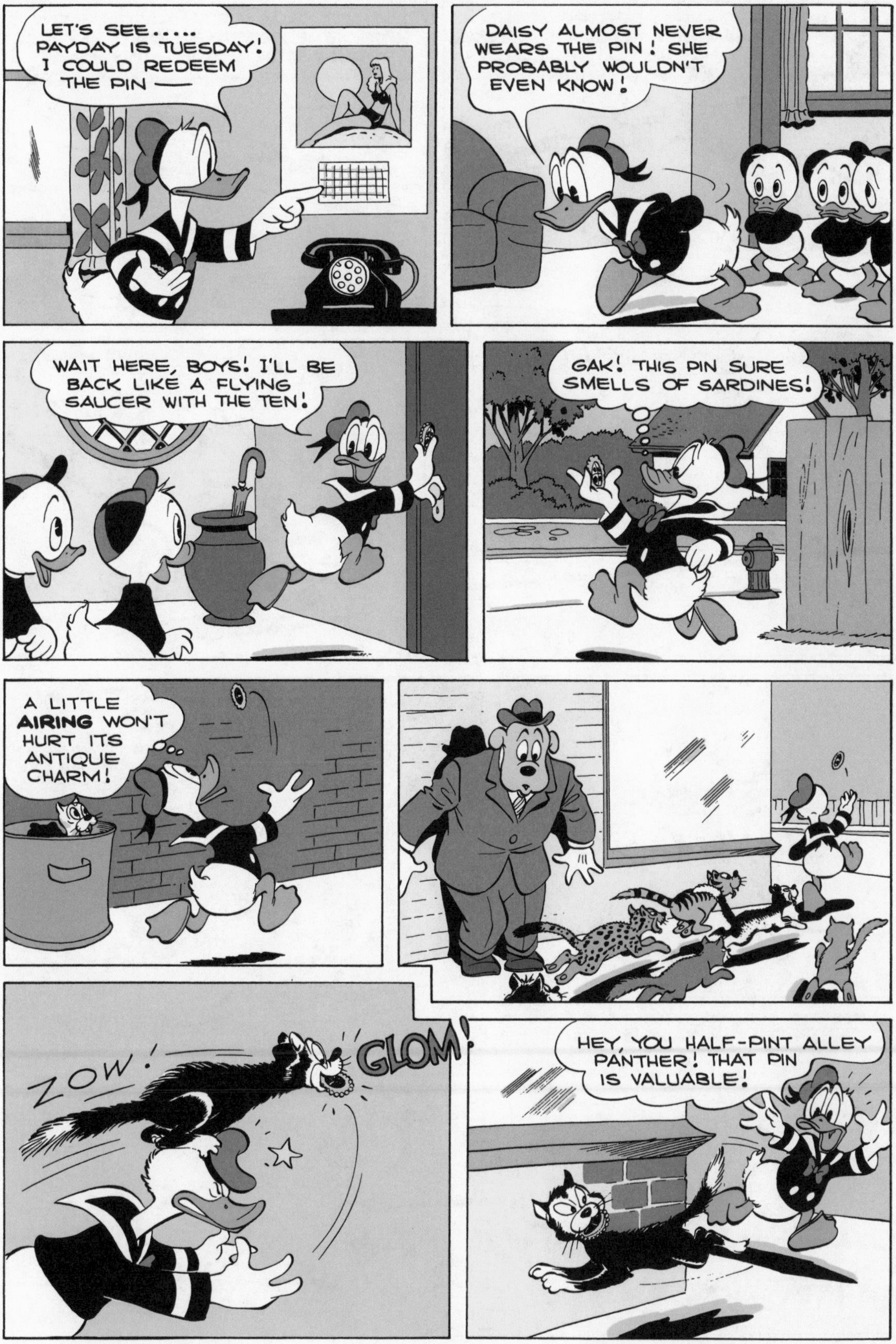
LET'S SEE..... PAYDAY IS TUESDAY! I COULD REDEEM THE PIN —
DAISY ALMOST NEVER WEARS THE PIN! SHE PROBABLY WOULDN'T EVEN KNOW!
WAIT HERE, BOYS! I'LL BE BACK LIKE A FLYING SAUCER WITH THE TEN!
GAK! THIS PIN SURE SMELLS OF SARDINES!
A LITTLE **AIRING** WON'T HURT ITS ANTIQUE CHARM!
ZOW!
GLOM!
HEY, YOU HALF-PINT ALLEY PANTHER! THAT PIN IS VALUABLE!

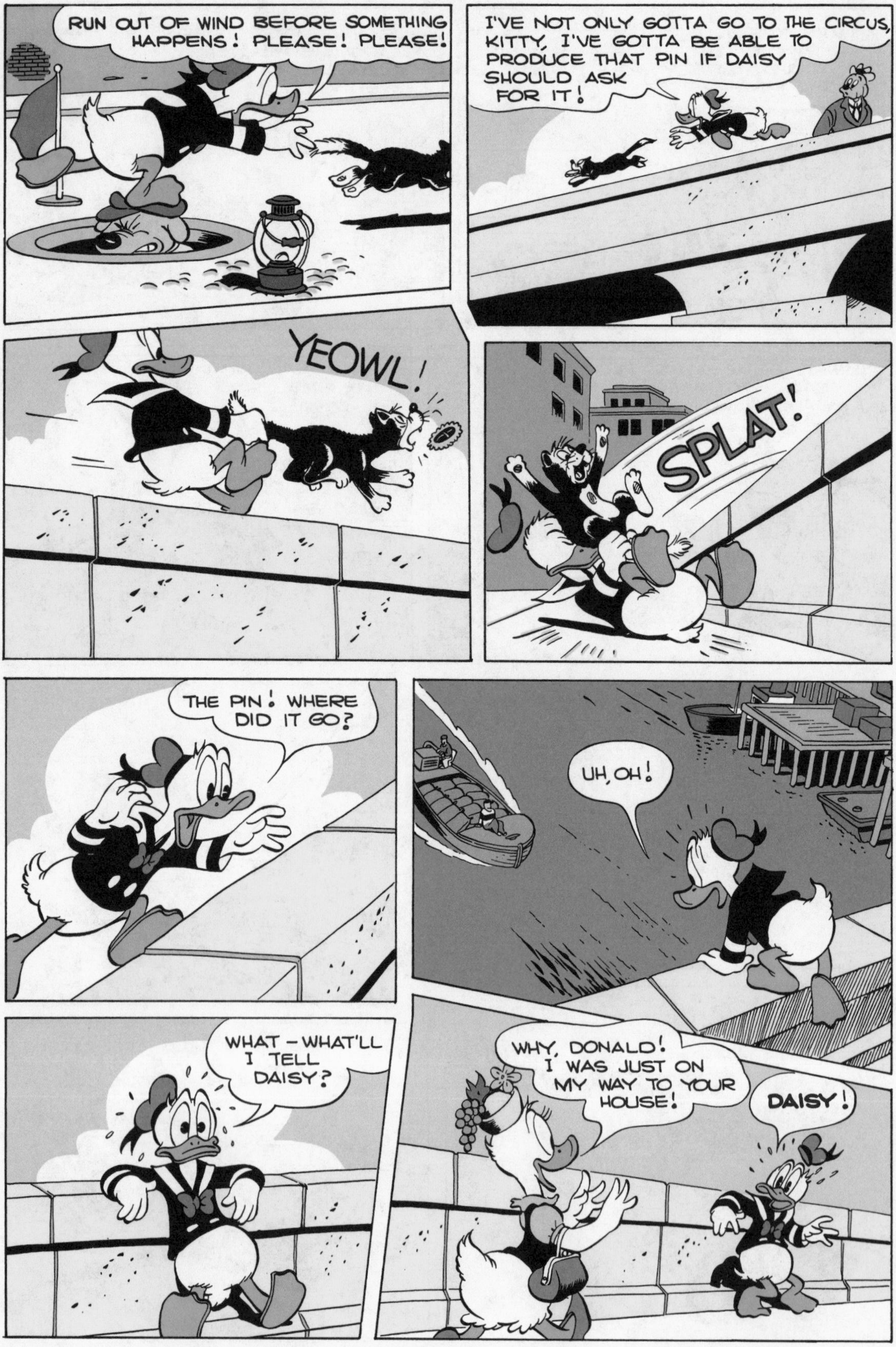
RUN OUT OF WIND BEFORE SOMETHING HAPPENS! PLEASE! PLEASE!
I'VE NOT ONLY GOTTA GO TO THE CIRCUS, KITTY, I'VE GOTTA BE ABLE TO PRODUCE THAT PIN IF DAISY SHOULD ASK FOR IT!
YEOWL!
SPLAT!
THE PIN! WHERE DID IT GO?
UH, OH!
WHAT - WHAT'LL I TELL DAISY?
WHY, DONALD! I WAS JUST ON MY WAY TO YOUR HOUSE!
DAISY!

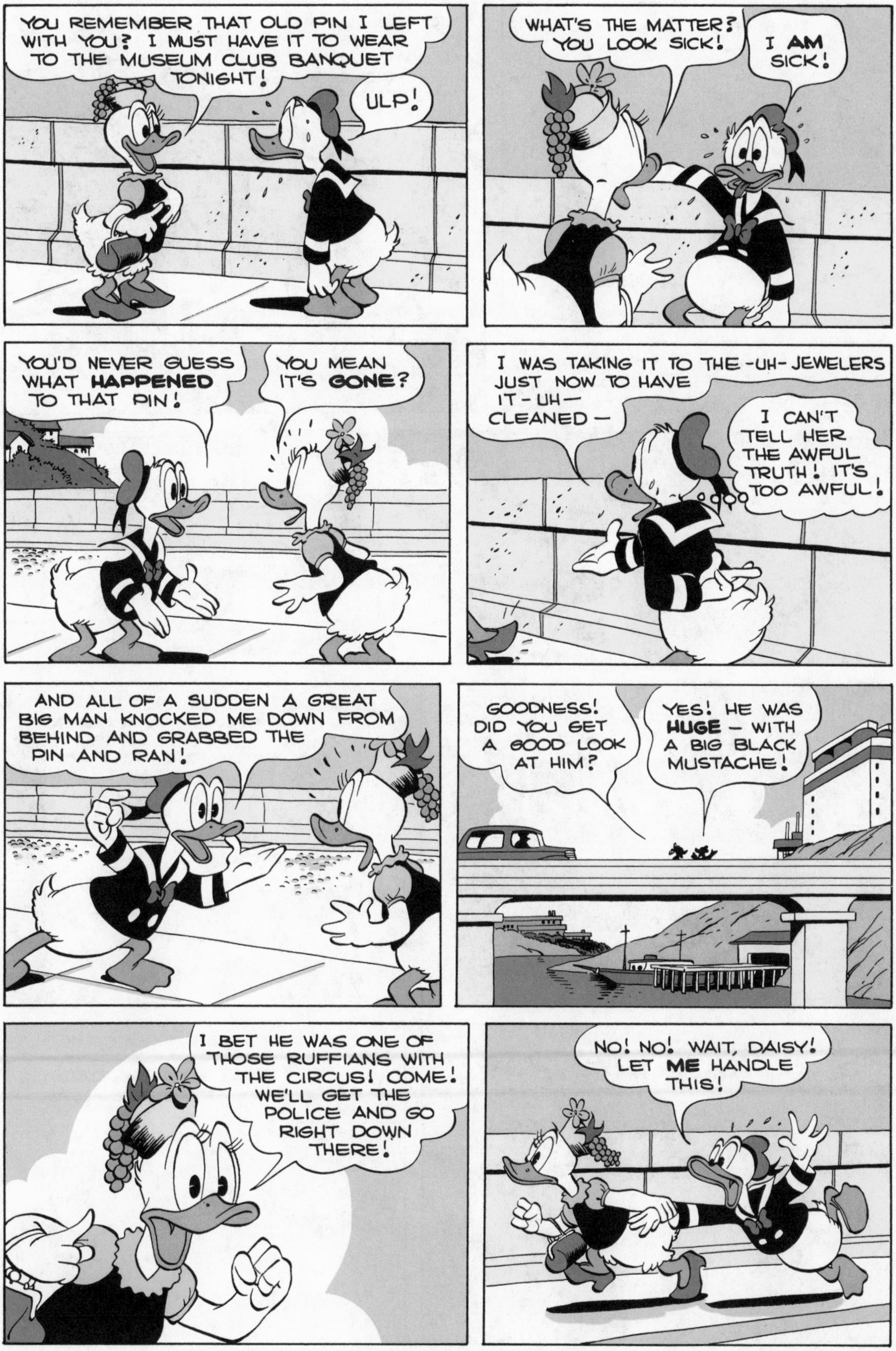
YOU REMEMBER THAT OLD PIN I LEFT WITH YOU? I MUST HAVE IT TO WEAR TO THE MUSEUM CLUB BANQUET TONIGHT!
ULP!
WHAT'S THE MATTER? YOU LOOK SICK!
I AM SICK!
YOU'D NEVER GUESS WHAT HAPPENED TO THAT PIN!
YOU MEAN IT'S GONE?
I WAS TAKING IT TO THE -UH- JEWELERS JUST NOW TO HAVE IT -UH- CLEANED -
I CAN'T TELL HER THE AWFUL TRUTH! IT'S TOO AWFUL!
AND ALL OF A SUDDEN A GREAT BIG MAN KNOCKED ME DOWN FROM BEHIND AND GRABBED THE PIN AND RAN!
GOODNESS! DID YOU GET A GOOD LOOK AT HIM?
YES! HE WAS HUGE - WITH A BIG BLACK MUSTACHE!
I BET HE WAS ONE OF THOSE RUFFIANS WITH THE CIRCUS! COME! WE'LL GET THE POLICE AND GO RIGHT DOWN THERE!
NO! NO! WAIT, DAISY! LET ME HANDLE THIS!

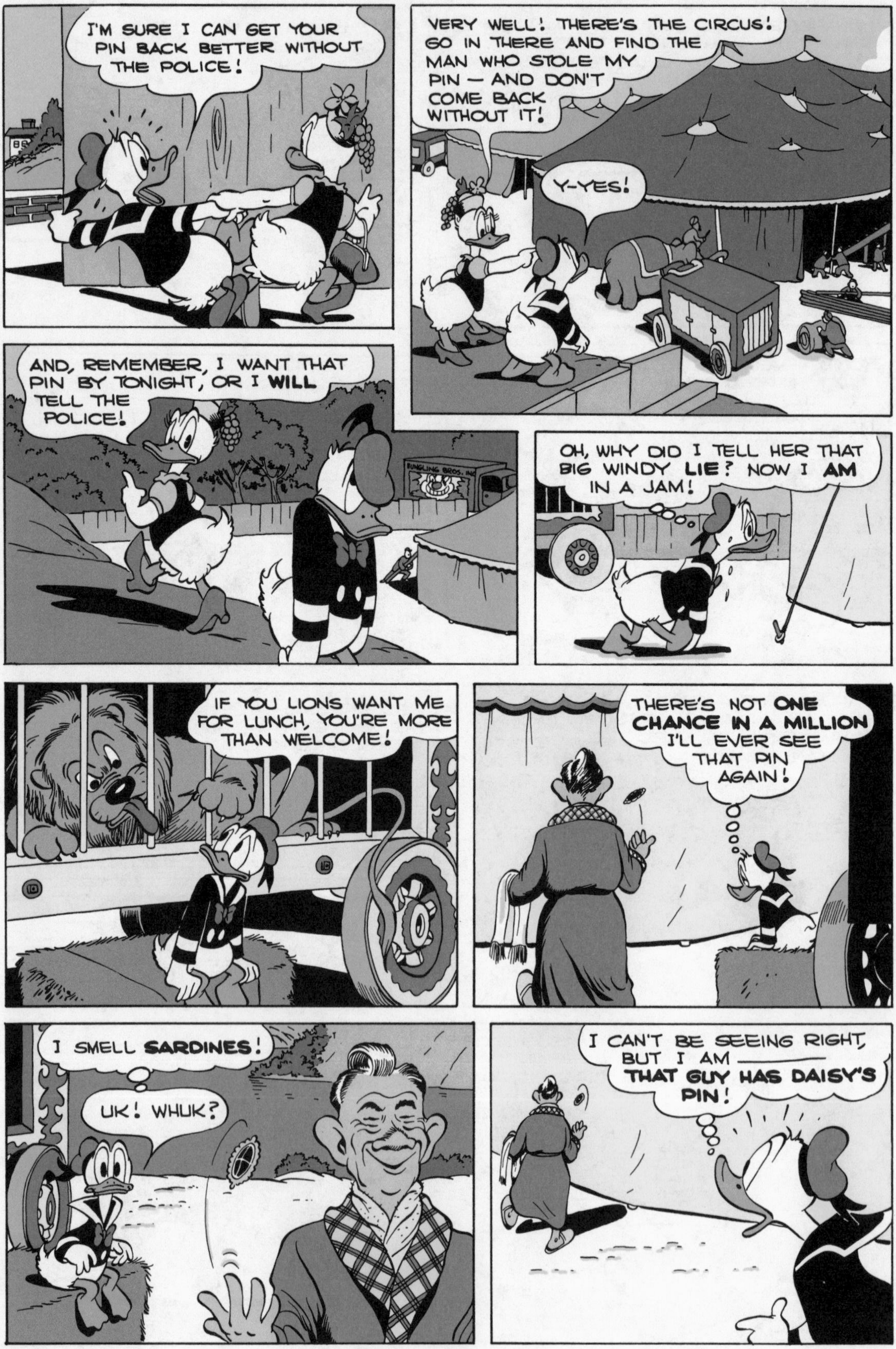
I'M SURE I CAN GET YOUR PIN BACK BETTER WITHOUT THE POLICE!
VERY WELL! THERE'S THE CIRCUS! GO IN THERE AND FIND THE MAN WHO STOLE MY PIN — AND DON'T COME BACK WITHOUT IT!
Y-YES!
AND, REMEMBER, I WANT THAT PIN BY TONIGHT, OR I **WILL** TELL THE POLICE!
BUNGLING BROS. INC
OH, WHY DID I TELL HER THAT BIG WINDY **LIE**? NOW I **AM** IN A JAM!
IF YOU LIONS WANT ME FOR LUNCH, YOU'RE MORE THAN WELCOME!
THERE'S NOT **ONE CHANCE IN A MILLION** I'LL EVER SEE THAT PIN AGAIN!
I SMELL **SARDINES**!
UK! WHUK?
I CAN'T BE SEEING RIGHT, BUT I AM ——— **THAT GUY HAS DAISY'S PIN**!

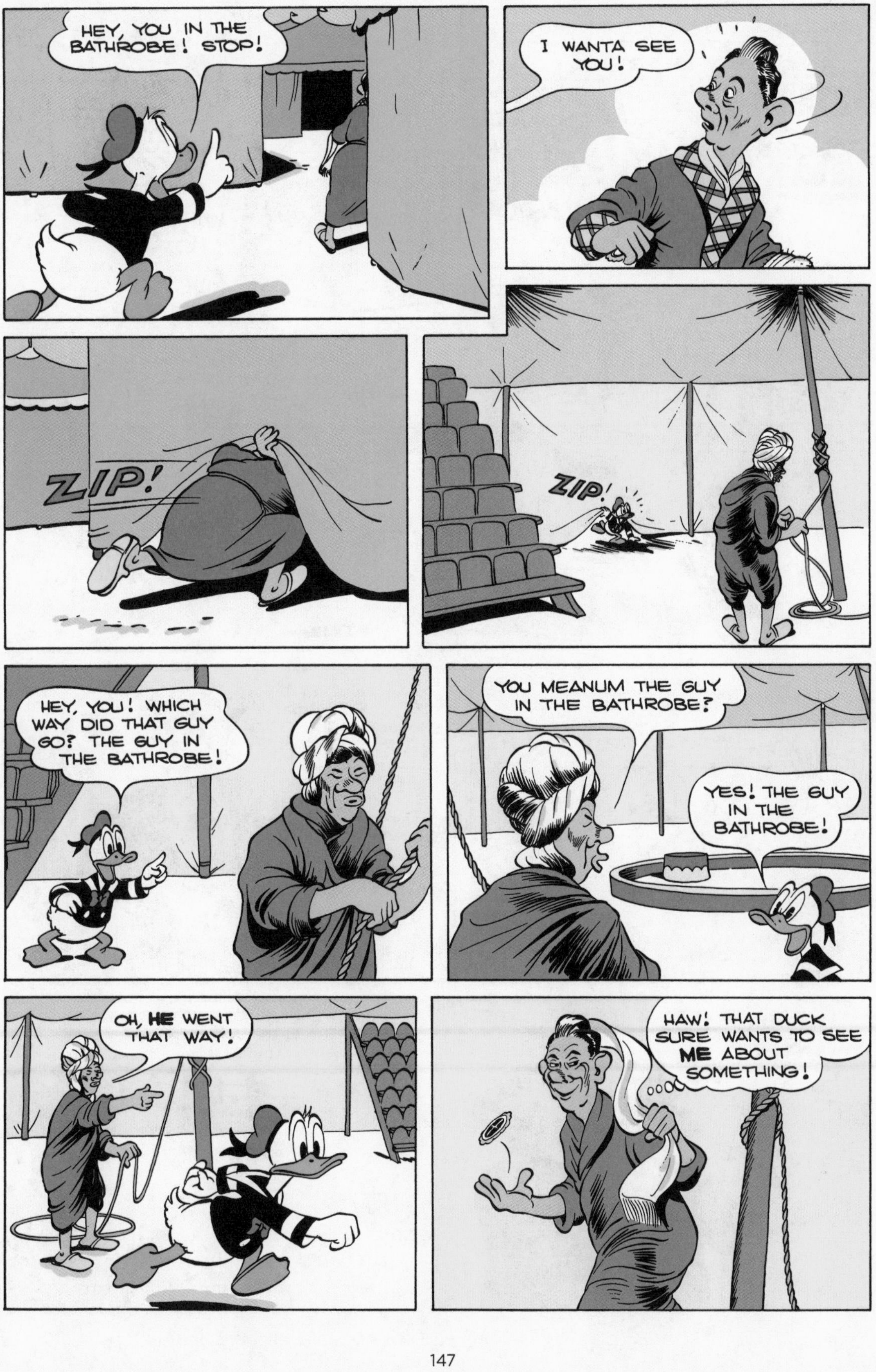
HEY, YOU IN THE BATHROBE! STOP!
I WANTA SEE YOU!
ZIP!
ZIP!
HEY, YOU! WHICH WAY DID THAT GUY GO? THE GUY IN THE BATHROBE!
YOU MEANUM THE GUY IN THE BATHROBE?
YES! THE GUY IN THE BATHROBE!
OH, HE WENT THAT WAY!
HAW! THAT DUCK SURE WANTS TO SEE ME ABOUT SOMETHING!

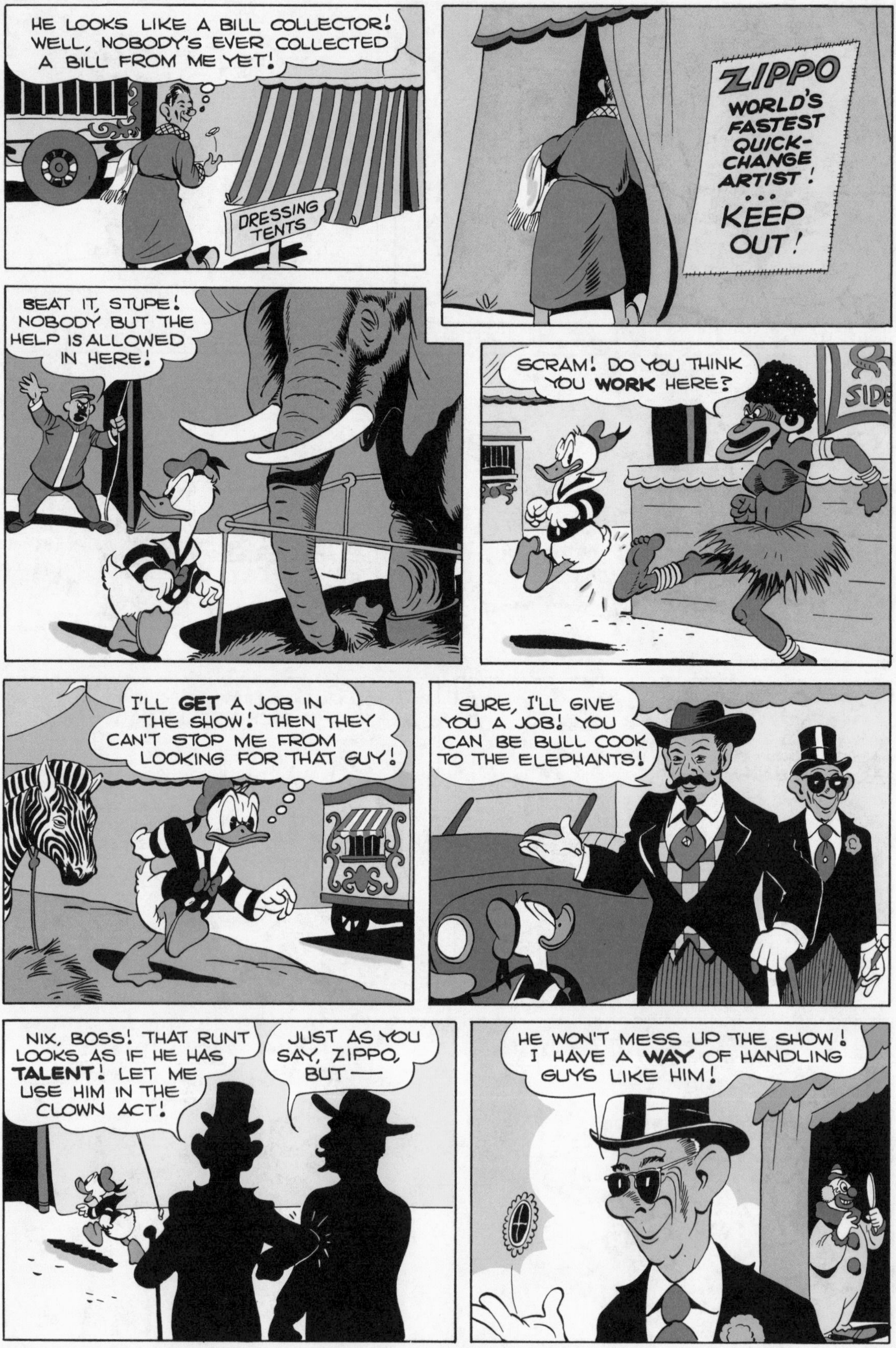
HE LOOKS LIKE A BILL COLLECTOR! WELL, NOBODY'S EVER COLLECTED A BILL FROM ME YET!
DRESSING TENTS
ZIPPO WORLD'S FASTEST QUICK-CHANGE ARTIST! ... KEEP OUT!
BEAT IT, STUPE! NOBODY BUT THE HELP IS ALLOWED IN HERE!
SCRAM! DO YOU THINK YOU WORK HERE?
I'LL GET A JOB IN THE SHOW! THEN THEY CAN'T STOP ME FROM LOOKING FOR THAT GUY!
SURE, I'LL GIVE YOU A JOB! YOU CAN BE BULL COOK TO THE ELEPHANTS!
NIX, BOSS! THAT RUNT LOOKS AS IF HE HAS TALENT! LET ME USE HIM IN THE CLOWN ACT!
JUST AS YOU SAY, ZIPPO, BUT—
HE WON'T MESS UP THE SHOW! I HAVE A WAY OF HANDLING GUYS LIKE HIM!

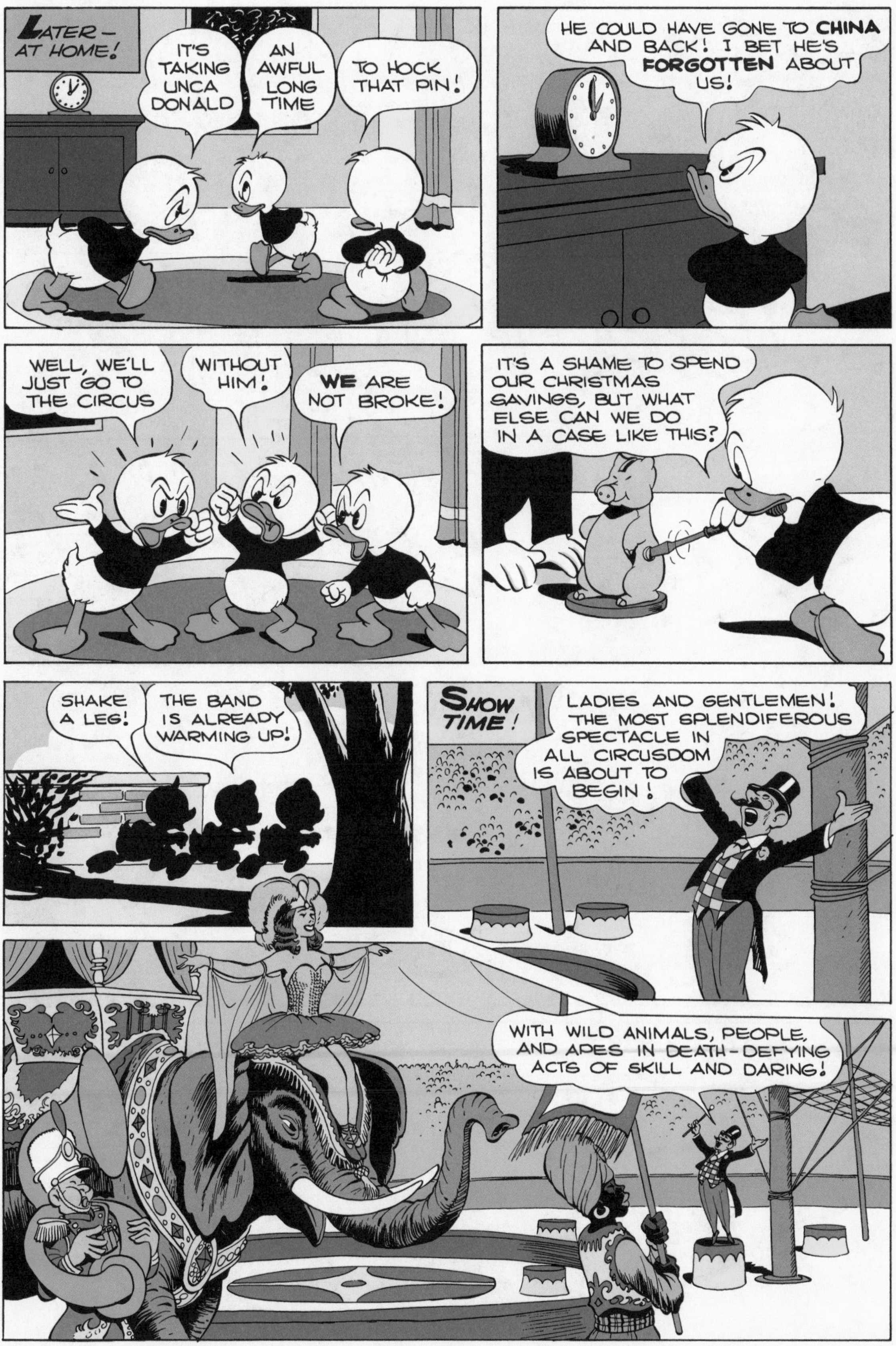
LATER—AT HOME!
IT'S TAKING UNCA DONALD
AN AWFUL LONG TIME
TO HOCK THAT PIN!
HE COULD HAVE GONE TO CHINA AND BACK! I BET HE'S FORGOTTEN ABOUT US!
WELL, WE'LL JUST GO TO THE CIRCUS
WITHOUT HIM!
WE ARE NOT BROKE!
IT'S A SHAME TO SPEND OUR CHRISTMAS SAVINGS, BUT WHAT ELSE CAN WE DO IN A CASE LIKE THIS?
SHAKE A LEG!
THE BAND IS ALREADY WARMING UP!
SHOW TIME!
LADIES AND GENTLEMEN! THE MOST SPLENDIFEROUS SPECTACLE IN ALL CIRCUSDOM IS ABOUT TO BEGIN!
WITH WILD ANIMALS, PEOPLE, AND APES IN DEATH-DEFYING ACTS OF SKILL AND DARING!

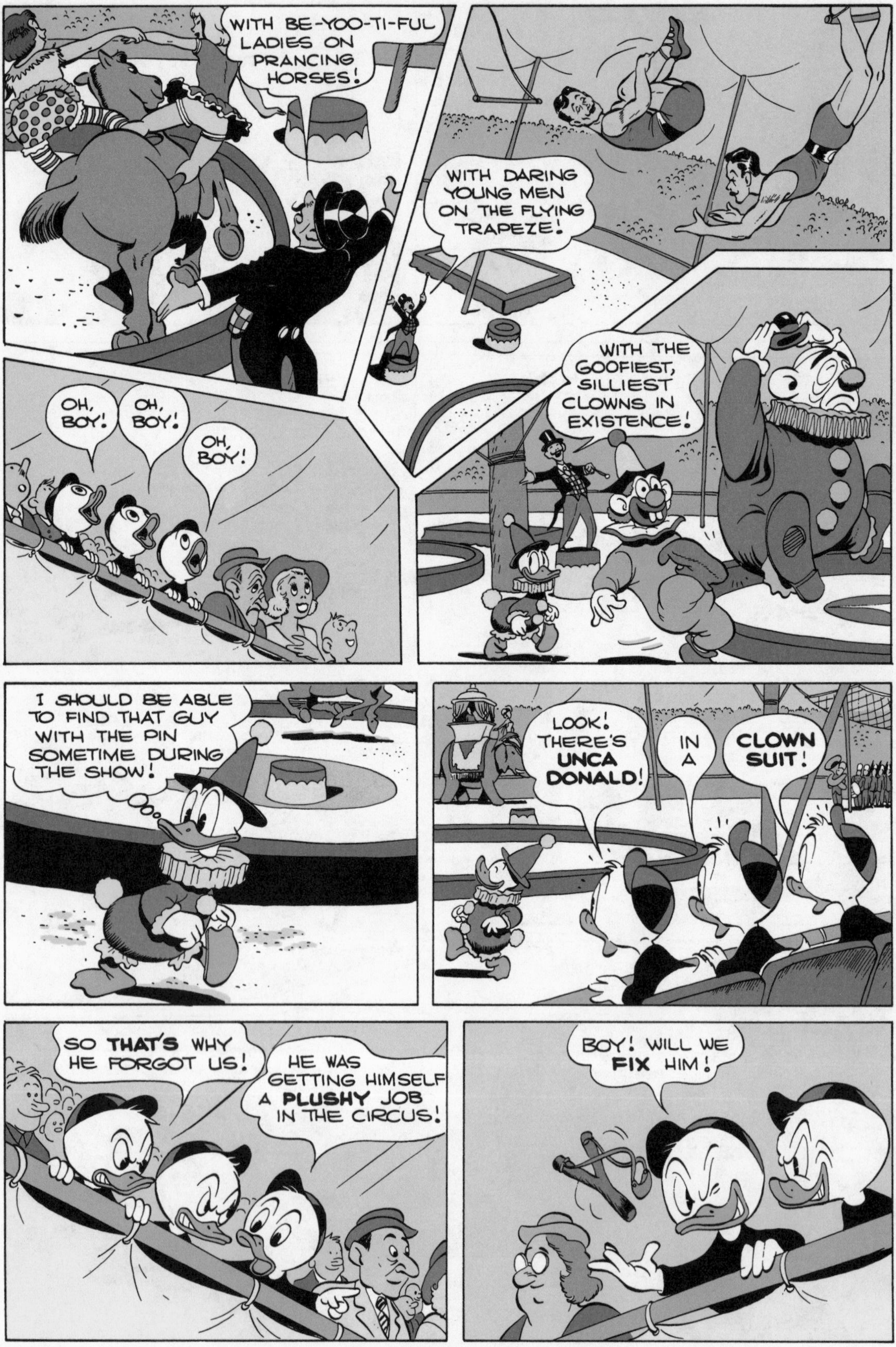
WITH BE-YOO-TI-FUL LADIES ON PRANCING HORSES!
WITH DARING YOUNG MEN ON THE FLYING TRAPEZE!
WITH THE GOOFIEST, SILLIEST CLOWNS IN EXISTENCE!
OH, BOY!
OH, BOY!
OH, BOY!
I SHOULD BE ABLE TO FIND THAT GUY WITH THE PIN SOMETIME DURING THE SHOW!
LOOK! THERE'S **UNCA DONALD**!
IN A
CLOWN SUIT!
SO **THAT'S** WHY HE FORGOT US!
HE WAS GETTING HIMSELF A **PLUSHY** JOB IN THE CIRCUS!
BOY! WILL WE **FIX** HIM!

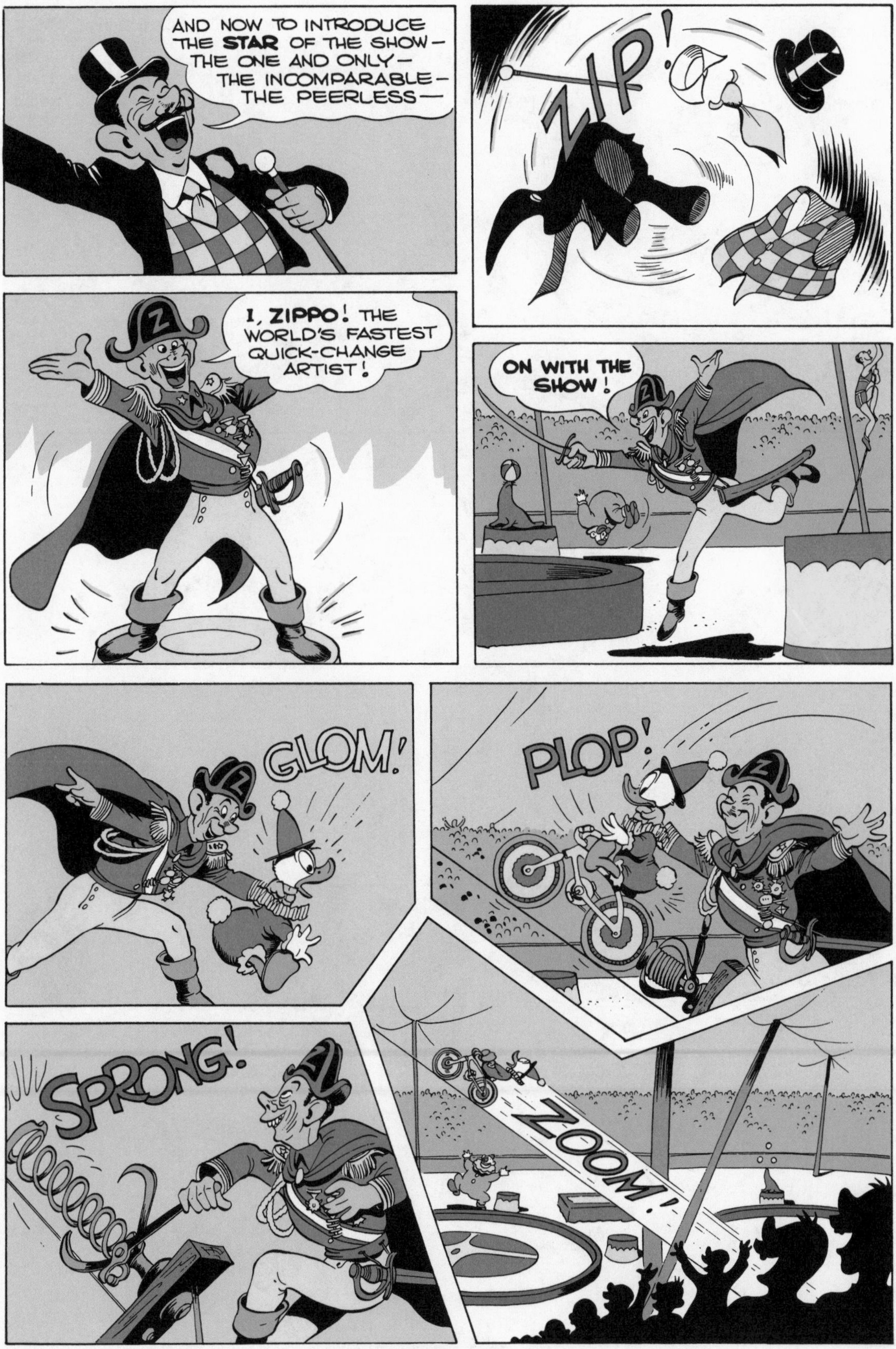
AND NOW TO INTRODUCE THE STAR OF THE SHOW— THE ONE AND ONLY— THE INCOMPARABLE— THE PEERLESS—
ZIP!
I, ZIPPO! THE WORLD'S FASTEST QUICK-CHANGE ARTIST!
ON WITH THE SHOW!
GLOM!
PLOP!
SPRONG!
ZOOM!

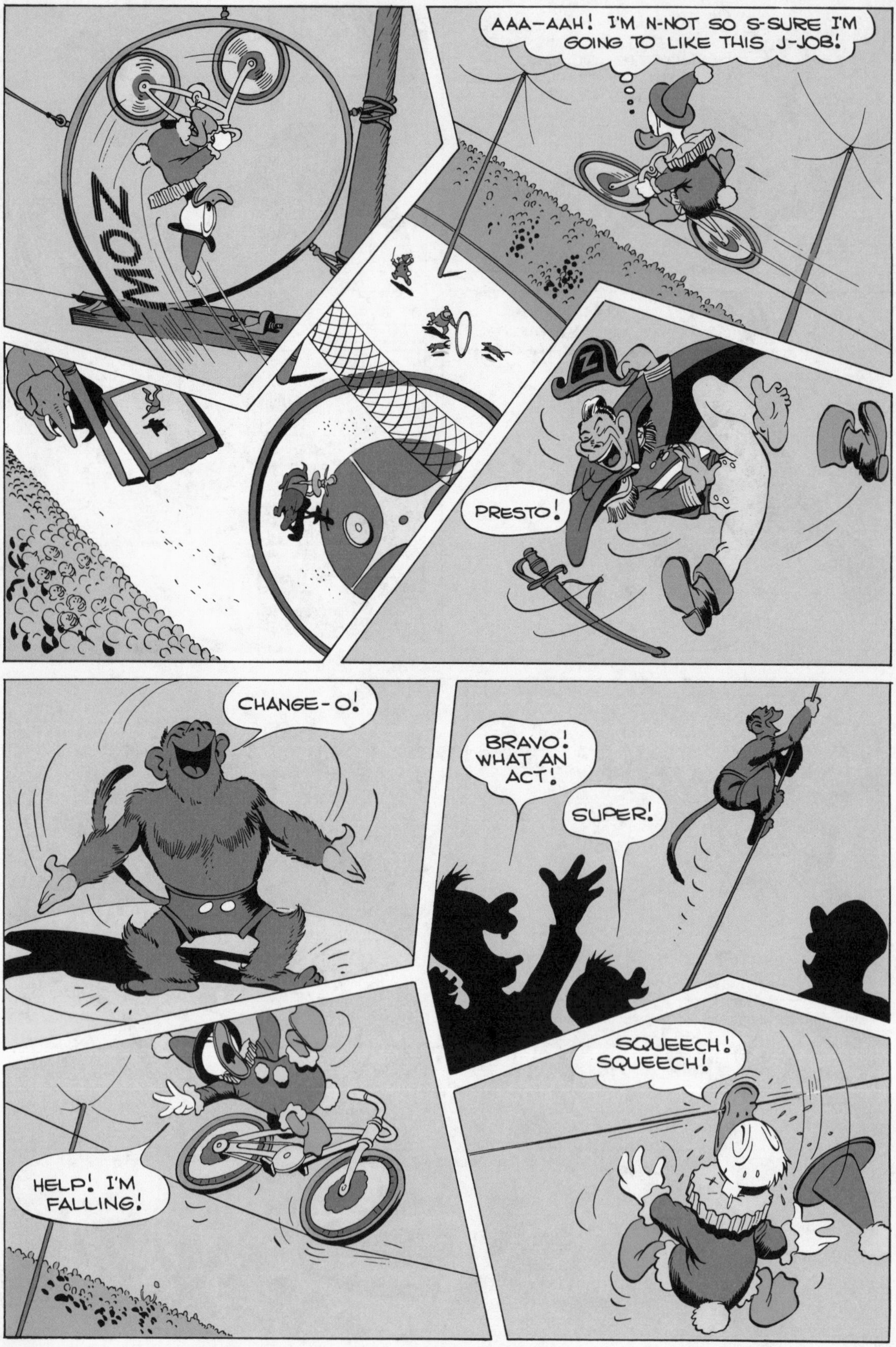
ZOW
AAA-AAH! I'M N-NOT SO S-SURE I'M GOING TO LIKE THIS J-JOB!
PRESTO!
CHANGE-O!
BRAVO! WHAT AN ACT!
SUPER!
HELP! I'M FALLING!
SQUEECH! SQUEECH!

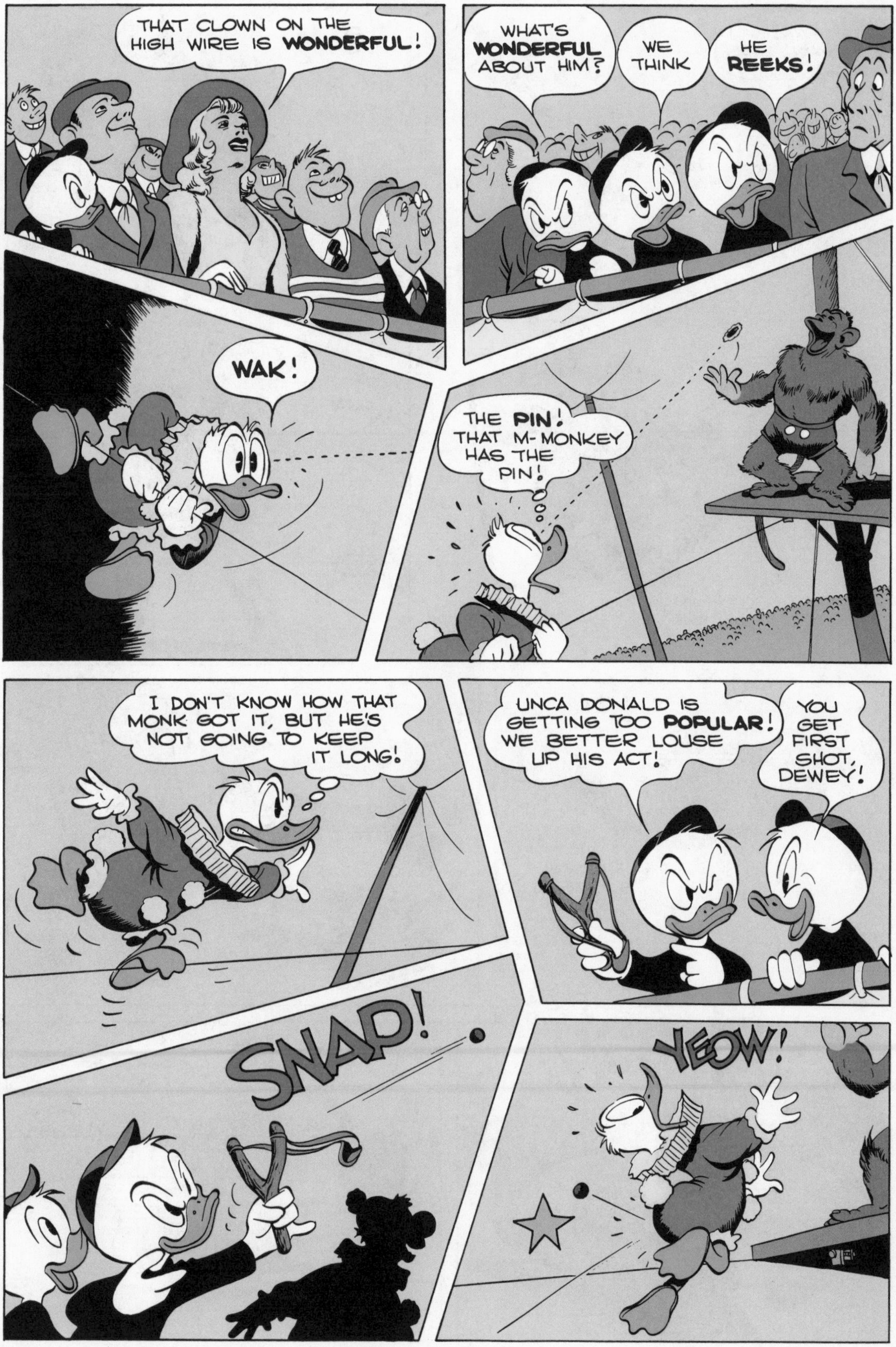
THAT CLOWN ON THE HIGH WIRE IS **WONDERFUL**!
WHAT'S **WONDERFUL** ABOUT HIM?
WE THINK
HE **REEKS**!
WAK!
THE **PIN**! THAT M-MONKEY HAS THE PIN!
I DON'T KNOW HOW THAT MONK GOT IT, BUT HE'S NOT GOING TO KEEP IT LONG!
UNCA DONALD IS GETTING TOO **POPULAR**! WE BETTER LOUSE UP HIS ACT!
YOU GET FIRST SHOT, DEWEY!
SNAP!
YEOW!

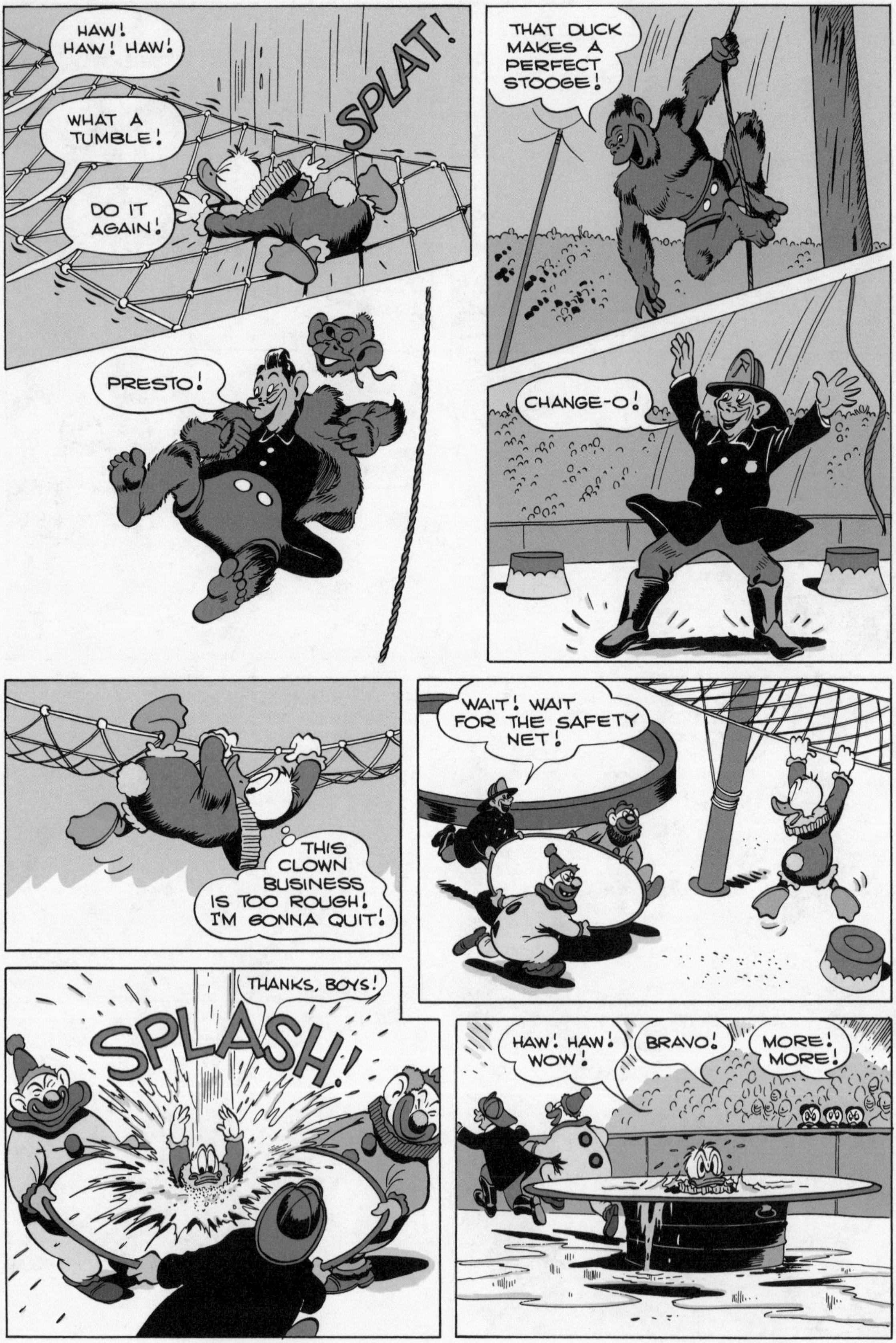
HAW! HAW! HAW!
WHAT A TUMBLE!
DO IT AGAIN!
SPLAT!
THAT DUCK MAKES A PERFECT STOOGE!
PRESTO!
CHANGE-O!
THIS CLOWN BUSINESS IS TOO ROUGH! I'M GONNA QUIT!
WAIT! WAIT FOR THE SAFETY NET!
THANKS, BOYS!
SPLASH!
HAW! HAW! WOW!
BRAVO!
MORE! MORE!

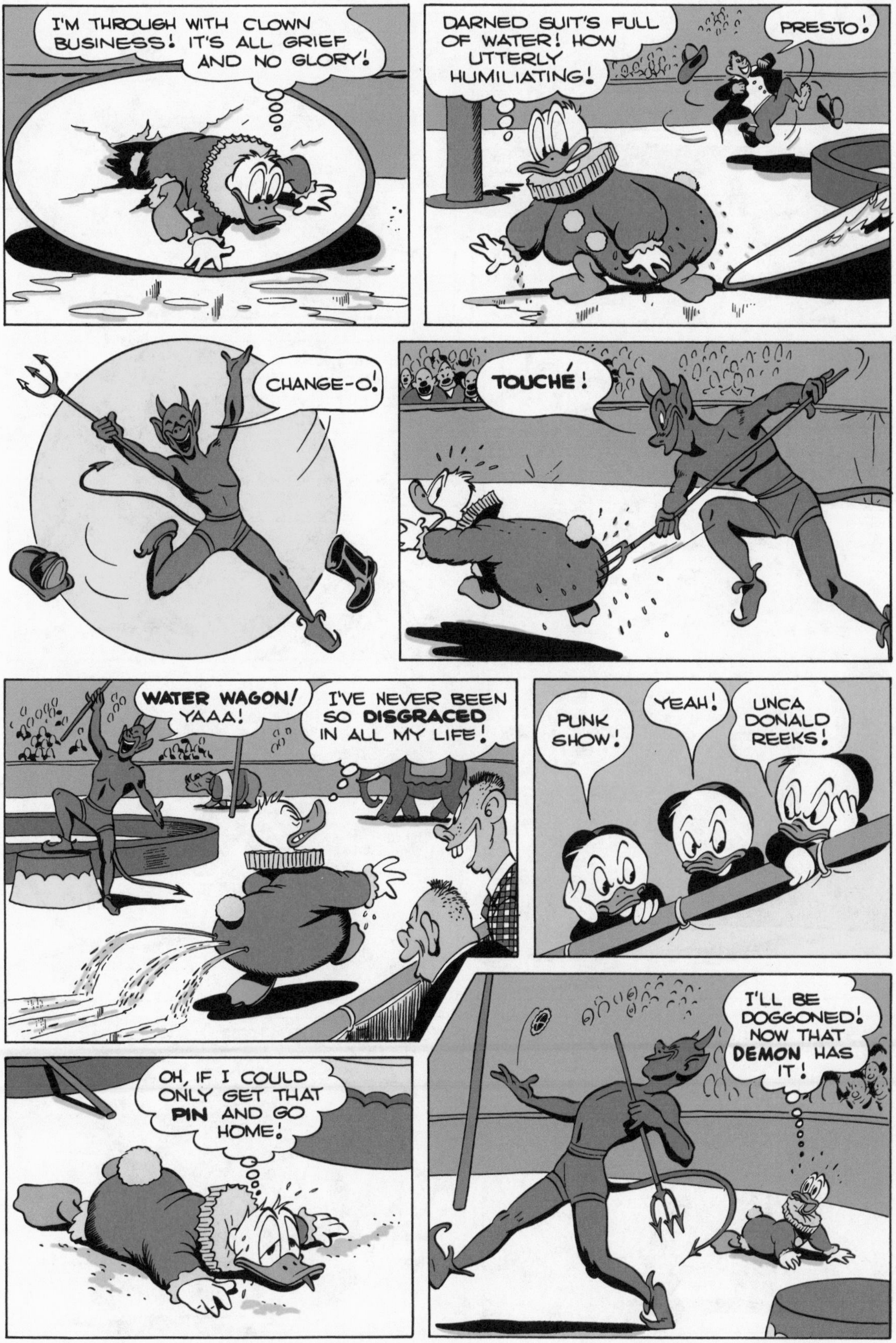

I'M THROUGH WITH CLOWN BUSINESS! IT'S ALL GRIEF AND NO GLORY!
DARNED SUIT'S FULL OF WATER! HOW UTTERLY HUMILIATING!
PRESTO!
CHANGE-O!
TOUCHÉ!
WATER WAGON! YAAA!
I'VE NEVER BEEN SO DISGRACED IN ALL MY LIFE!
PUNK SHOW!
YEAH!
UNCA DONALD REEKS!
OH, IF I COULD ONLY GET THAT PIN AND GO HOME!
I'LL BE DOGGONED! NOW THAT DEMON HAS IT!

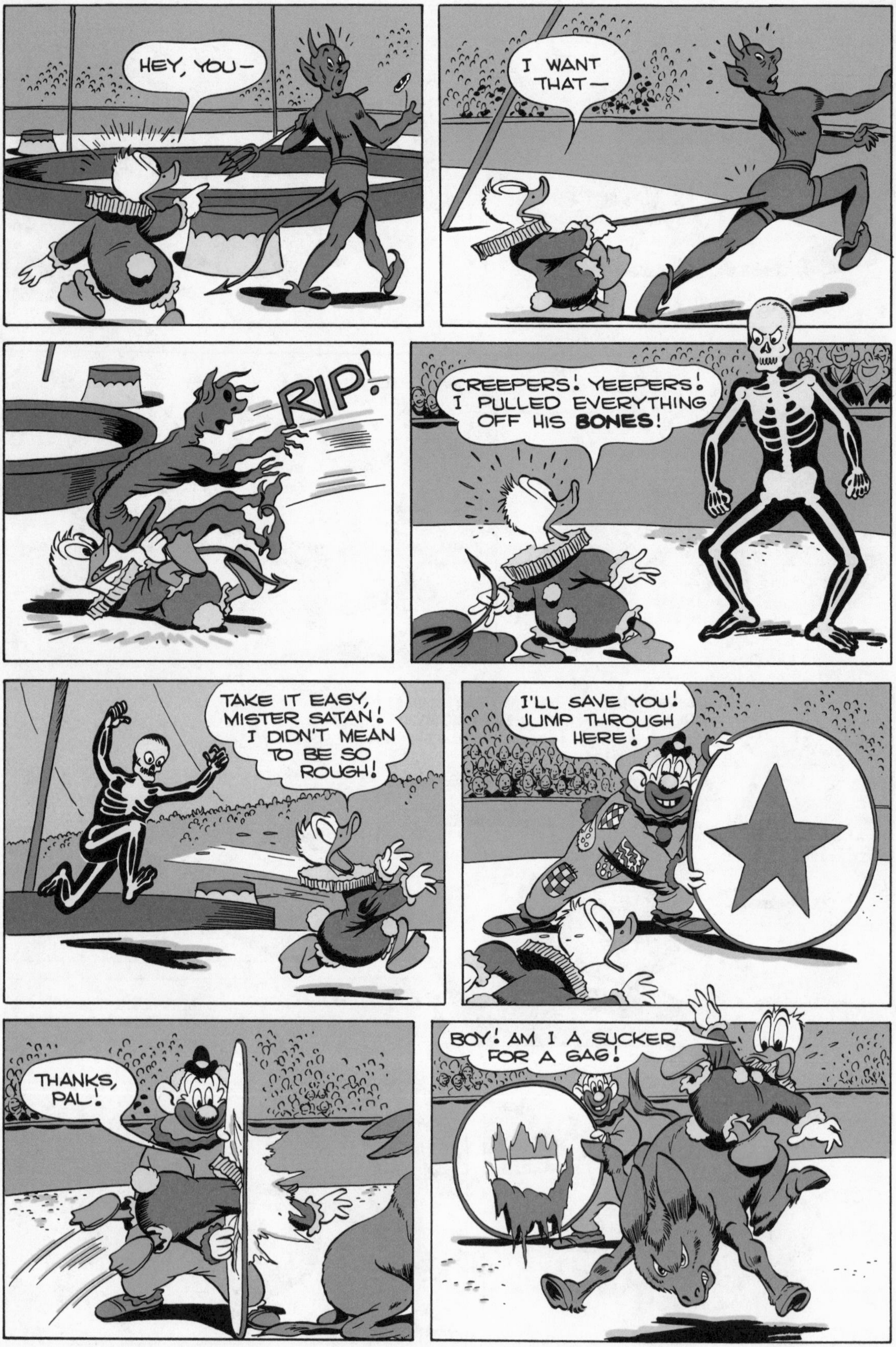
HEY, YOU—
I WANT THAT—
RIP!
CREEPERS! YEEPERS! I PULLED EVERYTHING OFF HIS BONES!
TAKE IT EASY, MISTER SATAN! I DIDN'T MEAN TO BE SO ROUGH!
I'LL SAVE YOU! JUMP THROUGH HERE!
THANKS, PAL!
BOY! AM I A SUCKER FOR A GAG!

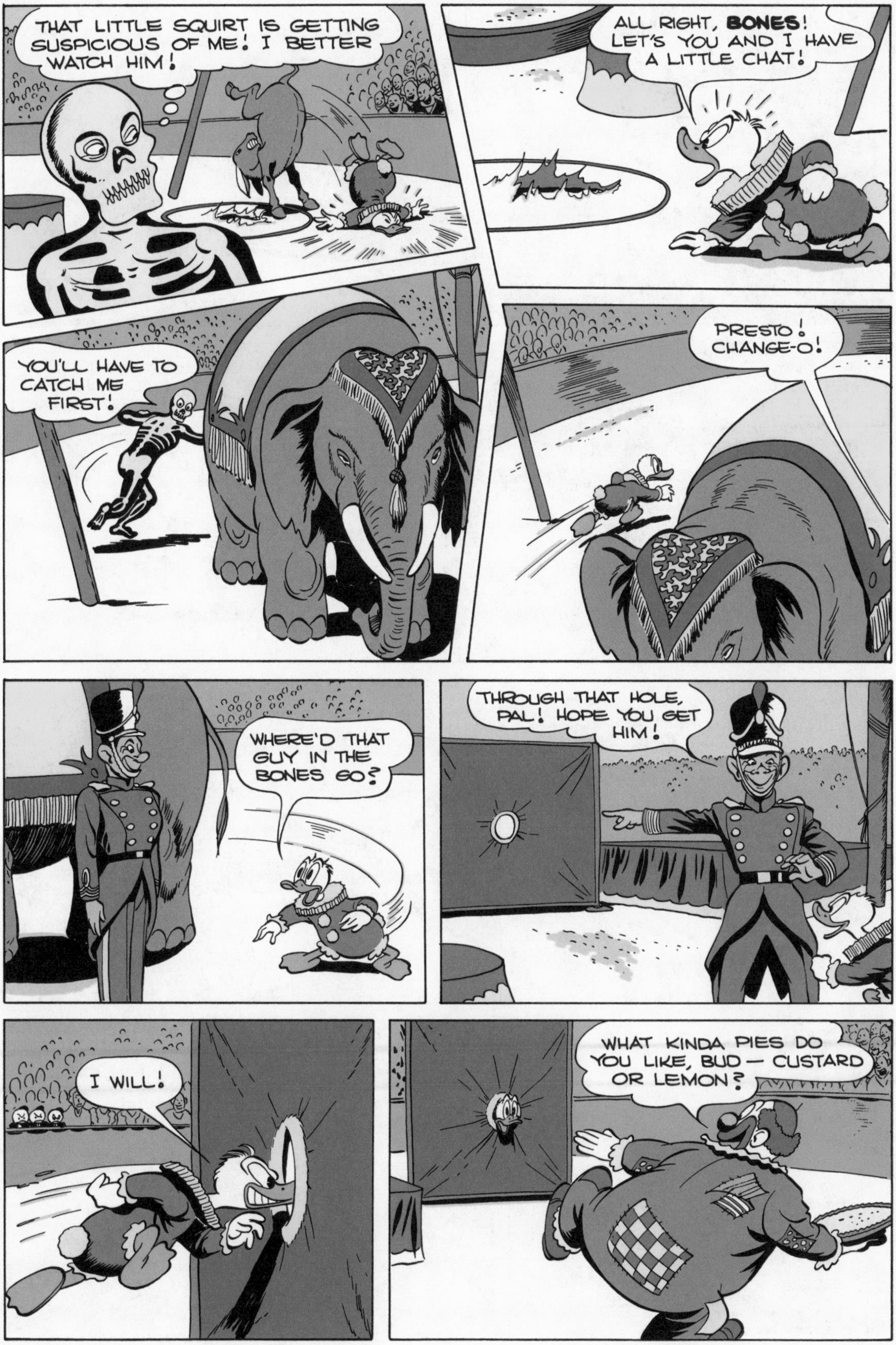
THAT LITTLE SQUIRT IS GETTING SUSPICIOUS OF ME! I BETTER WATCH HIM!
ALL RIGHT, **BONES**! LET'S YOU AND I HAVE A LITTLE CHAT!
YOU'LL HAVE TO CATCH ME FIRST!
PRESTO! CHANGE-O!
WHERE'D THAT GUY IN THE BONES GO?
THROUGH THAT HOLE, PAL! HOPE YOU GET HIM!
I WILL!
WHAT KINDA PIES DO YOU LIKE, BUD — CUSTARD OR LEMON?

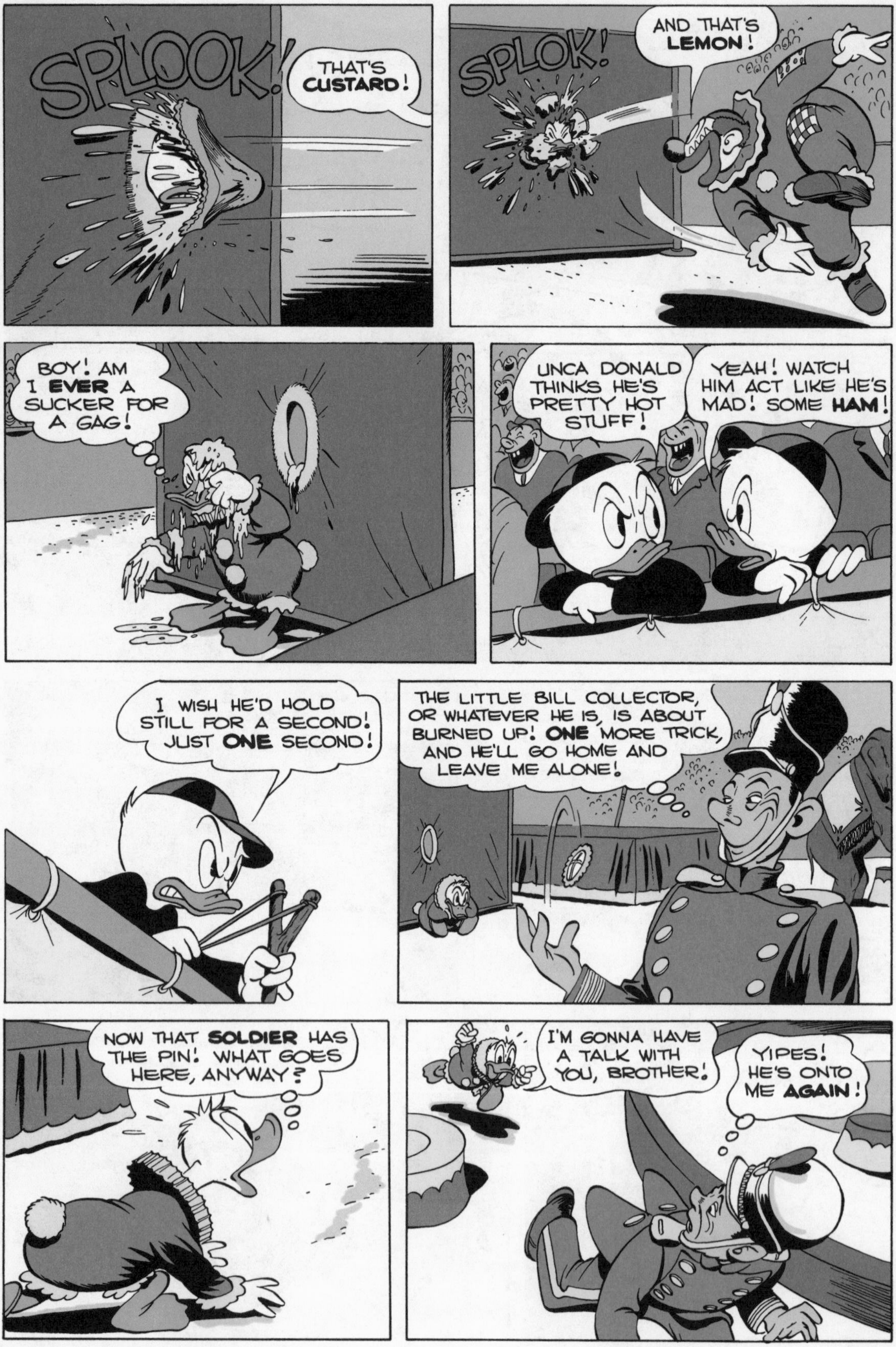
SPLOOK!
THAT'S CUSTARD!
SPLOK!
AND THAT'S LEMON!
BOY! AM I EVER A SUCKER FOR A GAG!
UNCA DONALD THINKS HE'S PRETTY HOT STUFF!
YEAH! WATCH HIM ACT LIKE HE'S MAD! SOME HAM!
I WISH HE'D HOLD STILL FOR A SECOND! JUST ONE SECOND!
THE LITTLE BILL COLLECTOR, OR WHATEVER HE IS, IS ABOUT BURNED UP! ONE MORE TRICK, AND HE'LL GO HOME AND LEAVE ME ALONE!
NOW THAT SOLDIER HAS THE PIN! WHAT GOES HERE, ANYWAY?
I'M GONNA HAVE A TALK WITH YOU, BROTHER!
YIPES! HE'S ONTO ME AGAIN!

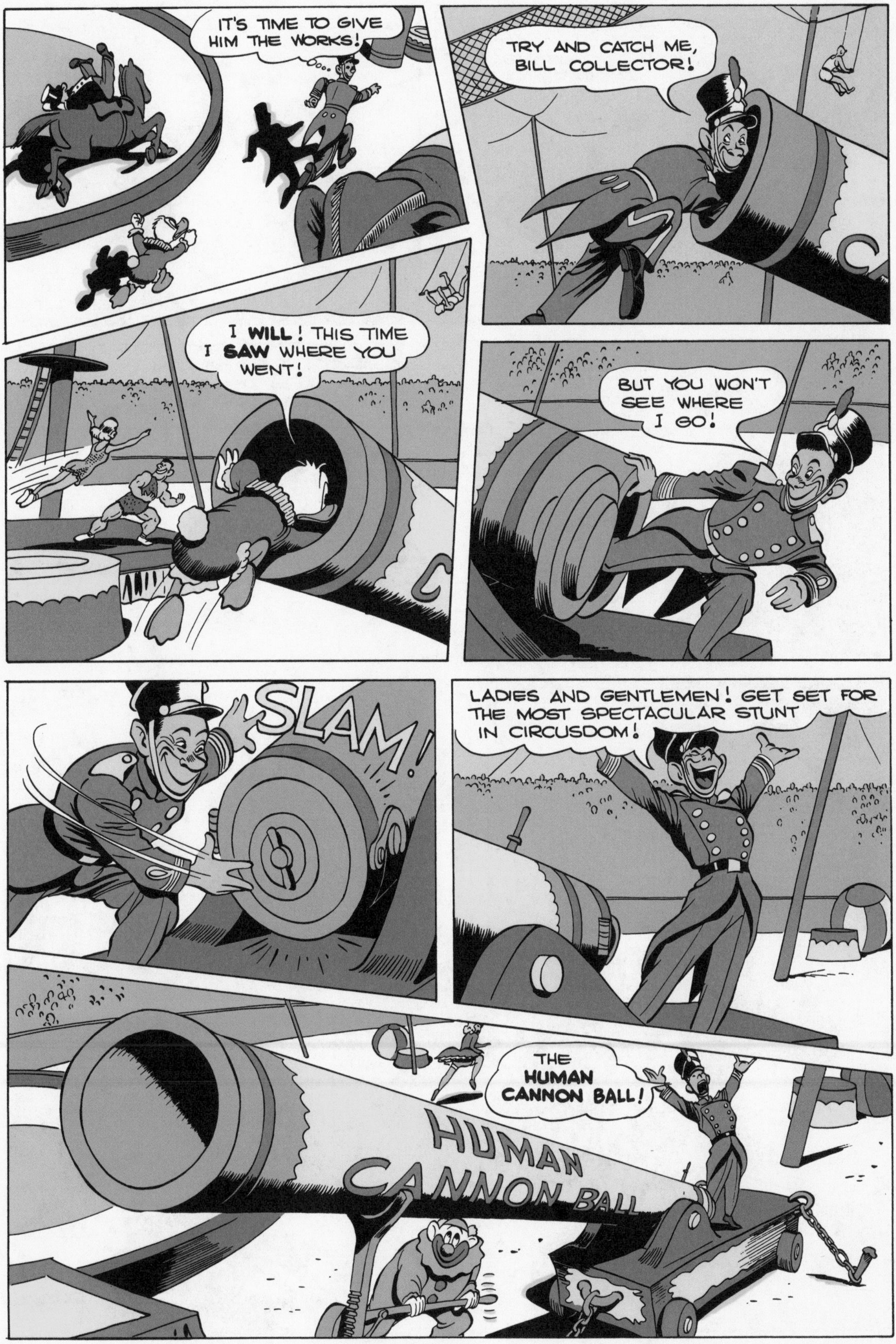
IT'S TIME TO GIVE HIM THE WORKS!
TRY AND CATCH ME, BILL COLLECTOR!
I WILL! THIS TIME I SAW WHERE YOU WENT!
BUT YOU WON'T SEE WHERE I GO!
SLAM!
LADIES AND GENTLEMEN! GET SET FOR THE MOST SPECTACULAR STUNT IN CIRCUSDOM!
THE HUMAN CANNON BALL!
HUMAN CANNON BALL

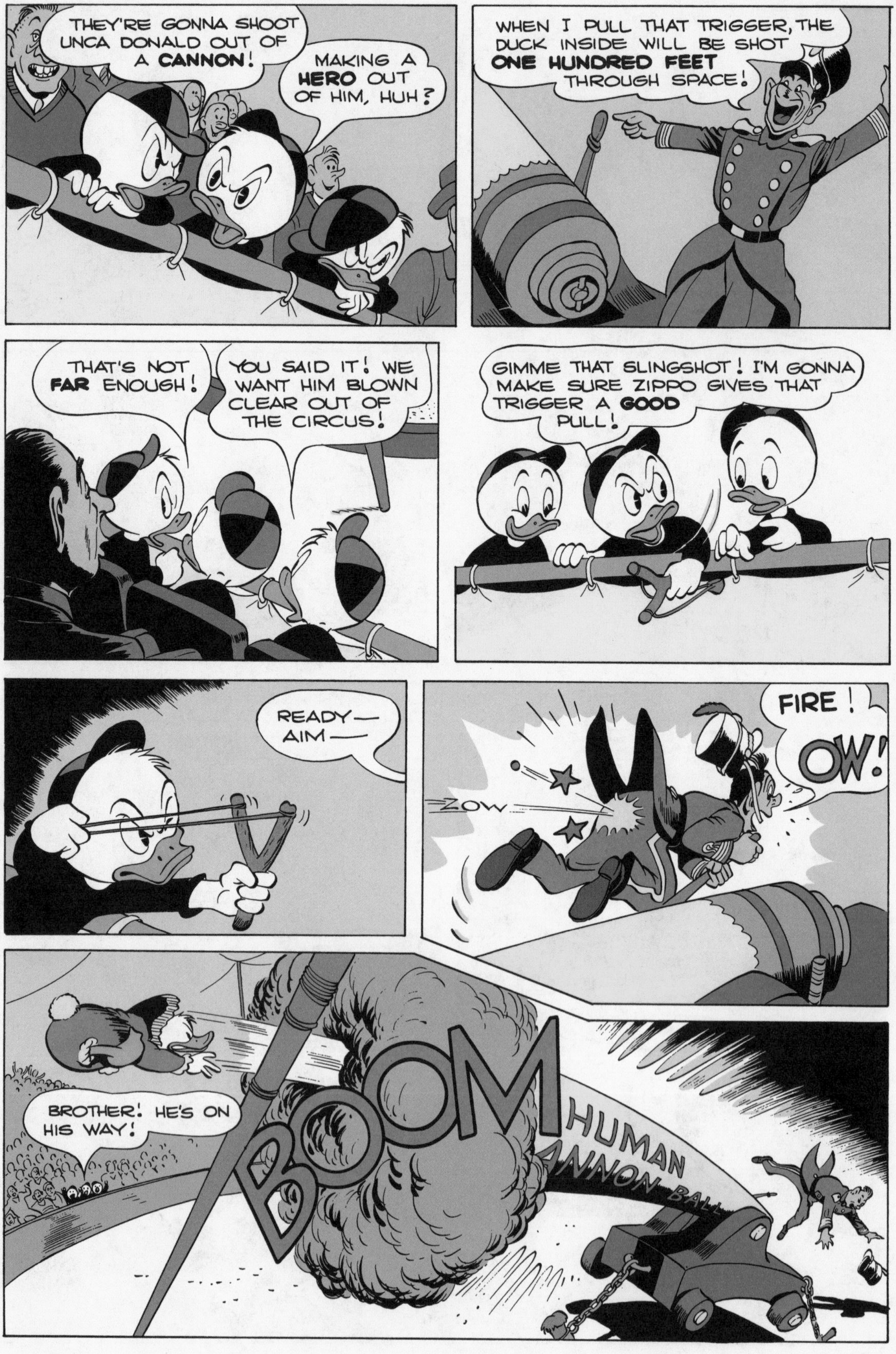
THEY'RE GONNA SHOOT UNCA DONALD OUT OF A CANNON!
MAKING A HERO OUT OF HIM, HUH?
WHEN I PULL THAT TRIGGER, THE DUCK INSIDE WILL BE SHOT ONE HUNDRED FEET THROUGH SPACE!
THAT'S NOT FAR ENOUGH!
YOU SAID IT! WE WANT HIM BLOWN CLEAR OUT OF THE CIRCUS!
GIMME THAT SLINGSHOT! I'M GONNA MAKE SURE ZIPPO GIVES THAT TRIGGER A GOOD PULL!
READY— AIM—
FIRE!
OW!
ZOW
BROTHER! HE'S ON HIS WAY!
BOOM
HUMAN
ANNON BALL

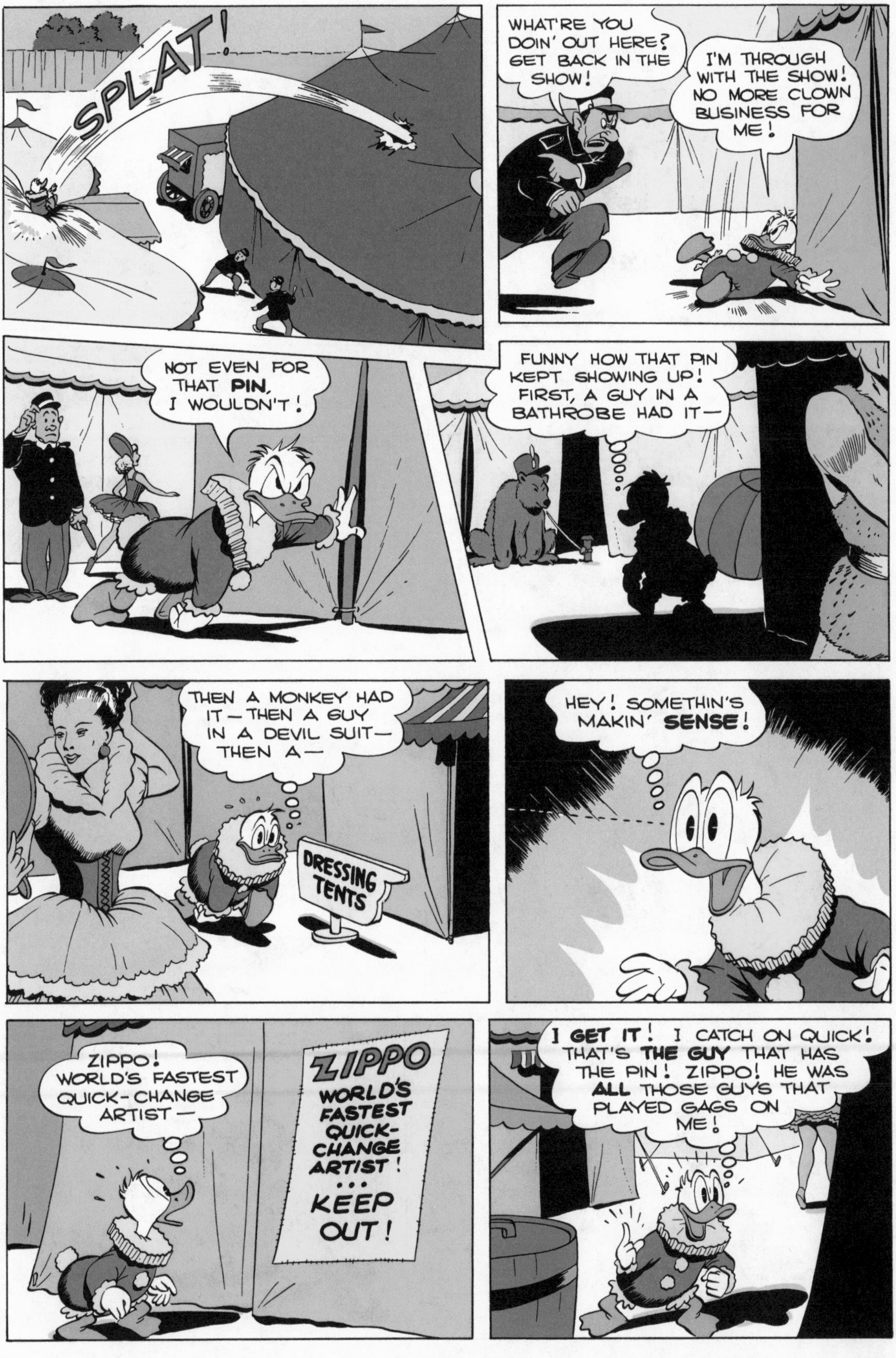
SPLAT!
WHAT'RE YOU DOIN' OUT HERE? GET BACK IN THE SHOW!
I'M THROUGH WITH THE SHOW! NO MORE CLOWN BUSINESS FOR ME!
NOT EVEN FOR THAT PIN, I WOULDN'T!
FUNNY HOW THAT PIN KEPT SHOWING UP! FIRST, A GUY IN A BATHROBE HAD IT—
THEN A MONKEY HAD IT—THEN A GUY IN A DEVIL SUIT—THEN A—
DRESSING TENTS
HEY! SOMETHIN'S MAKIN' SENSE!
ZIPPO! WORLD'S FASTEST QUICK-CHANGE ARTIST—
ZIPPO
WORLD'S FASTEST QUICK-CHANGE ARTIST! ... KEEP OUT!
I GET IT! I CATCH ON QUICK! THAT'S THE GUY THAT HAS THE PIN! ZIPPO! HE WAS ALL THOSE GUYS THAT PLAYED GAGS ON ME!

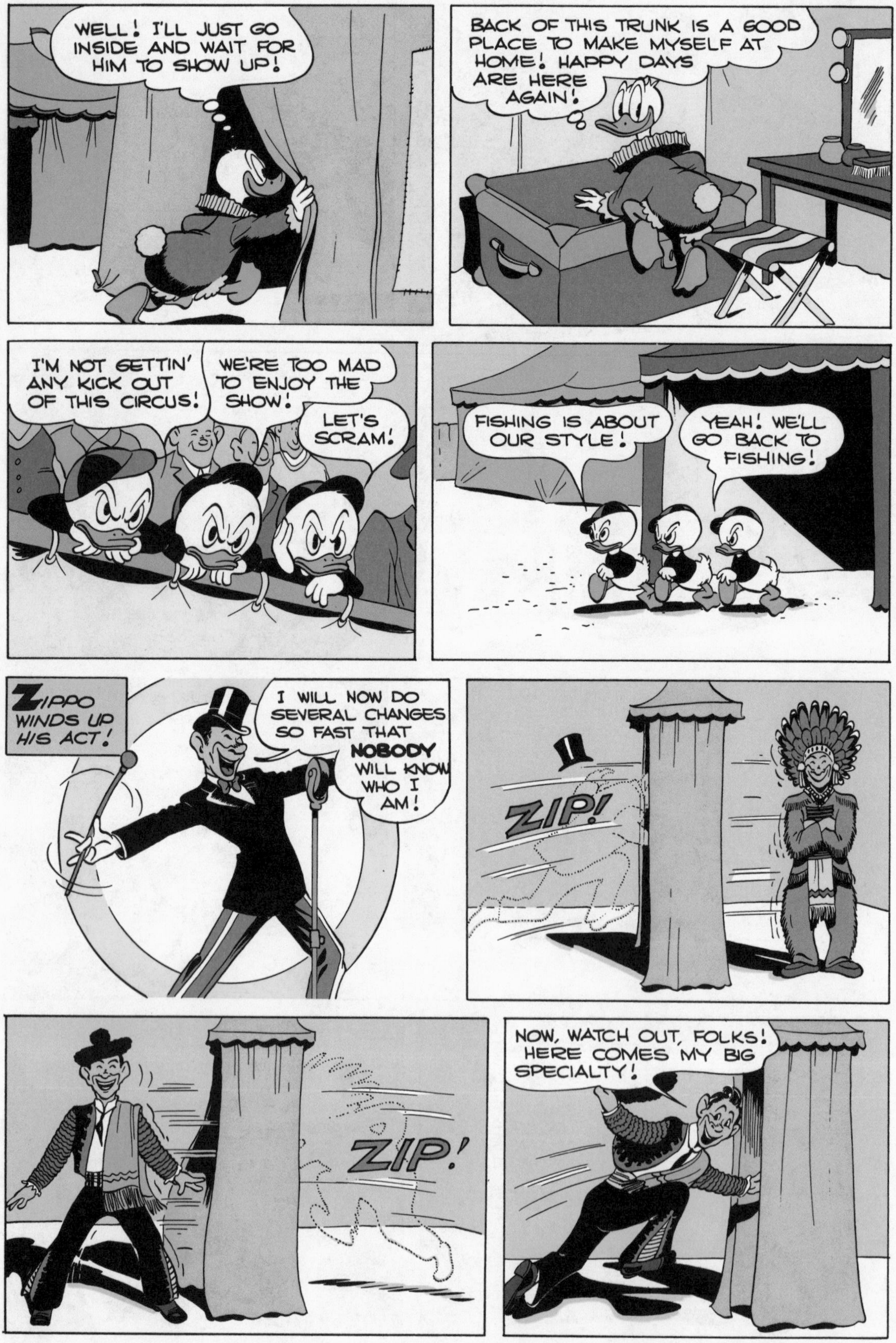
WELL! I'LL JUST GO INSIDE AND WAIT FOR HIM TO SHOW UP!
BACK OF THIS TRUNK IS A GOOD PLACE TO MAKE MYSELF AT HOME! HAPPY DAYS ARE HERE AGAIN!
I'M NOT GETTIN' ANY KICK OUT OF THIS CIRCUS!
WE'RE TOO MAD TO ENJOY THE SHOW!
LET'S SCRAM!
FISHING IS ABOUT OUR STYLE!
YEAH! WE'LL GO BACK TO FISHING!
ZIPPO WINDS UP HIS ACT!
I WILL NOW DO SEVERAL CHANGES SO FAST THAT NOBODY WILL KNOW WHO I AM!
ZIP!
ZIP!
NOW, WATCH OUT, FOLKS! HERE COMES MY BIG SPECIALTY!

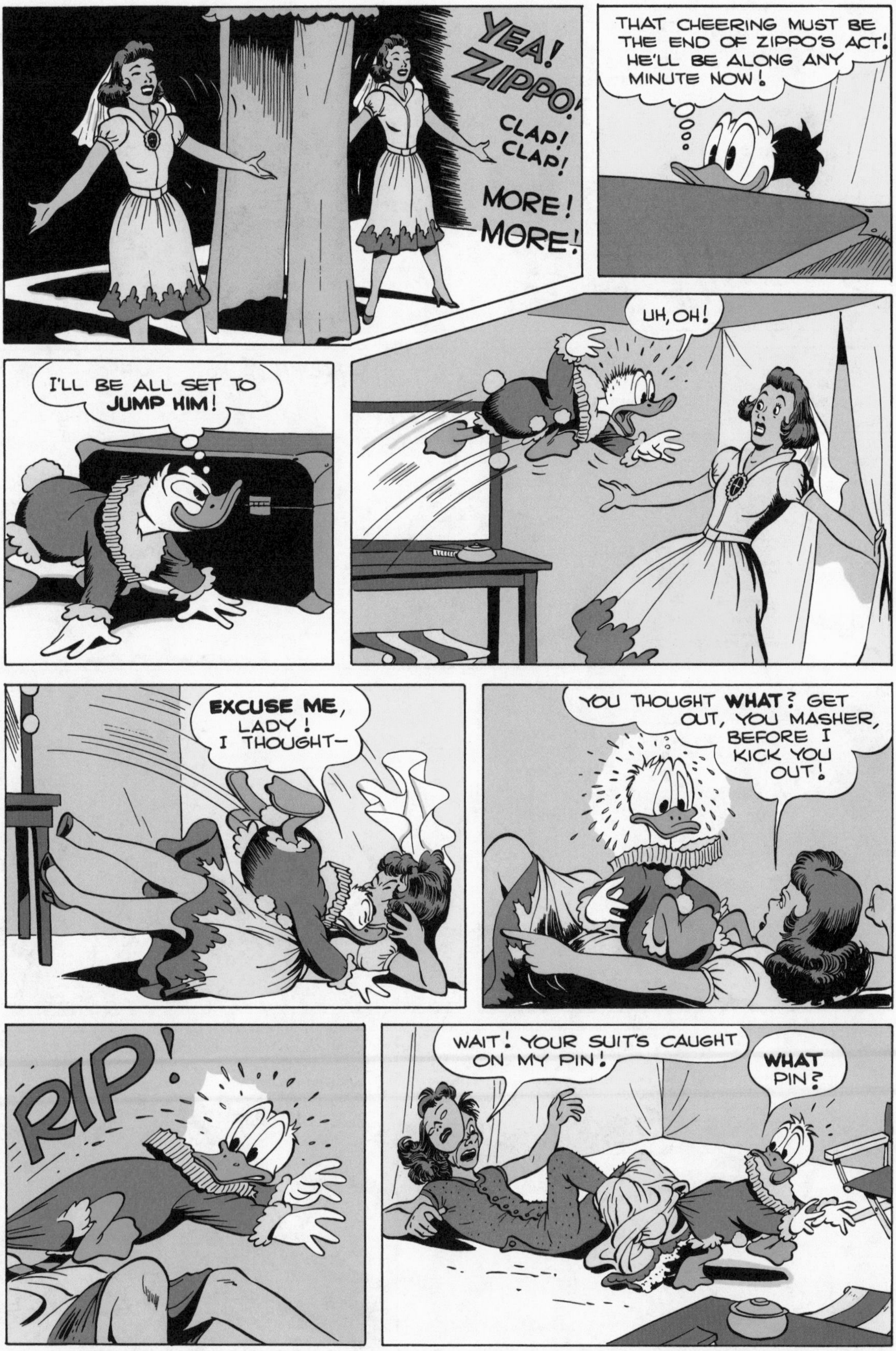
YEA! ZIPPO!
CLAP! CLAP!
MORE! MORE!
THAT CHEERING MUST BE THE END OF ZIPPO'S ACT! HE'LL BE ALONG ANY MINUTE NOW!
I'LL BE ALL SET TO **JUMP HIM**!
UH, OH!
EXCUSE ME, LADY! I THOUGHT—
YOU THOUGHT **WHAT**? GET OUT, YOU MASHER, BEFORE I KICK YOU OUT!
RIP!
WAIT! YOUR SUIT'S CAUGHT ON MY PIN!
WHAT PIN?

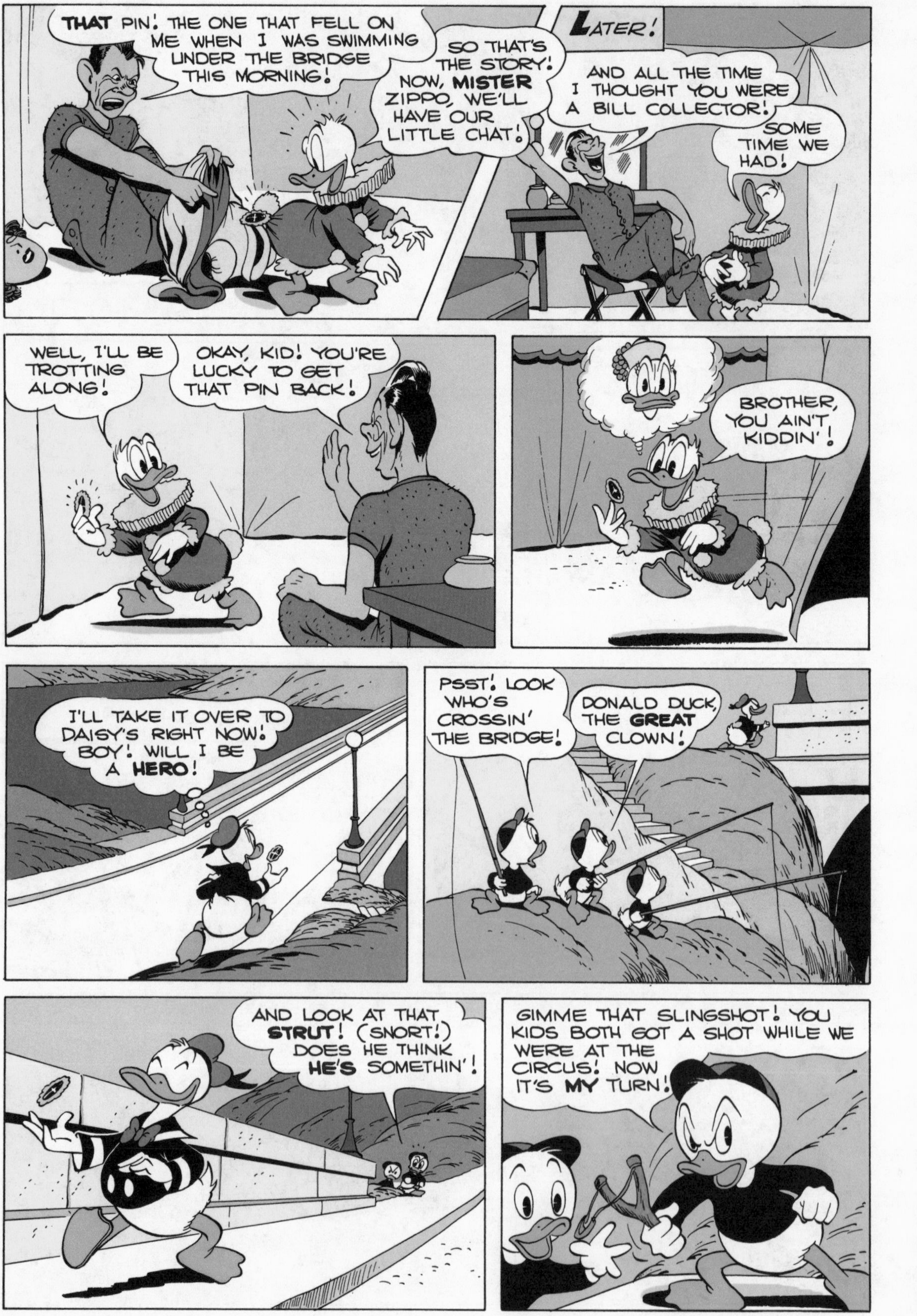
THAT PIN! THE ONE THAT FELL ON ME WHEN I WAS SWIMMING UNDER THE BRIDGE THIS MORNING!
SO THAT'S THE STORY! NOW, MISTER ZIPPO, WE'LL HAVE OUR LITTLE CHAT!
LATER!
AND ALL THE TIME I THOUGHT YOU WERE A BILL COLLECTOR!
SOME TIME WE HAD!
WELL, I'LL BE TROTTING ALONG!
OKAY, KID! YOU'RE LUCKY TO GET THAT PIN BACK!
BROTHER, YOU AIN'T KIDDIN'!
I'LL TAKE IT OVER TO DAISY'S RIGHT NOW! BOY! WILL I BE A HERO!
PSST! LOOK WHO'S CROSSIN' THE BRIDGE!
DONALD DUCK, THE GREAT CLOWN!
AND LOOK AT THAT STRUT! (SNORT!) DOES HE THINK HE'S SOMETHIN'!
GIMME THAT SLINGSHOT! YOU KIDS BOTH GOT A SHOT WHILE WE WERE AT THE CIRCUS! NOW IT'S MY TURN!

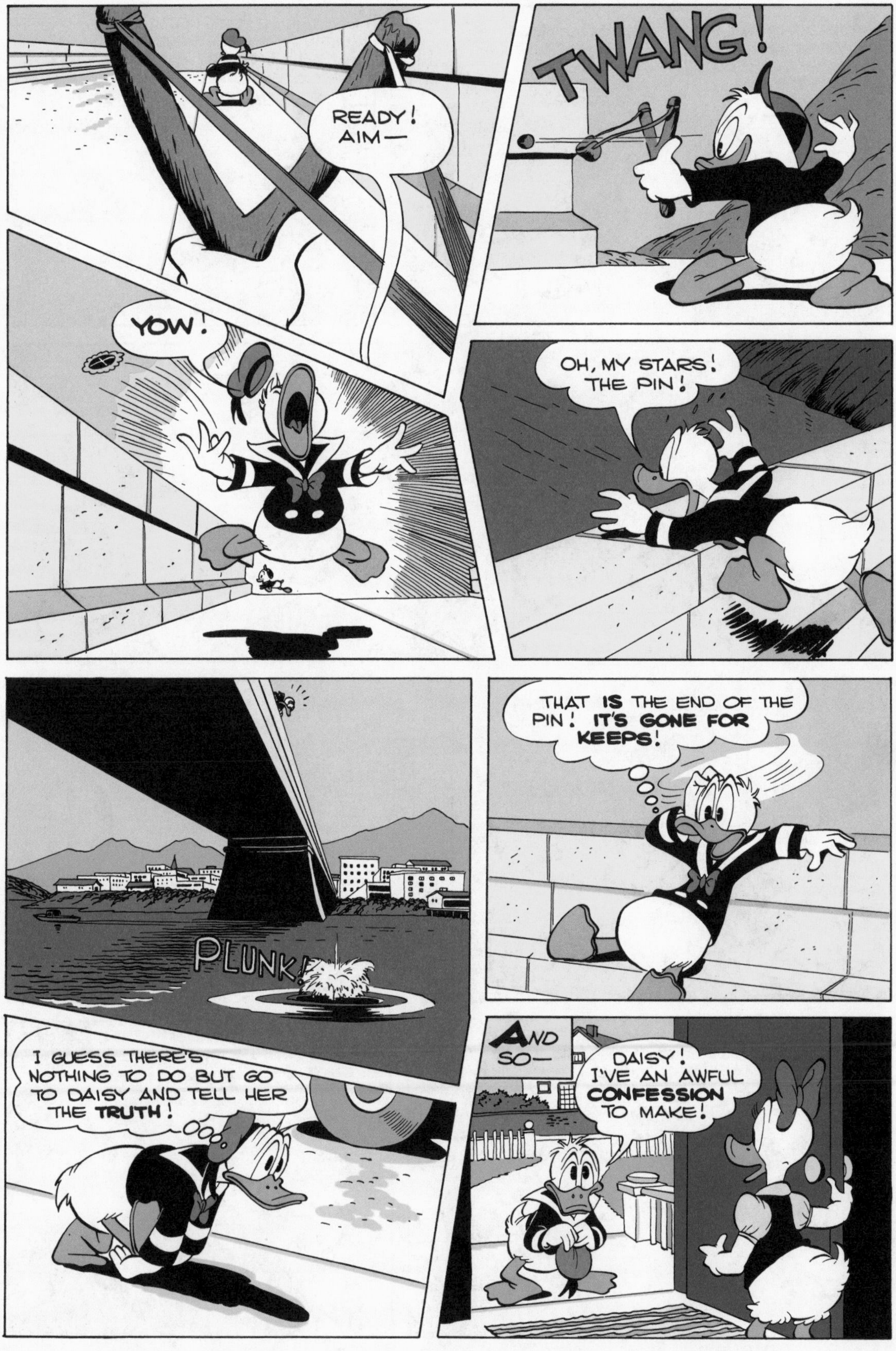
READY! AIM—
TWANG!
YOW!
OH, MY STARS! THE PIN!
PLUNK!
THAT IS THE END OF THE PIN! IT'S GONE FOR KEEPS!
I GUESS THERE'S NOTHING TO DO BUT GO TO DAISY AND TELL HER THE TRUTH!
AND SO—
DAISY! I'VE AN AWFUL CONFESSION TO MAKE!

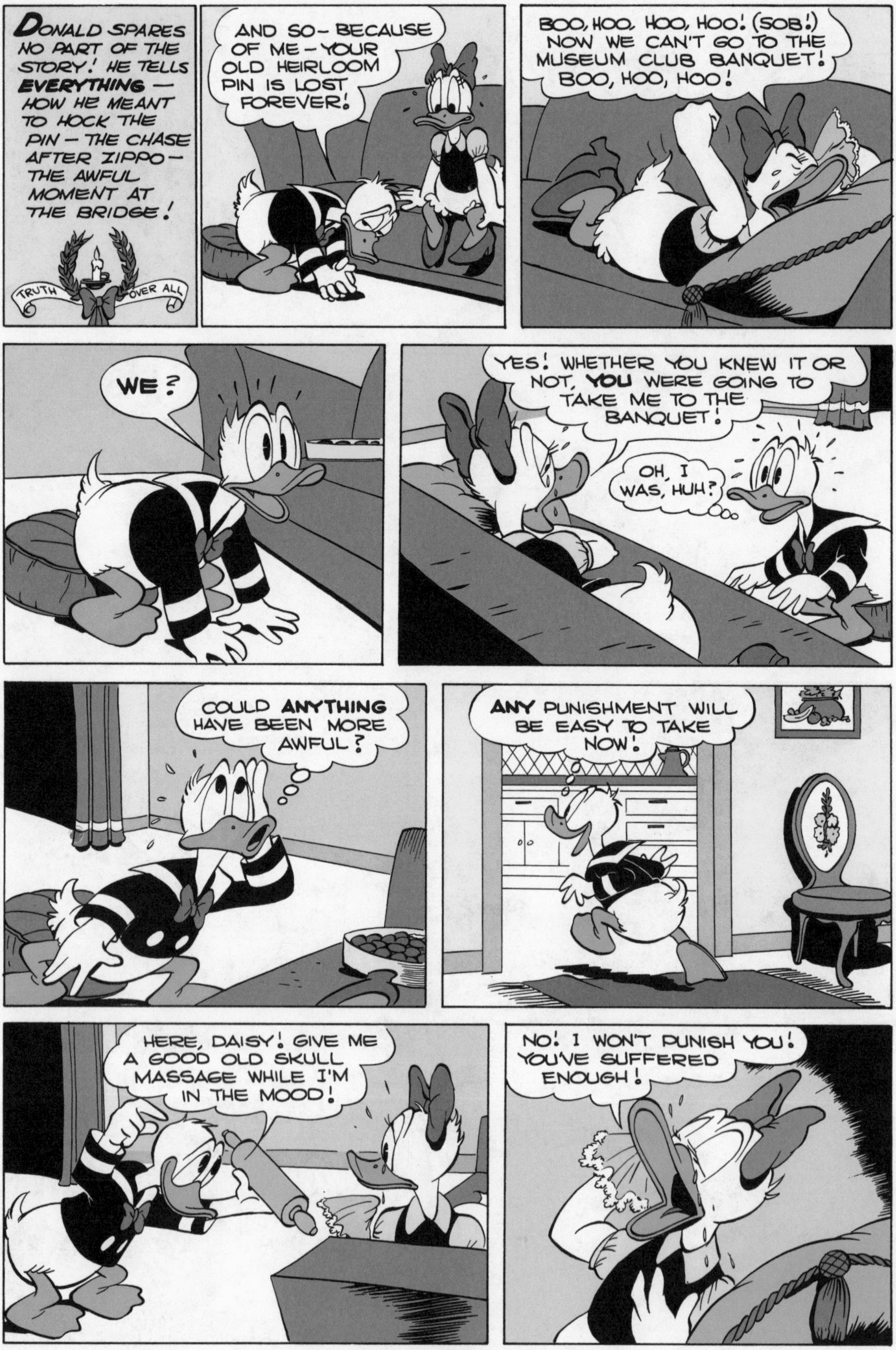
DONALD SPARES NO PART OF THE STORY! HE TELLS EVERYTHING — HOW HE MEANT TO HOCK THE PIN — THE CHASE AFTER ZIPPO — THE AWFUL MOMENT AT THE BRIDGE!
TRUTH OVER ALL
AND SO — BECAUSE OF ME — YOUR OLD HEIRLOOM PIN IS LOST FOREVER!
BOO, HOO, HOO, HOO! (SOB!) NOW WE CAN'T GO TO THE MUSEUM CLUB BANQUET! BOO, HOO, HOO!
WE?
YES! WHETHER YOU KNEW IT OR NOT, YOU WERE GOING TO TAKE ME TO THE BANQUET!
OH, I WAS, HUH?
COULD ANYTHING HAVE BEEN MORE AWFUL?
ANY PUNISHMENT WILL BE EASY TO TAKE NOW!
HERE, DAISY! GIVE ME A GOOD OLD SKULL MASSAGE WHILE I'M IN THE MOOD!
NO! I WON'T PUNISH YOU! YOU'VE SUFFERED ENOUGH!

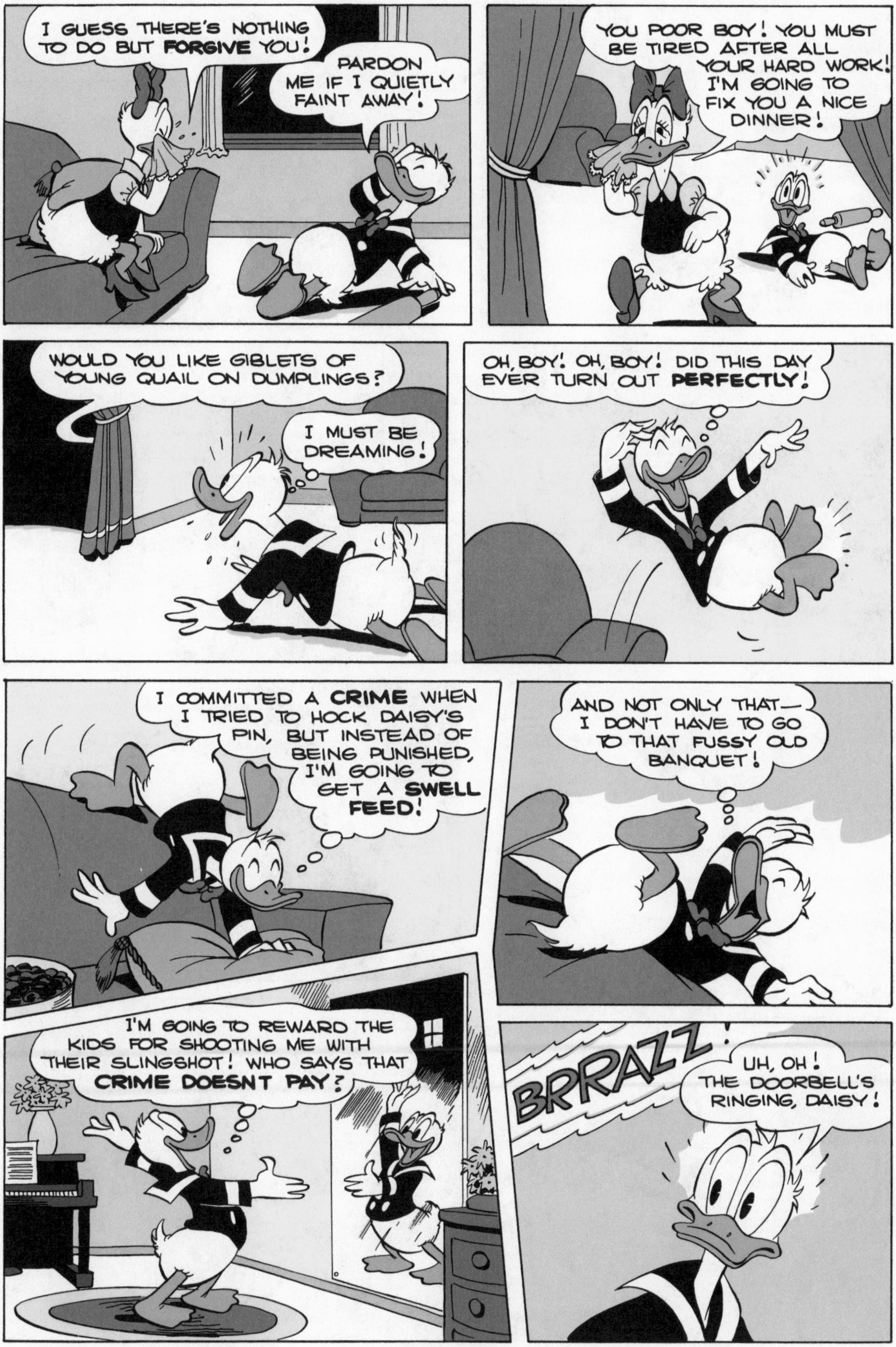
I GUESS THERE'S NOTHING TO DO BUT FORGIVE YOU!
PARDON ME IF I QUIETLY FAINT AWAY!
YOU POOR BOY! YOU MUST BE TIRED AFTER ALL YOUR HARD WORK! I'M GOING TO FIX YOU A NICE DINNER!
WOULD YOU LIKE GIBLETS OF YOUNG QUAIL ON DUMPLINGS?
I MUST BE DREAMING!
OH, BOY! OH, BOY! DID THIS DAY EVER TURN OUT PERFECTLY!
I COMMITTED A CRIME WHEN I TRIED TO HOCK DAISY'S PIN, BUT INSTEAD OF BEING PUNISHED, I'M GOING TO GET A SWELL FEED!
AND NOT ONLY THAT— I DON'T HAVE TO GO TO THAT FUSSY OLD BANQUET!
I'M GOING TO REWARD THE KIDS FOR SHOOTING ME WITH THEIR SLINGSHOT! WHO SAYS THAT CRIME DOESN'T PAY?
BRRAZZ!
UH, OH! THE DOORBELL'S RINGING, DAISY!

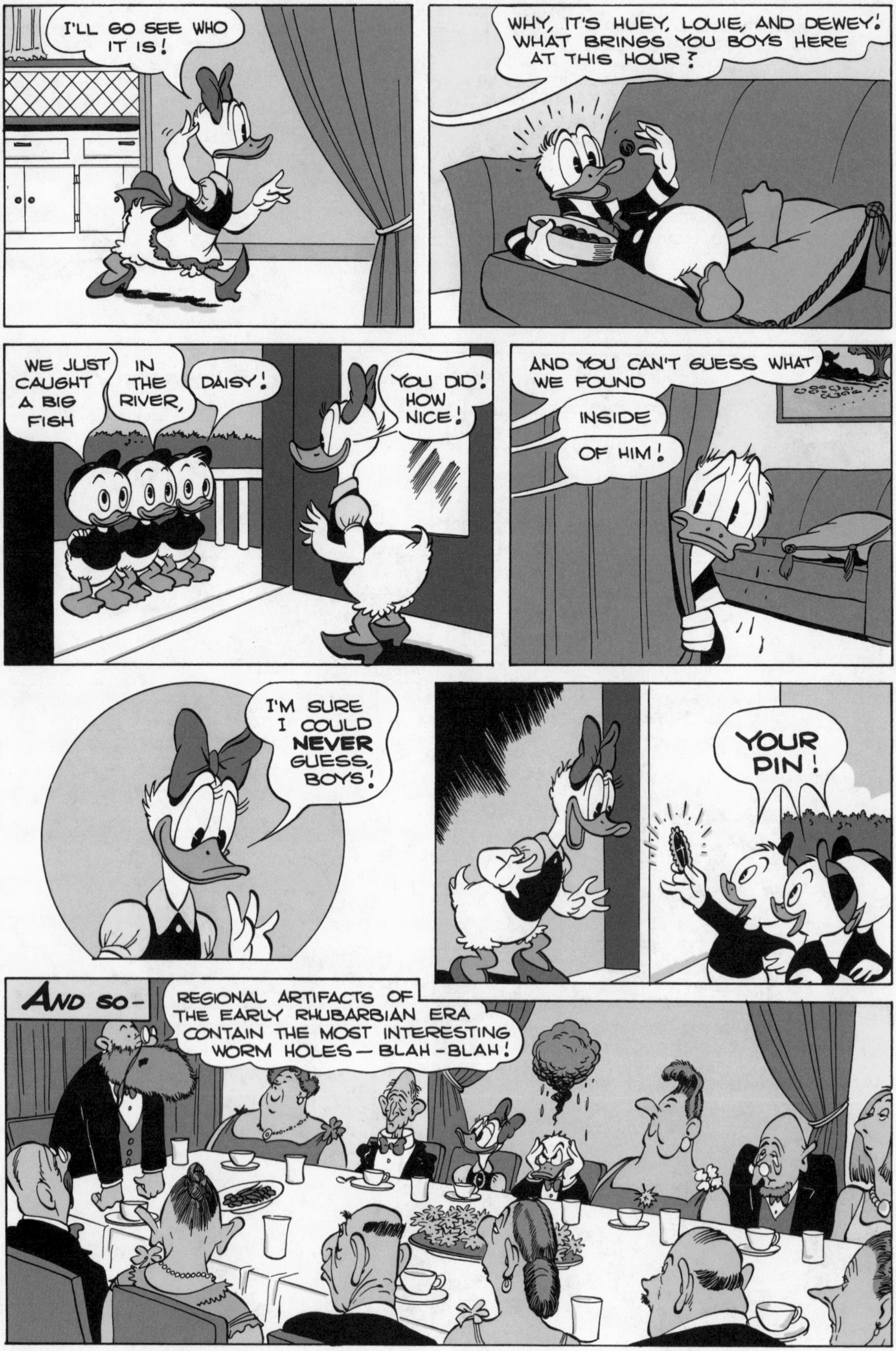
I'LL GO SEE WHO IT IS!
WHY, IT'S HUEY, LOUIE, AND DEWEY! WHAT BRINGS YOU BOYS HERE AT THIS HOUR?
WE JUST CAUGHT A BIG FISH
IN THE RIVER,
DAISY!
YOU DID! HOW NICE!
AND YOU CAN'T GUESS WHAT WE FOUND
INSIDE
OF HIM!
I'M SURE I COULD **NEVER** GUESS, BOYS!
YOUR PIN!
AND SO-
REGIONAL ARTIFACTS OF THE EARLY RHUBARBIAN ERA CONTAIN THE MOST INTERESTING WORM HOLES—BLAH-BLAH!

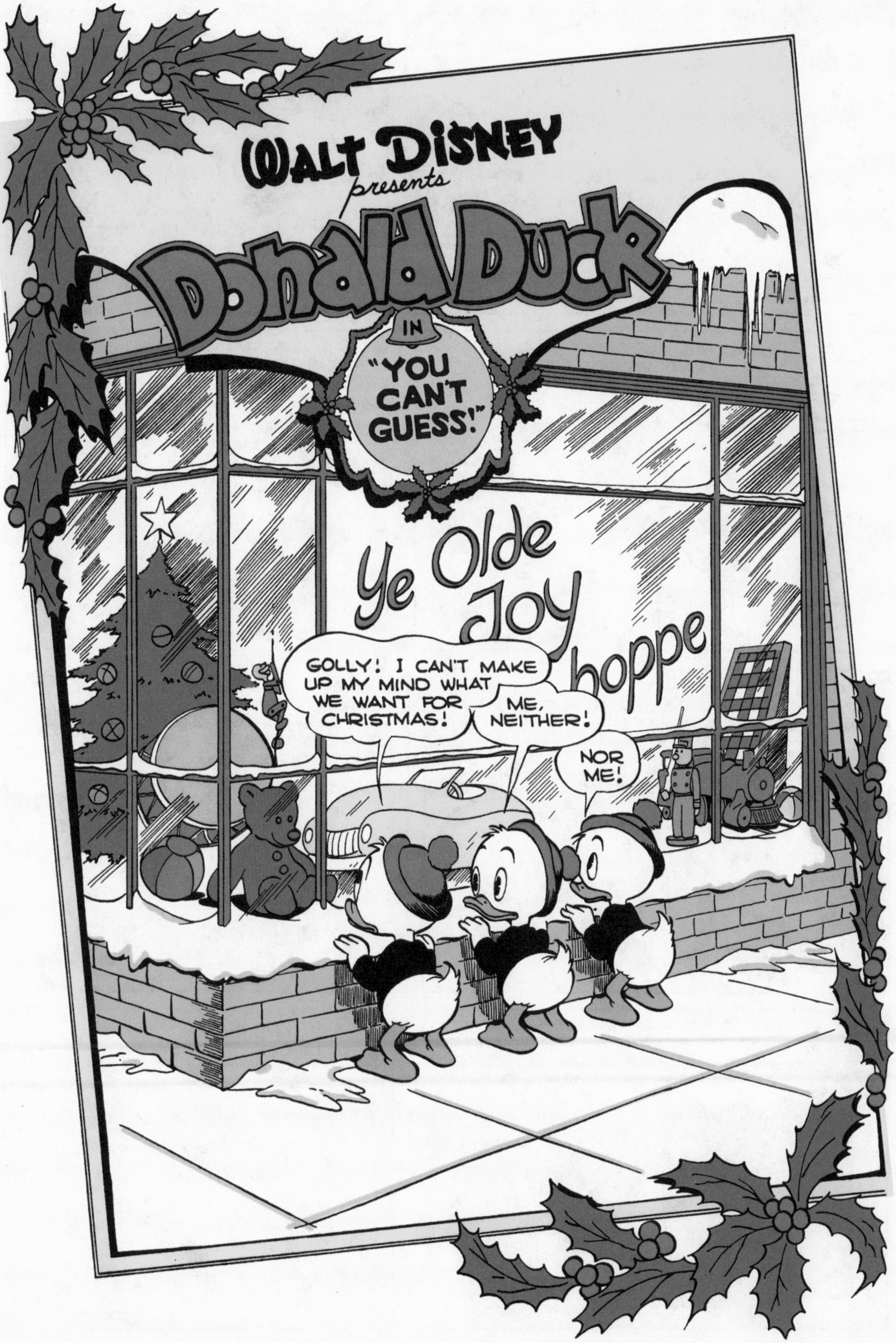
WALT DISNEY
presents
Donald Duck
IN
"YOU CAN'T GUESS!"
Ye Olde Joy Shoppe
GOLLY! I CAN'T MAKE UP MY MIND WHAT WE WANT FOR CHRISTMAS!
ME, NEITHER!
NOR ME!

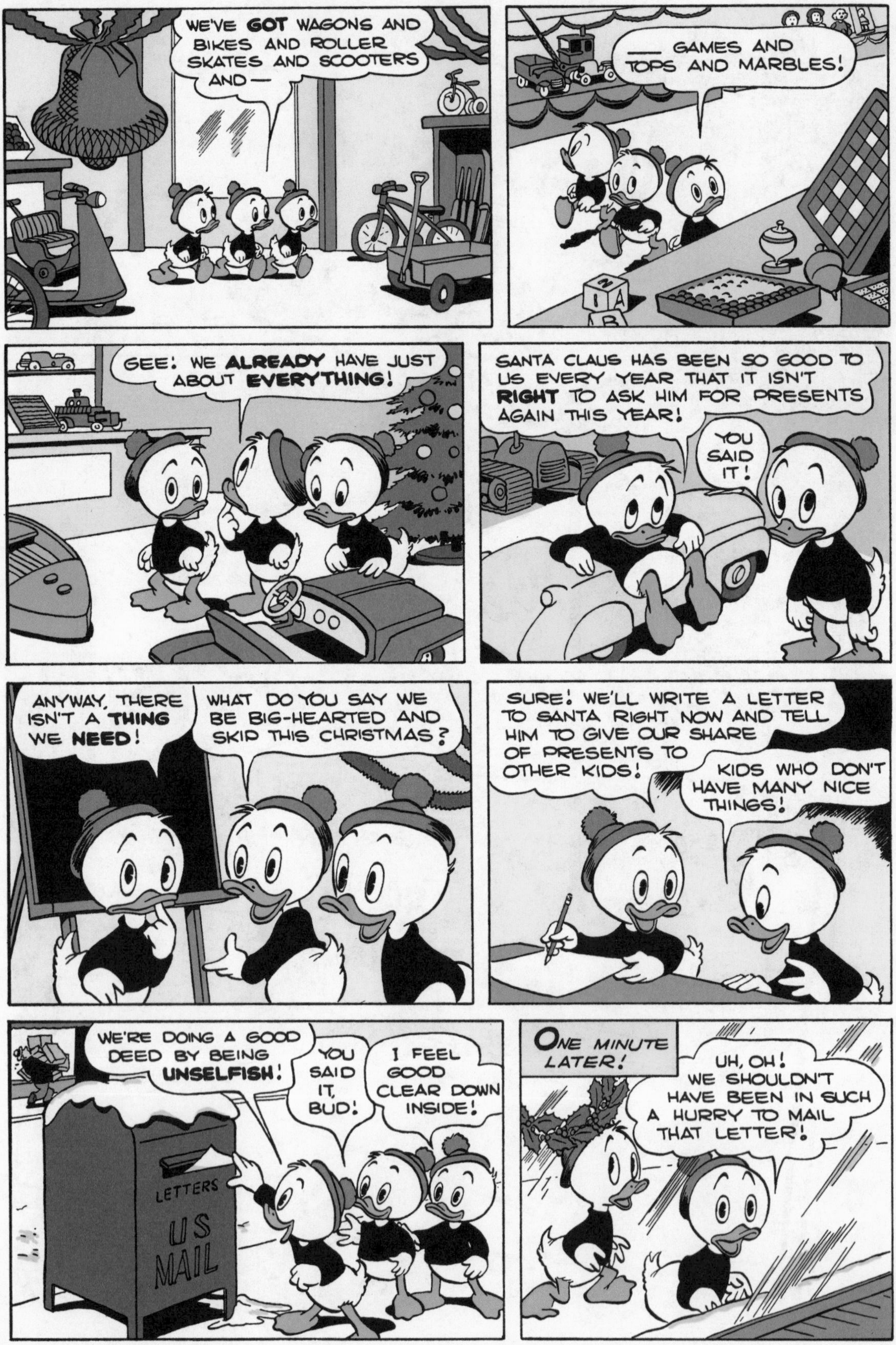
WE'VE GOT WAGONS AND BIKES AND ROLLER SKATES AND SCOOTERS AND—
— GAMES AND TOPS AND MARBLES!
GEE! WE ALREADY HAVE JUST ABOUT EVERYTHING!
SANTA CLAUS HAS BEEN SO GOOD TO US EVERY YEAR THAT IT ISN'T RIGHT TO ASK HIM FOR PRESENTS AGAIN THIS YEAR!
YOU SAID IT!
ANYWAY, THERE ISN'T A THING WE NEED!
WHAT DO YOU SAY WE BE BIG-HEARTED AND SKIP THIS CHRISTMAS?
SURE! WE'LL WRITE A LETTER TO SANTA RIGHT NOW AND TELL HIM TO GIVE OUR SHARE OF PRESENTS TO OTHER KIDS!
KIDS WHO DON'T HAVE MANY NICE THINGS!
WE'RE DOING A GOOD DEED BY BEING UNSELFISH!
YOU SAID IT, BUD!
I FEEL GOOD CLEAR DOWN INSIDE!
LETTERS
US MAIL
ONE MINUTE LATER!
UH, OH! WE SHOULDN'T HAVE BEEN IN SUCH A HURRY TO MAIL THAT LETTER!

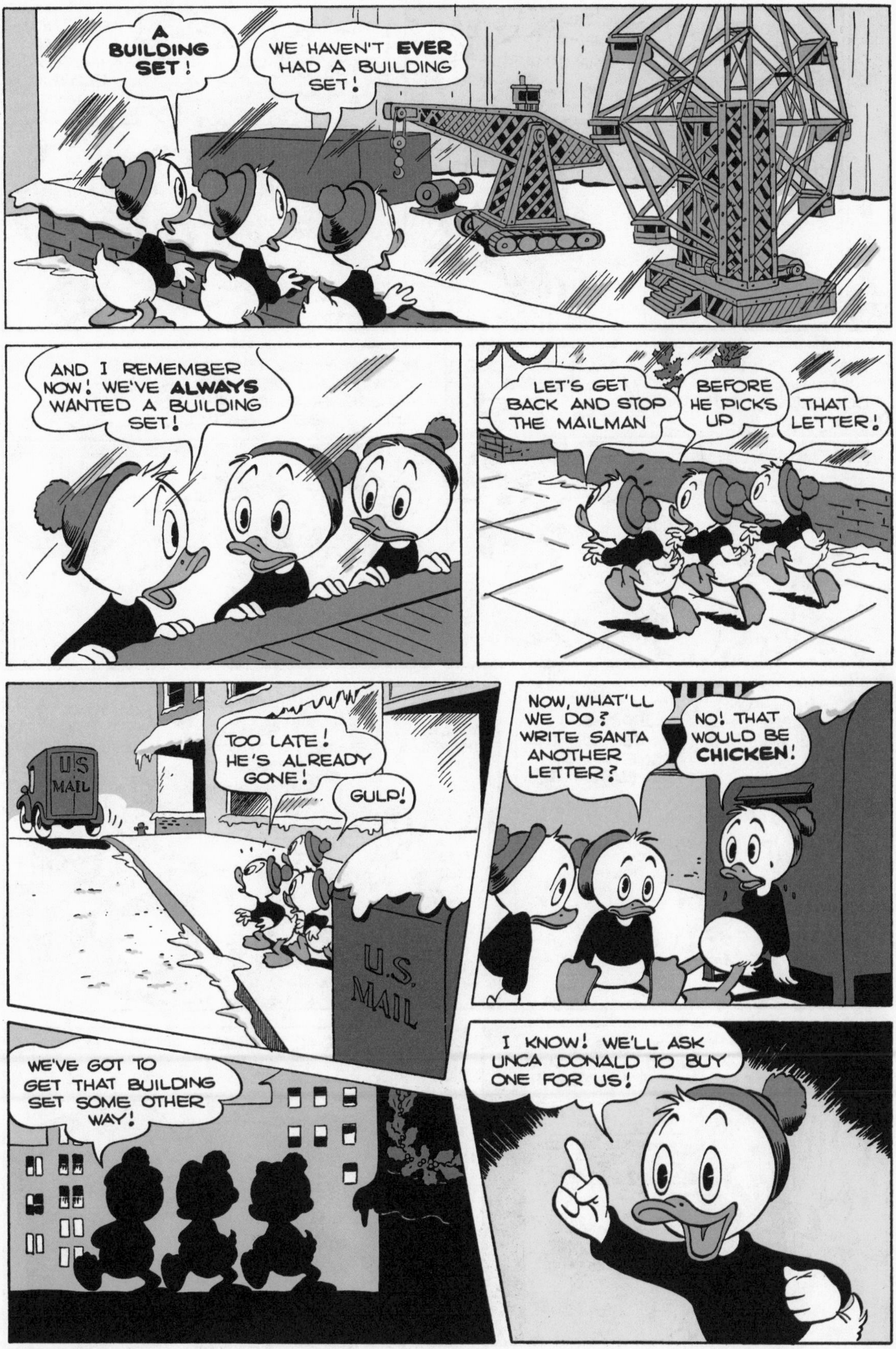
A BUILDING SET!
WE HAVEN'T EVER HAD A BUILDING SET!
AND I REMEMBER NOW! WE'VE ALWAYS WANTED A BUILDING SET!
LET'S GET BACK AND STOP THE MAILMAN
BEFORE HE PICKS UP
THAT LETTER!
U.S. MAIL
TOO LATE! HE'S ALREADY GONE!
GULP!
U.S. MAIL
NOW, WHAT'LL WE DO? WRITE SANTA ANOTHER LETTER?
NO! THAT WOULD BE CHICKEN!
WE'VE GOT TO GET THAT BUILDING SET SOME OTHER WAY!
I KNOW! WE'LL ASK UNCA DONALD TO BUY ONE FOR US!

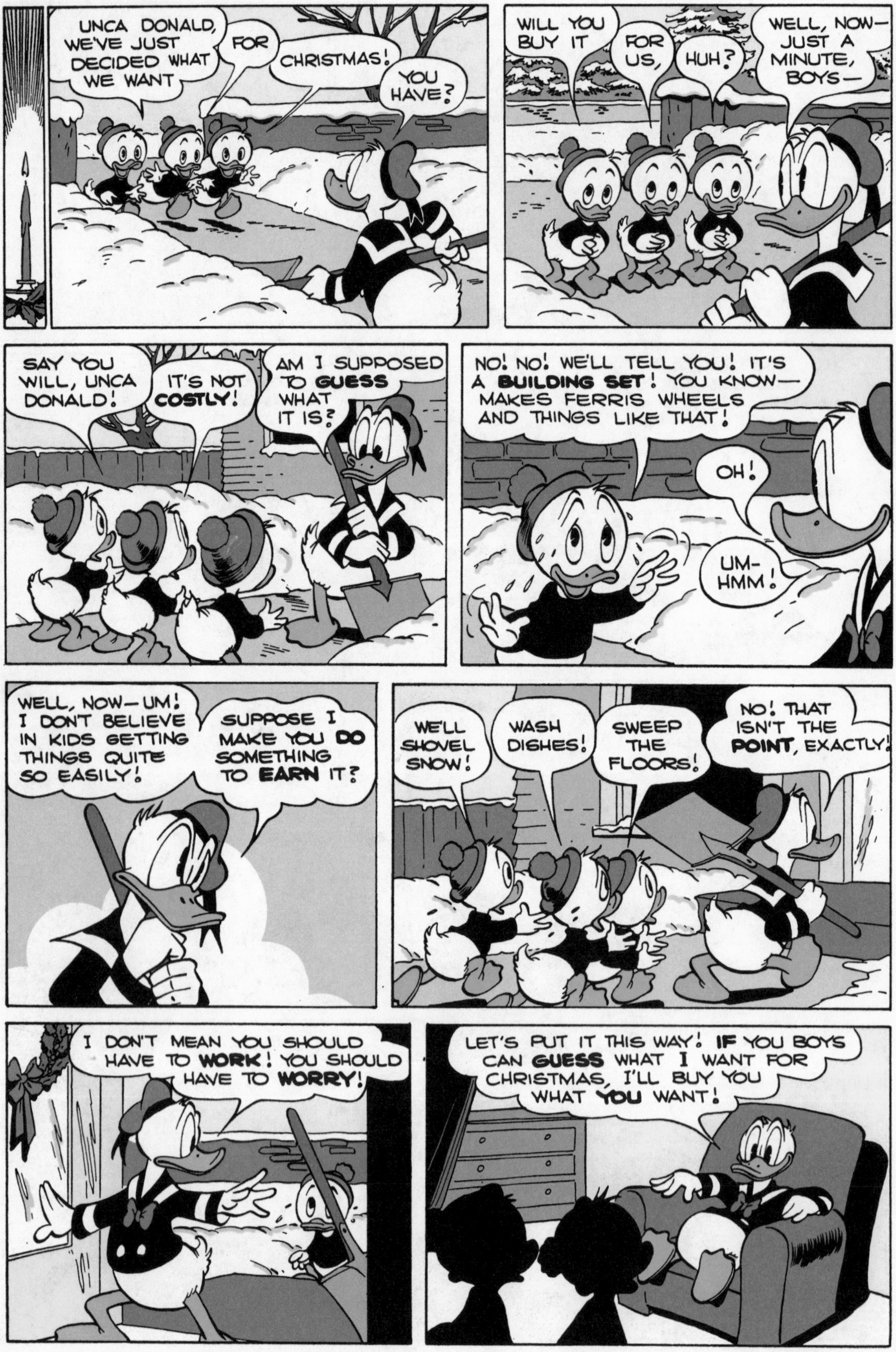
UNCA DONALD, WE'VE JUST DECIDED WHAT WE WANT
FOR
CHRISTMAS!
YOU HAVE?
WILL YOU BUY IT
FOR US,
HUH?
WELL, NOW— JUST A MINUTE, BOYS—
SAY YOU WILL, UNCA DONALD!
IT'S NOT **COSTLY**!
AM I SUPPOSED TO **GUESS** WHAT IT IS?
NO! NO! WE'LL TELL YOU! IT'S A **BUILDING SET**! YOU KNOW— MAKES FERRIS WHEELS AND THINGS LIKE THAT!
OH!
UM-HMM!
WELL, NOW—UM! I DON'T BELIEVE IN KIDS GETTING THINGS QUITE SO EASILY!
SUPPOSE I MAKE YOU **DO** SOMETHING TO **EARN** IT?
WE'LL SHOVEL SNOW!
WASH DISHES!
SWEEP THE FLOORS!
NO! THAT ISN'T THE **POINT**, EXACTLY!
I DON'T MEAN YOU SHOULD HAVE TO **WORK**! YOU SHOULD HAVE TO **WORRY**!
LET'S PUT IT THIS WAY! **IF** YOU BOYS CAN **GUESS** WHAT **I** WANT FOR CHRISTMAS, I'LL BUY YOU WHAT **YOU** WANT!

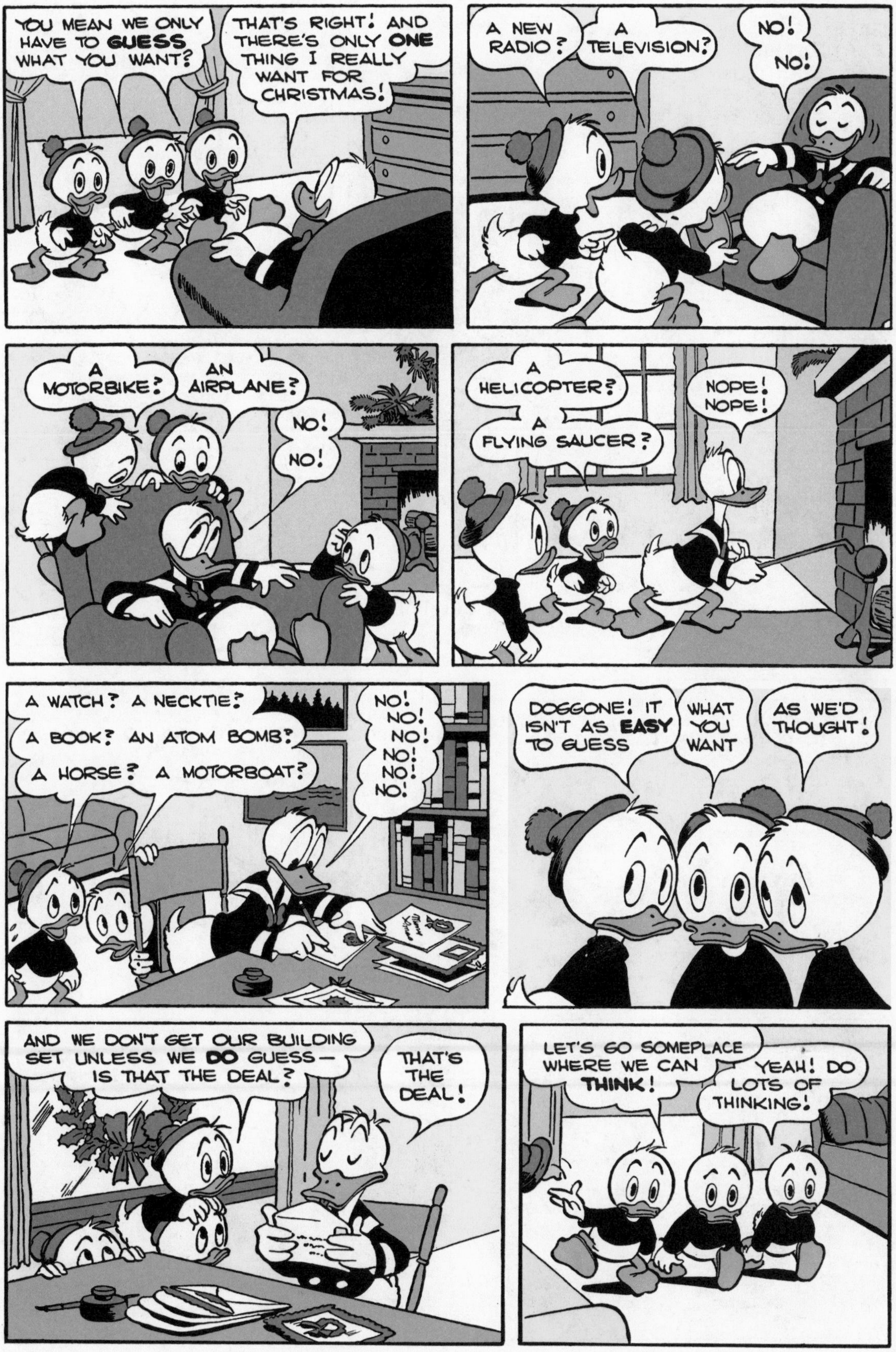
YOU MEAN WE ONLY HAVE TO **GUESS** WHAT YOU WANT?
THAT'S RIGHT! AND THERE'S ONLY **ONE** THING I REALLY WANT FOR CHRISTMAS!
A NEW RADIO?
A TELEVISION?
NO!
NO!
A MOTORBIKE?
AN AIRPLANE?
NO!
NO!
A HELICOPTER?
A FLYING SAUCER?
NOPE! NOPE!
A WATCH? A NECKTIE?
A BOOK? AN ATOM BOMB?
A HORSE? A MOTORBOAT?
NO! NO! NO! NO! NO! NO!
DOGGONE! IT ISN'T AS **EASY** TO GUESS
WHAT YOU WANT
AS WE'D THOUGHT!
AND WE DON'T GET OUR BUILDING SET UNLESS WE **DO** GUESS— IS THAT THE DEAL?
THAT'S THE DEAL!
LET'S GO SOMEPLACE WHERE WE CAN **THINK**!
YEAH! DO LOTS OF THINKING!

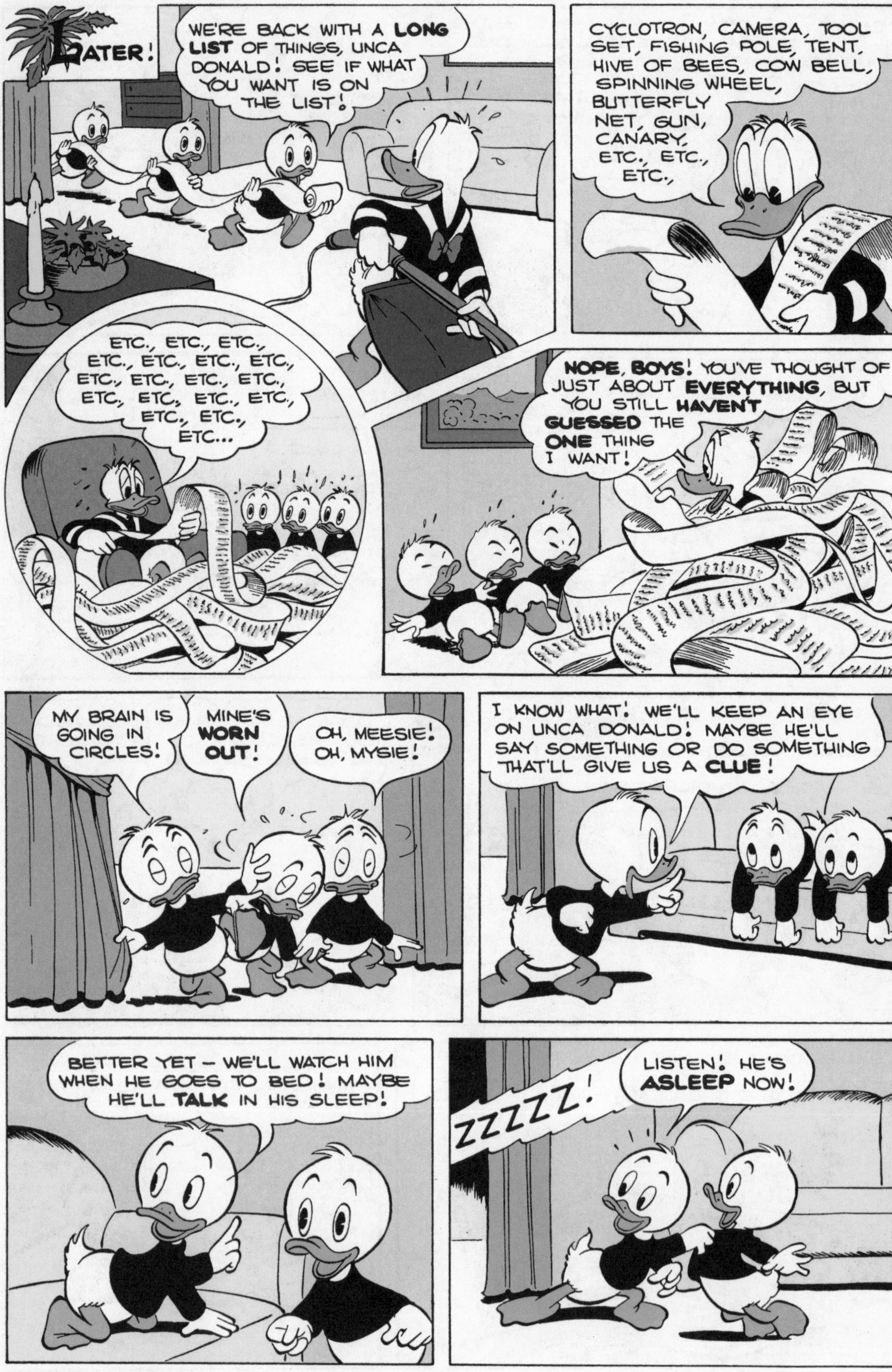
LATER!
WE'RE BACK WITH A LONG LIST OF THINGS, UNCA DONALD! SEE IF WHAT YOU WANT IS ON THE LIST!
CYCLOTRON, CAMERA, TOOL SET, FISHING POLE, TENT, HIVE OF BEES, COW BELL, SPINNING WHEEL, BUTTERFLY NET, GUN, CANARY, ETC., ETC., ETC.,
ETC., ETC., ETC., ETC., ETC., ETC., ETC., ETC., ETC., ETC., ETC., ETC., ETC., ETC., ETC., ETC., ETC., ETC., ETC...
NOPE, BOYS! YOU'VE THOUGHT OF JUST ABOUT EVERYTHING, BUT YOU STILL HAVEN'T GUESSED THE ONE THING I WANT!
MY BRAIN IS GOING IN CIRCLES!
MINE'S WORN OUT!
OH, MEESIE! OH, MYSIE!
I KNOW WHAT! WE'LL KEEP AN EYE ON UNCA DONALD! MAYBE HE'LL SAY SOMETHING OR DO SOMETHING THAT'LL GIVE US A CLUE!
BETTER YET – WE'LL WATCH HIM WHEN HE GOES TO BED! MAYBE HE'LL TALK IN HIS SLEEP!
ZZZZZ!
LISTEN! HE'S ASLEEP NOW!

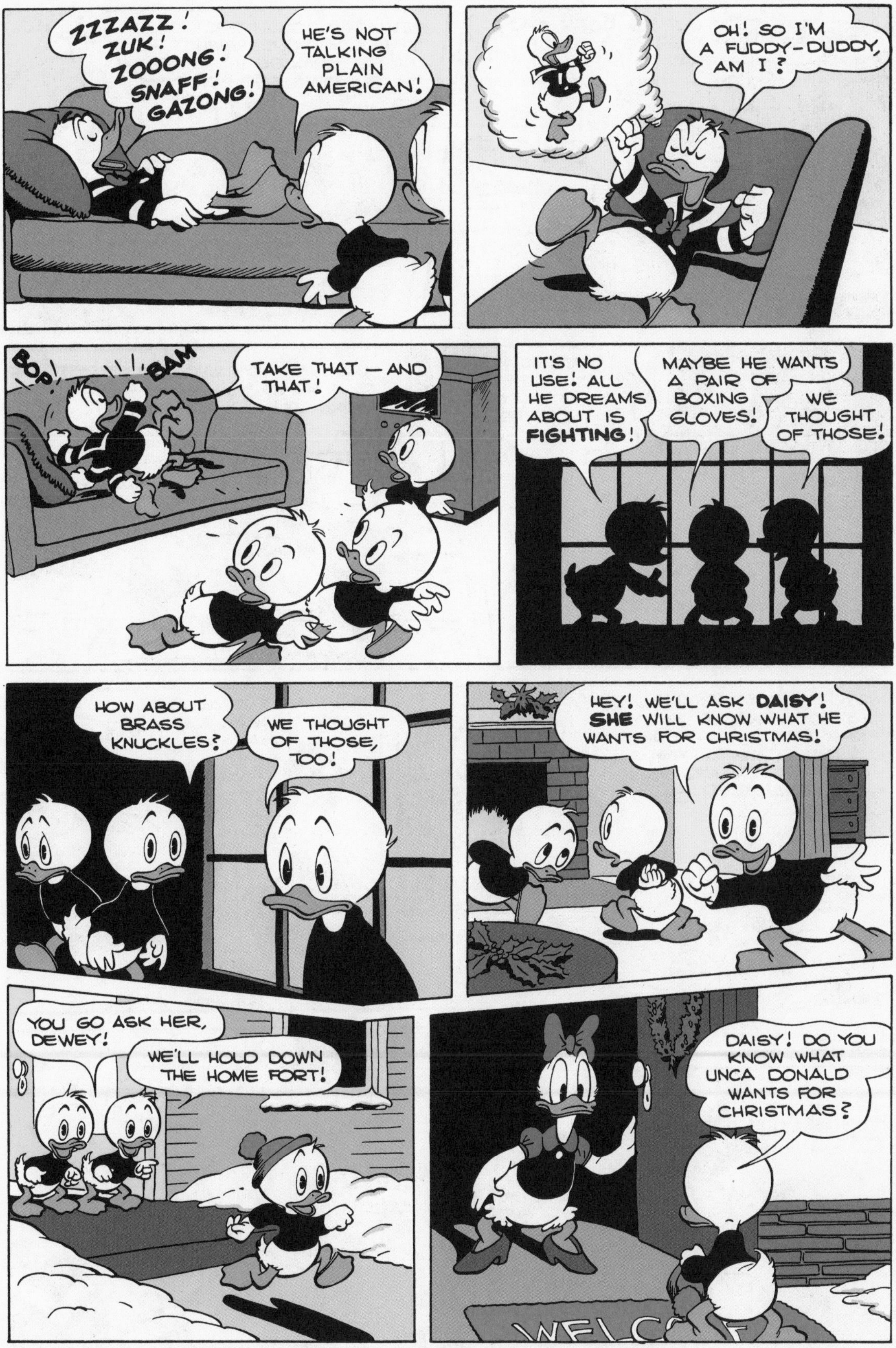
ZZZAZZ! ZUK! ZOOONG! SNAFF! GAZONG!
HE'S NOT TALKING PLAIN AMERICAN!
OH! SO I'M A FUDDY-DUDDY, AM I?
BOP!
BAM
TAKE THAT — AND THAT!
IT'S NO USE! ALL HE DREAMS ABOUT IS FIGHTING!
MAYBE HE WANTS A PAIR OF BOXING GLOVES!
WE THOUGHT OF THOSE!
HOW ABOUT BRASS KNUCKLES?
WE THOUGHT OF THOSE, TOO!
HEY! WE'LL ASK DAISY! SHE WILL KNOW WHAT HE WANTS FOR CHRISTMAS!
YOU GO ASK HER, DEWEY!
WE'LL HOLD DOWN THE HOME FORT!
DAISY! DO YOU KNOW WHAT UNCA DONALD WANTS FOR CHRISTMAS?

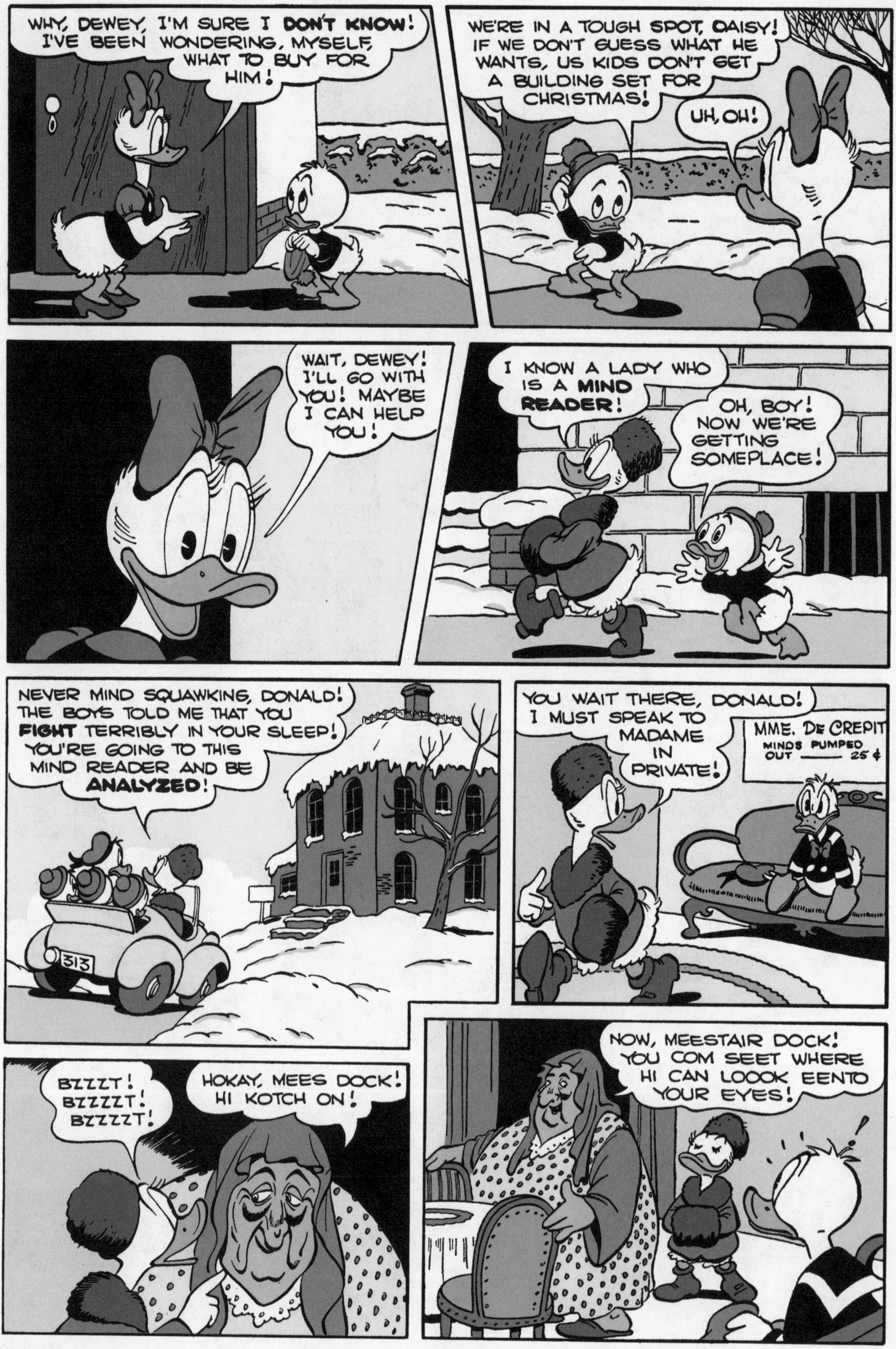
WHY, DEWEY, I'M SURE I **DON'T KNOW**! I'VE BEEN WONDERING, MYSELF, WHAT TO BUY FOR HIM!
WE'RE IN A TOUGH SPOT, DAISY! IF WE DON'T GUESS WHAT HE WANTS, US KIDS DON'T GET A BUILDING SET FOR CHRISTMAS!
UH, OH!
WAIT, DEWEY! I'LL GO WITH YOU! MAYBE I CAN HELP YOU!
I KNOW A LADY WHO IS A **MIND READER**!
OH, BOY! NOW WE'RE GETTING SOMEPLACE!
NEVER MIND SQUAWKING, DONALD! THE BOYS TOLD ME THAT YOU **FIGHT** TERRIBLY IN YOUR SLEEP! YOU'RE GOING TO THIS MIND READER AND BE **ANALYZED**!
313
YOU WAIT THERE, DONALD! I MUST SPEAK TO MADAME IN PRIVATE!
MME. DE CREPIT
MINDS PUMPED OUT —— 25¢
BZZZZT! BZZZZT! BZZZZT!
HOKAY, MEES DOCK! HI KOTCH ON!
NOW, MEESTAIR DOCK! YOU COM SEET WHERE HI CAN LOOOK EENTO YOUR EYES!

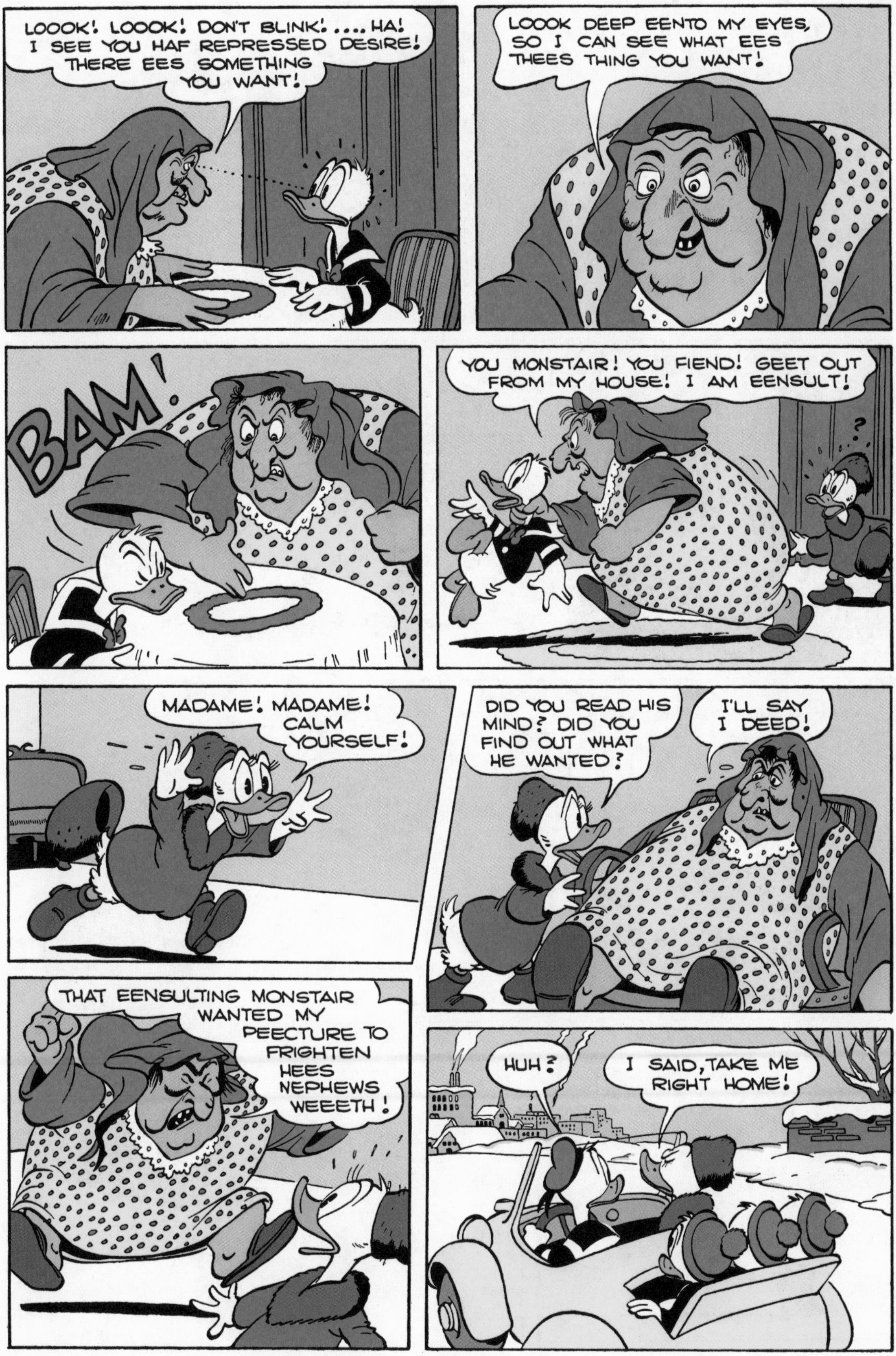
LOOOK! LOOOK! DON'T BLINK! ....HA! I SEE YOU HAF REPRESSED DESIRE! THERE EES SOMETHING YOU WANT!
LOOOK DEEP EENTO MY EYES, SO I CAN SEE WHAT EES THEES THING YOU WANT!
BAM!
YOU MONSTAIR! YOU FIEND! GEET OUT FROM MY HOUSE! I AM EENSULT!
?
MADAME! MADAME! CALM YOURSELF!
DID YOU READ HIS MIND? DID YOU FIND OUT WHAT HE WANTED?
I'LL SAY I DEED!
THAT EENSULTING MONSTAIR WANTED MY PEECTURE TO FRIGHTEN HEES NEPHEWS WEEEETH!
HUH?
I SAID, TAKE ME RIGHT HOME!

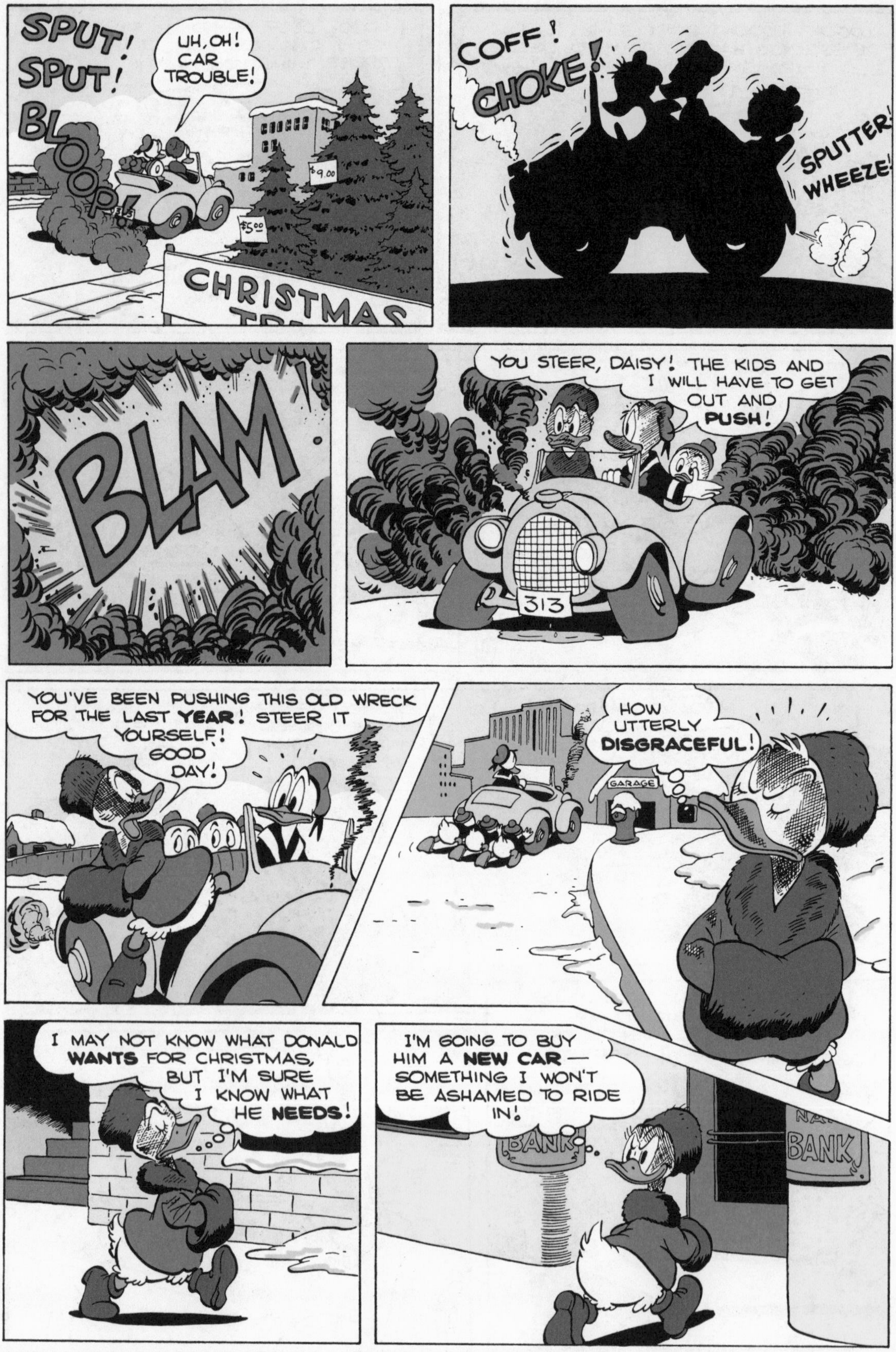
SPUT! SPUT! BLOOP!
UH, OH! CAR TROUBLE!
$9.00
$5.00
CHRISTMAS
COFF! CHOKE!
SPUTTER! WHEEZE!
BLAM
YOU STEER, DAISY! THE KIDS AND I WILL HAVE TO GET OUT AND PUSH!
313
YOU'VE BEEN PUSHING THIS OLD WRECK FOR THE LAST YEAR! STEER IT YOURSELF! GOOD DAY!
HOW UTTERLY DISGRACEFUL!
GARAGE
I MAY NOT KNOW WHAT DONALD WANTS FOR CHRISTMAS, BUT I'M SURE I KNOW WHAT HE NEEDS!
I'M GOING TO BUY HIM A NEW CAR — SOMETHING I WON'T BE ASHAMED TO RIDE IN!
BANK
BANK

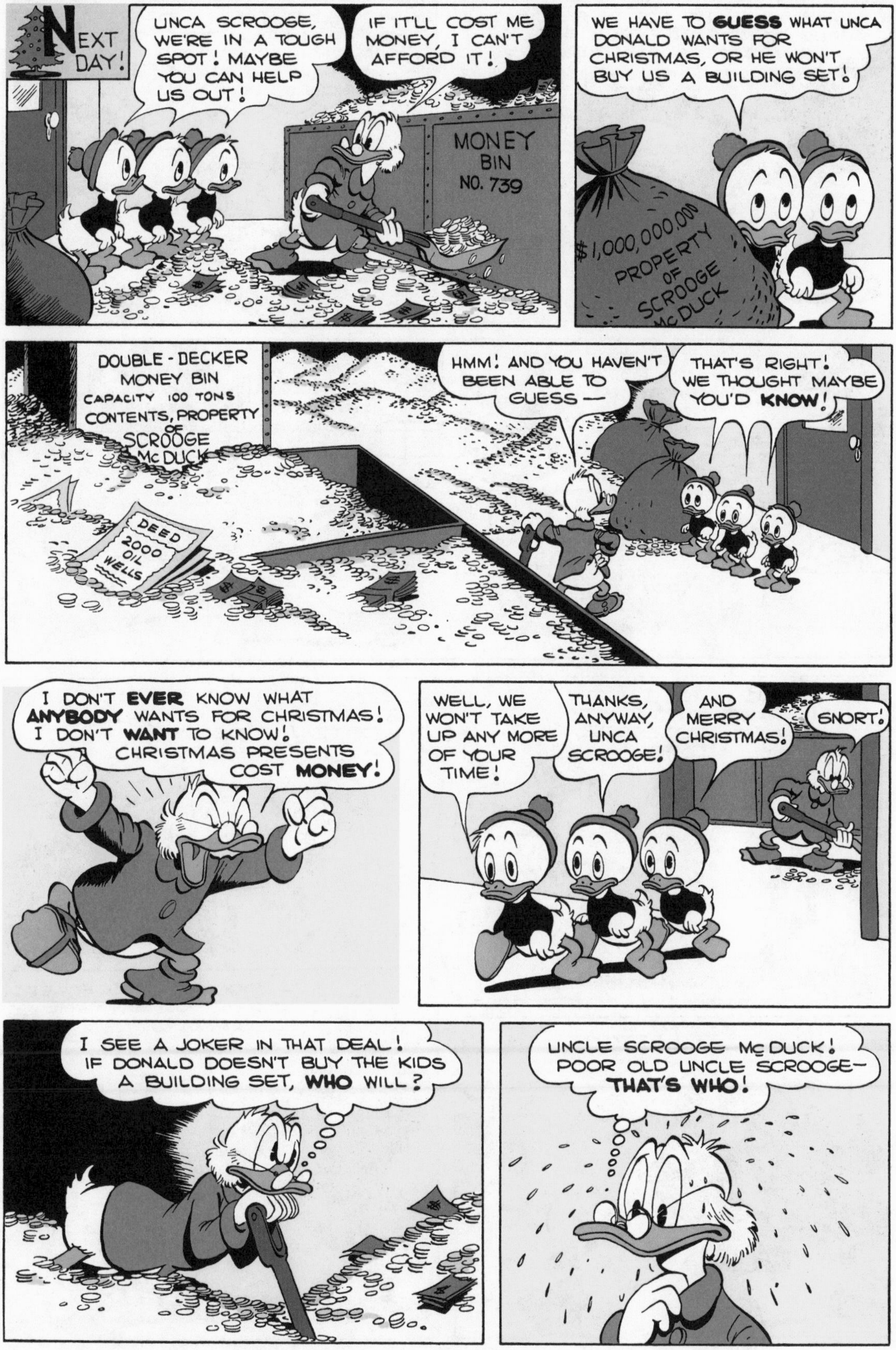
NEXT DAY!
UNCA SCROOGE, WE'RE IN A TOUGH SPOT! MAYBE YOU CAN HELP US OUT!
IF IT'LL COST ME MONEY, I CAN'T AFFORD IT!
MONEY BIN NO. 739
WE HAVE TO GUESS WHAT UNCA DONALD WANTS FOR CHRISTMAS, OR HE WON'T BUY US A BUILDING SET!
$1,000,000,000 PROPERTY OF SCROOGE McDUCK
DOUBLE-DECKER MONEY BIN CAPACITY 100 TONS CONTENTS, PROPERTY OF SCROOGE McDUCK
DEED 2000 OIL WELLS
HMM! AND YOU HAVEN'T BEEN ABLE TO GUESS—
THAT'S RIGHT! WE THOUGHT MAYBE YOU'D KNOW!
I DON'T EVER KNOW WHAT ANYBODY WANTS FOR CHRISTMAS! I DON'T WANT TO KNOW! CHRISTMAS PRESENTS COST MONEY!
WELL, WE WON'T TAKE UP ANY MORE OF YOUR TIME!
THANKS, ANYWAY, UNCA SCROOGE!
AND MERRY CHRISTMAS!
SNORT!
I SEE A JOKER IN THAT DEAL! IF DONALD DOESN'T BUY THE KIDS A BUILDING SET, WHO WILL?
UNCLE SCROOGE McDUCK! POOR OLD UNCLE SCROOGE— THAT'S WHO!

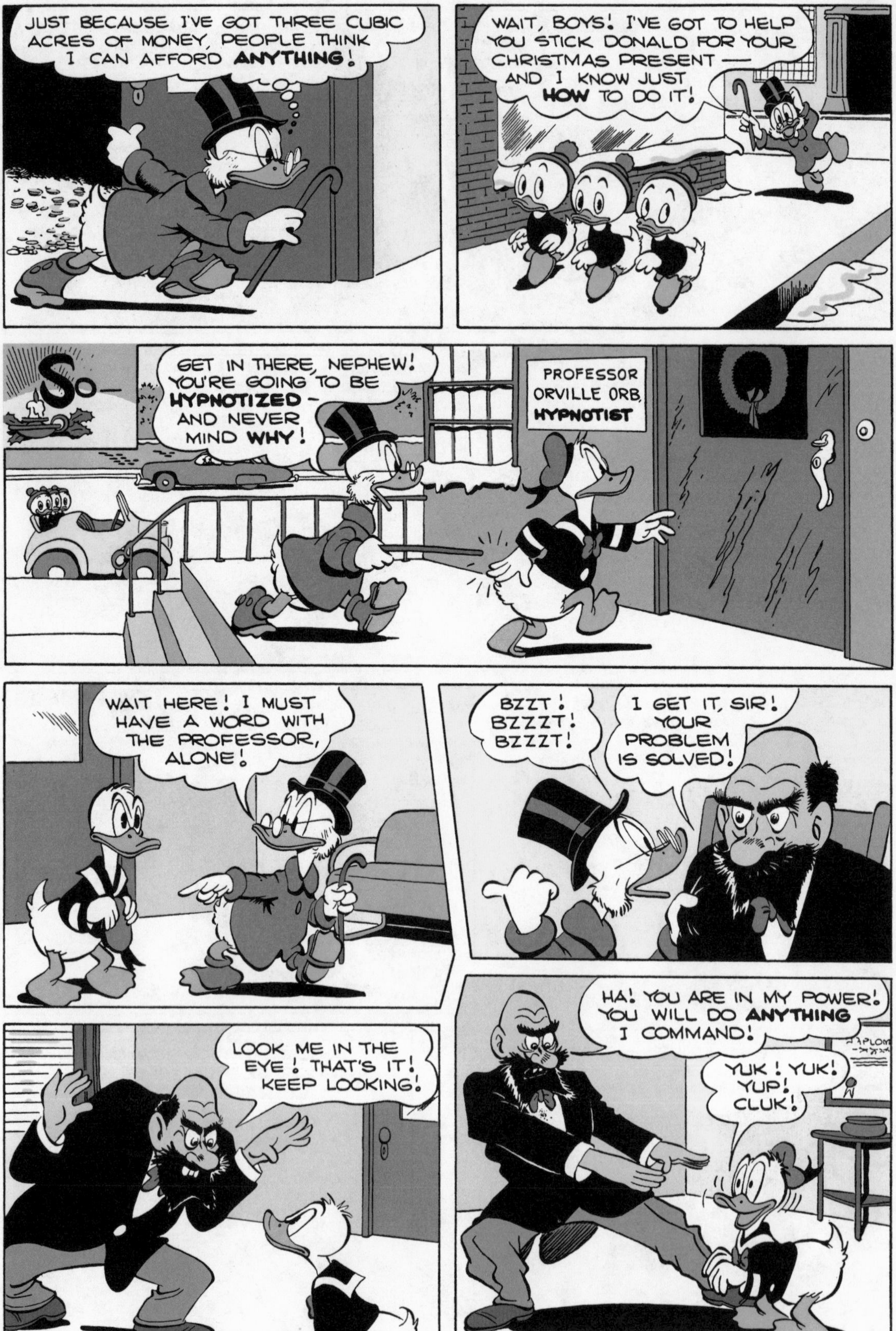
JUST BECAUSE I'VE GOT THREE CUBIC ACRES OF MONEY, PEOPLE THINK I CAN AFFORD **ANYTHING**!
WAIT, BOYS! I'VE GOT TO HELP YOU STICK DONALD FOR YOUR CHRISTMAS PRESENT — AND I KNOW JUST **HOW** TO DO IT!
SO—
GET IN THERE, NEPHEW! YOU'RE GOING TO BE **HYPNOTIZED** — AND NEVER MIND **WHY**!
PROFESSOR ORVILLE ORB, **HYPNOTIST**
WAIT HERE! I MUST HAVE A WORD WITH THE PROFESSOR, ALONE!
BZZT! BZZZT! BZZZT!
I GET IT, SIR! YOUR PROBLEM IS SOLVED!
LOOK ME IN THE EYE! THAT'S IT! KEEP LOOKING!
HA! YOU ARE IN MY POWER! YOU WILL DO **ANYTHING** I COMMAND!
YUK! YUK! YUP! CLUK!

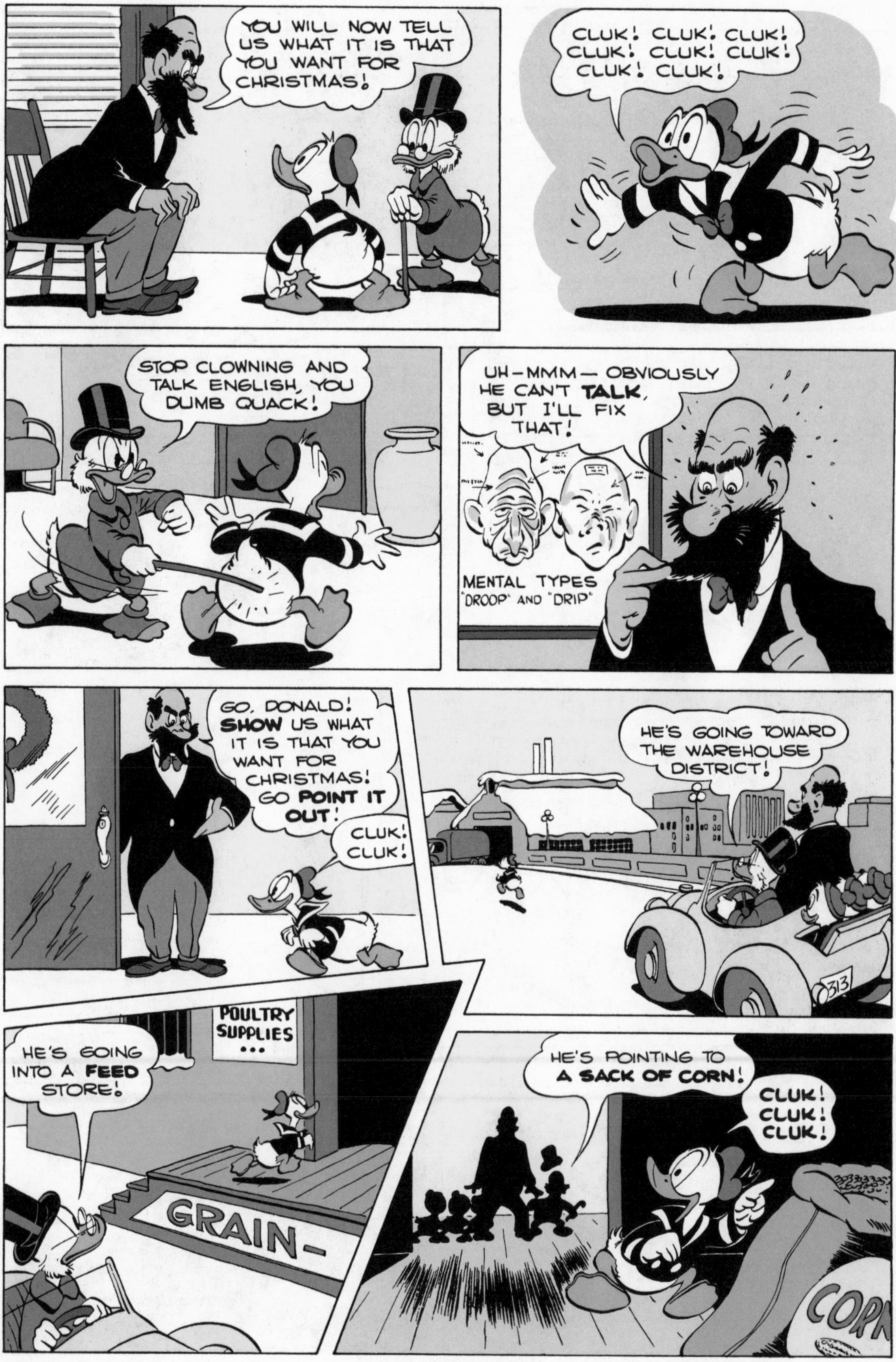
YOU WILL NOW TELL US WHAT IT IS THAT YOU WANT FOR CHRISTMAS!
CLUK! CLUK! CLUK! CLUK! CLUK! CLUK! CLUK! CLUK!
STOP CLOWNING AND TALK ENGLISH, YOU DUMB QUACK!
UH-MMM— OBVIOUSLY HE CAN'T TALK, BUT I'LL FIX THAT!
MENTAL TYPES "DROOP" AND "DRIP"
GO, DONALD! SHOW US WHAT IT IS THAT YOU WANT FOR CHRISTMAS! GO POINT IT OUT!
CLUK! CLUK!
HE'S GOING TOWARD THE WAREHOUSE DISTRICT!
313
POULTRY SUPPLIES ...
HE'S GOING INTO A FEED STORE!
GRAIN-
HE'S POINTING TO A SACK OF CORN!
CLUK! CLUK! CLUK!
CORN

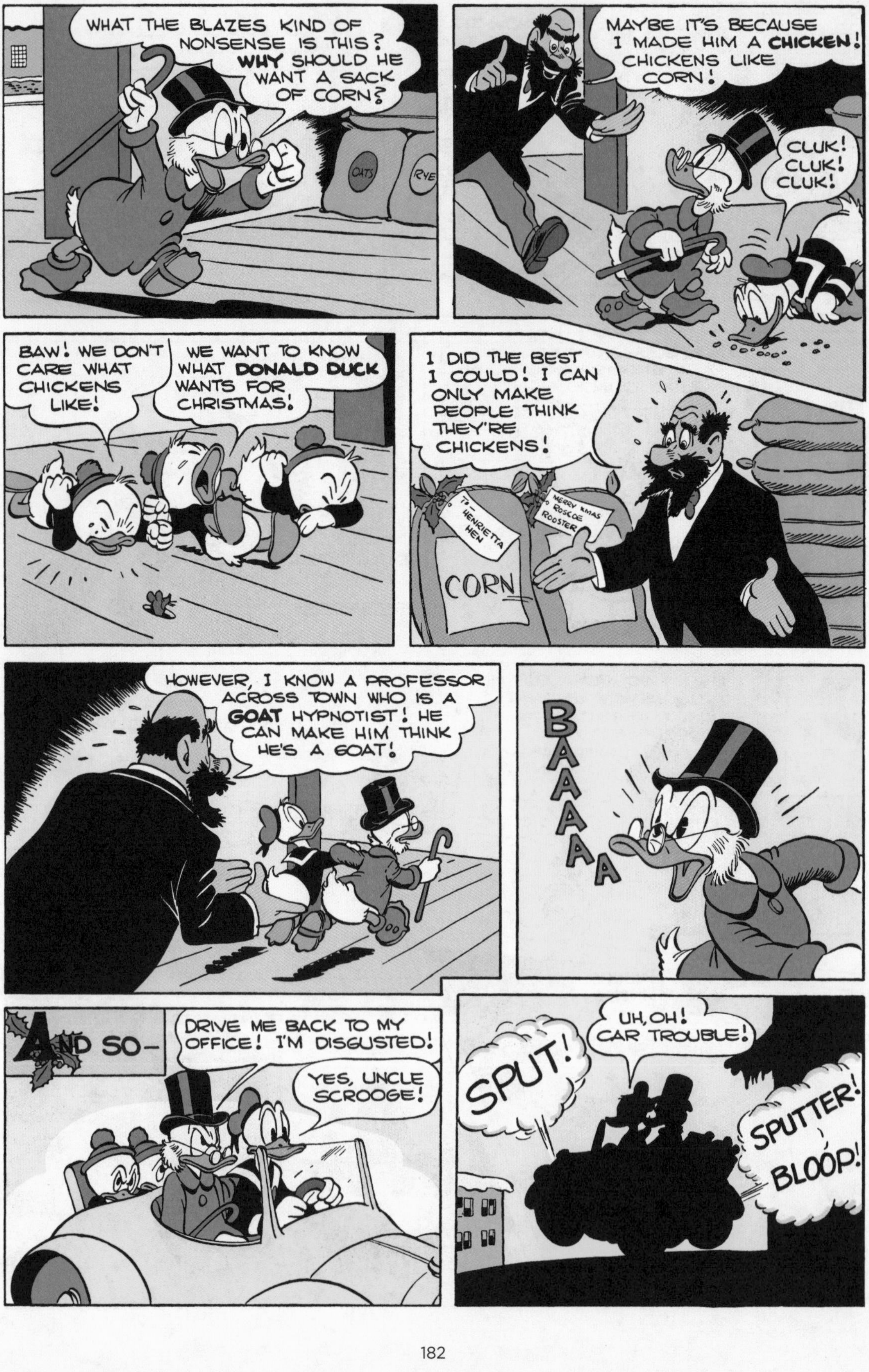
WHAT THE BLAZES KIND OF NONSENSE IS THIS? WHY SHOULD HE WANT A SACK OF CORN?
OATS
RYE
MAYBE IT'S BECAUSE I MADE HIM A CHICKEN! CHICKENS LIKE CORN!
CLUK! CLUK! CLUK!
BAW! WE DON'T CARE WHAT CHICKENS LIKE!
WE WANT TO KNOW WHAT DONALD DUCK WANTS FOR CHRISTMAS!
I DID THE BEST I COULD! I CAN ONLY MAKE PEOPLE THINK THEY'RE CHICKENS!
TO— HENRIETTA HEN
MERRY XMAS TO ROSCOE ROOSTER
CORN
HOWEVER, I KNOW A PROFESSOR ACROSS TOWN WHO IS A GOAT HYPNOTIST! HE CAN MAKE HIM THINK HE'S A GOAT!
BAAAAA
AND SO—
DRIVE ME BACK TO MY OFFICE! I'M DISGUSTED!
YES, UNCLE SCROOGE!
UH, OH! CAR TROUBLE!
SPUT!
SPUTTER!
BLOOP!

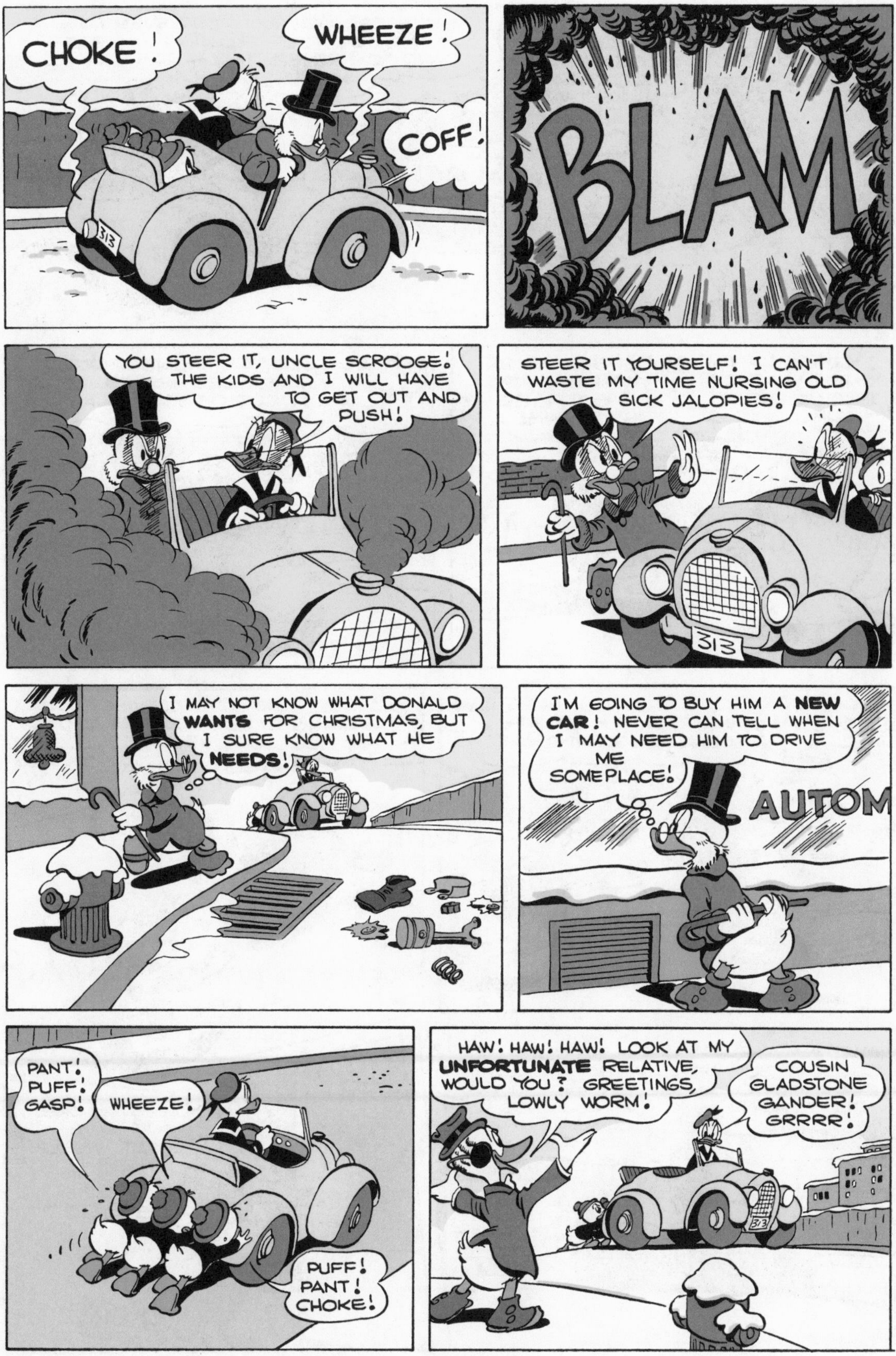
CHOKE!
WHEEZE!
COFF!
BLAM
YOU STEER IT, UNCLE SCROOGE! THE KIDS AND I WILL HAVE TO GET OUT AND PUSH!
STEER IT YOURSELF! I CAN'T WASTE MY TIME NURSING OLD SICK JALOPIES!
I MAY NOT KNOW WHAT DONALD WANTS FOR CHRISTMAS, BUT I SURE KNOW WHAT HE NEEDS!
I'M GOING TO BUY HIM A NEW CAR! NEVER CAN TELL WHEN I MAY NEED HIM TO DRIVE ME SOMEPLACE!
AUTOM
PANT! PUFF! GASP!
WHEEZE!
PUFF! PANT! CHOKE!
HAW! HAW! HAW! LOOK AT MY UNFORTUNATE RELATIVE, WOULD YOU? GREETINGS, LOWLY WORM!
COUSIN GLADSTONE GANDER! GRRRR!

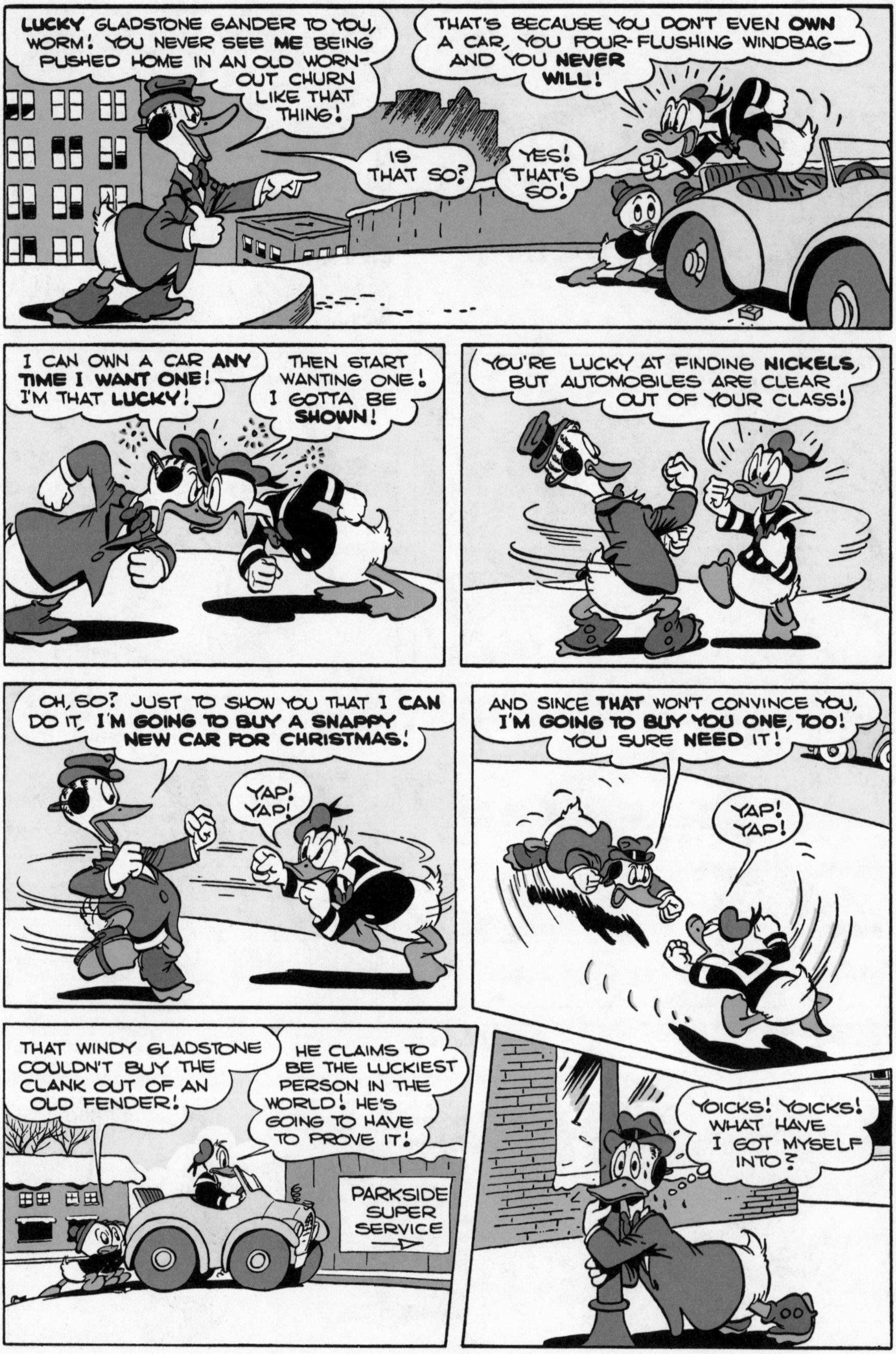

LUCKY GLADSTONE GANDER TO YOU, WORM! YOU NEVER SEE ME BEING PUSHED HOME IN AN OLD WORN-OUT CHURN LIKE THAT THING!
THAT'S BECAUSE YOU DON'T EVEN OWN A CAR, YOU FOUR-FLUSHING WINDBAG— AND YOU NEVER WILL!
IS THAT SO?
YES! THAT'S SO!
I CAN OWN A CAR ANY TIME I WANT ONE! I'M THAT LUCKY!
THEN START WANTING ONE! I GOTTA BE SHOWN!
YOU'RE LUCKY AT FINDING NICKELS, BUT AUTOMOBILES ARE CLEAR OUT OF YOUR CLASS!
OH, SO? JUST TO SHOW YOU THAT I CAN DO IT, I'M GOING TO BUY A SNAPPY NEW CAR FOR CHRISTMAS!
YAP! YAP!
AND SINCE THAT WON'T CONVINCE YOU, I'M GOING TO BUY YOU ONE, TOO! YOU SURE NEED IT!
YAP! YAP!
THAT WINDY GLADSTONE COULDN'T BUY THE CLANK OUT OF AN OLD FENDER!
HE CLAIMS TO BE THE LUCKIEST PERSON IN THE WORLD! HE'S GOING TO HAVE TO PROVE IT!
PARKSIDE SUPER SERVICE
YOICKS! YOICKS! WHAT HAVE I GOT MYSELF INTO?

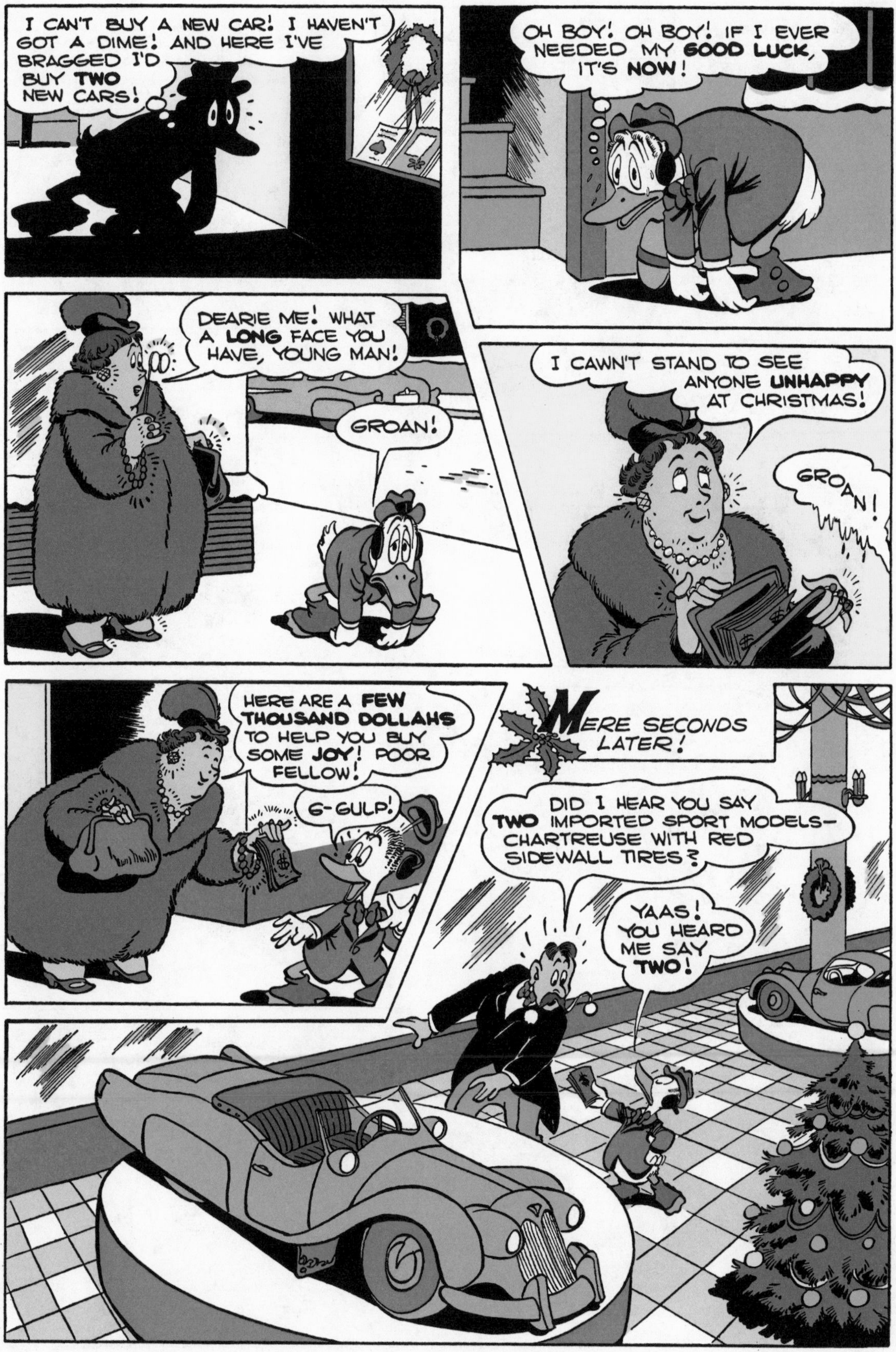

I CAN'T BUY A NEW CAR! I HAVEN'T GOT A DIME! AND HERE I'VE BRAGGED I'D BUY **TWO** NEW CARS!
OH BOY! OH BOY! IF I EVER NEEDED MY **GOOD LUCK**, IT'S **NOW**!
DEARIE ME! WHAT A **LONG** FACE YOU HAVE, YOUNG MAN!
GROAN!
I CAWN'T STAND TO SEE ANYONE **UNHAPPY** AT CHRISTMAS!
GROAN!
HERE ARE A **FEW THOUSAND DOLLAHS** TO HELP YOU BUY SOME **JOY**! POOR FELLOW!
G-GULP!
MERE SECONDS LATER!
DID I HEAR YOU SAY **TWO** IMPORTED SPORT MODELS—CHARTREUSE WITH RED SIDEWALL TIRES?
YAAS! YOU HEARD ME SAY **TWO**!

NEXT MORNING THE WORRIED KIDS GO TO SEE GRANDMA DUCK!

GRANDMA, WE'RE IN A TOUGH SPOT!

DO TELL!

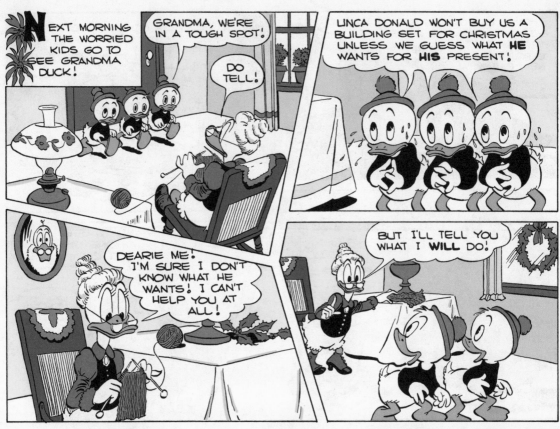

UNCA DONALD WON'T BUY US A BUILDING SET FOR CHRISTMAS UNLESS WE GUESS WHAT HE WANTS FOR HIS PRESENT!

DEARIE ME! I'M SURE I DON'T KNOW WHAT HE WANTS! I CAN'T HELP YOU AT ALL!

BUT I'LL TELL YOU WHAT I WILL DO!

IF YOU DO FIND OUT WHAT HE WANTS, I'LL BUY IT FOR HIM!

WELL, THAT'S THAT!

WE'RE ABOUT LICKED, MEN!

YEAH! WE MIGHT AS WELL GO HOME AND GIVE UP!

HONK! HONK!

SIGH!

GOING HOME, BOYS? HOP IN! I'LL GIVE YOU A LIFT!

UH, OH! CAR TROUBLE!

SPUT!

BLOOP!

SPUTTER!

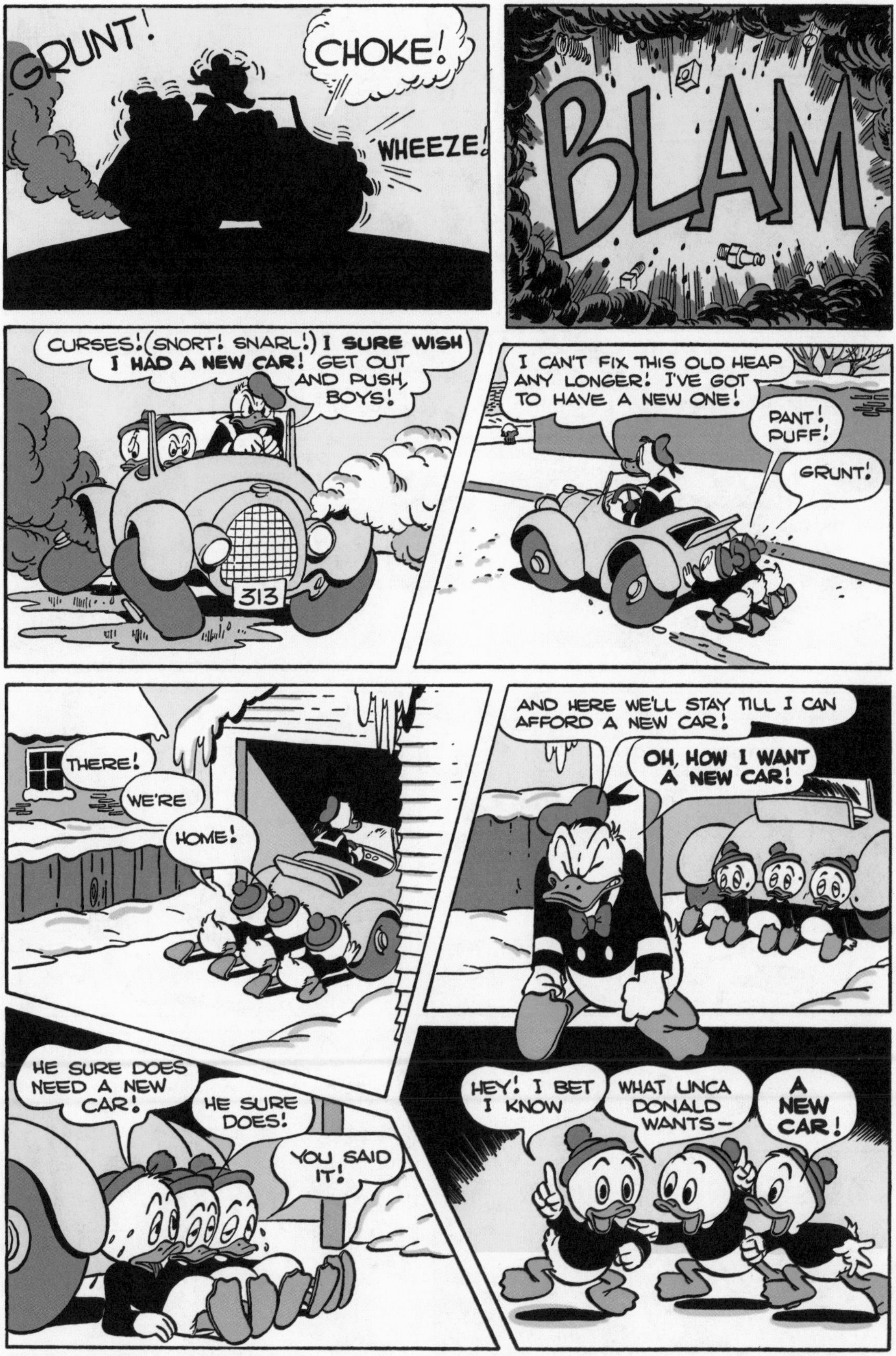
GRUNT!
CHOKE!
WHEEZE!
BLAM
CURSES! (SNORT! SNARL!) I SURE WISH I HAD A NEW CAR! GET OUT AND PUSH, BOYS!
313
I CAN'T FIX THIS OLD HEAP ANY LONGER! I'VE GOT TO HAVE A NEW ONE!
PANT! PUFF!
GRUNT!
THERE!
WE'RE
HOME!
AND HERE WE'LL STAY TILL I CAN AFFORD A NEW CAR!
OH, HOW I WANT A NEW CAR!
HE SURE DOES NEED A NEW CAR!
HE SURE DOES!
YOU SAID IT!
HEY! I BET I KNOW
WHAT UNCA DONALD WANTS—
A NEW CAR!

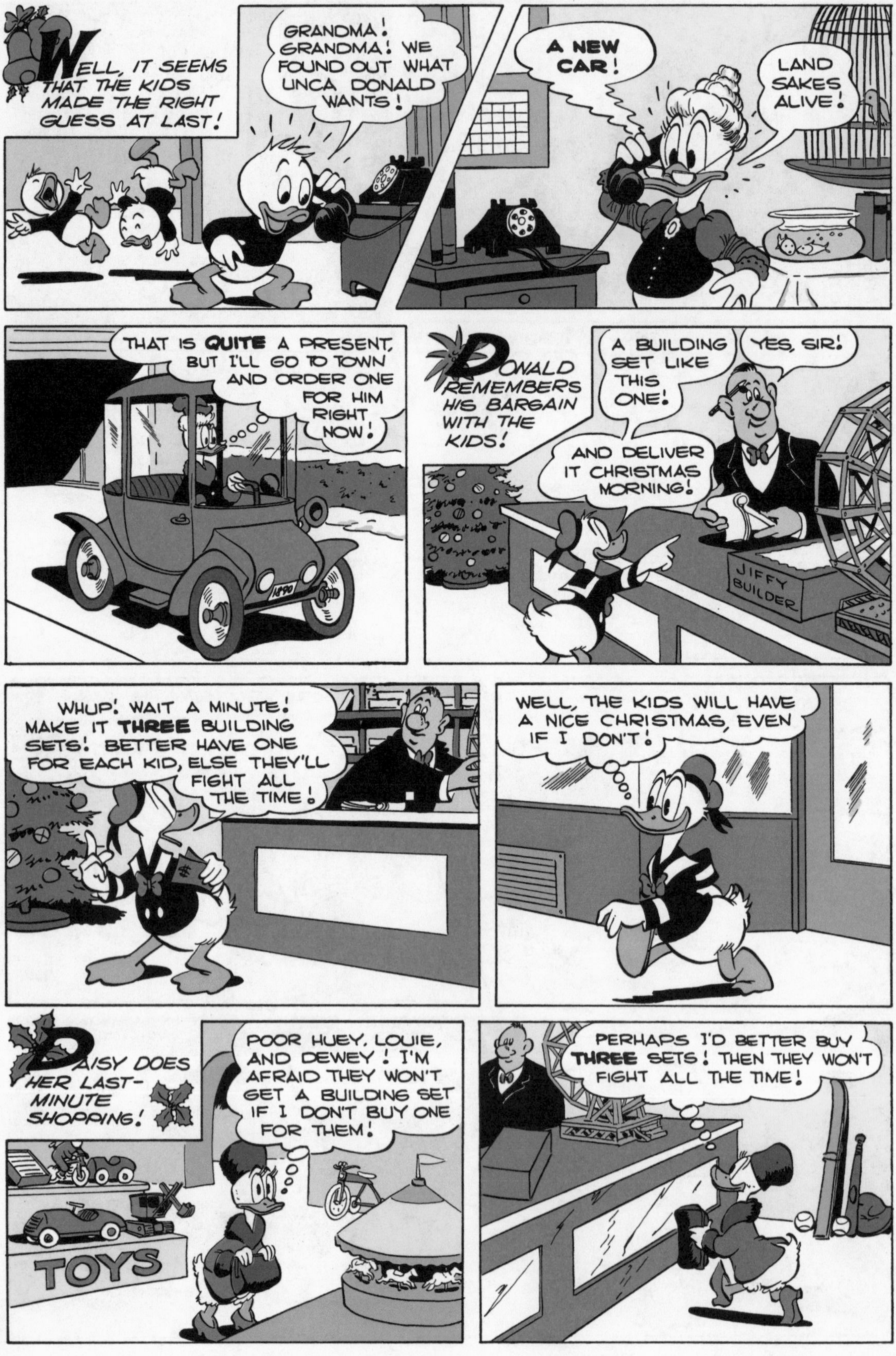
WELL, IT SEEMS THAT THE KIDS MADE THE RIGHT GUESS AT LAST!
GRANDMA! GRANDMA! WE FOUND OUT WHAT UNCA DONALD WANTS!
A NEW CAR!
LAND SAKES ALIVE!
THAT IS QUITE A PRESENT, BUT I'LL GO TO TOWN AND ORDER ONE FOR HIM RIGHT NOW!
1890
DONALD REMEMBERS HIS BARGAIN WITH THE KIDS!
A BUILDING SET LIKE THIS ONE!
YES, SIR!
AND DELIVER IT CHRISTMAS MORNING!
JIFFY BUILDER
WHUP! WAIT A MINUTE! MAKE IT THREE BUILDING SETS! BETTER HAVE ONE FOR EACH KID, ELSE THEY'LL FIGHT ALL THE TIME!
WELL, THE KIDS WILL HAVE A NICE CHRISTMAS, EVEN IF I DON'T!
DAISY DOES HER LAST-MINUTE SHOPPING!
POOR HUEY, LOUIE, AND DEWEY! I'M AFRAID THEY WON'T GET A BUILDING SET IF I DON'T BUY ONE FOR THEM!
TOYS
PERHAPS I'D BETTER BUY THREE SETS! THEN THEY WON'T FIGHT ALL THE TIME!

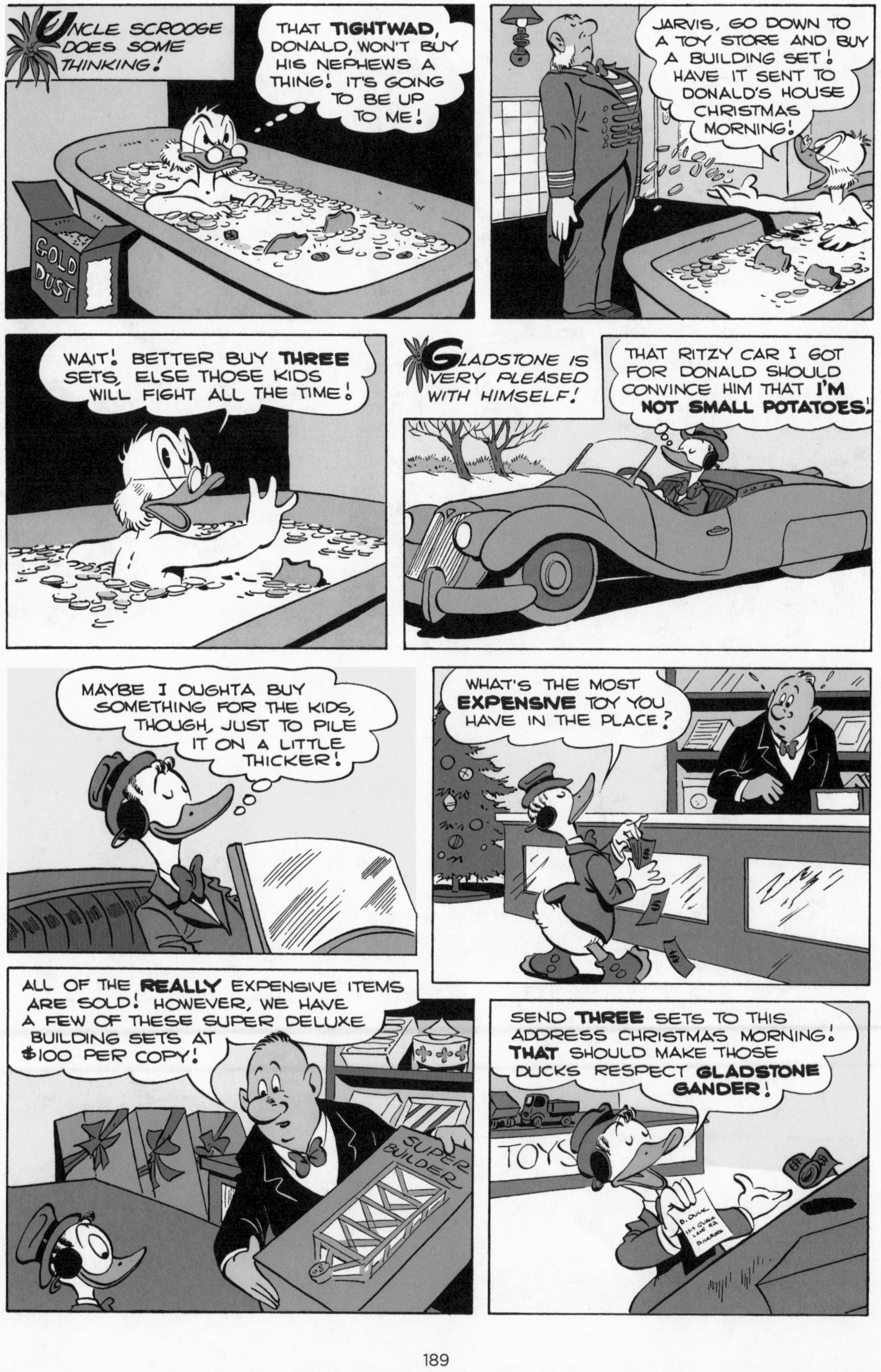
UNCLE SCROOGE DOES SOME THINKING!
THAT TIGHTWAD, DONALD, WON'T BUY HIS NEPHEWS A THING! IT'S GOING TO BE UP TO ME!
GOLD DUST
JARVIS, GO DOWN TO A TOY STORE AND BUY A BUILDING SET! HAVE IT SENT TO DONALD'S HOUSE CHRISTMAS MORNING!
WAIT! BETTER BUY THREE SETS, ELSE THOSE KIDS WILL FIGHT ALL THE TIME!
GLADSTONE IS VERY PLEASED WITH HIMSELF!
THAT RITZY CAR I GOT FOR DONALD SHOULD CONVINCE HIM THAT I'M NOT SMALL POTATOES!
MAYBE I OUGHTA BUY SOMETHING FOR THE KIDS, THOUGH, JUST TO PILE IT ON A LITTLE THICKER!
WHAT'S THE MOST EXPENSIVE TOY YOU HAVE IN THE PLACE?
ALL OF THE REALLY EXPENSIVE ITEMS ARE SOLD! HOWEVER, WE HAVE A FEW OF THESE SUPER DELUXE BUILDING SETS AT $100 PER COPY!
SUPER BUILDER
SEND THREE SETS TO THIS ADDRESS CHRISTMAS MORNING! THAT SHOULD MAKE THOSE DUCKS RESPECT GLADSTONE GANDER!
TOYS

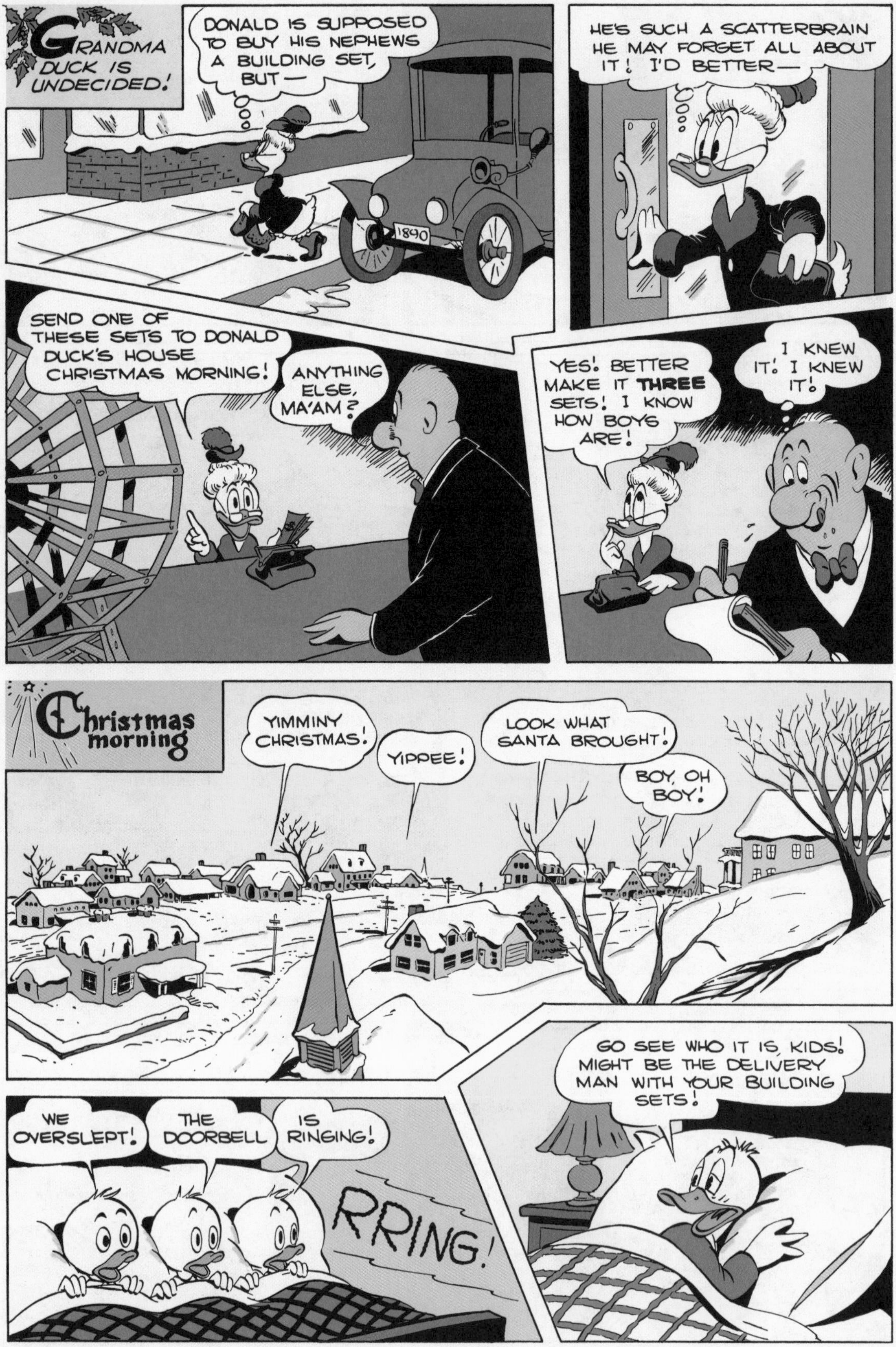
GRANDMA DUCK IS UNDECIDED!
DONALD IS SUPPOSED TO BUY HIS NEPHEWS A BUILDING SET, BUT—
1890
HE'S SUCH A SCATTERBRAIN HE MAY FORGET ALL ABOUT IT! I'D BETTER—
SEND ONE OF THESE SETS TO DONALD DUCK'S HOUSE CHRISTMAS MORNING!
ANYTHING ELSE, MA'AM?
YES! BETTER MAKE IT THREE SETS! I KNOW HOW BOYS ARE!
I KNEW IT! I KNEW IT!
Christmas morning
YIMMINY CHRISTMAS!
YIPPEE!
LOOK WHAT SANTA BROUGHT!
BOY, OH BOY!
WE OVERSLEPT!
THE DOORBELL
IS RINGING!
RRING!
GO SEE WHO IT IS, KIDS! MIGHT BE THE DELIVERY MAN WITH YOUR BUILDING SETS!

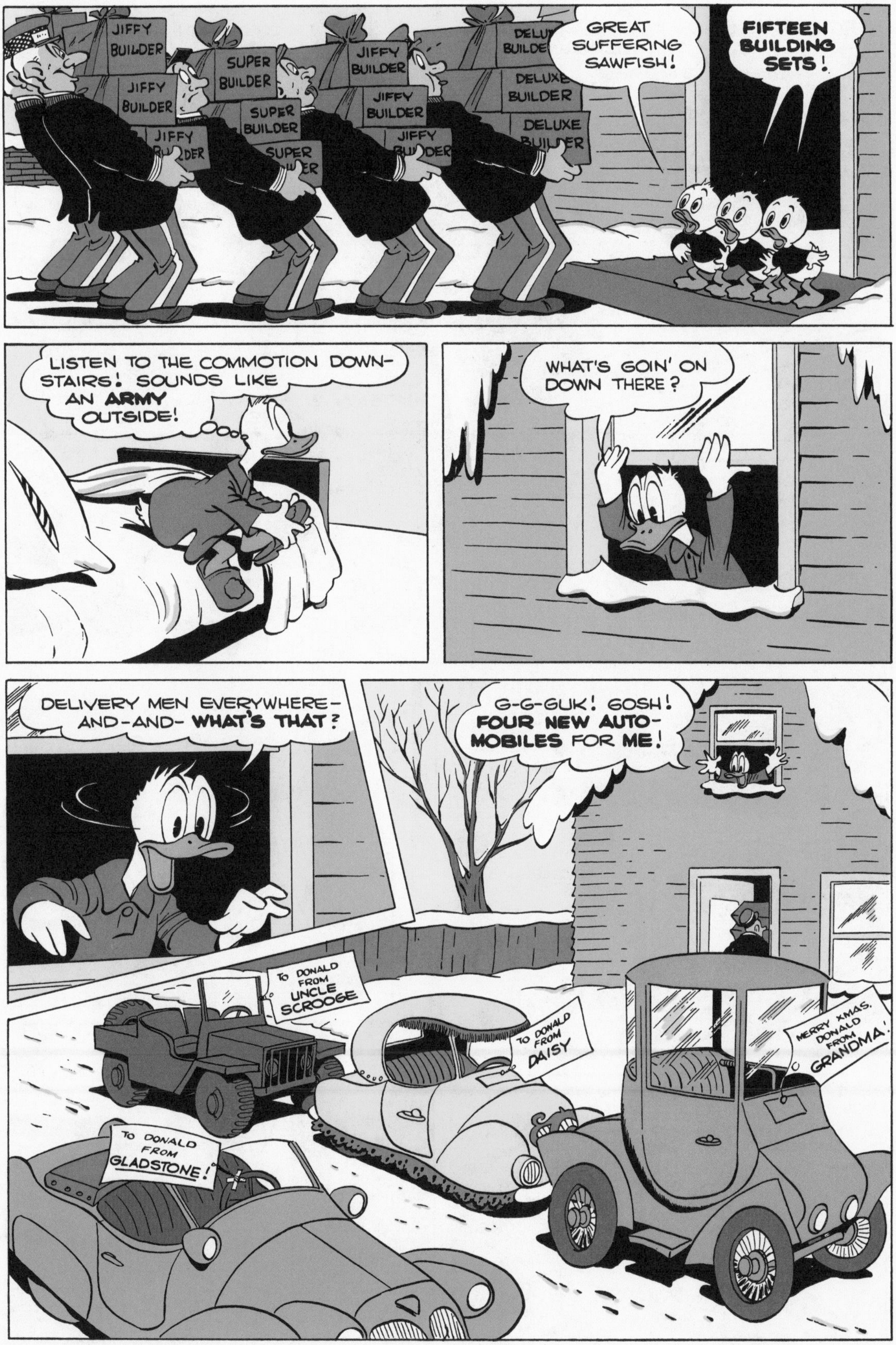
JIFFY BUILDER
SUPER BUILDER
DELUXE BUILDER
GREAT SUFFERING SAWFISH!
FIFTEEN BUILDING SETS!
LISTEN TO THE COMMOTION DOWN-STAIRS! SOUNDS LIKE AN ARMY OUTSIDE!
WHAT'S GOIN' ON DOWN THERE?
DELIVERY MEN EVERYWHERE-AND-AND- WHAT'S THAT?
G-G-GUK! GOSH! FOUR NEW AUTO-MOBILES FOR ME!
TO DONALD FROM UNCLE SCROOGE
TO DONALD FROM DAISY
MERRY XMAS, DONALD FROM GRANDMA!
TO DONALD FROM GLADSTONE!

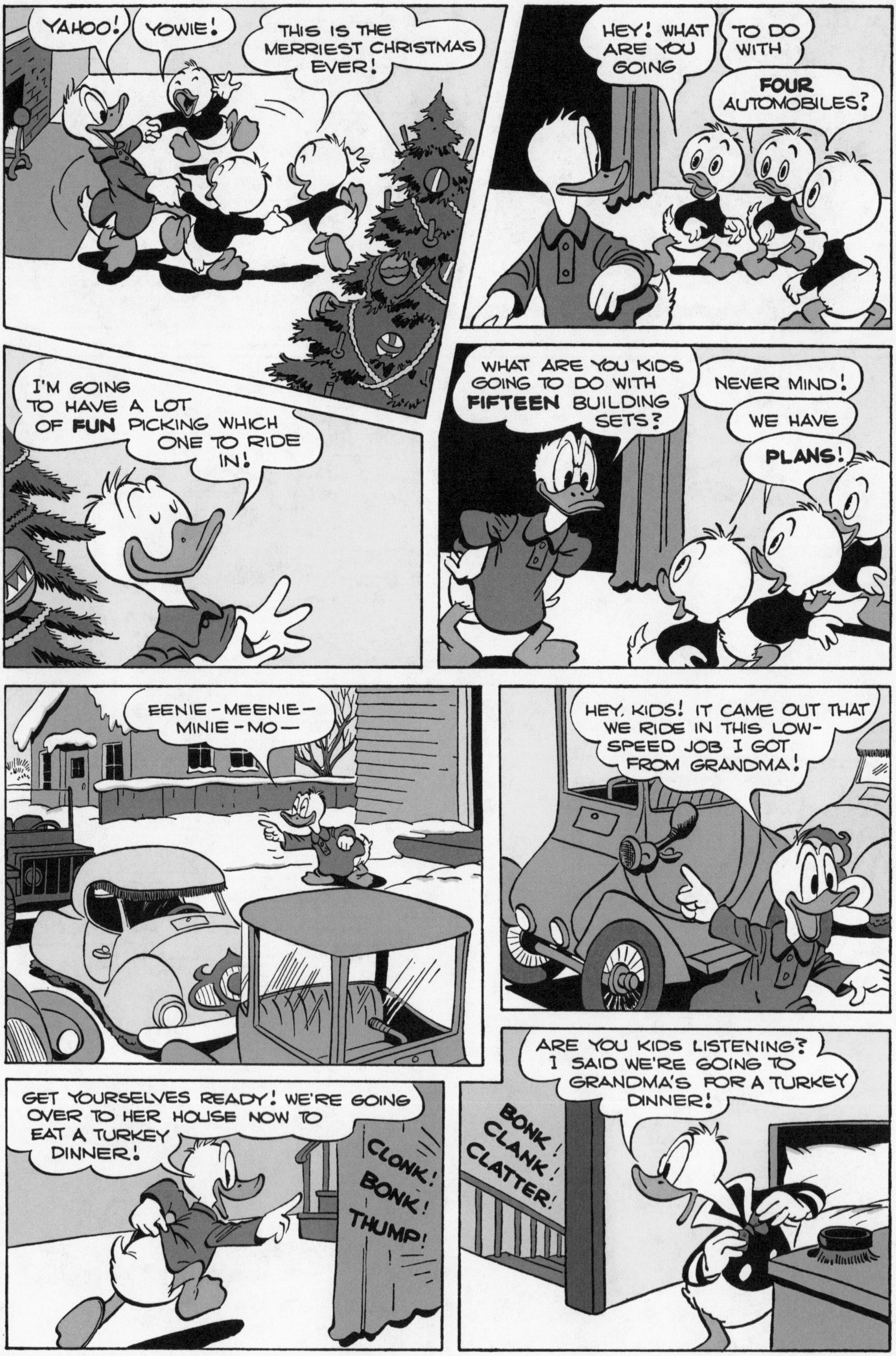
YAHOO!
YOWIE!
THIS IS THE MERRIEST CHRISTMAS EVER!
HEY! WHAT ARE YOU GOING
TO DO WITH
FOUR AUTOMOBILES?
I'M GOING TO HAVE A LOT OF FUN PICKING WHICH ONE TO RIDE IN!
WHAT ARE YOU KIDS GOING TO DO WITH FIFTEEN BUILDING SETS?
NEVER MIND!
WE HAVE
PLANS!
EENIE-MEENIE-MINIE-MO-
HEY, KIDS! IT CAME OUT THAT WE RIDE IN THIS LOW-SPEED JOB I GOT FROM GRANDMA!
GET YOURSELVES READY! WE'RE GOING OVER TO HER HOUSE NOW TO EAT A TURKEY DINNER!
CLONK! BONK! THUMP!
ARE YOU KIDS LISTENING? I SAID WE'RE GOING TO GRANDMA'S FOR A TURKEY DINNER!
BONK! CLANK! CLATTER!

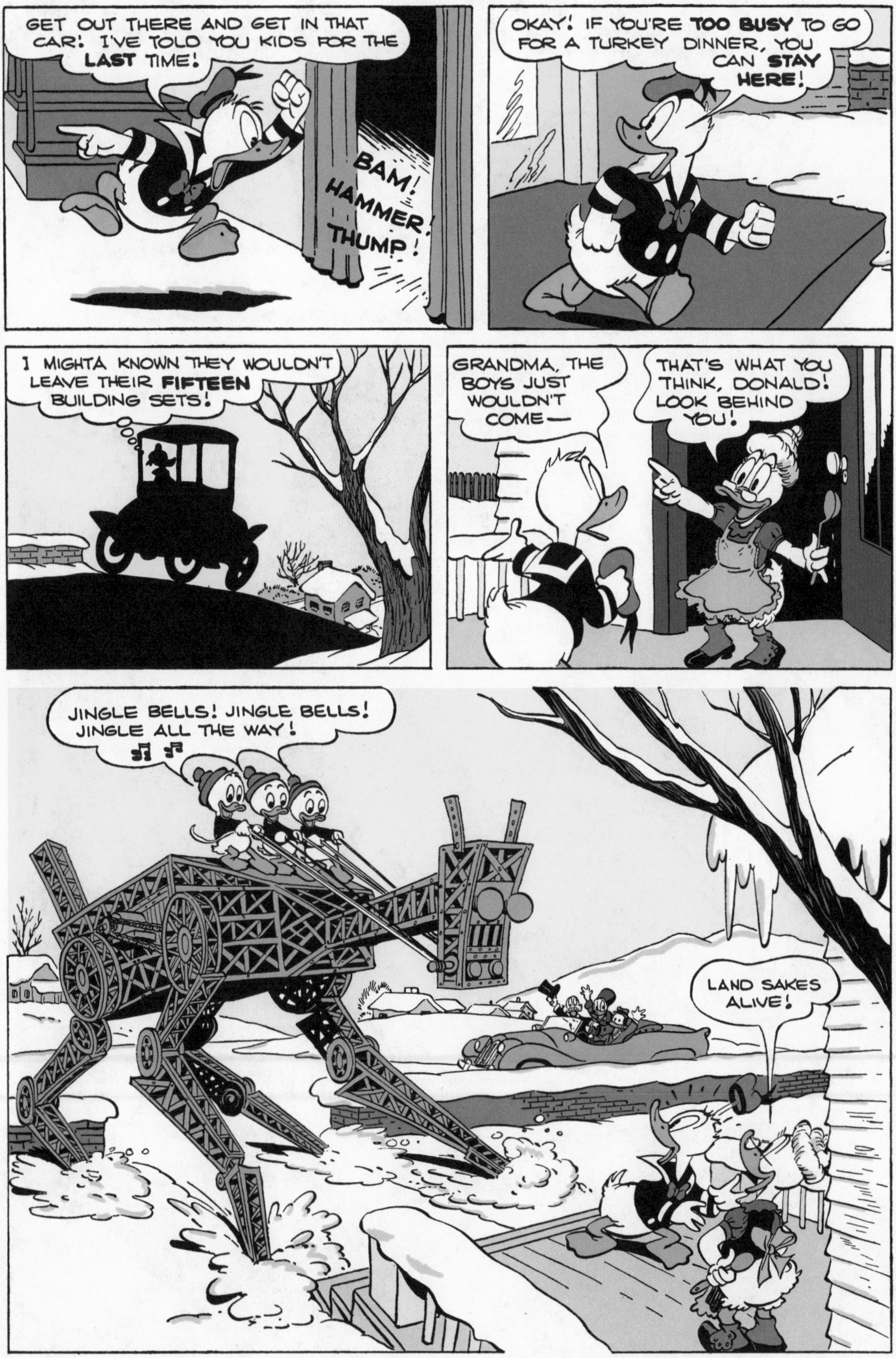
GET OUT THERE AND GET IN THAT CAR! I'VE TOLD YOU KIDS FOR THE **LAST** TIME!
BAM! HAMMER! THUMP!
OKAY! IF YOU'RE **TOO BUSY** TO GO FOR A TURKEY DINNER, YOU CAN **STAY HERE!**
I MIGHTA KNOWN THEY WOULDN'T LEAVE THEIR **FIFTEEN** BUILDING SETS!
GRANDMA, THE BOYS JUST WOULDN'T COME—
THAT'S WHAT YOU THINK, DONALD! LOOK BEHIND YOU!
JINGLE BELLS! JINGLE BELLS! JINGLE ALL THE WAY!
LAND SAKES ALIVE!

NO. 282
WALT DISNEY'S
10¢
Donald Duck
and THE PIXILATED PARROT
$
52 pages
ALL COMICS!

Story Notes

THE PIXILATED PARROT *p. 1*

On its own merits, "The Pixilated Parrot" is an entertaining romp that unfolds like a trapeze performance: one absorbing maneuver swings directly into and even necessitates the next, with everything based on considerable planning beforehand.

That compelling momentum carries the story over its curious rhythmic arc. It begins with a relaxed — almost protracted — introduction and ends with a rapid-fire resolution. In between, humorous skits can erupt anywhere, and do — dockside, in jungles, aboard ship, and out on a flagpole.

Within a larger survey of Carl Barks's work, the tale is a mix of the familiar and the unusual. There's an excursion to an exotic land, but it is brief and happens relatively late in the story. Instead of it being the highlight that colors and sets the tone for the action, it's a side trip.

Scrooge's money bin is emptied. Normally this would be the precipitating event of any narrative, with fortune's recovery being the focus of the rest of the proceedings. But here the principals don't know the riches are missing for half the story. Nor is it even the terrible, terrible Beagle Boys — Scrooge's perpetual nemeses — who do the pilfering.

Yet, like a trapeze act, everything has its own purposeful design (the Beagle Boys, for instance, would have sufficient manpower to divvy up Scrooge's loot in far less time than the month it took for the Ducks' journey out and back). Plus there's a crucial element that very much ties all the tempo punctuation and diverse scenes together: that talented parrot.

He appears on every page, an abnormality for a guest star, even a titular one. Typical for Barks, the parrot's "gimmick," that incessant

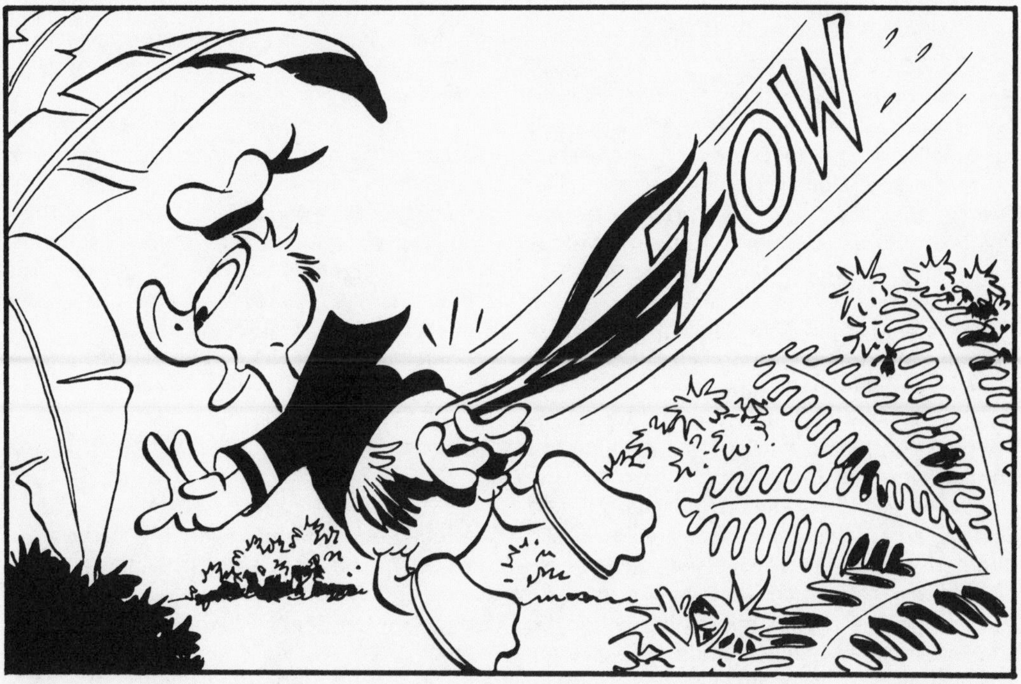
ZOW

counting, performs multiple functions. Like background music or a metronome's beat, it carries over panels, pages, and shifting venues throughout much of the story. It's a source of gags and, more importantly to the plot, doubles as an audio-locator at several critical junctures.

Nor can Barks let the parrot's numerical prowess rest with "mere" tabulation. (Actually, it's easy to lose track of how many different things the bird tallies in the story. I was always forgetting one. How many do you recall?) Naturally the parrot's additional ability — reciting strings of overheard numbers — also proves essential.

But isn't it odd that a counting parrot, chosen by Donald specifically for that skill and given to Scrooge who is first shown counting away in his money bin, is never actually employed by Scrooge for that purpose? Here mercy, not plot, dictates. For the longest time, the bird looks sad and resigned as he perfunctorily catches up on his banana count. Look at those bags under his eyes! If he were to tote up Scrooge's vast wealth, his solitary labors would have had no end. No, he's a social animal: apart from his brief tropical flirtation, he never seems happier than at story's end, counting along with company.

— RICH KREINER

WILD ABOUT FLOWERS *p. 23*

Having created Gladstone Gander in 1948, Carl Barks is still refining the annoying goose's personality in this 1950 story. From a seed he planted in "Donald's Love Letters" (*Walt Disney's Donald Duck: Trail of the Unicorn*, Vol. 8 of this series), Barks further develops the rivalry between the two cousins, as Gladstone cheekily announces to Donald that he will steal his girl. This sets up a true love triangle, whose background is a caricature of the social rituals of the time.

In this vanity fair, Daisy offers herself as the prize for the most valiant of the chivalrous contestants. The reader might wonder why, since she clearly seems to prefer Donald. Barks, sarcastically ambiguous, allows two alternative readings. Maybe she really wants Donald to win, but also wants him to work for it, giving her a proper courtship. Or maybe she doesn't really know whom she prefers, and will change her mind depending on the moment's mood. Indeed, Daisy's annoying fickleness will continue to be a feature of her personality for decades, even after Barks. The cartoonist behind the scenes is simultaneously participating and disenchanted as he observes and describes this battle of the sexes.

The tone is lightened by unrelated gags: literal visual renderings of flower names; semantic wordplay and alliteration on three meanings of the word "Daisy"; and the mute mini-saga of the mice riding the bottle, evoking memories of George Herriman's

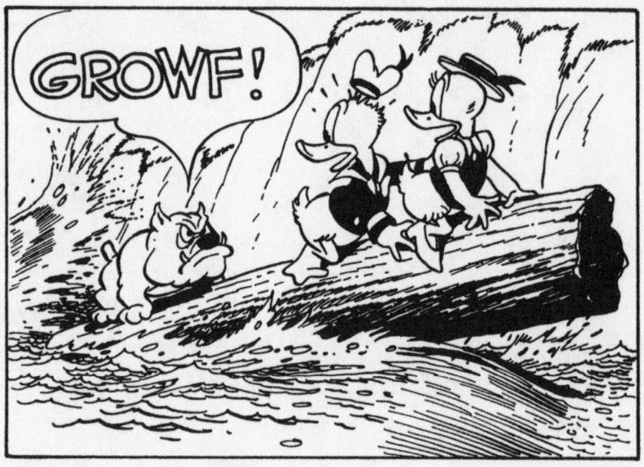
GROWF!

"The Dingbat Family," which Barks knew well, where the strips were footnoted by gags of a mouse and a cat that would later evolve into Krazy Kat. Barks would later perfect the "mute mini-saga" style after creating Gyro Gearloose and his Helper.

The story ends with a classic Barks moral: Gladstone's smug arrogance finally provokes Donald ("I've took all I could take!") to off-panel fisticuffs — thus alienating both of them from Daisy's good graces ("You disgraceful ruffians!"). The only worthy "gentlemen" turn out to be Huey, Dewy, and Louie: not even contestants, they emerge as the winners.

— FRANK STEJANO and LEONARDO GORI

ANCIENT PERSIA *p. 33*

"Ancient Persia" begins with the cadaverous, never-named mad scientist passing the Ducks' house and heading for his laboratory in the old house on the hill, where the nephews watch as he studies cuneiform tablets and activates exotic ingredients with "one small

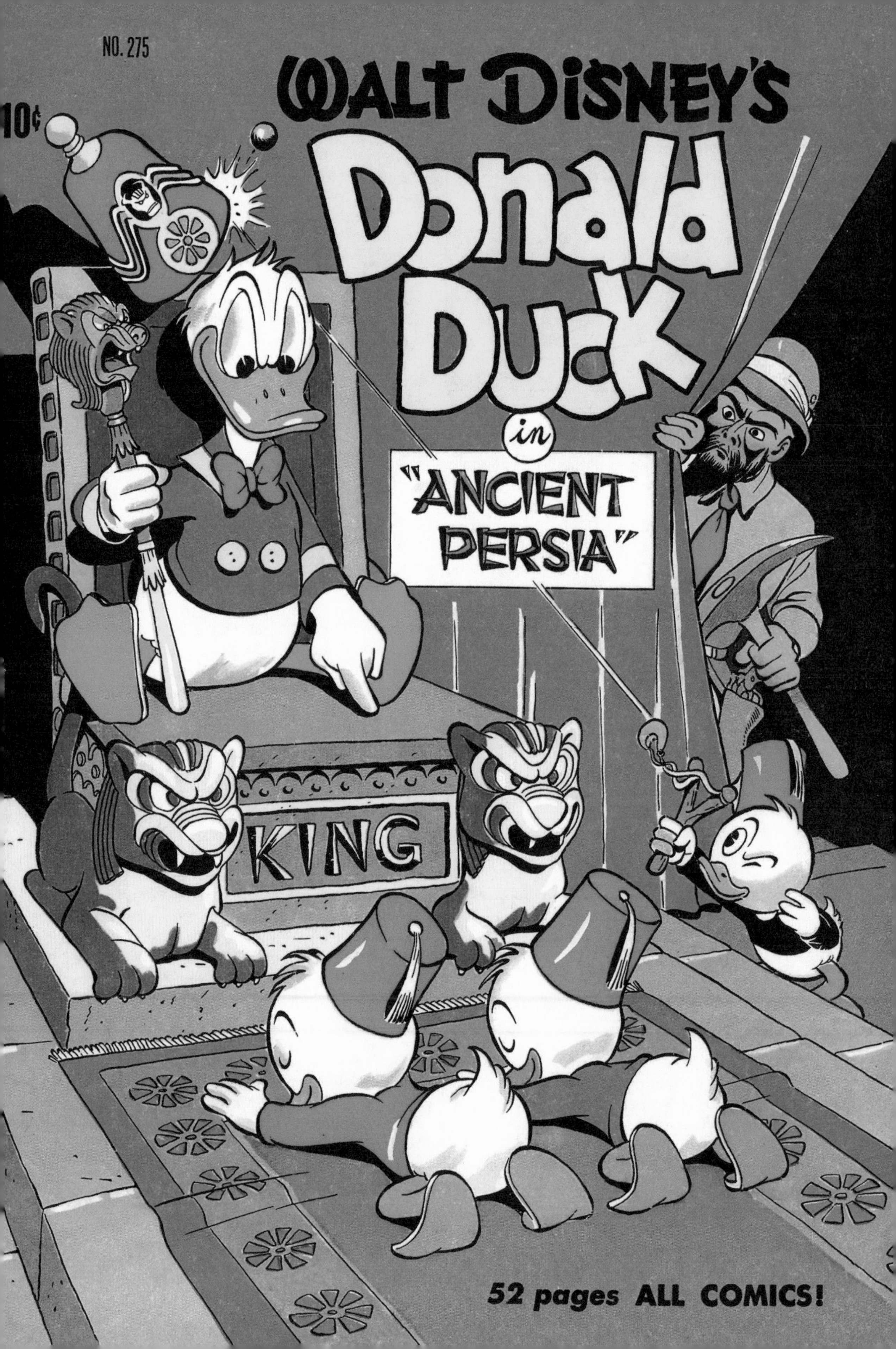
NO. 275
10¢
WALT DISNEY'S
Donald Duck
in
"ANCIENT PERSIA"
KING
52 pages ALL COMICS!

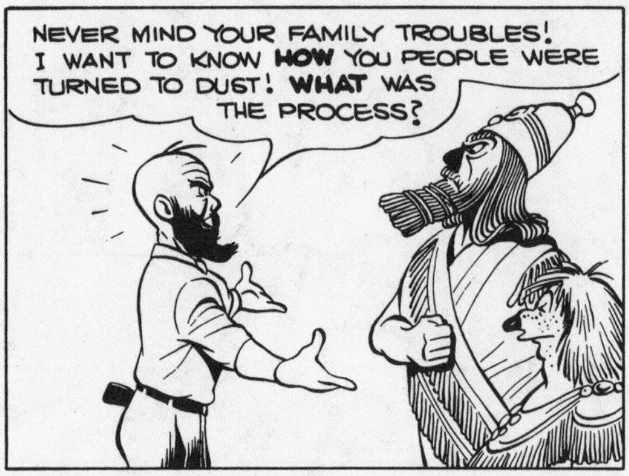
NEVER MIND YOUR FAMILY TROUBLES! I WANT TO KNOW HOW YOU PEOPLE WERE TURNED TO DUST! WHAT WAS THE PROCESS?

fraction of a thunderbolt." The scientist is a mixture of opposing qualities — sometimes sinister and thuggish, sometimes a friendly and knowledgeable guide to the cities of the ancient world: "Babylon, Kish, Susa, and so forth!"

The Ducks are soon flying over sculpted images of winged, bearded griffins and snarling lions. They explore, in a spectacular chiaroscuro page, the royal palace of the lost kingdom of Itsa Faka. And what youthful Barks reader would not be delighted by the torch-lighting scene, the perfumed water of the royal bathtub, or the effect on the Ducks of inhaling "some of the thought processes of those reviving people?"

We are deep inside a world of magic and enchantment that only Carl Barks could have created.

The ill-tempered king, with his tall Persian hat and unprepossessing daughter, now takes center stage in a complicated and farcical subplot involving Donald's double, the trickster Prince Cad Ali Cad, and a forced marriage to the princess.

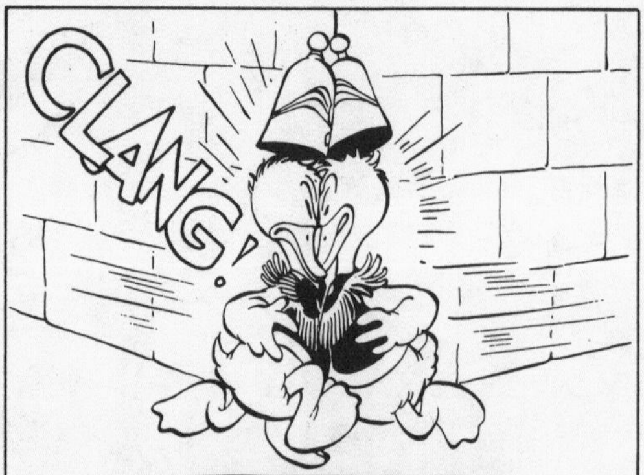
CLANG!

Barks handles the narrative tangle with his usual lightness of touch: Prince Cad remains a smiling impostor to the end, the mad scientist goes mad for real when he discovers "the substance that turns people to dust," the king does his last irritated double-take, and Donald hides out safely in the still-full royal bathtub. Everyone else turns to dust with a Barksian lettering trick that is visually satisfying and as close to the absoluteness of death as anyone could come in a Disney comic book.

The final panel is a variant of Barks's favorite ending: Donald chasing the boys with a switch, all the Ducks in silhouette.

— BILL MASON

VACATION TIME *p. 57*

The extra-long "Vacation Time" affords Carl Barks an unusual luxury: a full-height introductory splash panel/page. Normally, Barks's full-page drawings were limited to the covers: quick-hit gags composed to be easily and immediately appealing. But it takes a while to drink in all the details on the opening splash of "Vacation Time." Our eyes are funneled down from the wild beasts through the centrally positioned car — all its wheels aloft — then down into the waterfall, over its edge into the whirlpool, and back up to the rickety bridge about to be crossed. It's the perfect visual lead-in to the second page's equally imaginative string of one-panel jokes, which poke ironic fun at the perils of city life.

In the wilderness, Barks renders the woods with a real affection, from comfy campsites to grand panoramas, with a similar warmth animating forest creatures. Majestic trees abound. Lush greens and cool aquas are the calming backdrop for Donald's frenetic mishaps center stage.

Into this bucolic merriment Barks slips a true viper, one of the most heinous villains in a long line of memorable bad guys. He goes unnamed, as if nobody special. Likewise, his initial rudeness (and poor diction) can appear

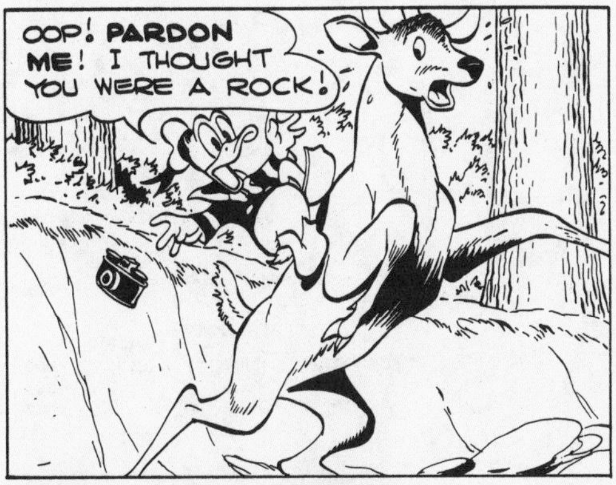
OOP! PARDON ME! I THOUGHT YOU WERE A ROCK!

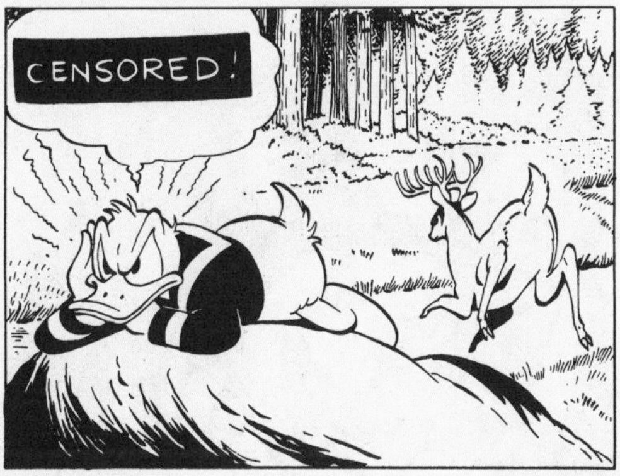
CENSORED!

pedestrian, commonplace, at least until he starts muscling Donald around. The early indifference in that casually flicked match establishes merely a baseline for his disdain, a contempt that grows to include a murderous disregard for others.

As a wildlife photographer Donald may play the buffoon, but when it comes to fire prevention, he is all business. His knowledge of smokejumpers' last-ditch survival tactics saves the day. While the unthinkable has been avoided, what has been lost is crushing. Over his long career, Barks presented few panels as woeful as Donald's initial sight of the smoldering landscape in which he manages to convey both a survivor's relief and genuine grief.

Afterward, the Ducks traverse a wasteland. Trees are charred stalks. The rivers run brown. The ground smokes and the sky is streaked with plumes. The guilty party is ultimately exposed, thanks to the evidence that Barks, ever fair to his readers, has hinted existed within the camera at several points earlier in the story.

So justice triumphs, yet the upbeat ending probably reads a little flatter today than it did in 1950. Then it might have been easier to conceive of nature as an inexhaustible bounty and of an America with unlimited wilderness. After the destruction of Eagleclaw Canyon, the Ducks can relocate their camp and frolic and relax in a fresh forest primeval — equivalent to the last one, right down to its fauna. That's an optimism no longer so easy for us to embrace.

— RICH KREINER

TALKING PARROT *p. 90*

Carl Barks didn't draw "Talking Parrot," so what is it doing in this book? Well, although opinions may differ, it does appear that this one-page gag was *written* by Barks and then drawn by someone else. That someone is Frank McSavage, who produced numerous stories and covers for Western Publishing. "Talking Parrot" appeared in *Four Color* #356, November 1951, which featured a cover by Barks but no other interior work by him. But Barks indexer and scholar Kim Weston notes, "There is a listing in Barks's work records for a one-page gag for that comic book." Could Barks's original art have been lost or damaged in the editorial offices, thus requiring it to be quickly re-drawn by someone close by? We may never know, but the main evidence that the gag originated with Barks is that 15 years later, a similar gag *was* written and drawn by Barks. ("Wasted Words," *Uncle Scrooge* #61,

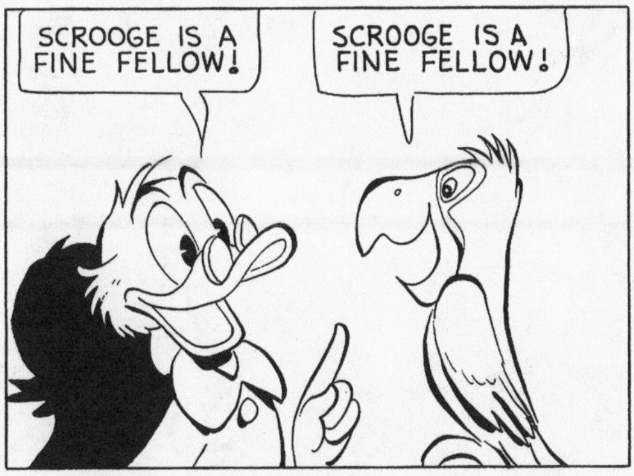
SCROOGE IS A FINE FELLOW!
SCROOGE IS A FINE FELLOW!

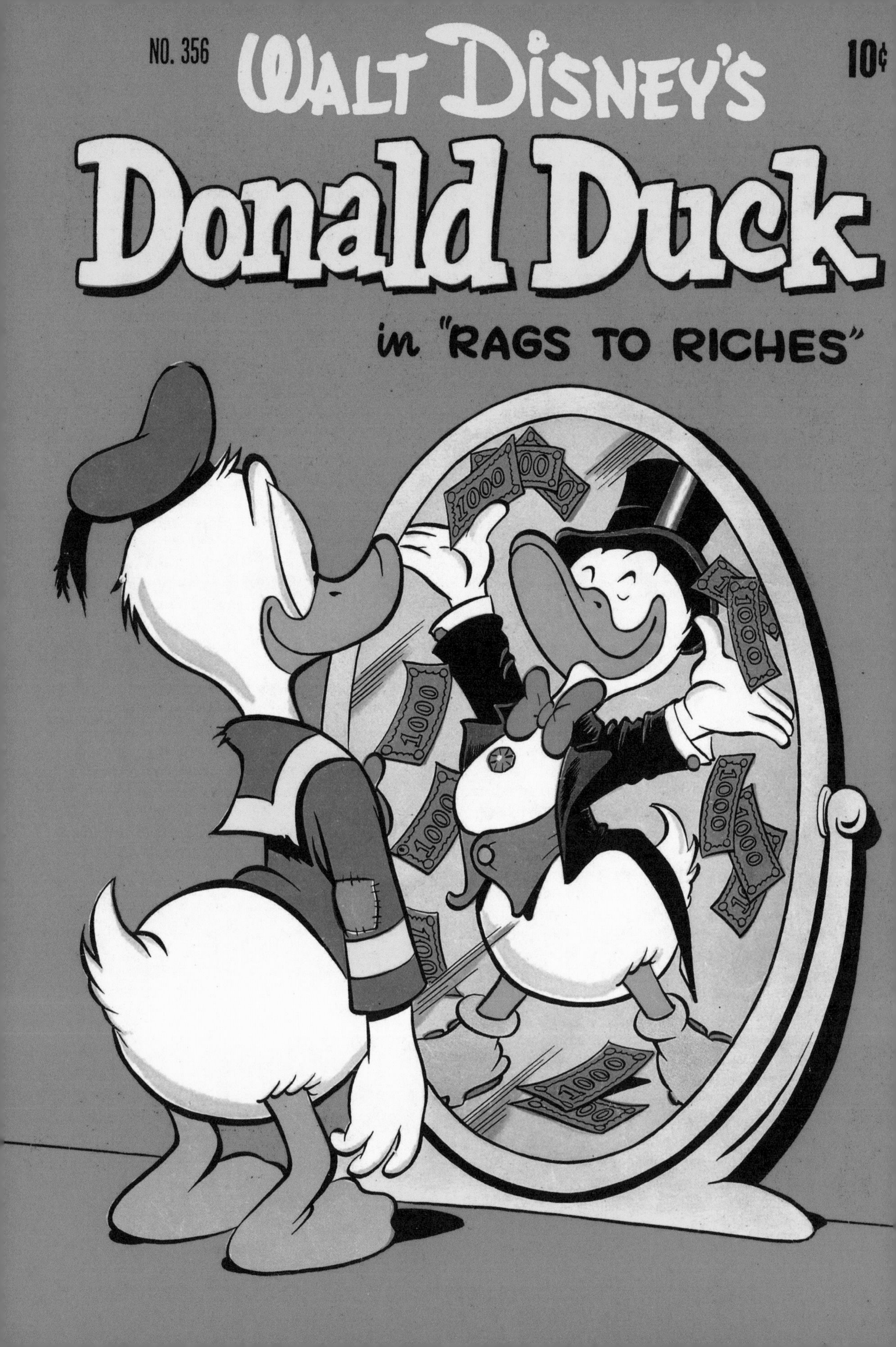
NO. 356
WALT DISNEY'S
10¢
Donald Duck
in "RAGS TO RICHES"

January 1966, currently scheduled for Volume 31 of *The Complete Carl Barks Disney Library*).

It may be, Weston notes, that "Barks reached into his file of ideas and used one that he never saw in print." A panel from that later gag is shown here. (Scan courtesy of Kim Weston).

— JOSEPH COWLES

DONALD'S GRANDMA DUCK *p. 91*

The years immediately after World War II saw a resurgence — in films, popular culture, and the then-new medium of TV — of sentimental depictions of the early 20th century, as if North America was taking a deep breath before leaping headlong into the glittering post-war world. Films like *When My Baby Smiles at Me* (1948) and *In the Good Old Summertime* (1949) recreated the pre-World War I era in bright-hued Technicolor, while pop songs like "Cruising Down the River (On A Sunday Afternoon)" (1946) and "Chi-Baba, Chi-Baba (My Bambino Go To Sleep)" (1947) exuded a good-old-days nostalgia that helped set the tone for late-1940s American popular culture. Such was the setting for the first comic book appearance of Grandma Duck and Gus Goose in "Donald's Grandma Duck."

Grandma had been around since 1943, when she appeared in a *Donald Duck* daily strip by Al Taliaferro (1905–1969) giving Donald a scrub behind the ears. In "Donald's Grandma Duck" it's the good-natured Gus Goose who gets the scrubbing, much to the delight of Huey, Dewey, and Louie, who have just arrived in "the country" — i.e., outside of Duckburg — for a visit.

When I first read it in 1950, the high point of "Donald's Grandma Duck" was the joke about Grandma's new TV, a Christmas present from Donald that Grandma has covered with a tablecloth and moved into a corner of her parlor. This was especially delightful to me because my parents had just gotten their first TV. It was only the third one in our apartment building, and it was a great source of pride to us kids — we were now as up-to-date as Grandma Duck!

Grandma's old-fashioned treasures — the still-in-mint-condition electric car, oil lamps with painted shades for all the tables, a grandfather's clock decorated with Victorian curlicues, a bowl of wax fruit, and a stereoscope with slides of Niagara Falls and "President Taft speaking on the Corn Tax" — are a source of amazement to the boys. None of these objects was a "nostalgia item" in 1950, since nostalgia for the cultural artifacts of the recent past did not yet exist.

Grandma spoils the boys with multi-scoop dishes of ice cream, anticipating the expanding coffee cup Uncle Scrooge was to use at lunch counters a few years later (see *Walt Disney's Uncle Scrooge: "The Seven Cities of Gold,"* Vol. 14 in this series).

"Donald's Grandma Duck," which was not written by Barks, is mostly a collection of jokes about the nephews getting used to country life and Gus finding ways to conceal his laziness. A letter from "Ezra Scrooge" threatening to foreclose the mortgage on Grandma's farm loses its point when Gus discovers the checks to pay Grandma's unpaid

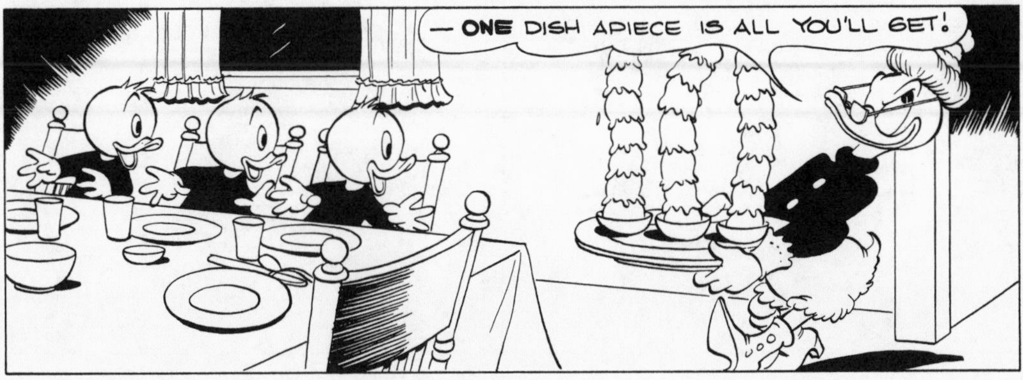
— ONE DISH APIECE IS ALL YOU'LL GET!

bills in his vest pocket and saves the farm by making a trip to town in the electric car.

Aside from two well-staged scenes involving the nephews stealing fresh eggs from the hen house and getting tossed in a muddy hog-wallow, all ends well for the boys — except that the farm is too quiet at night and they can't sleep. The anonymous scriptwriter supplies a graphically striking ending worthy of a TV sitcom, with Grandma and Gus providing a late-night shivaree while they sit on the platform of a windmill and the boys snore happily and peacefully.

— BILL MASON

CAMP COUNSELOR *p. 105*

"Camp Counselor," which at first glance might look like a minor short story, was drawn — but not written — by Carl Barks. The script may have been by Nick George, a Disney animator and story man who also wrote scripts for Dell's Disney comic books from 1950 to 1970. "Camp Counselor" has the feel and rhythm of an animated short. Specifically, it looks like it was inspired by *Good Scouts*, a Donald Duck animated short (released July 8, 1938) whose story directors were Harry Reeves — and Carl Barks.

In *Good Scouts*, scoutmaster Donald awkwardly tries to teach his nephews wilderness skills at Yellowstone National Park. They end up being chased by a grizzly bear on a boulder rotating on top of the stream of water erupting from the geyser "Old Reliable."

In "Camp Counselor," Donald also shows his clumsiness at setting up a tent and, in general, proves himself to be a bumbling scoutmaster. Both in the film and in the comic, Donald is the victim of his own joke on the nephews. On screen, he pours ketchup over himself and pretends to have been injured, only to end up bandaged from head to toe. On paper, to impress the kids, Donald pretends to be fighting with a bear (actually a bearskin) before the nephews, dressed up as a bear, scare him in return.

Yet the most interesting detail about "Camp Counselor" is that, unlike the animated short, it features three other scouts besides Huey, Dewey, and Louie. This, then, may be considered the original nucleus of the Junior Woodchucks, the upright Boy Scouts–like organization that Barks would introduce just seven months later in "Operation St. Bernard" (scheduled for Volume 10 of *The Complete Carl Barks Disney Library*).

— ALBERTO BECATTINI

THE MAGIC HOURGLASS *p. 113*

When asked about the art in his Duck stories, Carl Barks frequently discussed the way he drew characters. The Ducks' faces and bodies, he believed, needed to telegraph a story's action, emotion, and humor — a bold approach to figure drawing he developed while working at Walt Disney animation studios. Barks talked far less about another, yet equally compelling, aspect of his art: settings. "The Magic Hourglass," like many of the cartoonist's long stories, displays his ability to represent all kinds of environments with grace and sophistication, making them

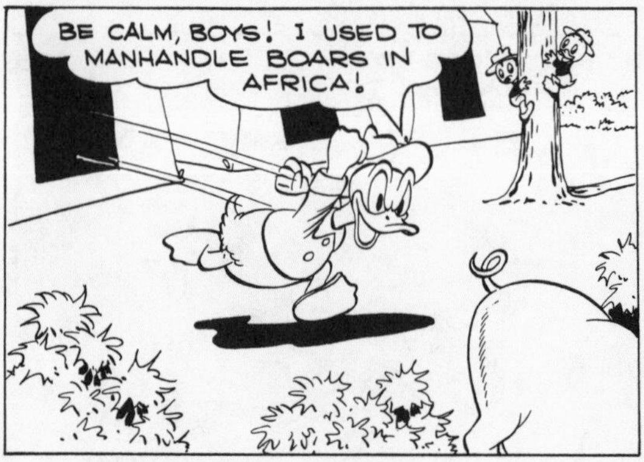
BE CALM, BOYS! I USED TO MANHANDLE BOARS IN AFRICA!

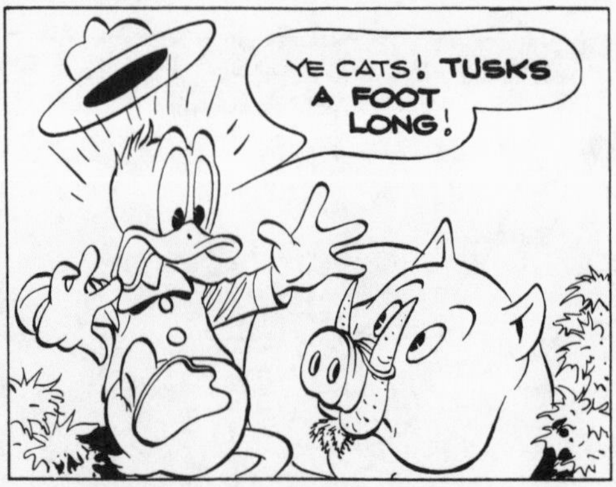
YE CATS! TUSKS A FOOT LONG!

as important to the comic's humor and drama as the Ducks themselves.

While Barks gives his protagonists a cartoony appearance, he typically draws a setting's manufactured and natural objects with realism and restraint, at times evoking the accuracy of an architectural drawing. A Barks story might even appear as if drawn by two artists: one energetically cartooning the characters and another meticulously illustrating the environments. Barks knew that, for his comics to be engaging, he must think

IT'S ONLY US KIDS PLAYIN' HIDE-AND-GO-SEEK IN A BED SHEET!

not only like a comedic actor, but like a film's location scout and theater's set designer.

The plot of "The Magic Hourglass" cycles through a dozen locations, each a marked departure from the one before it. The story begins with the Ducks enjoying a panoramic urban view of realistically drawn skyscrapers, warehouses, train yards, and ships. The setting quickly shifts from high and outside to low and inside, from a dense view of industries owned by Scrooge to the old miser himself, who's alone in a home adorned only by dollar signs. Often employing scene-to-scene transitions in comical and philosophical ways, Barks uses the first transition in "The Magic Hourglass" to evoke a tension at the heart of Scrooge's troubled psychology, playing the duck's outsized greed against his Spartan lifestyle. (Barks also hints at this opposition when he switches from the urban scene's rectangular panels to the off-kilter ones of Scrooge's home.) In the rest of the tale, settings continue to shift dramatically, moving, for example, from a barren desert

to a lush oasis and then to an underground cavern filled with rugs, pillows, tapestries, and clothing that the design-conscious Barks decorates with a wide variety of geometric patterns.

Barks's adventure comics often portray his belief that environments affect and even dominate us in ways we fail to understand. In the first panel of "The Magic Hourglass," the sometimes cynical cartoonist shows that, as we grow older, we lose the ability to directly engage the world around us. The nephews experience the urban splendor with uncompromised awe, but Donald is fully compromised by an adult obsession: ownership. The vista impresses him solely as "property." By pointing out the "swell view," the nephews alert us to the considerable effort Barks invested in the impressive and ever-changing environments that drive his adventurous plots.

— KEN PARILLE

BIG-TOP BEDLAM p. 141

At the beginning of the 20th century, upwards of a hundred circuses were in operation coast-to-coast across the country. They were the dominant source of live entertainment in America. When the circus came to town, folks in the backcountry traveled great distances to attend.

Records of the *Circus Historical Society* show that Barnum & Bailey's Traveling Circus (Ringling Bros., Proprietors) played in Oregon in six alternate years between 1908 and 1918. Included in this period were three bookings in Medford — about 80 miles from the Barks residence in Midland (near Klamath Falls), and another 15 miles from the family farm in Merrill.

The performance dates were August 29, 1910, August 29, 1914, and September 11, 1916. The Barks family was in California in 1914, and while strictly conjecture, it is possible that young Carl may have found a way to attend either or both of the other two performances: in 1910 at age 9, or in 1916 when he would have been old enough to earn his ticket to the circus by working as a roustabout. Or perhaps he only wistfully watched the circus train pass by on the rail line between Klamath Falls and Medford.

However it happened, Carl Barks developed an appreciation of circuses that led to the rousing "Big-Top Bedlam."

"Oh, Boy! The circus is coming to town!" exclaims one of Donald's nephews upon seeing the "Bungling Bros." circus train crossing the bridge over a wide river. "Park these fishing rods someplace and let's go!"

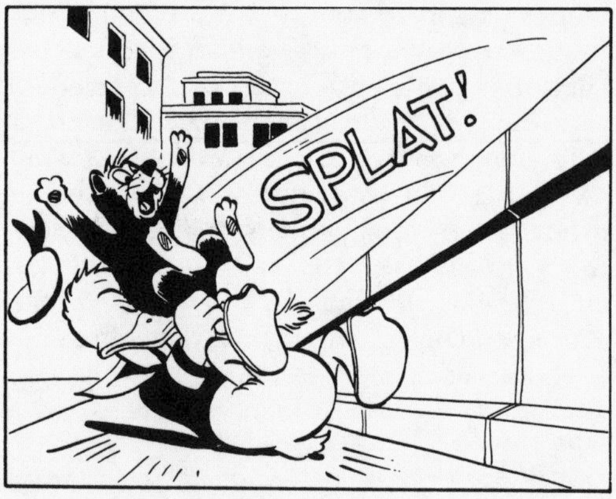
SPLAT!

replies Donald. "If we hurry over to the circus lot now, we can watch them set up the tents."

When the circus rolled into town, most of the citizenry turned out to watch the trains being unloaded, followed by a parade down main street (with elephants and other exotic animals pulling the circus wagons), followed by the performers and crew setting up the huge tents, exhibits, and sideshows on vacant land at the edge of town. Factories shut down, stores and schools closed, and suddenly it was a holiday.

American circus performances were originally held in outdoor amphitheaters, but early in the 19th century huge portable pavilions of waterproof canvas — the big-top tents — became the hallmark of traveling circuses. This development enabled the show to go on regardless of weather conditions.

Bark's "Big-Top Bedlam" gives readers a look back at the glory years of the American circus. By 1950, circuses were on the wane, due in no small part to the advent of television. From about one million American homes with televisions in 1949, the number exploded to 50 million in the next decade. Families quickly became accustomed to getting their entertainment right in their own living rooms.

As reported by *The New York Times*, when "The Greatest Show on Earth" played under canvas for the final time on July 16, 1956, it was a front-page story in newspapers across the land. "Clowns wept. The ringmaster actually sobbed. A thousand roustabouts, aerialists, and equestrians began looking for work."

"Big-Top Bedlam" is another of Barks's little morality tales in which Donald's willingness to do something a bit underhanded quickly boomerangs and proves his undoing. In this case, a plan to pawn Daisy Duck's heirloom brooch for ticket money to see the circus leads to 28 delightful pages of fast-paced mayhem. Along with having to deal with an unhappy (and uncharacteristically understanding) girlfriend, Donald ultimately ends up attending Daisy's boring (blah blah blah) museum club banquet. But for half the story, Donald is the butt of a rapid series of clown gags inflicted by Zippo, "the world's fastest quick-change artist." Not only does Donald fall on his prat, he gets it shot from a cannon right through the peak of the big top.

Of special interest to Barks enthusiasts is the fact that this tale from early 1950 is one in which Barks was still allowed to mix the Disney Ducks with characters that are clearly

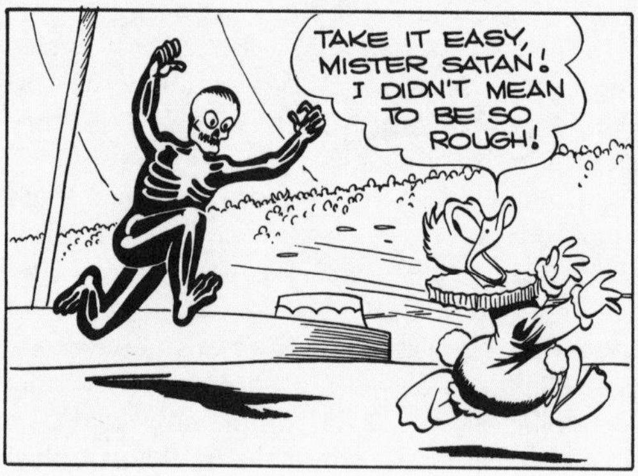
TAKE IT EASY, MISTER SATAN! I DIDN'T MEAN TO BE SO ROUGH!

human beings — rather than adorning them with dog noses and drooping ears (as was later decreed by higher-ups at either Disney Studios or Western Publishing). Readers of "Big-Top Bedlam" will note that dog noses appear in only three panels early in the story. By the time Barks presents us with action scenes at the circus, the characters have unmistakably human features, including hands with four fingers and a thumb. And when Barks draws beautiful women, they can be stunning — even those who turn out not to be quite the ladies they appear to be.

— JOSEPH COWLES

YOU CAN'T GUESS *p. 169*

"You Can't Guess" shamelessly (and for the reader, refreshingly) wallows in Christmas materialism without veering off into the sentimentality typically associated with the holiday. The premise established at the story's beginning — that Huey, Dewey, and Louie need to guess what Donald wants for a present, and have trouble doing so — could easily end with a treacly punch line: "You kids! All I wanted was a hug from each of you!"

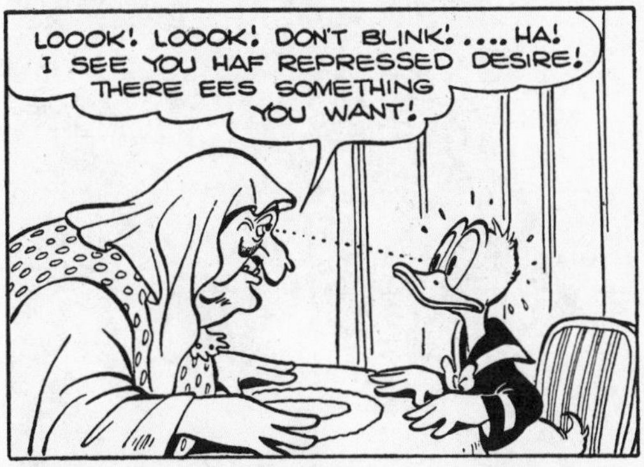
LOOOK! LOOOK! DON'T BLINK! .... HA! I SEE YOU HAF REPRESSED DESIRE! THERE EES SOMETHING YOU WANT!

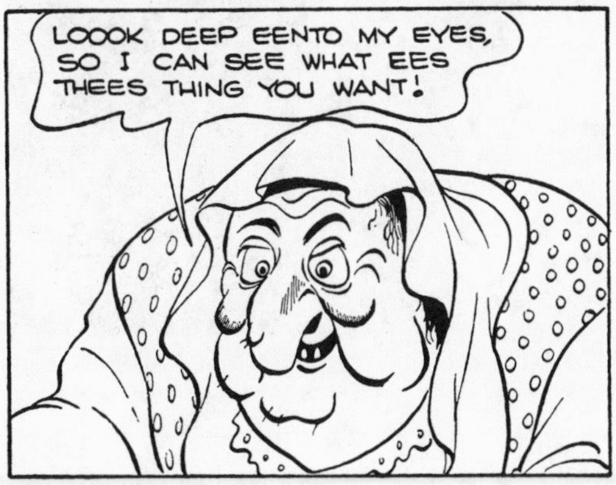
LOOOK DEEP EENTO MY EYES, SO I CAN SEE WHAT EES THEES THING YOU WANT!

But no. Barks gives us a Donald who's "going to have a lot of *fun*" wandering among all the cars given to him, as if he's shopping in the lot of a luxury car dealer, until an arbitrary "eenie-meenie" count lands on the "low-speed job" from Grandma.

Excess is the order of the day with the nephews too, who abandon their platitudes about the less fortunate as soon as they spot the erector set in the window of the department store; at the story's conclusion the nephews aren't interested at all in giving away any of the 15 sets they receive on Christmas morning to poor kids. Instead, they build their own monstrous transportation, even though there are plenty of cars available to ferry them over to Grandma's house. More, more, more presents are better than fewer, Barks seems to be arguing, gently subverting the heartfelt, spiritual Christmas feelings we might expect from a Disney tale.

Much of "You Can't Guess" reads like a compendium of Barks's most successful aesthetic elements. Barks's love for repetition — for replayed comedy situations, usually with variations — is manifest in the similar-but-slightly-different visits to the mind reader and the hypnotist, and in the panels of Donald's perpetually-malfunctioning car (*Blam!*) threaded through the story.

Barks's capacity for playful self-awareness is also present here. It's supremely ironic that Donald, a *duck*, is hypnotized into believing that he is a chicken, hungry for corn. (On page 182, panel 4, bags of corn are gifts for "Henrietta Hen" and "Roscoe Rooster," alliterative, anthropomorphic names just like "Donald Duck." Barks habitually and humorously juxtaposes his three-dimensional fowls with less "human" birds like the Andean chickens that lay square eggs (see *Lost in the Andes*, Vol. 7 in this series).

Finally, Barks often includes one or two panels per story where he places one character (or a group of characters) in the distant background and others in the extreme foreground. In "You Can't Guess," one such composition occurs on page 178, panel 6, where Daisy is close to the surface of the picture plane — perhaps to emphasize how she's been dirtied by exhaust? — while the nephews push Donald's car toward a garage. Maybe Donald's car is always breaking down, but Barks's storytelling motors along.

— CRAIG FISCHER

Carl Barks

LIFE AMONG THE DUCKS

by DONALD AULT

ABOVE: *Carl Barks at the 1982 San Diego Comic-Con. Photo by Alan Light.*

"I was a real misfit," Carl Barks said, thinking back over an early life of hard labor — as a farmer, a logger, a mule-skinner, a rivet heater, and a printing press feeder — before he was hired as a full-time cartoonist for an obscure risqué magazine in 1931.

Barks was born in 1901 and (mostly) raised in Merrill, Oregon. He had always wanted to be a cartoonist, but everything that happened to him in his early years seemed to stand in his way. He suffered a significant hearing loss after a bout with the measles. His mother died. He had to leave school after the eighth grade. His

father suffered a mental breakdown. His older brother was whisked off to World War I.

His first marriage, in 1921, was to a woman who was unsympathetic to his dreams and who ultimately bore two children "by accident," as Barks phrased it. The two divorced in 1930.

In 1931, he pulled up stakes from Merrill and headed to Minnesota, leaving his mother-in-law, whom he trusted more than his wife, in charge of his children.

Arriving in Minneapolis, he went to work for the *Calgary Eye-Opener*, that risqué magazine. He thought he would finally be drawing cartoons full time, but the editor and most of the staff were alcoholics, so Barks ended up running the whole show.

In 1935 he took "a great gamble" and, on the strength of some cartoons he'd submitted in response to an advertisement from the Disney Studio, he moved to California and entered an animation trial period. He was soon promoted to "story man" in Disney's Donald Duck animation unit, where he made significant contributions to 36 Donald cartoon shorts between 1936 and 1942, including helping to create Huey, Dewey, and Louie for "Donald's Nephews" in 1938. Ultimately, though, he grew dissatisfied. The production of animated cartoons "by committee," as he described it, stifled his imagination.

For that and other reasons, in 1942 he left Disney to run a chicken farm. But when he was offered a chance by Western Publishing to write and illustrate a new series of Donald Duck comic book stories, he jumped at it. The comic book format suited him, and the quality of his work persuaded the editors to grant him a freedom and autonomy he'd never known and that few others were ever granted. He would go on to write and draw more than 6,000 pages in over 500 stories and uncounted hundreds of covers between 1942 and 1966 for Western's Dell and Gold Key imprints.

Barks had almost no formal art training. He had taught himself how to draw by imitating his early favorite artists — Winsor McCay (*Little Nemo*), Frederick Opper (*Happy Hooligan*), Elzie Segar (*Popeye*), and Floyd Gottfredson (*Mickey Mouse*).

He taught himself how to write well by going back to the grammar books he had shunned in school, making up jingles and rhymes, and inventing other linguistic exercises to get a natural feel for the rhythm and dialogue of sequential narrative.

Barks married again in 1938, but that union ended disastrously in divorce in 1951. In 1954, Barks married Margaret Wynnfred Williams, known as Garé, who soon began assisting him by lettering and inking backgrounds on his comic book work. They remained happily together until her death in 1993.

He did his work in the California desert and often mailed his stories into the office. He worked his stories over and over "backward and forward." Barks was not a vain man but he had confidence in his talent. He knew what hard work was, and he knew that he'd put his best efforts into every story he produced.

On those occasions when he did go into Western's offices he would "just dare anybody to see if they could improve on it." His confidence was justified. His work was largely responsible for some of the best-selling comic books in the world — *Walt Disney's Comics and Stories* and *Uncle Scrooge*.

Because Western's policy was to keep their writers and artists anonymous, readers never knew the name of the "good duck artist" — but they could spot the superiority of his work. When fans determined to solve the mystery of his anonymity finally tracked him down (not unlike an adventure Huey, Dewey, and Louie might embark upon), Barks was quite happy to correspond and otherwise communicate with his legion of aficionados.

Given all the obstacles of his early years and the dark days that haunted him off and on for the rest of his life, it's remarkable that he laughed so easily and loved to make others laugh.

In the process of expanding Donald Duck's character far beyond the hot-tempered Donald of animation, Barks created a moveable locale (Duckburg) and a cast of dynamic characters: Scrooge McDuck, the Beagle Boys, Gladstone Gander, Gyro Gearloose, the Junior Woodchucks. And there were hundreds of others who made only one memorable appearance in the engaging, imaginative, and unpredictable comedy-adventures that he wrote and drew from scratch for nearly a quarter of a century.

Among many other honors, Carl Barks was one of the three initial inductees into the Will Eisner Comic Awards Hall of Fame for comic book creators in 1987. (The other two were Jack Kirby and Will Eisner.) In 1991, Barks became the only Disney comic book artist to be recognized as a "Disney Legend," a special award created by Disney "to acknowledge and honor the many individuals whose imagination, talents, and dreams have created the Disney magic."

As Roy Disney said on Barks's passing in 2000 at age 99, "He challenged our imaginations and took us on some of the greatest adventures we have ever known. His prolific comic book creations entertained many generations of devoted fans and influenced countless artists over the years.... His timeless tales will stand as a legacy to his originality and brilliant artistic vision."

Contributors

Donald Ault is Professor of English at the University of Florida, founder and editor of *ImageTexT: Interdisciplinary Comics Studies*, author of two books on William Blake (*Visionary Physics* and *Narrative Unbound*), editor of *Carl Barks: Conversations,* and executive producer of the video *The Duck Man: An Interview with Carl Barks*.

Alberto Becattini was born in Florence, Italy. He has taught high school English since 1983. Since 1978, he has written essays for Italian and U.S. publications about comics, specializing in Disney characters and American comics generally. Since 1992 he has been a freelance writer and consultant for The Walt Disney Company-Italy, contributing to such series as *Zio Paperone, Maestri Disney, Tesori Disney, Disney Anni d'Oro, La Grande Dinastia dei Paperi*, and *Gli Anni d'Oro di Topolino*.

Joseph Robert Cowles is a lifelong Donald Duck fan who became friends with Carl and Garé Barks while a teenager working at Disneyland in the 1950s. He writes for the quarterly newsletter of the Carl Barks Fan Club, contributed materials and commentary to Egmont's *Carl Barks Collection,* and is the author of *Recalling Carl,* a pictorial dissertation contending that Disney should be making feature films of Barks's stories. His Carl Barks website is TheGoodArtist.com.

Craig Fischer is Associate Professor of English at Appalachian State University. His Monsters Eat Critics column, about comics' multifarious genres, runs at *The Comics Journal* website (tcj.com).

Leonardo Gori is a comics scholar and collector, especially of syndicated newspaper strips of the '30s and Italian Disney authors. He wrote, with Frank Stajano and others, many books on Italian "fumetti" and American comics in Italy. He has also written thrillers, which have been translated into Spanish, Portuguese, and Korean.

Rich Kreiner is a longtime writer for *The Comics Journal* and a longertime reader of Carl Barks. He lives with wife and cat in Maine.

Bill Mason has been a teacher in the Humanities Department at Dawson College, Montreal, Canada, since 1971. The first Carl Barks story he remembers reading is "The Old Castle's Secret," which was originally published when he was in the second grade.

Ken Parille is the author of *The Daniel Clowes Reader* (Fantagraphics, 2012) and has published essays on Louisa May Alcott and boyhood, the mother-son relationship in antebellum America, TV bandleader Lawrence Welk, and, of course, comics. His writing has appeared in *The Nathaniel Hawthorne Review*, *The Journal of Popular Culture*, *The Boston Review*, *The Believer*, and *The Comics Journal.* He teaches literature at East Carolina University.

Francesco ("Frank") Stajano began reading Disney comics in preschool and never grew out of it — the walls of his house are covered in bookshelves and many of them hold comics. He has written on Disney comics, particularly with Leonardo Gori, and had the privilege of visiting Carl Barks at his home in Oregon in 1998. In real life he is an associate professor at the University of Cambridge in England.

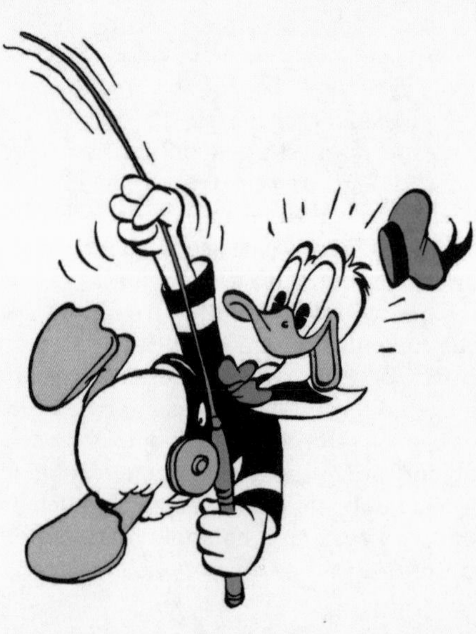

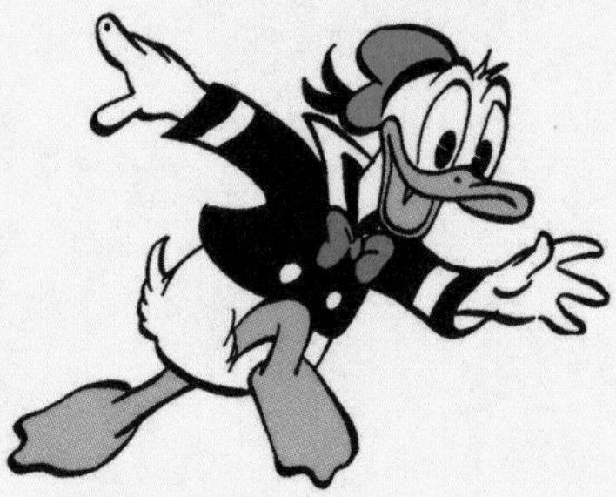

Where did these Duck stories first appear?

The Complete Carl Barks Disney Library collects Donald Duck and Uncle Scrooge stories by Carl Barks that were originally published in the traditional American four-color comic book format. Barks's first Duck story appeared in October 1942. The volumes in this project are numbered chronologically but are being released in a different order. This is volume 9.

Stories within a volume may or may not follow the publication sequence of the original comic books. We may take the liberty of rearranging the sequence of the stories within a volume for editorial or presentation purposes.

The original comic books were published under the Dell logo and some appeared in the so-called *Four Color* series — a name that appeared nowhere inside the comic book itself, but is generally agreed upon by historians to refer to the series of "one-shot" comic books published by Dell that have sequential numbering. The *Four Color* issues are also sometimes referred to as "One Shots."

Most of the stories in this volume were originally published without a title. Some stories were retroactively assigned a title when they were reprinted in later years. Some stories were given titles by Barks in correspondence or interviews. (Sometimes Barks referred to the same story with different titles.) Some stories were never given an official title but have been informally assigned one by fans and indexers. For the untitled stories in this volume, we have used the title that seems most appropriate. The unofficial titles appear below with an asterisk enclosed in parentheses (*).

The following is the order in which the stories in this volume were originally published.

***Four Color* #275 (May 1950)**
- Cover
- Ancient Persia

***Walt Disney's Comics and Stories* #117 (June 1950)**
- Wild About Flowers (*)

***Vacation Parade* #1 (July 1950)**
- Vacation Time
- Donald's Grandma Duck
- Camp Counselor

***Four Color* #282 (July 1950)**
- Cover
- The Pixilated Parrot

***Four Color* #291 (September 1950)**
- The Magic Hourglass

***Four Color* #300 (November 1950)**
- Big-Top Bedlam

***Walt Disney's Christmas Parade* #2 (November 1950)**
- You Can't Guess!

***Four Color* #356 (November 1951)**
- Cover
- Talking Parrot (*)